P9-CCF-056

FLORIDA STATE
UNIVERSITY LIBRARIES

MAY 12 1998

TALLAHASSEE, FLORIDA

Morel Tales

GARY ALAN FINE

Morel Tales

The Culture of Mushrooming

HARVARD UNIVERSITY PRESS

CAMBRIDGE, MASSACHUSETTS

LONDON, ENGLAND

1998

GF
50
·F53
1998

Copyright © 1998 by the President and Fellows
of Harvard College
All rights reserved
Printed in the United States of America

Library of Congress Cataloging-in-Publication Data

Fine, Gary Alan.
Morel tales : the culture of mushrooming / Gary Alan Fine.
p.   cm.
Includes bibliographical references and index.
ISBN 0-674-08935-9 (alk. paper)
1. Human ecology.   2. Mushrooms, Edible—Social aspects.
3. Nature.   I. Title.
GF50.F53   1998
304.2'7—dc21   97-37201

Designed by Gwen Nefsky Frankfeldt

To Lee Muggli (1943–1994),
for teaching me to see
what was at my feet

Contents

Preface

The search. The hunt. Ethnographers enter uncharted realms, lashed by our muses, our guilts, our striving to find that Truth that turns the pain of the voyage into the apotheosis of our desires, perhaps into our souls, attempting to find the words and form to capture the reader. Escaping our confining offices into a "natural" world is a chill tonic, a quaff of equilibrium.

I present a simple ethnographic narrative, told about nature, meaning, humanity, society, living, and the world. A story about fungus, and simultaneously a peopled sociology. Told by a tourist—a tourist with guides and comrades. This then is my tale. How a little patch of the world becomes known, is given value and worth, and what this suggests about how we understand our world.

Stories set the foundation for understanding. Having completed years of research on the lives of cooks, relating how organizations direct and channel the creation of aesthetic objects and interpersonal relationships, I became—I confess—fond of gourmet foodstuffs. One day I read a journalistic squib about hobbyists who collected morel mushrooms. At first I merely wanted to learn *where* to collect these delicacies without cost. Not only was this question naive, but it became fundamental to my research. How can a group coalesce when secrecy is so central to their activities?

As is often the case with ethnography, my focus expanded, but in the process of collecting data I learned to collect morels, and I have become quite as secretive of my spots as my friends are of theirs. I do eat wild mushrooms, not only morels, but chanterelles, puffballs, sulphur shelves, honeys, corals, and boletes. I have even shared some with doubting colleagues. All have survived.

As I spent time with these "naturalists," I became intrigued by how their attitudes toward nature developed. Mushrooming is largely unknown and mistrusted by many Americans. How do our attitudes toward nature reveal themselves in our responses to nature? This problem is particularly acute because, on some level, mushrooming is an extractive enterprise. Mushroomers wish not only to appreciate the fields and woods, but also to pluck parts of those fields and woods, bringing them home to sauté. They violate the naturalist's maxim to "take nothing but memories." Should amateur ornithologists eat the species for which they search (as John J. Audubon did in an earlier age)? What does the natural environment *mean* to these men and women, and how can they justify their actions?

For many, mushrooms are meaningless and often unseen; yet hobbyists have developed an extensive set of meanings and beliefs about these natural phenomena. How to explain the development of these meanings? How does this correspond to what all leisure participants do in their own small corners of the world?

As most nonmushroomers realize, eating the wrong mushroom can be fatal. Even though gathering mushrooms can hardly be considered strenuous, it involves a degree of danger. How do collectors cope with this danger in their culture, and how does their subsociety help in this effort? Through stories, jokes, warnings, slogans, and folk beliefs, the world is made provisionally safe.

Finally, these individuals are enmeshed in a *leisure organization;* I hoped to understand how an established organization contributes to personal satisfactions, as well as, on occasion, contributing to the tensions within this diverse hobby. Leisure organizations help *provision* leisure, and this process, akin to resource mobilization theory in social movement research, demands elaboration. Leisure events do not just happen; they must be facilitated through individual or group resources.

From a simple desire to learn where I could pick gourmet mushrooms, from a desire to escape a stuffy office, I found a strange, robust, natural world. It was a foray of discovery, with the goal of finding objects of symbolic potency.

During my research I was supported and advised by many fine individuals. I worked most closely with the Minnesota Mycological Society. I particularly thank several friends for their generosity of time and spirit: Lee Muggli, Herb and Norma Harper, Bruce Auerbach, Steve Langston, Erma and Bill Lechko, Gene and Lillian Crandall, Steve Benson, Bill Jasper, Doris Johannes, Pat Leacock, Mitch Metcalf, Judy and Dick O'Connor, and Peg Mossberg. I assign them pseudonyms in this volume, but my appreciation is real. I also received help from several colleagues associated with the North American Mycological Association and the Mycological Society of San Francisco, especially Bill Freedman, Don Huffman, Gary Lincoff, Larry Stickney, and Michael Boom. I am grateful for many acts of hospitality.

Friends and colleagues in the academic enterprise hid their shock that I had selected such an esoteric topic. These critics are surely justified in their skepticism; I only hope that I have done something with this social world that demonstrates that truth is in all matter. I appreciate the advice of Elizabeth Brumfiel, Kathy Charmaz, Carolyn Ellis, Kai Erikson, Doug Harper, Lori Holyfield, Thomas Hood, Jennifer Hunt, Donna King, Sherryl Kleinman, Edward Lawler, Richard Lempert, Tanya Luhrmann, Jeylan Mortimer, Kent Sandstrom, Neil Smelser, Robert I. Sutton, Jim Thomas, Leigh Thompson, C. B. Wolfe, and Robert Wuthnow. Portions of Chapter 5 were written with the collaboration of Lori Holyfield. The Center for Advanced Study in the Behavioral Sciences provided a home for the writing of a draft of this manuscript. I am grateful for the marvelous library assistance provided by Joy Scott and Jean Michel, and the financial support provided by National Science Foundation grant no. SBR-9022192. I also thank my editors at Harvard University Press, Michael Aronson, Jeff Kehoe, and Christine Thorsteinsson, and my indexer, Lori Lathrop.

Portions of the manuscript previously appeared in: "Community and Boundary: Personal Experience Stories of Mushroom Collectors," *Journal of Folklore Research* 24, 1987, 223–240; "Dying for a Laugh: Negotiating Risk and Creating Personas in the Humor of Mushroom Collectors," *Western Folklore* 47, 1988, 177–194; "Mobilizing Fun: Provisioning Resources in Leisure Worlds," *Sport Sociology Journal* 6, 1989, 319–334; "Wild Life: Authenticity and the Human Experience of Natural Places," in *Investigating Subjectivity,* ed. Carolyn Ellis and Michael Flaherty (Newbury Park, Calif.: Sage, 1992); "Secrecy, Trust, and Dangerous Leisure: Generating Group Cohesion in Voluntary Organizations," *Social Psychology Quarterly* 59, 1996, 22–38 (with Lori Holyfield); "Naturework and the Taming of the Wild: The Problem of 'Overpick' in the Culture of Mush-roomers," *Social Problems* 44, 1997, 66–88.

For four years my wife tolerated my stunt well enough that after a few occasions she actually consumed, and sometimes picked, wild mushrooms. She endures. My relatives still haven't succumbed to the charms of the fungal world, at least as I have presented them. They may have read too many murder mysteries.

For myself, I feel the wild urge to traverse the fields once again.

Author's Note

Unattributed quotations are from personal interviews and field notes. All names of persons referred to in these excerpts have been changed to protect the privacy of individuals. I use GAF when referring to my comments in interviews.

Introduction

To put it bluntly, man is not unnatural, the bear natural; buildings unnatural and beaver lodges natural.

—GREGORY STONE AND MARVIN TAVES[1]

Of the changes during the past quarter century that have altered human conceptions of our place in the universe, perhaps none has had more impact than the attention that we—as individuals, as societies, and as a species—give to our "environment," to nature. Although concern with the meaning of nature has not been absent during the past millennia,[2] the relationship between humans and nature had not been considered sufficiently.

Thankfully, this is no longer the case. Throughout the academic community and in public discourse, theorizing about the natural environment is epidemic. Discussions of the meaning of "nature" and the relationship between humans and the natural environment flourish. Likewise, the growth in size and number of environmental organizations in the past thirty years[3] suggests that public concern matches academic interest.[4] Perhaps not surprisingly, given the political and cultural stance of academics and environmentalists, wide agreement exists that all is not well with how humans "treat" nature. Some argue that the villain is corporate (reform environmentalists),[5] oppressive social control (anarcho-socialist social ecologists),[6] anthropocentrism (deep ecologists),[7] or androcentrism (ecofeminists).[8] Each approach, arguing for a reduced impact on "nature," hectors humans to be more considerate, leaving animals and plants in peace. The anthropologist Mary Douglas asserts: "Always and everywhere it is human folly, hate, and greed which put the human environment at risk."[9]

Although there is much to be said for an approach that frets about degradation to the "natural environment," such a view ignores the images through which social actors understand their environment as a meaningful other, linked to a set of social values, and ignores the processes by which this interpretation of nature is transformed into a set of action claims.

I examine how individuals define the meanings of the environment in light of cultural images and then define their relationship to that environment: a process I term "naturework." Naturework is a rhetorical resource by which social actors individually and collectively make sense of their relationship to the environment. As ideological work conveys the process by which individuals transform the here-and-now into broader moral concerns,[10] naturework conveys how natural objects are given cultural meaning. This process is linked to a set of ideologies that specify the relationship between culture and nature, and the moral value of the relationship. From childhood, we are exposed to claims about how nature is to be treated, and from these texts and images—our ideological toolkit[11]—we present environmental "concerns." My argument is not that every individual has a single, consistent ideology, but that we draw from extant cultural images.

Ideological perspectives on nature provide pools of images by which individuals establish models both for experiencing the wild (and describing that experience) and for analyzing the existence and severity of natural social problems. Human-nature "interaction" and its interpretation—naturework—deserve sociological analysis.

Through naturework human actors interpret the natural environment and situate themselves within this world. Natural objects are transformed from things into symbols.[12] In George Herbert Mead's[13] sense, the environment becomes a "generalized other," providing a lens by which we interpret and direct our actions. This process of construing meaning transforms nature into culture, while channeling and organizing our cultural choices. Naturework involves interpretations of the wild, justified through moral purpose and ratified in emotional response.[14]

This approach does not deny the biological reality of trees, plants, or streams; nor does it deny that alterations to an ecosystem may have effects (although we must specify our values and who or what will benefit or lose). Nor do I deny that large-scale social actors (institutions or organizations) may have a consequential impact on ecosystems; indeed, as the sociologist Andrew Weigert[15] asserts, environmental events can be consequential. One would be foolhardy to deny the effects of a natural disaster or toxic mushroom. The results are real, even though they must still be interpreted. But given that the environment is an obdurate reality, I assert that the labels "nature," "the wild," and "the environment" as categories of objects are socially constructed, linked to "environmental" ideologies.[16] From classes of objects we build value-laden ideas. Together natural objects—and their uses in society—provide a set of constraints or capacities that allow nature to be formulated in particular ways, and not in others. As we discuss the meanings of individual mushrooms and of the process of collecting, we see both the process by which nature is made like culture and the boundaries and limits of that process. Nature is thus known by the fact that it can be seen as like society (with fungi interpreted as people), but that it also provides a distinctly authentic realm that reflects everything that human culture cannot be.

No matter how egalitarian one may wish to be, plants and animals do not participate in a dialogue: we embrace either *laissez faire* or social control. As a result, each of these theories by virtue of its audience and its targets of change is human-centered. We don't fret about how owls should treat field mice or how beavers should treat pines. Protecting the environment implies limiting human action, leaving natural selection and the food chain to do the rest.

Ultimately we cannot speak to other species, although we often speak for them. *Homo sapiens* find the claims of other *homo sapiens* more or less plausible, but other species make no claims on us, although we often read their claims through role-taking. By virtue of the demands of discourse, environmental ethics are anthropocentric. Even though humans and (nonhuman) "nature" mutually influence each other's behaviors, no meeting of minds is possible. Nature must be mediated in order to be meaningful, dependent on human values, specified through communication.[17] Anthony Giddens[18] writes of "socialised nature," the ongoing process by which nature is given meaning. The ideas that human beings assign to those objects that they classify as "wild" vary, and the definitions that are selected are based on and then affect human interaction and nature.

How nature is interpreted is not "natural." Nature is a cultural creation,[19] despite our gut feeling that nature and culture are different kinds of realities. As the social critic Lewis Mumford notes: " 'Nature' as a system of interests and activities is one of the chief creations of the civilized man."[20] We interpret and experience nature as a deep or authentic reality. Yet, as environmental historians emphasize, the meaning of nature is not inherent in the environment itself, but requires a human template. David Scofield Wilson remarks: "Persons brought up in western culture know nature when they see it. And culture."[21]

To state the matter baldly: "Nature" does not exist. Whereas individual trees, birds, and fungi exist, nature as a concept is a function of cognition, cultural activity, and social organization. The lumping of diverse objects together within a category (nature) is a human creation. The environment is enacted.[22] My goal, then, is to explore the implications of a cultural perspective for the construct of nature.

In practice, our definition of nature often excludes human impact. We are likely to define the extent of human transformation as crucial to what nature means, enshrining "wildness." Yet this view is not without challenge, as we may force nature to live up to our expectations. In our national parks[23] and our gardens[24] we transform and manipulate nature to make it feel authentic. In our leisure we search for "nature," even if that reality is presented and organized by entrepreneurs in settings that are not fully authentic.[25] Arcadia is mythic in an interrelated biosystem.

Consider the odd little word "nature." Closest to our meaning among three dense pages of the *Oxford English Dictionary* is definition thirteen: "the material world, or its collective objects and phenomena, especially those with which man is most directly in contact; frequently the features and products of the earth itself, *as contrasted with* those of human civilization" (emphasis added).[26] We contrast the features and products of the earth with those of human civilization, as if the latter were not a feature and product of the earth.[27] When Bill McKibben[28] writes of the "end of nature," he refers to the fact that nature can no longer be separated from human society. Now that nature no longer exists, say some, we have rediscovered it.[29]

We speak of people in society and "in nature." What does it mean to be "in nature"? Where is nature? Presumably it is to be found in those places that have not been shaped by the human hand, but all earth has been affected by humankind, and some of the areas that we consider to be most natural, such as Yosemite, Yellowstone, and the Shenandoah National Parks, are in their ecological structure profoundly human creations.[30] The ecologist Walter Truett Anderson[31] argues that humans cannot escape responsibility to direct nature—to engage in "evolutionary governance." Should we now wash our hands of intervention and no longer participate in the creations of environments that support our moral visions?

Most Americans—more than three-fourths of the population if surveys can be believed—identify themselves as environmentalists. The label is a badge of honor. We claim that we love nature, but what does this love entail? Can nature love us in return? We suggest that we must treat nature with respect, but respect implies a social, hierarchical vision.

The idea of "nature" suggests in practice a contrasting reality of "culture."[32] Yet is it self-evident that a beaver dam should be classified as "nature" and that a child's treehouse made of logs and branches (much less a human dam) should be seen as "culture"? For good or ill, beavers do not fill out environmental impact statements, whereas human dam builders do, and some parents constructing treehouses must complete building permits in accordance with state law. We could imagine a world in which a beaver's dam and a human dam— both purposive constructions—could be considered the same class of object. Yet this is not our world.

The ultimate meaning of nature is shaped by humans, not by Mother Nature. Although nature has agency in its own right, meanings of nature reflect human templates.[33] We need not accept a monist or radical phenomenological perspective that denies that the environment has real effects.[34] Natural disasters have dramatic consequences, yet these effects are known within an interpretive matrix. Is a natural disaster a sign from God, a warning of the dangers of overbuilding, or mere actuarial chance? The cosmic reality of nature is mediated through culture, personal experience, and the institutional order.

We can use nature to justify nothing or anything.[35] This recognition is central to an interpretivist approach to understanding the environment. In this sense, the nature-culture division is, at its heart, deceptive.[36] The preference for preserving nature is a cultural choice, as is the willingness to see nature transformed. I am not claiming that alterations in the natural environment are not consequential; they are. Human actions have real effects, but interpretations are grounded in cultural templates and human values.

Why do we distinguish between culture and nature? This social differentiation has become traditional, unthought, and accepted without self-reflection. Belief in the separate reality of nature is central to modern environmentalism. The claim that an autonomous realm of nature exists is taught by parents to preschoolers, and is bolstered by the ideology of children's books and elementary education.[37] We learn to experience natural settings differently from cultural settings.

Some even suggest that the nature-culture distinction is instinctive. Thomas McNamee writes in *Nature First* that "our conception of [nature] springs from the darkest depths of our unconscious sense of life itself."[38] Ultimately some, such as the naturalist John Livingston,[39] claim that "there can be no 'rational' argument for wildlife preservation. . . . There is no 'logic' in feeling, in experiencing, in states of being." The valuation of nature is, in this view, a decision not grounded in rational choice.

Understanding nature involves embracing metaphor.[40] The question becomes not "What is nature?" but "What is nature like?" or, put another way, "What are the boundaries of nature, and how should they be policed?" To answer I suggest three distinct metaphorical visions of nature: a protectionist view, an organic view, and a humanist view. These visions are, self-evidently, social constructions that do not perfectly capture nature discourse. For instance, the protectionist view and rights discourse do not perfectly intersect; the latter is a much more recent view, and it is entirely possible to see the need for protection without according standing in a polity (and, hence, rights). Similarly, even an area of ecological thought such as ecofeminism has several distinctly different strands[41]: some protectionist, some organic. My analysis is merely a convenient heuristic for three strands of thought. These strands do not exhaust how nature could be conceptualized, although they do encapsulate major environmental positions. Further, in practice few embrace a position with such zeal that their passion blinds them to other visions and to pragmatic concerns. Even Rachel Carson did not oppose the use of all pesticides;[42] even the animal rights advocate Tom Regan[43] recognizes that on occasion causing an animal harm may be justified.

Ultimately, humans are active meaning-creators and can devise their own set of images that do not perfectly correspond with those outlined here. One should think of these not as ways that people actually conceptualize nature, but as metaphorical resources by which interpretations of nature are created. These images seem plausible to many, given the continuing debate over the boundaries between culture and nature, and whether those boundaries should be crossed. Implicit in these models are directives for state action. Images of social control derive from the metaphors one uses. Those who embrace some form of protectionism are more likely to condone or demand state action (controlling the actions of wayward individuals) than are those whose humanism may border on libertarianism. Thus the personal images of nature are inevitably tied to larger concerns about the legitimacy of social organization.

A PROTECTIONIST VISION: RIGHTS FOR NATURE

A protectionist vision argues that nature is a special realm—authentic and uncontaminated, fundamentally distinct from the built environment. A bright and shining line separates nature and culture, leading the radical environmental theorist Christopher Manes to conclude *Green Rage: Radical Environmentalism and the Unmaking of Civilization* with a call to action: "the time to make the choice between the natural and cultural worlds has come."[44] This view implies that nature is a preserve that human beings could easily spoil. Our goal is not to manage ecosystems, but to protect them.[45] We protect nature from our own incursions and instincts. This view is evident in the chosen label of the radical environmentalist movement Earth First! If earth first, then who second?: humans, of course. Charles Rubin suggests provocatively that environmentalism is an evangelical movement, heir to temperance crusades that attempt to "save us from ourselves."[46] The desire to protect the wild represents the claim of a moralist who wishes to convert others.[47] We must sacrifice our own interests.[48]

We need to set aside wilderness areas, prevent acid rain, and limit the human "built" environment. This view is evident in the naturalist's slogan that in nature "one should take nothing but memories, and leave nothing but footprints," and in Barry Commoner's[49] Third Law of Ecology: "Nature knows best." Even the smallest transformation is potentially harmful. We must restrain our activities to protect nature. As one mushroomer averred: "Life on earth could exist very nicely without people, a hell of a lot better without people, but it couldn't exist without fungi. Human beings are the biggest threat to nature. . . . We should try to have as little impact on the environment as possible."

Just as social order is premised on a social contract between dissimilar equals, those who compete on common ground with conflicting interests, so it seems to follow that the relationship between humanity and nature can fit within a metaphor of a polity of competing interests, not an organic, systemic, seamless unity or a conquered land. Rights theorists, such as Tom Regan in *The Case for Animal Rights*, emphasize the dignity of each agent rather than each species.[50] These attempts to ensure rights for nature seemingly erase boundaries between humans and others, in line with an organic approach, but in practice establish humans as the protectors of the rights of nature. Rights discourse does not fully fit within a protectionist model, but by virtue of nature's need for protection by humans, I include it here. For instance, Dave Foreman of Earth First! proclaims:

> The other beings—four-legged, winged, six-legged, rooted, flowing, etc.—have just as much right to be in that place as we do, they are their own justification for being, they have inherent value, value completely apart from whatever worth they have for . . . humans.
>
> You protect a river because it's a river. For its own sake. Because it has a right to exist by itself. The grizzly bear in Yellowstone Park has as much right to her life as any one of us has to our life.[51]

Foreman's plea is to expand rights, a characteristic of contemporary social systems.[52] We give corporations the legal status of "persons" but have not yet done the same for plants and animals.[53] But rights cut several ways. If community includes all interests, we humans, too, have the rights gainsaid by this community of equals. Yet humans are treated as distinct—for example, by virtue of being able to distinguish right from wrong—and have extra responsibilities and limitations. Animals (and plants) are not concerned with the rights of others, whereas humans are constrained. This model maximizes the restrictions on human action.

If plants and animals are to be protected, how and by whom are their rights defended? The answer must involve the human perception of the inadequacies of nonhuman nature. Rights are structured to protect the powerless or unaware, demanding that the powerful mitigate the full extent of their control. Humans have extensive power to alter nature, but the powerlessness of nature with regard to human expansiveness becomes a moral virtue. Nature is among the oppressed. Thus some speak of nature as a "Green Nigger."[54] Theodore Roszak writes: "The natural environment is the exploited proletariat, the downtrodden nigger of everybody's industrial system. . . . Nature must also have its natural rights."[55] This virtue is evident in that portion of the environmental movement that can be read as a civil rights movement for trees.[56]

We live in an age characterized by an "ethic of tolerance," particularly among intellectual and cultural elites. Elites insistently question their place, asking whether the status structure is just and whether special virtues adhere to the oppressed—what Tom Wolfe[57] cynically lambasted as *nostalgie de la boue*. This is an undercurrent in social movements that question the established power structure on behalf of minorities, women, children, animals, and now nature. Such movements can be read as making a moral claim that these groups demonstrate a purity that stems from a mix of innocence and exploitation.

AN ORGANIC VISION: AT ONE WITH NATURE

The organic vision, the oldest and youngest perspective, presupposes that no firm line divides human life and natural life. This is a key element of many ancient, non-industrial tribal societies, and is lately embraced by "new-age" postmoderns. It denies that human beings are separate from nature and seems to suggest that humans have no special importance. According to this perspective, human beings are "merely" part of nature—part of an organic whole.[58]

A substantial proportion of environmental writers emphasize an organic perspective, even while stressing the authenticity of nature (as distinct from civilization). Although an organic view need not always be romantic,[59] it often emphasizes the love and mutual caring of each to each ("nature green in tooth and claw"), stressing the pastoral. The perspective of natural man residing in the Garden of Eden is a core image of what the environmental historian Donald Worster terms the "Arcadian" vision, which postulates a pastoral and harmonious link between man and nature, while underlining the authenticity of the natural environment. In their distinctive ways, much of deep ecology, ecofeminism, and the Gaian philosophy accept this model, while disputing the source of blame for environmental degradation (anthropocentrism, androcentrism, or population pressures).

Yet if human beings truly are part of nature, humans logically should have no greater need to restrain their own action than should any creature. As Walter Truett Anderson puts it: "Earth itself brought forth human intelligence and . . . all the biopolitical events of our time . . . are part of nature."[60] We can no more condemn the human hunter than the feline hunter, the developer than the nest maker, or the engineer than the beaver. Can we say that when an animal builds a home, altering the ecosystem, that is natural, and when humans do the same, nature has been violated? The philosopher Robert Nelson explains: "If the lion is not to be condemned morally for wanton acts of cruelty against other creatures, why should mankind be judged harshly for making practical use of the natural world?"[61] Each is operating on the basis of genetic and material capabilities, following instrumental goals. James Lovelock, the author of the Gaian hypothesis, when suggesting that earth is a living entity, noted: "Our species with its technology is simply an inevitable part of the natural scene"[62]: we are mechanically advanced beavers.[63] This perspective, then, could erase the division between nature and culture, incorporating the latter into the former.

This argument, as I have mischievously presented it, would be abhorrent to most self-defined environmentalists. The organic view assumes that humans should accept a set of affirming values—the values of "nature," which are often linked to various forms of feminist ideology. We perceive some values to be more in keeping with an organic, Gaian approach than others.

A HUMANIST VISION: USING NATURE

A common, "pre-environmentalist" view of the relationship between humanity and nature postulates what Donald Worster[64] terms the "Imperial" vision, and what I label, less pejoratively, a humanist vision,[65] emphasizing the priority of the needs and desires of *homo sapiens*. This perspective emphasizes a sharp distinction between culture and nature, suggesting that nature is to be used for human purposes. This anthropocentric view once felt right, and still does in most societies that have not reached a postcapitalist plateau: those that cannot afford the luxury of scorning necessity. The humanist vision gives no special moral weight to nature, except, in some versions, when defining nature as a force to be "tamed": wilderness is seen as a "dark and sinister symbol . . . a cursed and chaotic wasteland."[66]

Surely it is understandable why for millennia, and even today, nature is seen as a source of danger: consider volcanos, radon, rabid raccoons, the Ebola virus, and an army of intestinal parasites.[67] Sometimes human society and the natural order battle. Human actions have primacy, and environmentalists may be attacked for "scorning" human life[68] and embracing an ethic of scarcity, curtailing liberty.[69]

John Stuart Mill expressed this perspective, suggesting that "conformity to nature has no connection whatever with right and wrong,"[70] a view echoed by the psychologist William James:

> Visible nature is all plasticity and indifference,—a moral multiverse
> . . . and not a moral universe. To such a harlot we owe no allegiance;
> with her as a whole we can establish no moral communion; and
> we are free in our dealing with her several parts to obey or to destroy,
> and to follow no law but that of prudence in coming to terms
> with such of her particular features as will help us to our private
> ends.[71]

Many turn-of-the-century supporters of nature preserves were business leaders who saw no contradiction between their capitalist ventures, often dependent on extracting natural resources, and their support of environmental preserves. Humans had the right to dominate nature and to make choices about its place and boundaries. To the extent that this model is linked with environmentalism—for instance, in the "Wise Use Movement"[72]—it is grounded in an ethic of balance and conservation.

Conservation suggests that we are naturalists from our own interest; our interests are "vested" in nature (through agriculture, hunting, fishing, mining, recreation, or aesthetic appreciation), and we protect what benefits us.[73] The wild can in this sense be thought of as a market in which all manners of taste are to be satisfied, through private financial commitments or governmental policy: it should not be set aside for a few elite "nature fakirs."[74]

As a result, a prime consideration of the humanist is to preserve nature for posterity, linking generational equity to environmentalism. The nineteenth-century geologist and explorer John Wesley Powell argued that people are obliged to use natural resources prudently to ensure that they will be available for future human generations,[75] husbanding resources for a later day. Our goal is not to maximize our interests, but to satisfice them.

My goal is not to claim that any of these broad ideological perspectives is uniquely adequate as a theoretical model or that humans accept only one, ignoring the others. In fact, these perspectives are resources from which one can draw to make claims about the good and well-lived life. These ideological perspectives are backdrops by which we understand and experience the natural world. That human contact with nature has ecological effects underlines the importance of understanding how humans conceptualize their place in nature. Despite our talk about being at one with nature or giving full rights to it, the visions and decisions are, and must be, social choices.

THE SOCIOLOGY OF NATURE

As is their right, philosophers specialize in grand pronouncements about what the relations between humans and the natural environment ought to be. Sociologists ask rather different questions, more specific and empirical: how do humans conceive of nature and how do they interact with the natural environment? By looking at behavior instead of ideals, I present a *peopled sociology*: an analysis of what individuals actually do and say. Sociologists did not always define the study of nature within their domain, but slowly and fitfully they have claimed the environment.[76]

In the past twenty years environmental sociology has become a central topic, both theoretically and in applied terms. Much research explores human attitudes and the effects of behavior in a cultural arena: popular attitudes toward pollution and environmentalism,[77] the growth and development of social movements protecting the environment,[78] the effects of pollution and environmental degradation on human communities,[79] and the development of technologies and population patterns that have an ecological impact.[80] Models of appropriate relations between human society and the environment (for example, the human exceptionalism paradigm vs. the new environmental paradigm)[81] are laden with strategic interest for the organization of communities and social systems.

These are worthy topics, but my concerns are different—less directly tied to pressing social problems, but equally related to how morality and society are linked. I examine how individuals and groups understand, experience, and interact with the natural environment, not so much in their theoretical pronouncements as in practice, what I term "naturework." I connect the appreciation of nature to its social organization and to the cultural system in which it is embedded.

Often we casually speak of nature as a totality and refer to "attitudes about nature." By doing this we lose sight of the fact that people deal not with a global nature, but rather with a local environment. Our experiences are with small corners of the world we label nature. A natural environment is a set of objects, meanings, and experiences classified together. Yet merely because we label a set of objects or a space as nature does not mean that this object or space will be meaningful. As a thought experiment, consider a walk in the woods. How many birds did you hear? How many mushrooms did you spy? How many flowers did you recognize? How many animal tracks did you spot? How many insects were crawling or flying nearby? What minerals did you step over? Nature is a "booming, buzzing confusion." The potential for cognitive overload[82] is as real in the clearing as on the corner.

THE SOCIOLOGY OF FUNGUS

To explore the relationship between humans and their environment, I observed a group that specializes in a small slice of the natural world. Specifically, I came to know people who as part of their leisure activities choose to walk through fields and forests, and who value this expressive activity: amateur mycologists, or mushroomers. I observed these men and women and gradually came to share their knowledge and their passion.

Not surprisingly, plants[83] are seen as even more different from humans than are animals. Since animals move and respond in ways that seem under volitional control, we comfortably suggest that they think, act, and interact. Plants, being "rooted" and lacking human-like organs, are harder to role-play. We assume that plants do not think, although they respond to stimuli. The relationship between humans and animals is now examined by sociologists and other social scientists,[84] but one would be thought odd to suggest that plants interact with each other or with humans—despite some hopeful, if inconclusive, attempts to converse with plants.

Examining the human relationship with nature is only one focus of this research project; often people who wish to interact with nature do so in the company of others who facilitate that connection—a voluntary grouping that creates a sense of communion.[85] Mushroomers see themselves as sharing interests, and this provides the basis of ongoing affiliation. Experiencing nature is frequently a collective enterprise—a sociality that provides satisfaction.

Some nature lovers, like other hobbyists, explore their interests in the context of a formal organization. One need not pay dues to explore the woods, but many who do so have made that choice. Organizations can provide things that personal action and interpersonal ties alone cannot. In all spheres of leisure activity, and particularly in ecoleisure, people join organizations to facilitate their goals and to provide a community in which to share their experience.

A WORLD OF FUNGUS

Those unfamiliar with mushroom collecting might be surprised to learn that there exists a national (or, more precisely, a continental) organization of some 1800 members who share a common interest in learning about and collecting mushrooms. According to the organization's founder's story,[86] the North American Mycological Association (NAMA) grew out of the interest of a sheet metal worker, Harry Knighton,[87] who,

> while sitting on an old log, watching the fall migration of birds in 1957 . . . noticed a brilliant orange growth along the log and promptly photographed it. The idea was to take the finished photo to the local library, look up the fungus in Nina Marshal's Mushroom Book. Alas it wasn't there!

This frustration led Knighton to contact prominent professional mycologists, such as Alexander Smith and William Bridge Cooke; eventually Knighton's need for comradeship led him to participate in the People-to-People program of the Eisenhower administration, which attempted to facilitate "international friendship and understanding"[88] through personal contacts, and grew out of a recognition of "the American predilection" for leisure groupings.[89] In November 1959 a meeting was held at the Botany Department at Ohio State University, which led to the formation of the North American Mycological Association. The organization currently publishes a biannual journal, *McIlvanea,* named for Charles McIlvane, a turn-of-the-century collector and fieldguide author. The scientific articles in this journal, unlike those in professional journals such as *Mycologia,* are written in a style comprehensible by serious amateurs. In addition, NAMA publishes a bimonthly newsletter, sponsors a slide contest, provides educational slide-shows and speakers, maintains a registry of mushroom poisoning cases, and, most significantly, sponsors an annual five-day mycological foray.

A network of smaller, local or regional organizations bolsters the larger organization. In most major metropolitan areas, particularly in the Northeast, Midwest, and West, groups of amateurs have banded together for support and community. According to a NAMA list of affiliated state and local organizations, seventy-seven mycological clubs operated in the United States and Canada in 1993. Total membership has been estimated at ten thousand.[90] These clubs vary in size, with more than one thousand in the San Francisco Mycological Society; six hundred in the Colorado Mycological Society; seventy-five in the Illinois Mycological Association; and a few dozen in smaller clubs, such as the Northwestern Wisconsin Mycological Society.

The Minnesota Mycological Society,[91] the site of the bulk of my observations and interviews, was founded in 1898, making it the second oldest continuously active mushroom society in the United States. Although professional mycologists are welcome to join, none were active during my observation.

As in many voluntary organizations, interest groups exist under the banner of the larger organization. Some of the approximately two hundred members are primarily interested in examining mushrooms from a quasi-scientific perspective (these members are sometimes labeled amateur mycologists); some enjoy compiling lists or collections of the mushrooms they find; and others, known as pot hunters, collect mushrooms to eat (for the pot). Still others have photography as their first love. Although the members of the organization are friendly and mutually supportive, tension occasionally flares over the proper division of club resources.

The Minnesota Mycological Society meets one evening a week for approximately two hours during the prime mushroom-picking months in Minnesota: May, June, September, and October. At these meetings the president describes the mushrooms that members bring and that the Identification Committee[92] has identified. Members also describe their memorable mushroom finds, and, consistent with norms of secrecy (discussed in Chapter 5), describe where and how their caches were discovered. At some meetings, members give talks (for example, on cultivating mushrooms, mushrooms in other nations, or foreign travel) or present show slides. In addition to these weekly meetings, the club also organizes approximately half a dozen forays to state and county parks and to private property. Two of these forays last for a weekend. The club also holds a banquet during January and organizes a mycology study group that meets once a month to examine mushrooms with microscopes and chemicals.

To learn how mushroom collectors understand nature, I employed several methods: participant observation, in-depth interviews, surveys, and document analysis. For three years I attended most of the meetings, forays, and banquets of the Minnesota Mycological Society and compiled detailed field notes. These notes were supplemented by a questionnaire sent to all members (with a 66 percent response rate), and with in-depth interviews of approximately two dozen active members of the group, lasting approximately ninety minutes each. In the course of my research I also attended a national foray organized by the North American Mycological Association, and two regional forays—one in the Midwest and one in the Northeast. I later mailed a survey to a 10 percent sample of the members of NAMA (with a 60 percent response rate). These data are supplemented by copies of newsletters published by some two dozen mycological societies, personal correspondence, and fieldguides for mushroom collecting and other publications (memoirs, cookbooks, and collections of essays). I also examined the first twelve years of *Mushroom: The Journal of Wild Mushrooming,* a national periodical aimed at amateur mushroomers with a circulation of approximately two thousand. Finally, I included questions on a random survey of residents of the Twin Cities, asking whether these respondents had ever picked wild mushrooms and eaten those mushrooms that they picked.

My focus is not on all mushroom collectors, but on those who have chosen to join voluntary organizations. I do not examine in depth commercial pickers, who represent a sizable segment of West Coast pickers; those who collect in the context of ethnic group activity, notably Southeast Asians; nor professional mycologists. Although I discuss these groups at various points, my ethnographic focus is on hobbyists. The site of my ethnography in Minnesota affects some of my conclusions, as it affects the species of mushrooms that were collected.[93]

THE HISTORY AND GEOGRAPHY OF MUSHROOM COLLECTING

We know little of what our cave-dwelling ancestors chose to consume and why. But there is no doubt that the consumption of mushrooms has a long history. In 300 B.C. Theophrastus recorded that mushrooms were valued as food and for trade. Pliny, Juvenal, Martial, and Cicero each considered mushrooms to be great delicacies, and the Roman emperor Claudius was allegedly poisoned by a plate of mushrooms.[94] Mushrooms are also mentioned in the Hindu Rig Vega, and were eaten on the Indian subcontinent.[95] Mushrooms were probably consumed for food and for their psychedelic properties in Mesoamerica, Siberia, and Scandinavia.[96]

The fact that mushrooms can literally appear overnight makes them seem a gift from the divine. Indeed, some believe that God provided the Israelites with "manna from heaven" in the form of a fungus.[97] Others interpret the miraculous appearance of mushrooms as indicative of an evil origin, such as the spit of witches.[98] Still others—Hindus, Greeks, Romans, ancient Mexican tribes[99]—attributed their sudden appearance to the effects of lightening or thunder. Through much recorded history mushrooms have been recognized as food, medicine, a psychoactive plant, and a source of divine or evil powers.

By the eighteenth century mushrooms began to be tamed. Mushrooms were first cultivated in caves near Paris in the reign of Louis XIV. By the end of the nineteenth century, mushrooming had become a popular leisure pursuit in Europe and America. In 1884 the first mycological society, the Société Mycologique de France, was organized by a group of local naturalists. A decade later in 1895 the Boston Mycological Club was established, apparently the first such group in the United States. The Mycological Society of America, the organization of professional mycologists, was founded in 1932.[100] Although Americans (and the English)[101] do not have the same rage for mushrooms as do the French and Eastern Europeans,[102] a mistrust that some label as "mycophobia," mushrooming has become more respectable in this country,[103] as an ecological orientation is taking hold. Living in harmony with nature (including eating wild foods) is becoming part of the cultural capital of many young, upwardly mobile Americans. This, combined with more free time among some population segments, with the availability of fieldguides and other resources for collecting, and with immigration from Asia, the Americas, and Eastern Europe, has led to the increased interest in mushroom collecting.

Who are mushroomers? The members of every leisure group differ in some measure from those who select other activities.[104] One estimate places the number of mushroomers at thirty million in the United States,[105] a figure made credible by survey research. According to a random sample of the Twin Cities metropolitan area, 22 percent of those polled have collected wild mushrooms,[106] and 15 percent have, at least once, consumed mushrooms that they picked in the wild. In this sample, there were no age or income differences, although compared with the rest of the population mushroom collectors were more likely to be male (Chi Square = 7.1, $p < .01$) and college graduates (Chi Square = 2.9, $p < .10$).[107] The number of regularly active collectors is surely substantially lower, though many more than the two hundred members of the Minnesota Mycological Society.[108]

The folk beliefs of many mushroomers suggest that they have a distinct personality, although there is not total agreement on these characteristics. Many note their interest in the outdoors, with one man commenting on how they are "generally quieter, more gentle people"; another notes that "they're free. They enjoy life. . . . They are more down-to-earth." Some comment that mushroomers like to collect things, love a treasure hunt, and are curious about the world. One mushroomer combined these themes, suggesting that "they like to try new things. I think they like to be self-sufficient a little bit. . . . Most people who like mushrooms also like to gather other wild food, and they are interested in other plants."

In a more self-critical vein, some suggest that mushroomers are introverted. One commented that "people interested in inanimate objects have difficulty dealing with people. . . . It's a solitary occupation. . . . So often the topic of conversation is about the mushroom, rather than, 'Does your husband have cancer?' or 'How are your children?'" Mushrooming can be an eccentric compulsion:

> Bruce Horn, who . . . is currently serving as president of the Kaw Valley Mycological Society [in Kansas] thinks that mycology attracts people who, if not exactly eccentric, are not afraid to be seen as such. The people who like mushrooms do, he thinks, simply because most people don't, and liking mushrooms sets you apart from everybody else.[109]

One should be cautious in accepting these ingroup folk interpretations as anything other than rhetorical resources that help participants define themselves. Still, the emphasis on loving nature, being down-to-earth, desiring to collect objects, being curious about the world, and being willing to be seen as eccentric are traits that—if they do not necessarily distinguish mushroomers in fact—contribute to their personal identity.

SCOPE

I examine the link between nature and community as expressed through leisure activity, that is, people choosing to spend time in a natural environment. In order to examine how the wild is made social, I divide the work into three sections addressing the lived experiences of persons, the social engagement of friends, and the structure of organizational affiliation. Each represents a different level of analysis by which we can understand how humans tame nature into their models, connecting the images of nature described above (protectionism, organicism, and humanism) to the actual doing of naturework.

"Nature" is inevitably a cultural construction, and being "in nature" implies being in culture. I treat the sociology of nature as a branch of the sociology of culture, confronting the claim that nature is an autochthonous realm that has a unique claim on our attention. Nature does, of course, claim our attention: not because of what it is, but rather because of what we make of it.

Nature and Lived Experience

It is now widely accepted that what we experience is not objective but must be created, both through previous experience (termed "socialization") and through immediate experience. A budding flower, a bird in flight, or a decaying carcass will not inevitably produce a fixed set of sensory evaluations or cognitive meanings. We share evaluations and meanings, but this collective knowledge speaks to the power of our culture to impress itself on us. Nature is a social construction. Yet to say this is to say little. The larger issue is how in practice we perceive and interpret stimuli that we are taught to experience in particular ways. What are the processes by which we invest objects with meaning and emotion, what are the features of social organization that affect our reaction to an "authentic," "unmediated" experience, and how does this social construction affect us?

In depicting nature as an experienced reality, I focus on the perspectives of human actors describing what they label "nature." Although nature is an imprecise category, most of us have little difficulty knowing whether we are in a natural setting. If we are surrounded by grass, trees, or water in an environment that we do not consider to have been created by human hands, then we are experiencing "nature." The fewer human objects (and the fewer human bodies), the more the location is said to be natural. These settings routinely generate emotions that, depending on the characteristics of the natural environment, can include rapture, fear, or calm. Transactional emotions, such as anger, are rarely experienced. One can hardly be angry at poison ivy, nettles, swamp gas, or copperheads, although one might be angry at oneself (or one's companions) for not avoiding them. The anger that arises in natural environments occurs when one comes across human detritus (for example, a beer can) in an otherwise pristine (natural) setting.

In addition to the emotional reactions to the natural environment, humans also organize nature into a set of cognitive categories, often providing elaborate metaphorical and moral constructions to help understand what they have just experienced. For instance, mush-roomers define certain mushrooms as good and others as bad; some are referred to with the male pronoun and others with the female pro-noun; some are considered beautiful and others are dismissed as homely. These meanings are not inherent in the objects; we cannot say with certainty the divine's intention in their creation.

Finally, being "in nature" contributes to identity work.[110] How do individuals present their identity by virtue of their leisure pursuits? What does it mean to one's self-image to be the sort of person who spends time in a natural environment, and how are others categorized by virtue of their leisure activities? To be a nature lover is not simply to do something but to be someone. The moral virtue of being one with the environment rubs off on the visitor, attaching itself like net-tles. Nature shapes self-definition.

Nature and Social Engagement

When we encounter nature, it is frequently in the company of other humans, as part of a group. This groupness channels behavior. Ad-mittedly, people on occasion venture into nature alone, and they may treasure that encounter, but frequently we bring our social world along. Encountering nature is often an event, as when families or friends plan a camping trip. For many, the social surround deepens and enlivens the ecological surround, and transforms it: just as drink-ing alone is seen as quite different from drinking with a group.

The significance of a network of contacts is magnified when indi-viduals recount the highlights of their experiences in nature. As Richard Mitchell[111] notes, speaking of mountain climbers, the climb is not over until the tale has been told.

In Chapters 3 and 4, I examine how sociability and relationships process and facilitate natural experiences. Nature is made meaningful through the existence of a social group. My goal is to analyze the con-tent and context of these shared occasions. A mushroom foray is a so-cial event that, if successful, can involve culture and nature, sociabil-ity and authenticity derived from unmediated exposure to ultimate reality. Building on my previous research on group culture,[112] I exam-ine how, through narrative, people talk about their experiences. Na-ture serves as a "staging area" for the development of culture.

I am particularly interested in the narratives that follow natural experience, making it socially real. In collecting subcultures, participants describe their finds and missed finds, presenting narratives that create an empathetic community. Nature is a storied realm—as populated by narratives as by trees. These stories dip into several emotional and cognitive streams.

Some narratives can be likened to *war stories,* in which participants depict their common efforts to overcome obstacles, emphasizing their solidarity and collective understanding of a world that does not appreciate or understand them. In these stories, tellers differentiate their communities from those of outsiders.

A second set of narratives, labeled *sad tales,* includes instances in which triumph becomes failure. As with the fish that gets away, a collector may return to a patch of mushrooms to discover that they have been picked, can no longer be found, or have decayed. Mushroomers share the emotional let-down with the teller, and, through the act of commiseration, establish the reality of the community. These tales emphasize the uncontrolled, authentic quality of the natural environment.

A third set of stories—richly told and personally satisfying—is *treasure tales.* They depict triumphs in which mushroomers unexpectedly encounter a remarkable cache of specimens. These stories are akin to those that antique collectors narrate about their purchases, comedians tell about great audiences, archival researchers tell about their discoveries, or birders tell about the species found out of place. These narratives exemplify shared identity and reflect communal feelings, relying on collective values and emotions. That discovery occurs within a context of scarcity, a lack of control, and group competition gives the narratives power that might be absent in conditions of abundance.

Narratives can be told in several emotional and interpretive registers. For each of these types, one can find narratives that transform the events into humor. Jocular discourse plays with the emotions that are embedded in the untransformed texts. Some narratives are told specifically as humorous talk (such as stories that satirize danger or public hostility), but more frequently a "doubling" of meaning occurs in which the narrative will be heard as thematically serious, while humorous remarks comment on the events.

In accounts about experiences in nature, one is reminded that what seems at first to be personal and authentic is based on shared understandings and values. Narratives play upon other narratives and depict events in light of other accounts and forms of narration. Nature is not only a space to be experienced, but a space to be talked about.

Nature and Organizational Affiliation

Many have noted the American penchant for forming voluntary organizations to support collective interests.[113] These organizations extend beyond work, politics, and religion to include leisure organizations; organizations that promote sociability and facilitate leisure.[114] Organizations designed to provide natural experiences were among the earliest and most popular leisure groups.[115] Although individuals can experience nature without collective facilitation, Americans find that organizations are not only efficient but, more significantly, provide an arena in which one's self-image may be formulated, relations of communal trust developed, and competition organized and harnessed. Such groups, in some circumstances, provide participants or resources for social movements or collective action. In the case of the Audubon Society or the Sierra Club, the goals of the organization include both leisure facilitation and political activism, a mix that may provoke organizational tension.

In this study I examine the Minnesota Mycological Society as a nature organization, a position that it shares with organizations devoted to butterfly collecting, herpetology, rock hounding, birdwatching, hiking, skiing, diving, and other pursuits. That enthusiasts often establish organizations to achieve their ends leads me to ask, how are these groups organized and stabilized? What purposes are they perceived as serving in a community that could survive without them?

Merely to establish an organization does not in itself facilitate a satisfying experience. Bringing together people who have different claims upon the resources of the group may provoke competition, and, potentially, may splinter the organization. Although most leisure organizations, by virtue of their voluntary character, are fairly harmonious, conflicts do develop and may strain members' sense of belonging to the same moral community. The group must be organized to provide not only knowledge about and access to nature, but also satisfying social experiences that overwhelm debate about the use of organizational resources.

Voluntary organizations have problems different from those of organizations that rely on social control. Surely one can understand the worker who continues to toil at an unpleasant job in a difficult environment. Such cannot be said of organizations that facilitate leisure. Although instrumental resources are often provided to members of nature groups, it is equally critical that participants receive a continual stream of nonmaterial benefits in the form of self-confirmation and emotional satisfaction: identity work. This is provided through social ties, which are seen as constituting the organization. Membership should be identity-affirming and members *by their presence* should provide benefits.

Their provisioning of resources for leisure activity, their potential for ideological socialization, and their ability to create community make nature organizations socially significant. The focus on the natural environment by these groups reminds us of the linkage of culture and nature. It is not only through the human technologies that environments are altered, but through collective action and organizational life.

Chapter 1 explores how individuals experience the natural environment. I begin by discussing the importance to naturalists of being "apart" from the built environment, asking how people distinguish between the social world and the natural world, describing what it means to be outside the social world. For all their discussion about the desirability of respecting nature, mushroomers (like other naturalists) use nature for their own ends. Despite this utilitarian orientation, most naturalists wish to be at one with the world. In line with the organic vision, they define nature as an authentic environment. Some naturalists claim to experience a mystical relationship—with God, nature, the universe—in the wild. Finally, I examine sources of danger that validate the authenticity and nonhuman quality of the wild, even while danger is limited and the environment has been tamed and defanged.

Chapter 2 expands personal interpretations of nature by connecting them to the process by which amateur mycologists think and talk about the mushrooms they collect. I begin by examining the professed need for a focus for naturework. I then address the metaphors that are used to interpret mushrooms. These metaphorical constructions are most apparent in the personifications of mushrooms, in which the moral valuation of these natural objects becomes explicit.

Chapters 3 and 4 deal with how nature becomes central to social interaction. In Chapter 3, I explore the social features of searching for, identifying, and consuming mushrooms. Although mushroomers sometimes do these activities alone, part of the satisfaction of mushrooming comes in taking one's community into the woods. Collective decisions characterize this nature pursuit, as they do other leisure activities. Chapter 4 moves the discussion from the woods. Leisure activities consist of bundles of narratives. I focus on the social discourse involved in naturework—how individuals share their commitment to the wild through their accounts: war stories, sad tales, treasure tales, and a set of jokes that situate and tame collective danger.

In Chapter 5 I return—with a twist—to the issues of the first chapter. At the beginning of the book I was interested in how individuals experience nature; here my concern is with how organizations are experienced: not all organizations, but those that deal with a nature pursuit that is both potentially dangerous and competitive, even though this argument applies to a wide range of leisure organizations. I present a model of how leisure organizations need to provide sufficient rewards for members so that they continue their affiliation. This approach, borrowing from Resource Mobilization Theory in social movements, I have termed Provisioning Theory. I argue that leisure organizations need to provide knowledge, sociability, and identity for members. The division of the book into sections dealing with lived experience, social engagement, and organizational affiliation is patterned on this claim.

Further, I argue that mushroom societies, like other groups, may be split by segmental interests. Individual mushroomers have different concerns, and this often plays itself out in attempts to obtain organizational resources. Despite the communal concern, organizational politics may make the group fragile. How are members tied to one another in the face of centrifocal forces? Organizations need to develop trust in the competence of members and in the organization as a corporate entity. Mushroomers place faith in the judgments and advice of peers, and, under some circumstances, risk their lives, without little worry. Much trust and confidence in the competence of others characterize the mushrooming community. Yet this community also depends on competition in finding mushrooms, and this leads to secrecy. How is secrecy compatible with the equally visible trust?

Chapter 6 extends the structural analysis. In this chapter I describe how amateur mushroomers perceive and interact with the general public (ignorant, and perhaps fearful, of their pursuit), commercial mushroom collectors (who compete for the same patches of desired mushrooms), and professional mycologists (who simultaneously are esteemed for their knowledge and scorned for their esoteric specialization). Amateur mushroomers operate within a structured and differentiated social arena, filled with group typifications and stereotypes. Many groups have a stake in the interpretation of this natural realm.

Ultimately, as I describe in Chapter 7, this project is an attempt to develop and expand the construct of naturework in order to demonstrate that nature is in itself not an essential reality, but a cultural category that is constructed from essential, real objects. Nevertheless, I emphasize throughout the book that nature is not "merely" cultural; the authenticity of nature (as it is and as it is perceived) forces us to treat it as real, even though we continue to shape its meaning for our own ends. The world exists and is consequential, but we struggle to make it meaningful and to provide guidelines for the choices that we, as members of society, inevitably make in preserving and altering our ecosystems. Although nature may be a cultural construction, the choices that we make are powerful and have lasting, reverberating effects that channel our built environment and our quality of life.

CHAPTER
ONE

*Being
in Nature*

Nature, praise be, neither talks nor is rational,
and therein is comfort.

—JOHN LIVINGSTON[1]

The early autumn air was crisp and bright. After a brace of damp, chill days, the sun had broken through the clouds on this Saturday morning in September. Some two dozen men and women, dressed in jeans and sweaters, milled around a small parking lot near a county park in southeastern Minnesota. With the mild weather following cool, wet days, the group's hopes were high that they would find caches of edible boletes, hen of the woods, oyster mushrooms, and honey mushrooms. Sadly, it was too late in the year for chanterelles. This year the weather had not been kind to Minnesota mushroomers, although some wondered whether the cause was really pollution. It had been another bad year for morels—too cold and wet during May, with a little snow. Even the summer was too hot for many chanterelles. But we were hopeful on this first foray of the fall, and our attention was focused on the promisingly gloomy weather of the past few days. Mushroomers frequently remind themselves that they welcome cool rains and cloudy days. We shared accounts of the mushrooms found over the summer, narrated humorous stories about the large national foray that three members had attended, and questioned those who had recently found edible species about promising locations.

Finally, the foray leader arrived, and as a group we entered the woods, each clutching a basket, knife, bags, and fieldguides. Some carried whistles in case they strayed from the group. Within minutes, like bugs roused from an overturned log, we separated, at first in groups of two or three, and then individually. Whenever one of us found a notable mushroom—a large patch of shaggy manes, a giant puffball, a brilliant chicken of the woods, a lacy stinkhorn, a magnificent hedgehog mushroom, a log loaded with oyster mushrooms, or a perfectly preserved, poisonous, fiery orange *Amanita muscaria*[2]—those within earshot would be called to gather and examine the treasure.

After two hours tromping through the woods, we straggled back to a picnic area near our meeting place. The search was successful—the rain of the previous week had produced a fresh and plentiful crop of mushrooms, and simply being in the woods on this beautiful fall day lifted our spirits. Still, we had found no honey caps, disappointing, since honeys were a favorite edible of several forayers. Perhaps it was still early, we consoled ourselves.

After examining one another's finds, hearing about the adventures in the woods, and taking photographs, we hungrily turned to lunch. Several members of the group shared fungal delectables: a cream of wild mushroom soup, pickled mushrooms, and a mushroom pâté. No one questioned their edibility: the cooks were veterans.

After lunch we turned to the task of identifying the mushrooms. Many were old friends and took no more than a quick glance. Several, particularly those brought in by novices, were too small, dull, or dried out for the serious identifiers, and these were unceremoniously dumped in the trash. Our attention was directed to about a half dozen brightly colored or large mushrooms. There were a few vivid red and orange waxy caps, for which we needed the aid of a fieldguide. One brownish amanita provoked a lively debate as to its precise species—*pantherina* or *rubescens*. The color wasn't quite right for either; a potentially important matter, given that the former was deadly, the latter edible. Partisans for each position mercilessly teased their rivals. Finding *Lactarius* specimens is always fun in that the taste, color, and amount of the milk permit identification. Then there were some specimens—a yellow-green bolete and a large bracket fungus—that, after considerable time and frustration, we awarded uncertain labels. Since we were not planning to consume them, some name, however incorrect, was better than none. By mid-afternoon, our identification complete, our jokes told, and our feet sore, we turned to our cars. We shared a day: even if the mushrooms would not stay with us, our experiences would. So ended our time in the woods. For a few hours our fellowship was encircled by nature.

Being surrounded by stately trees can provoke many sentiments. Some become claustrophobic, feeling lost or trapped, soon to be crushed by a wayward branch. Others experience pressured anxiety: too many pines to be cut for the mill at an inhuman pace. Still others feel at peace; standing in a sylvan glade is perfection—a mystic link to the divine in a green cathedral.

Although mushrooms do not have the same cultural resonance as trees, parents of young children may feel anxious surrounded by brightly colored toadstools, whereas amateur mycologists may exult in these rough treasures.

The experience of nature may be mundane, frightening, or richly emotional depending upon circumstance and upon cultural beliefs. This is dramatically evident when Edmund Burke[3] connects nature to the sublime, linking the astonishment of the unknown and uncontrolled to an experience of terror. Today's wild is no longer quite so dangerous; as a result, nature now affords the luxury of calm contemplation and fosters a desire to preserve a tamed other.

Because nature is now widely viewed as "pleasant," many Americans desire to "experience" it for their leisure.[4] The past decade has witnessed a rise in organized authentic experiences: "ecotourism."[5] For some this involves days camping in a wilderness area, for others a morning of hunting or fishing, and for still others a brief excursion to the park with one's kin. The attraction of nature is so potent that landscaping is a critical selling point for homes, colleges, and apartment complexes, even if pesticides and herbicides must be slathered around to maintain the pastoral scene. Human-created environments, such as zoos or amusement parks, simulate, imperfectly, a natural environment for their patrons. The desire to share one's life with "natural" objects is widespread, as it has been in most times and places, albeit in different forms. Nature is not simply a matter of fact but an insistent and live reality.[6] In this belief that nature is central to what we are as humans, to our "nature," attitudes to the wild differ in kind from reactions to other scenes.

Understanding nature requires recognizing how natural objects are linked to experiences that are felt as authentic but are actually culturally privileged. Humans justify their satisfactions,[7] perhaps as a consequence of the Puritan ethic: free time without purpose is waste.[8] We insist that we "get something" for our leisure.[9] The experience of being in nature generates sensual and cognitive satisfactions that overwhelm costs. Yet for all this, naturalists are challenged to describe their emotional trill so that others can appreciate this internal sensibility.

In this chapter I explore how mushroomers feel and speak about their activity, justifying their pursuit. I focus on three issues—being away from civilization, being at one with nature, and the pragmatic use of nature—that resonate with the visions of nature described in the Introduction, linking the experience of nature to the ways that human-nature interaction is organized. Although I do not postulate a direct link between how nature is perceived in light of core images and policy prescriptions and the way that nature is personally experienced, the templates described above (the protectionist, organic, and humanist views) are theoretically tied to how nature is to be experienced. I do not claim that individuals who share a vision of nature necessarily experience nature identically; views of nature and modes of experience are cultural toolkits that individuals and groups draw upon to interpret their world. One's orientation toward nature influences modes of experience, but this is an imperfect connection for active meaning creators.

The protectionist view sees nature as separate from human society. To be "in nature" sets one apart from humanity, and this awayness is central to the justifications of naturework. Civilization is scorned and nature is enshrined. Benefits—emotional and cognitive—derive directly from being apart from an oppressive, built environment. In contrast, to embrace an organic metaphor suggests that the boundary between humanity and nature is artificial and blurred, and that humans can become one with the surrounding world. To feel at one with nature connects one to the "unity of the planet." Finally, a humanist view of nature implies that the natural environment is to be consumed and used by humans for their own satisfaction. One's emotions and goals justify an orientation to the wild. Although this does not imply that humans should destroy the planet (indeed, many choose to conserve it for later pleasures), it does elevate the desires of human actors over "nature's own" desire. This humanist orientation also suggests that danger is inherent in nature. Danger implies that nature is an authentic and uncontrolled reality, one of which humans must be aware in organizing their activities. Ultimately, naturework depends on culturally validated metaphors and must be interpreted *in light of* (and often *in contrast to*) the experience of human society.

BEING AWAY

According to many nature enthusiasts, the world is too much with us. We need to get away. This image of escape, found throughout naturalist writing, emphasizes that nature contrasts with "civilization." As Bill McKibben recognizes in *The End of Nature,* "We feel the need for pristine places, places substantially *unaltered* by man."[10] McKibben notes, astutely, that unaltered places no longer exist—no natural streams, no natural autumns; it is the recognition of *alteration* that provides the basis for the search for the pristine. Preserved wildness expresses the value of the superimposed culture: the continued existence of the bald eagle in its wilderness environs symbolizes—emotionally and powerfully—the very society that altered much of its habitat.[11] By preserving the eagle (and the elk, the condor, and the spotted owl), we legitimate ourselves. Being away provides emotional richness by contrast: the rejection of the Mundane in the face of the Other—an Orientalism of place.

For many naturalists the implicit rule seems to be "the further away the better." One's time in the wild brings discovery and exploration. This awayness was put graphically by Hal Borland, the nature essayist for the *New York Times* Sunday editorial page, who described his role as "like a foreign correspondent reporting an alien scene."[12]

The possibility of natural experience depends upon the existence of places that can be defined as unaltered, wrong though that categorization may be objectively. Nature is real, not artificial, in that "the hand of man is excluded from it."[13] Wilderness (*pure* nature) is a place that produces a mood, feeling, or state of mind. These emotions depend on one's experience of place: one person's wilderness may be another's roadside picnic ground. Civilization for the Yukon trapper is wilderness for the Chicago banker.[14] As Thoreau recognized, wilderness does not exist apart from us.[15] Wilderness is a place where it is good to think: an arena that, no longer threatening, is viewed sentimentally with affection, utopianism, and nostalgia.[16] Harold Ickes, Franklin Roosevelt's secretary of the interior, remarked after viewing Yosemite: "One should get away once in a while as far as possible from human contacts. To contemplate nature, magnificently garbed as it is in this country, is to restore peace to the mind."[17] Human contact, in contrast, is laden with conflict.

Nature rejuvenates humans after the demands of civilization—temporal and material stressors. This is in the tradition of Henry David Thoreau's *Walden,* John Muir's writings, and, from a different tradition, Sigmund Freud's *Civilization and Its Discontents.* Wilderness is an antidote for the poisons and detritus of industrial society. Human society, in this view, is infected by conflict and materialism.

Writing in an Emersonian tradition, the nineteenth-century naturalist George Evans, esteeming the moral benefits of nature, captured the belief in the emotional rejuvenation that wilderness supposedly provides:

> Whenever the light of civilization falls upon you with blighting power . . . go to the wilderness. . . . Dull business routine, the fierce passions of the market place, the perils of envious cities become but a memory. . . . The wilderness will take hold of you. It will give you good red blood; it will turn you from a weakling into a man. . . . You will soon behold all with a peaceful soul.[18]

Evans is prescient in his image of wilderness as a tonic for the disease of civilization. Modern life is imbued with stress, which nature dissipates through a "rite of simplification."[19] We speak of "restorative" environments that lead to the recovery of effective psychological functioning, including a sense of wholeness and a positive view of life.[20] We claim that children *need* wildness for healthy development and self-esteem.[21] William Gibson, a neurological researcher, describes parklands as "the greatest mental health guardians we have."[22] Wilderness therapy and adventure therapy are now in the arsenal of metal health professionals—removing patients from civilization removes them from neurosis and psychopathology, producing a "complete human being" again.[23] Some evidence suggests that providing hospital patients with a view may speed recovery,[24] and being in the wild may even cure "irregular bowel movements."[25]

Humans lack the soul of nature. They fill their world with meaningless objects. The naturalist Paul Gruchow speaks of the "necessity of empty places."[26] Humanness for him represents an ugly fullness:

> It is an odd irony that the places that we call empty should retain some memory of the diversity of life, while the places we have filled up grow emptier and emptier. If we knew what we were getting rid of, we might have some premonition of the things we were going to miss.

The fullness needs to be drained for the natural world to be appreciated. As the sociologist Alex Inkeles[27] has observed, a reliable indicator of modernity is the ratio of animate to inanimate objects in the everyday environment—the more modern one's society, the more one's space is filled with things. The biologist Edward O. Wilson sardonically notes: "Lawn grass, potted plants, caged parakeets, puppies, and rubber snakes are not enough."[28] Fullness is auditory as well as visual and tactile. Bernard DeVoto justifies being in the wilderness "to learn again what quiet is. I believe that our culture is more likely to perish from noise than from radioactive fallout."[29]

The emptiness in nature is not a literal emptiness but an emptiness of value, filled with the detritus of human activity. It is a space known by what is absent. When one says in frustration, "I've had it up to here," or "I can't take any more," what is had or taken are the demands of a routinized social order: demands that contrast with the absence of similar demands in nature.

Mushroomers readily accept this desire to stand apart from a troubling humanity as justification for their activities. One successful professional told me: "Like many people who are overcommitted, I often need at least a psychological boost. I mean, this next couple of weeks, I'm going to be spending a lot of time in the woods." Said another: "After a week in the office as a dentist, [I find that] the woods are a fresh and new world."[30] A third reported:

> When I think about being in the city, I usually think of concrete and traffic lights, schedules, and limitations on time, being dressed up, and usually have something to do with work one way or another.

When I'm out in nature, I think of being relaxed, and being dressed either to keep warm or to keep cool, instead of what it looks like, and being someplace where I want to be, where something is growing, whether it's in the meadow or in the woods or in the lake or something. Someplace where nature hasn't been wiped out for the sake of civilization. Usually away from all the noises of the city.

Humanity fosters alienation, which is assuaged by an encounter with the "authentic":[31] an antidote to the dangers of overcivilization.[32] One mushroomer remarked on "the need to feel there is more to life than bringing home the evening paper and the paycheck."[33] The distinction between nature and civilization is embedded in these mushroomers' appreciation of the set-apart quality of their leisure. By virtue of their rapid and unexpected appearance, mushrooms represent "patches of anarchy . . . [revealing] nature at work."[34]

This distinction between nature and culture is evident in the objects of the hunt: wild mushrooms are valued over those purchased, not from blind taste tests, but through the emotional experience of naturework. This is particularly true for species such as morels that entrepreneurs attempt to cultivate:

> The taste of the cultivated morels may please the palate, but they will not satisfy like a meal of wild morels and fiddleheads gathered among wildflowers in the spring sunshine. Wild morels and the experience of searching for them cannot be packaged and sold.[35]

Nature lures the hobbyist away from quotidian commitments. One notes that "the urge to be outdoors transcends any of the lesser urges,"[36] even leading to psychological distress:

> In winter many of my mushroomy friends succumb to a malady called mycological cabin fever. Its symptoms include anxiety, deep depression, even stomach cramps and sweating. It is a direct result of "not getting out there."[37]

"Out there" cures "in here." This distinction is evident on forays, when the parking lot represents the transition between civilization and the woods. Mushroomers frequently talk about the weather, their eagerness to get into the field, and their expectations. The mundane experiences of careers and families are rarely mentioned. I learned little about my comrades' personal lives on these gatherings. It was at meetings and meals that personal matters could be discussed and institutional identities displayed. Entering the foray site, one sets aside one's mundane life in favor of the identity of "mushroomer."

Many find that they need a justification for being away. Amateur mycologists stress that "mushrooming is one of the best excuses to get into the woods at one of the most beautiful times of the year,"[38] or "I figured mushrooms would give me an excuse to be out in the woods, and there's nothing to haul around like there is with fishing."[39] That individuals demand a justification to be in the woods suggests that a stigma adheres to those who reject the social world without "reason."

Being away requires reveling in the oppression of one's quotidian existence and embracing a Thoureauvian scorn. This recognition of a dramatic contrast gives the desire to escape emotional resonance. Scorn is not a "fast emotion," easily readable, as are anger and fear, but a "slow" one, long-lasting and linked to stable perception—a majestic idea that can be expressed rhetorically when appropriate and hidden behaviorally when not. The rejection of civilization is not a displayed emotion; one can judge that naturalists reject civilization only from their words. Yet this rhetoric is believed to provide a clear path to their hearts. The satisfactions of being away depend upon the necessity of returning and the impossibility of permanently shedding civilization.

Respecting Nature: Erasing the Self

A paradox is inherent in the desire to insert oneself into nature while treasuring its wildness, emptiness, and nonhumanness. Doesn't human presence pollute the wild? Mushroomers must *use* nature instrumentally for their own ends, but they simultaneously feel guilty. To assuage the damage from their presence, naturalists speak of treating nature "with respect." The theme of self-erasure is prominent in the rhetoric of mushroomers. One should be in nature, but it should be as if one were not present: humans do not really belong to—or with—nature.

Being in the woods is a magical time in which all share a focus on nature. When the mood is broken, we recognize a sharp malaise. On one occasion, foraying in a deep forest, we stumbled upon a clearing where houses were to be built. Our leader commented sarcastically, "I think we're back in the real world." Remnants of human presence are a "desecration." Garbage is often jokingly transformed into "authentic" nature, as if to deny human presence while condemning it. Jay commented when he found an oil filter can: "There's an oil filter fungus." When we found a nail embedded in a tree, Dennis called it a "steelhead," and Jay joked that it had "rusty spores." After finding tin cans in the area we were foraying, Dave joked, "You can't see the cans for the mushrooms."

Civilization and nature are seen as fundamentally incompatible. Although one could imagine that finding a beer can in a pristine wilderness might be seen as a postmodern evocation of bricolage, it never is.

Mushroomers are continually exhorted to treat the woods with respect and to erase their presence. The New Jersey Mycological Association advises mushroomers: "Always try to leave the site as though you had not been there." This theme was apparent in my interviews:

> Try to do as little damage [as possible] in the woods when you walk. Watch very carefully where you put your feet. Try not to disturb too much of the habitats . . . When you find [mushrooms], put back the dirt. If you made a little hole in the ground, push the leaves back.

This mushroomer expresses the irony of respecting nature. The issue is one of presentation: to make the scene appear as if it had not been disturbed.

The importance of appearance is evident when a foray leader tells his "troops" (recognizing the military images of a foray) that they "should try to affect the area as little as possible. Use discretion in beating down the bushes so [it doesn't] look like an army went through." Another leader, using an equally violent image, remarks: "One is not there to rape the forest scene. One is there to appreciate the beauty of the moment and perhaps, if lucky, take a few treasured remembrances home with one."[40] If image is important, heroes are those who alter the scene to make it prettier and more "natural":

> As I see it, 1000 [Mycological Society of San Francisco] members can be out in the field with their families, and at least a simple majority of them will be doing more harm than good. Most of the rest will take enough for their own needs and leave behind an aura of appreciation, which is all Nature has ever asked of us anyway. But then there are the few petit heroes among us who bring along a litter bag, and who

leave an area just a little prettier than they found it. . . . Envision strolling through clean fields and unspoiled woods, no beer cans or candy wrappers to mar the simple beauty for which we make long journeys! It's a wonderful dream, and it will be ours, if we will only stoop to conquer—trash.[41]

The ambivalence between using nature for one's own ends and the belief that nature is to be protected is expressed in the injunction by one mycological society to "foray softly":

Cave explorers realize how delicate the environment of a cave really is, and they try to make others aware of how easily the cave environment can be damaged or destroyed by the slightest acts of man. Sometimes the actions are intentional, but often they are just thoughtless actions. The motto of cavers is: Take nothing but pictures; Leave nothing but footprints; Kill nothing but time. Another of the favorite sayings is: Cave Softly. . . . If we are collecting specimens for identification, we should pick only those specimens that will be used in the identification, and should leave everything else undisturbed. If we are collecting edible mushrooms, we naturally will be collecting larger numbers of a given species. Collecting for one's personal use is not likely to cause so much damage as to endanger the species, but we still should be careful to do no more damage than necessary. . . . All of us should take a lesson from the Cavers, and learn to Foray Softly![42]

An unstated tension exists between a sincere belief in respecting nature and the desire to justify collecting for personal consumption.

We respect animate objects, and typically those that we see as having higher moral value than ourselves. Humans are polluters in both our presence and our artifacts. The tragedy of the naturalist is that of the person whose presence is simultaneously reverential and destructive, and who to treasure the environment has to erase all signs of his or her presence.

AT ONE WITH NATURE

Being away from civilization is part of the natural experience. One goes from and goes to. One can use nature (as collecting mushrooms entails) or experience it, becoming a full part of the ecosystem, linked to the organic vision. Most naturalists wish, to some degree, to become incorporated within the alien system, becoming "at one" with nature. Naturalists experience the marvels of the Other, enchanting a disenchanted world. This unity can be primarily emotional or more explicitly cultural (and institutional), as when nature is linked to the divine.

As noted, naturalists often reject civilization because of its bustle: the absence of empty places. The balanced human strives for peace, calm, and tranquility. Being away from civilization is necessary, but so is the embrace of nature. As the fieldguide author David Arora exhorts: "Mushroom hunting is not simply a matter of traipsing through the woods in winter. It is an art, a skill, a meditation, and a process."[43] This emphasis on the centrality of process, in contrast to the content of what is experienced, contributes to naturework being seen as magical and mystical. Being part of nature provides this equanimity, although admittedly it is a tamed, defanged nature. When mushroomers are asked to explain what it is about the environment that they treasure, they emphasize this peace:

> Early in the season, hunting in the cool, magnificent giant redwood forests . . . can produce both many choice edible mushrooms . . . and an exquisite sense of beauty, tranquility and exultation from the deep silence and sheer size of the trees. Right next to a thousand-year-old 300-foot-tall giant, you can find tiny, fragile, elegant Lepiotas . . . and Mycenas, which can set your sense of proportion and perspective atingle.[44]

> ---

> It is impossible to know [mushrooms] and to wander in their environment, through woods and pastureland, without the pace of mind slowing down to their enduring serenity; and when the mind relaxes the eyes and ears gain a new awareness of the microscopic detail of other small miracles.[45]

On one occasion Stuart told me that he and his wife have stressful jobs. He commented that one day when he was standing outside looking for mushrooms, a deer came up to them, and they felt calmed by the experience.

The philosopher Erazim Kohak[46] in *The Embers and the Stars,* an inquiry into the moral status of nature, claims that primordial awareness is a lived reality: it is subjective but not "merely subjective." As one mushroomer suggests, it represents a deep subjectivity, an experienced oneness:

I can feel Nature. I feel warmth from the sun. Cold from the snow. I can move in nature and I like to jump on rocks and go mountain climbing in the summertime. It's physical oneness.

One can easily parody this nature talk, noting that the speaker also gets warmth from space heaters and cold from air conditioners, and can jump on trampolines. Yet parody denies what is unquestionably a mental reality.

Emotional reality is attached to places that have power in generating deep, often inexpressible emotional responses:

> Every hunter and angler had his own favorite microcosm composed of woodlots, swamps, ponds, and other topographical features. . . . Whatever and wherever his "territory," it was part of the fiber of every sportsman's existence. While in its midst, he watched the change of seasons, shared the joys of friends, made discoveries about nature and himself, and experienced other sensations too mystical to put into words.[47]

As a consequence, mushroomers, like birders or hikers, return to the same spots, not only for instrumental reasons, but because the places *mean* something. For some mushroomers, having a "sacred spring" where they meditate is as real as having a special song. Nature is filled with spaces imbued with metaphorical meanings.

For many, an identity as naturalist is core to one's self. As two mushroomers write after a long winter:

> Over winter some of us stare at the bare, hard ground and dream of mushrooms past and to come. Those of us who define ourselves by our actions believe that, as mushroom hunters, either we hunt mushrooms or we are nothing.[48]

To be at one with nature is to "know thyself," a process of self-actualization.[49] The environmental persona is core to one's identity. As one student of mountaineering notes, "For the romantic the essence of mountaineering lay in an unmediated and intensely personal relationship between the individual and the mountains."[50] In fact, the creation of the meaning of the mountain is grounded in culturally constructed images, constantly mediated. One's natural identity is bolstered by a sense of accomplishment and competence that simultaneously provides satisfaction in itself and satisfaction in light of the establishment of community.[51] A mushroomer muses:

One progresses at his own pace, rewarded constantly by correct identifications, and the ever-changing panorama of the seasonal fruitings. It is probably for some of these reasons that Gary Lincoff [then the president of NAMA] says, "Mushroom hunting gets in your blood"; . . . If one dares to eat the mushrooms he finds, his identification is tested in this very personal cauldron. Mistakes are quick to appear. What remains soon accumulates into a personal kind of confidence, arrogance, or authority, depending, of course, upon one's own perspective.[52]

With time, one embraces nature and begins to see oneself as a "mushroomer."

Whenever nature is linked to a social institution, that institution is religion. The emotions involved are deep and mystical: not a passionate love but pure enchantment. This perspective can be explained either in traditional religious terms or as a pantheistic, mystical vision. In either case, the underlying metaphor suggests that the individual is incorporated into an organic vision: Gaia in principle. Many mushroomers speak of forgetting mundane reality:

> [Being in nature] actually kind of humbles me a little bit. If I wasn't standing in the woods, [plants and animals] wouldn't know the difference. When you're alone, you're more quiet because you are not with anybody, and you can just stand there and watch one bird for a while. I watched a deer and it didn't even know I was there. . . . You do feel like a nobody out there in the big world.

In an account of the joys of hunting, the *New Yorker* essayist Vance Bourjaily emphasizes the fading of time in the woods:

> I think of the old tag . . . "Allah does not count, in a man's allotted span, the hours spent in hunting." . . . In the inevitable way of old tags, this one seems sometimes to be true: there are such hours, marvelous, absorbed, stolen from time.[53]

One can contrast the realities of clock time, meteorological time, and biological time with *lived time*.[54] Temporality exists in nature, but often one is not reminded of it:[55] it is time transfixed.[56] When time becomes noticeable, oppressive or insistent, something is amiss. Few wish to remain away for unlimited periods—the experience of *durée* eventually intrudes.[57]

God—and Gods—in the Woods

Religion as a social institution is constituted by several domains: spatial (the church, synagogue), cultural (the Bible, Cabala), emotional (reverence, awe), and mystical (the divine, spirit). The significance of the religious metaphor for natural activity is evident in the fact that each of these domains contributes to the rhetoric of mushrooming. Nature is a religious "resource,"[58] the world sacralized, enshrined through rites and cults. Being in the wild is a "sacred act," likened to participating in organized religion.[59]

CHURCH

Sylvan glades are often referred to as green cathedrals, and naturalists find that wilderness is imbued with the sanctity of God.[60] We speak of nature sanctuaries. For some people, to view the wild is to appreciate God's design before sin entered into the world. We can venerate Him in our blessings of his places and creations. One mushroomer makes this explicit: "[The woods are] my church. I even love the trees. When things get tight, I need to go to the woods." Nature is a place where some can communicate with God—meditating, praying, or just being by His side.

SCRIPTURE

Postmodern literary critics are fond of saying that everything is a text: if so, nature is the Bible. The philosopher Holmes Rolston in *Environmental Ethics* argues that the woods can be read as a sacred text, and sacred texts can be read as wilderness tracts:

> Wild nature becomes something like a sacred text. . . . Analogies with the natural world fill the Book of Job and Jesus's parables. The wilderness elicits cosmic questions, differently from town.[61]

Thoreau, in describing a local angler, suggested that fishing was "a sort of sacrament and withdrawal from the world, just as the aged read their Bibles." Knowing fish and fungus is reading the work of the divine hand:

> Suddenly [mushrooming] made me think of my Chassidic grandfather and his mystical belief in the Cabala. Coincidentally there is a "destroying angel" mentioned in the Cabala. This made me wonder about the combination of the beauty and deadly poison in the

Destroying Angel [the *Amanita virosa*—an "elegant" white mushroom]. There is indeed a mystique about mushrooms. Is there some mystery in the mushrooms from which man may learn, or in the past, has learned?[62]

RELIGIOUS IMPULSES

Given the Deist, pantheist impulse in much of modern life,[63] it is not surprising that many people feel a religious impulse in the forests and fields: a cosmic justification, occult relation, or deep humility. One morel collector notes:

> The morel is merely an excuse [for mushroomers] to devote themselves to their cult, to take a moment while picking to commune intimately with their Creator while admiring his handiwork. . . . The trees are no merely-tolerated decoration of the countryside, for it is they who make it a retreat, an asylum; it seems that without them poor souls couldn't even arrange an interview with God or find reason to rejoice in themselves.[64]

Nature provides a setting in which people can communicate with the divine, admiring His sublime handiwork.

THE DIVINE

Pantheists, deists, and feminist nature worshippers, among others, believe that nature is divine. As Charles R. Simpson puts it, "Through wilderness, one reached God."[65] We have resacralized the environment. Nature has power that civilized objects cannot match, in part because, as with the divine, "we will never fully understand it."[66] In the words of the psychedelic philosopher Andrew Weil:

> The energy of mushrooms is real and strong: remember, it can push up asphalt, unhinge the mind, kill, and permeate the darkness with eerie, heatless light. . . . I do not think it unreasonable that lunar energy is food for the unconscious, that mushrooms in the diet stimulate the imagination and the intuition. Wild mushrooms are stronger in this respect than cultivated ones. . . . Mushrooms are external symbols of those [unconscious] forces, and their invasion of our outward lives is a dramatic and encouraging sign of the progress of this great change.[67]

The revered student of mushrooms R. Gordon Wasson[68] argued that the *Amanita muscaria,* the psychedelic "Fly Agaric," was worshipped in Hindu culture as the god Soma.

Through metaphor we recognize the centrality of nature. For the naturalist, being in the woods is coming home to where our species began. The mystical transforms an ordinarily mundane social order.[69] Love for nature is one means by which we reenchant the world.

USING NATURE

Mushroomers are engaged in an extractive activity, though most would object to this characterization. To be sure, they are a sufficiently small band that this extraction has relatively little ecological effect compared with changes in global temperature, acid rain, housing construction, and industrial development. Still, mushroomers do affect the microecology of forests and fields, and most would not engage in their hobby were this not so. They borrow a term from agricultural cultivation in speaking of "harvesting mushrooms." Even the common terms used to describe mushroomers pay heed to their effects: collectors, pickers, and hunters (not fungus watchers). In their talk, the tension between picking mushrooms and preserving the environment is evident. Andy recounted how he found several hen of the woods in a local nature reserve. Molly noted that it is illegal to pick there, commenting, "If they catch you, you'll be one sorry person." Andy responded, "I told [the rangers] that there were kids picking flowers and when they went down there, I picked the mushrooms." At this, the other mushroomers laughed loudly. Someone joked, "You're evil," and Molly added, "That's the height of ingenuity." Such "ingenious" mushroomers are esteemed, but with a certain ambivalence.

Admittedly, not every activity has an identical effect. The environmental impact separates birdwatchers from mushroomers from rattlesnake collectors from gem collectors. Yet even birdwatchers alter the ecosystem, as those who specialize in photographing nests realize.[70] In practice, those who claim to do little damage (for example, birders) often demand restrictions on those whose impact is more evident (for example, dove hunters). Groups may resent each other because of distinct perspectives on nature.[71] Relatively unobtrusive groups—such as mushroom collectors—desire to minimize their effects, while criticizing those who are seen as doing more harm. In turn, they are criticized by others. One prominent mushroomer explicitly notes the similarity among all who enjoy nature activities—they all rely on the humanist vision of using nature for human ends:

> I'm not sure I'm all that happy with the concept of a nature lover. I'm not so sure that there are such things in America. . . . That is, after you have already denuded nature of all of the tooth and claw, you then go into a denatured nature, and you can sit there watching birds, and everything that could possibly harm you has already been taken out of the environment. . . . So I'm not sure that there's a difference between a birdwatcher and a mushroom hunter. A mushroom hunter is clearly out there picking things, and deer hunters are clearly out there shooting deer, and you can hear all kinds of stories from deer hunters why what they're doing is morally good.

Everyone alters the environment from self-interest, and all persuade themselves of their respect for it.

As noted above, mushroomers tell each other repeatedly and heatedly that they must treat the woods with respect. They are devoted to this idea. Any suggestion by an intrusive sociologist that this is not so is met with indignation. But they are equally devoted to gaining natural treasures. Humor reflects their unease, as when we are foraying for highly esteemed morel mushrooms in a nature area where we should only be picking for study, and one mushroomer jokes: "We might study them as they're cooking in the pan. We have to have a certain amount of respect for things."[72]

How can mushroomers justify what might seem naively to be behaviors that "serious" naturalists would oppose? They provide excuses and justifications. First, they minimize the extent of the harm, and second, they differentiate themselves from and stigmatize those who do more damage.

Minimization

We excuse damage by minimizing it, admitting the possibility of harm. Mushroomers say they are gathering food, much like animals do. We must eat *something,* and so one claims, somewhat implausibly but sincerely, that there is "no difference between the man who buys the mushrooms at the store and the person who picks the mushrooms out of the woods." Mushroomers note that there are sufficiently few of them that damage is limited. Further, the damage is minor. Many mushroomers assert that they avoid picking all the mushrooms in a locale, leaving some for future years.[73] One writer provides a humorous example of this process:

> Last fall's TV series . . . pictured Julia Child gathering huge chanterelles . . . When they were done picking, Julia and her guide crumbled up a giant mushroom and scattered it around—to appease the mushroom god. Many members of our club follow the practice of leaving a few mushrooms behind, when they are harvesting in the wild. It's nice for others who come later, it ensures some spores are released, and it augers well for a mycological future.[74]

Some mushroomers claim that because of the structure of fungi, picking mushrooms does not harm the environment. A mushroom growing on the forest floor appears to be a plant rooted in the soil. This is misleading, however, as a mushroom is actually a fruiting body of a "plant." This plant body consists of a mass of threadlike, microscopic filaments, called mycelium. The mycelium lives in earth, wood, or even animal dung. The thirty-seven-acre fungus (*Armillaria bulbosa*) discovered in the forests of Michigan a few years ago was not a monster mushroom but a gigantic network of filaments, producing numerous delicious honey cap mushrooms: a gigantic, underground apple tree. Mushroomers can say with some justice that they merely pick fruit. Done with care, all will be well. This comforts individuals doing what they would likely do otherwise, contributing to an ecological process:

> Since the mushroom we eat is only the fruiting body of the hidden plant, I have no more qualms about my harvest interrupting a valuable natural process. . . . Anybody who likes oysters (and many who do not) will like oyster mushrooms. So will anyone who likes to contemplate the recycling of nutrients in a forest. When I began eating oyster mushrooms from wasted logs, I became a part of that useful cycle.[75]

Mushroomers warn one another to avoid harming the mycelium when they pick their cache. One does not "rake" mushrooms, for that damages the mycelium and may prevent further fruitings.[76] Evidence of one's picking should be erased. One mycological newsletter exhorts morel hunters:

> One way to insure the preservation of your morel patches is correct harvesting procedures. The mycelium of the morel is the actual plant or "tree." The morel (as with all fungi) is the "fruit." Remember that mycelium is delicate and easily damaged. Plucking and raking mushrooms destroys the mycelium, and eventually there will not be enough surviving mycelium to continue producing fungi. It is comparable to cutting down the tree to pick the apples.[77]

This sounds nice, but a problem exists. The "fruit" contains the "seeds" (spores) of future plants. By picking mushrooms (or apples) one decreases the likelihood of new plants, leading some to worry about the dangers of overpicking (see Chapter 6). One prominent mushroomer explained:

> It's not just that a mushroom is a fruiting body, which it is. There's no question that there is legitimate controversy on whether or not if you pick all the mushrooms, you're going to reduce mushroom yield in an area. There are some people who are trying to suggest that it's possible that there is a threshold. That is, picking an individual mushroom doesn't do anything. If you've got an area, and you really calculatingly pick every fruiting body, does that so weaken the mycelium underneath that you can reduce the threshold for reproduction?

Another mushroomer made the same point:

> There is a general feeling that you're just picking apples off the tree, but I wonder if it may be like pulling the branches off the tree, because this is the reproductive organ of a plant, and if anyone goes along harvesting out the reproductive organ of the plant, obviously the plant is not going to be reproducing.

Overpicking becomes a problem after a mediocre year for collecting, and when one is confronted with those who do not embrace the communally understood limits on collecting.

Differentiation

Some mushroomers differentiate themselves from stigmatized others. At one extreme are those who pick mushrooms only for investigation, avoiding picking "for the pot." John Schaaf, the former editor of the

Mycena News, the newsletter of the San Francisco Mycological Society, expressed this position well:

> Just as the joy of birdwatching is enhanced by investigating the subject while disturbing it the least, so the mycologist can derive pleasure from the study of any fungus, edible or not, by observing it in its habitat over a time, watching its growth and succession patterns, discovering its higher purpose. A few specimens are sometimes taken, any one of which may provide the makings of a hundred microscope slides. . . . Some of our Council members don't even eat mushrooms; but then you wouldn't expect the head of the local Audubon chapter to go around biting cassowaries.[78]

Schaaf's position is not popular, as evidenced by the approximately 95 percent of mushroomers who eat wild mushrooms (indeed, for many, it is the main reason they collect them). More typically, mushroomers condemn as greedy those colleagues who scour the woods for every mushroom:

> Last fall Eileen and I met a man with a five-gallon white pail. He was picking everything he came across in a city park. If he ate everything in that bucket he probably got his due for despoiling the park.[79]
>
> ---
>
> [In *Boletus edulis* season] enthusiastic gatherers destroy every fruiting body to be found. Bushes are leveled, branches torn away, duff scattered. . . . Joan Plumb was collecting in the state of Washington and found hunted areas torn up as if furrowed by wild pigs. She was not surprised when the perpetrators asked her to direct them to other places where edible mushrooms were to be found.[80]

Once Joyce told me that she was angered by how some people pick all the mushrooms they can, and then drop the ones that are inedible by the side of the road. She gave the example of some people she knows who go through the woods kicking and picking up those mushrooms that they can't eat.

An implicit folk belief exists as to one's proper share, and these individuals have violated norms that are linked to assumptions about the carrying capacity of the natural environment. These examples emphasize the presence of aesthetic rules: the moral character of the woods is undermined by human remains. It is bad enough to pick all the mushrooms, but to level bushes and leave broken mushrooms further offends the mycological sensibility. Although during forays woods are not trashed, neither are they left in pristine condition; these criticisms, directed toward others, might also apply to group members.

The human use of the natural environment is critical to mushrooming and other nature pursuits. This reality makes each naturalist a conservationist who judges how much damage is too much. Despite their denial, naturalists cannot totally erase their presence from the wild.

ALARMS AND DANGERS

One charm of nature is that it is not totally under our control. Admittedly, we have removed much of its sting and pain, condemning our predators to a premature oblivion. We have tamed the wild. Still, we are anxiously aware that threats are real, if manageable. Kayakers, backpackers, even birders must accept what nature sends their way. The satisfaction of naturework is linked to an appropriate challenge. Too little challenge is as distressing as too much. Many activities in the wild pose a contest between man and nature.[81] Mushrooming is one of them, for there are species that are deadly, even if the number of cases of poisoning in the United States is comfortingly small.[82]

Mushroomers continually test the authentic reality of nature. Risk is perceived not as undesirable but as a means of measuring personal accomplishment. Can one cope with a nature that is untamed and unsympathetic? This humanistic view postulates that culture and nature are in opposition to each other: besting nature is the goal, even though respect for the *power* of nature is essential. As one mushroomer put it:

> I heard an old mushroom picker explain to his son that "in this world, everything has its mission. Boletes are here to be picked by mushroom pickers, and *Amanita phalloides* is here to reduce the excessive number of mushroom pickers."[83]

Another announced: "Sometimes you get the fungus; sometimes the fungus gets you."

The sociologist Georg Simmel remarked of adventure: "To the sober person adventurous conduct often seems insanity."[84] Yet this "insanity"—a willingness not to minimize danger—provides motivation. Edmund Burke recognized that danger is at the heart of the sublime:

When danger or pain press too nearly, they are incapable of giving any delight, and are simply terrible; but at certain distances, and with certain modifications, they may be, and they are delightful, as every day experience.[85]

Transcendence implies a measure of risk. One must transcend a challenge[86]—what the psychologist David Apter[87] terms the "dangerous edge." A meaningful nature experience must incorporate uncertainty. Pleasure and fear are unalterably linked, as the sociologists Norbert Elias and Eric Dunning[88] describe in *Quest for Excitement,* noting a "de-routinizing" function of leisure, a process that playful risk encourages. This is said to produce a "clarity of mind" unavailable to the safe and secure.[89]

Some mushroomers emphasize the thrill in confronting danger:

> Maybe there's a lure for some people about doing dangerous, exciting things. I would put myself in the category of courting disaster. . . . I could think of a lot of things I've done that other people say, "Oh, that's too dangerous," and don't dare do that. Maybe in this connection, some people pick unusual things.

> Certainly there's also a fear element. If you really got into mushrooms, and, like the Japanese blowfish, if you eat a bad one, you die. . . . Within the mycological society, there are people who are pressing the limits. So there's that kind of challenge in mycology.

This becomes even more explicit when nature is personified (see Chapter 2). Nature punishes the reckless. One mycologist suggests that morels, which often grow near prickly ash, "keep pretty tough company"; another notes that mushroomers call poisonous or questionable species "bad guys."[90]

Ultimately, many—although not all—mushroomers report a desire to "test" their knowledge. A well-known example is the amateur mycologist Greg Wright, who

> is engaged in a singlehanded and singleminded campaign to taste and test every species of "unknown" edibility. He doesn't eat mushrooms that in his view have been adequately proven to be toxic. But he insists on trying, at least once, almost everything else, including the foul-smelling, bitter, and unpalatable species.[91]

Wright may be an extreme case, but others have similar attitudes:

Howard: Once I was going to try some *Coprinus atramentarius* with some alcohol and see what the symptoms were like. [This species is edible, but causes severe reactions if consumed within several hours of alcohol.] Then someone reminded me of my heart condition and that a rapid heart rate might result, and that might not be a smart thing to do, so I thought I'd forgo that.

GAF: Why would you want to [try that combination]?

Howard: To see what it was like. To tell someone that this is what it was like. . . . I think you appreciate these things by the amount of effort you go through.

Brian talked about eating an edible amanita [a genus with deadly poisonous species]:

Brian: I'd like to say I've tried it, and it's my knowledge and my own control of my destiny, my fate. I make my own world. This is my confirmation that I do it, and be reasonably sure that I've taken care of what's necessary. . . . Much as I've tried, I've never been able to choke one down. Much as I've promised myself. I've collected them and brought them home, only to not be able to eat them. I hope to do it this year.

GAF: Will you do it on your own? Would you ask someone else?

Brian: I'd do it myself. I wouldn't even tell anyone until I started evidencing severe symptoms.

GAF: Why?

Brian: Because I want to think it's my own thing, own control. . . . It's kind of a scary feeling to hold your own death in your hand. You pick an *Amanita verna* or *virosa*, you are literally holding your own death, and an extremely painful one at that. It's an eerie feeling. Sense of power, controlling your own destiny.

Controlling risk is, for some, status-enhancing, with losing face a greater fear than suffering the physical consequences of a mistake. For those who embrace the risk of nature, the danger confirms their ultimate triumph over a world they understand and respect.[92]

Deciding which species to consume is a source of tension among mushroomers. Some are liberal in their willingness to experiment; others are more cautious. Should one mix edible and poisonous mushrooms in the same basket? Some claim that the spores of poisonous mushrooms contaminate edible ones. A few assert that they get headaches by walking near poisonous amanitas. Some claim that one must wash one's hands after picking amanitas, whereas others see this as excessive. When mushrooms were passed around at meetings, the amanitas were sometimes placed in plastic bags. On one foray Harvey, a novice, picked a bag of edible honey caps, but he put three unidentified mushrooms in with them. Molly, who is very cautious, told him to throw the whole bag away, even though the three mushrooms were probably not deadly poisonous. Harvey told me: "I learned a lesson. . . . I can't eat them. Here they go. I'm going to throw them in the garbage can."

Conservatives repeat common refrains: "There are old mushroom hunters; there are bold mushroom hunters, but there are no old, bold mushroom hunters"; "No mushroom is poisonous until you eat it." Some, however, believe that being daring is desirable within limits. On one trip an older man said to a younger woman: "They're always telling about someone getting sick from eating this or that. They overcaution you. If you don't want to eat them, you don't." As the Japanese say about eating the potentially deadly blowfish: "Those who eat fugu are stupid. But those who do not eat fugu are also stupid."[93]

The desire for risk is a social construction—a choice of the collector, an orientation to the natural environment. The question is how *certain* one must be about the identification of a mushroom and about its effects before it is consumed: some demand near certainty and safety, whereas others are willing to sample if the mushroom is unlikely to be deadly, even if it leads to intestinal discomfort. Indeed, a finely attuned balance exists between the satisfactions of taste and diarrhea.[94] The author of an article entitled "Eat Russulas in '86! (A Challenge)" touts a genus of edible but unappreciated mushrooms, encouraging his colleagues to be more adventurous:

> Some books have said that any Russula which does not taste acrid is edible. Others will say that even acrid species are OK after being parboiled. While these last two statements may sound a bit careless, there is no Russula known that can even come close to killing you. The worst that can happen is that you may be sick to your stomach or have a bit of looseness in the lower digestive tract. But hey, good chili does that![95]

Ultimately, competence and confidence are central for both "liberals" and "conservatives." No collector wishes to commit suicide, despite different thresholds of fungal risk. One eats those mushrooms with which one feels "reasonably" secure. This estimate is grounded not in an objective evaluation, but in personal assessments: judgments both cognitive and emotional. Thus one collector became more liberal after a severe automobile accident: "I am going to look at relative risks, because I may die tomorrow. I want to do all that I want to do right now. . . . The mushrooms I collected this past weekend, three years ago I would never have done that."

For those unfamiliar with mushrooms, "all mushrooms look alike," and "any mushroom could be deadly." Confidence is based on the ability to differentiate among specimens. One mushroomer links this to picking berries, an activity with which many feel comfortable:

> I always pose [to those who say that mushrooming is dangerous] the counterquestion, "How dangerous is berrying?" In the sense of going to look for berries. I look for blueberries. I have a currant and gooseberry hedge in my backyard. There are strange little green and red berries also, and I don't eat strange little green and red berries. But I do eat currants and gooseberries off my own bushes because I understand what they are.

Confidence in one's ability to differentiate among natural objects supports the belief in one's skill in mastering ambiguous nature. One is picking not only species but individual mushrooms. Just because a group of mushrooms are similar-looking does not mean that they all are the same species, as the club president commented: "You've got to look at them one at a time. . . . If you got one that doesn't look quite right, don't put it in with the good ones. Keep it separate and then identify it later." Of course, in the rush of mushroom collecting, snap judgments are routine, but they can haunt the collector, causing worry, if not abdominal distress. Confidence may be problematic when one consumes species that one has not tried previously, that one has not picked, or that don't look precisely right.

Once the mushroomer makes a tentative identification that suggests that a mushroom is edible, he or she must decide whether to act on that information. I found that even when I was "sure" of my identification of some species, I could not always bring myself to consume what I had picked. I was not alone in this. Lorelei Norvell recounts:

> A friend had taken me to a cluster of stately *Lepiota rachodes*, which I eagerly gathered. But as this delicious mushroom is usually listed as "edible with caution [because of a similar-looking mushroom]," my

collection aged gracelessly in our refrigerator and had to be thrown out before we gathered enough courage to eat them.[96]

A mushroomer in the Minnesota club told the other members: "I had been collecting mushrooms, boiling them, and freezing them, but I was scared of eating them." (There was knowing laughter in response to his remark.) Brian, the club president, told a similar story of how, when he was new in the society, he and Howard came upon some honey caps that were yellow rather than tawny. He later called Howard, who reassured him that they were edible, but Brian added: "You should always feel free to call someone if you're not sure. Don't ever be afraid of throwing them in the garbage can."

Consumption does not quell all uncertainty. Mushroom poisoning does not occur immediately, but may be noticeable several hours, several days, or, in one case, at least a week after consuming the mushroom. Nervous mushroomers worry about nature's "revenge," and their distress takes the thrill out of their triumph. Some careful mushroomers save specimens to aid the rescue squad in their treatment, and worry about their reckless abandon:

> The first time I ate a *Lepiota procera,* the parasol, and later on *Amanita rubescens,* the blusher, my family and I lived for twenty-four hours in mortal terror that I had made a dreadful error. The terror was unfounded, of course, for I knew the mushrooms well enough and had not mistaken them for any others. . . . The understanding that knowledge can conquer fear was a heady one.[97]

> I began wondering if we dared try to cook up a couple [of] Caesars [*Amanita caesarea*]. I had eaten [*Amanita caesarea*] when it was ID'ed and prepared by one whose judgment I trusted, but now confirmation was up to us. All the books caution beginners not to eat any Amanitas. Yet, I was more than Ivory 99-44/100th percent sure that these were the highly prized Caesars. . . . After another 24 hours, and then 36 hours had passed, and we were still feeling fine, we agreed they were indeed very, very good.[98]

> *Brian:* I remember picking some things I thought were shaggy manes growing in a park near Fridley. . . . Now I think they were long-stemmed [*Coprinus*] *atramentarius.* I fried them up and ate them, and I wasn't even smart enough to know better. I thought they were shaggies.

GAF: Once you realized your mistake, was it scary?
Brian: I realized it was stupid before, but not as much as after, when I
kept waiting for something to happen. When I didn't drop over
dead, I was amazed.

Anxiety can lead some individuals to experience psychosomatic reactions to mushrooms. Nature is ratified as mysterious and powerful,
outside the grasp of human knowledge. Several mushroomers told
me that their upset stomachs may have been caused not by the mushrooms but by the idea of mushrooms. Others note:

> The apprehension and fear of some people of being poisoned, even
> dying from the act of eating wild edible mushrooms, especially a first
> experience, often causes abdominal pains. No poison at all is
> involved in such mental disturbances.[99]

> You don't have to eat a poisonous mushroom to get ill; you only have
> to think you did. It's a very uncomfortable feeling, as I can testify
> from experience. I had been hunting 3 or 4 years, and I was following
> all the rules. I brought home some mushrooms and checked the iden-
> tification in two local field guides. I was sure I knew exactly what
> they were. After dinner, I was leafing through another field guide,
> and I saw my mushroom and a description that said, "Be absolutely
> certain that you do not confuse this with mushroom X." I'd eaten all I
> had. I thought, "Oh, my God. Could it be mushroom X?" My pulse
> rate shot up to 180. I started sweating. I became flushed.[100]

As students of probability emphasize, people overestimate the possibility of rare events,[101] leading to an exaggerated concern.

Of course, sometimes people do become ill after consuming mushrooms, and this illness cannot always be attributed to uncertainty
about one's identification. Yet illness subsequent to the consumption
of fungus is not evidence that the latter produced the former. Some
collectors will consider mushrooms "the culprit," attributing their
ailment to a challenging opponent. But other mushroomers will attempt to deflect blame, protecting themselves from the stigma of having engaged in such foolhardy behavior:

> Whenever you eat a new wild mushroom, there is always a slight
> doubt as to whether it will agree with you. Even the varieties with
> which you are familiar can disagree with you inexplicably on occa-

sion, but if you are a true wild mushroom aficionado, you will never attribute your discomfort to the mushrooms. Instead, you will believe it was due to some other aspect of the meal—the rich dessert, perhaps, or too much wine. After all, as one wild mushroom lover said to me, you get sick even if you never eat wild mushrooms.[102]

The former head of the NAMA Poison Registry argued that "the labeling of a mushroom is often a bum rap. The eating of a mushroom is a relatively notable event." NAMA does not list poisoning reports on mushrooms unless there are at least two cases, and little confidence is to be given to reports until there are four or five cases of poisoning. Single cases may be attributed to any source. On one foray a club member mentioned that she had diarrhea after eating a beaver stew with honey caps. She emphasized that her illness might not have resulted from the stew or might have been due to the beaver meat, not the mushrooms.

The source of poisoning is not taken for granted but must be assessed. Nature has consequences, but these effects are only known through our interpretations. The fact that we recognize the power and danger of nature suggests that it is active and competitive. This permits us to justify our use of the natural environment as something more than the instrumental use of a meaningless object: mushrooming, like other dangerous leisure pursuits, provides a test of human competence. The attribution of meaning—including the personification and assignment of agency—supplies a basis for emotional satisfaction. The Other is incorporated into our soul.

In this chapter I situated human beings within a natural environment, examining the metaphorical linkages that people make to nature writ large, as well as the emotions they associate with it. These orientations to natural experience are linked to general ideological perspectives described in the Introduction: being away reflects a protectionist view; being at one is organic, and orientations to the use and danger of nature are tied to a humanist orientation.

Naturalists feel a need to escape the "burdens" of civilization. They contrast nature with culture. They wish to be away from a negatively loaded emotional and cultural nexus. A well-developed rhetoric denigrates society, often focusing on the stresses and temporal pressures that constitute mundane life. In nature, in contrast to "civilization," stress and temporal pressure are minimized. Although dangers exist, they are defined as part of an authentic reality, a reality that validates experience. Time is defined as having a different, less compelling meaning in the wild than in our tame order.

Part of the naturalist's goal is to become one with nature—linking nature to authenticity, mysticism, or religion. The organic drive is powerful, just as in many "primitive" societies. Nature provides lessons that we use to live our postmodern lives. To feel at one with nature is to recapture the part of one's self that has been drained by the demands of civilization. We seek a sense of the environmental Other: what the sociologist Andrew Weigert[103] has labeled transverse interaction.

These sentiments are set within a behavior system that depends on the *use* of the natural environment for the achievement of personal satisfaction. Ultimately, people demand that their personal needs be met. People wish not for oneness with nature at all costs, but rather for a oneness on their terms. Emotional responses are filtered through human desires.

People experience emotional richness through their contacts with nature, and being in nature is part of the moral lives of many citizens, but it is a mistake to consider this connection socially unmediated. One's response to nature is a consequence of how one believes that one should feel and relate to an Other. To transform the Other into the Self is a fiction, no matter how fervently one wishes to believe that it is real.

CHAPTER
TWO

Meaningful Mushrooms

Have you not seen in the woods, in a late autumn morning, a
poor fungus or mushroom,—a plant without any solidity, nay,
that seemed nothing but a soft mush or jelly,—by its constant,
total, and inconceivably gentle pushing, manage to break its way
up through the frosty ground, and actually to lift a hard crust on
its head? It is the symbol of the power of kindness.

—RALPH WALDO EMERSON, *MAN THE REFORMER*[1]

When people elect to spend time in the wild, they typically establish a
focus or specialization.[2] This may involve action (hiking, kayaking,
or climbing) or things (butterflies, minerals, birds, or mushrooms),
or a combination of the two (hunting, fishing). This division is
blurred, as climbers collect "mountains" and birders treasure the act
of watching. Still, most people at most times are not simply experiencing nature but have targeted their activities. Nature is too broad a
domain to appreciate as a whole. As one mushroomer explained to me:

> I've always enjoyed nature, and I like to go out into the woods. When
> I was a young boy I very early noticed [mushrooms] all around, and
> learning a little bit about them, I think it became a focal point, some-
> thing to focus on when I went out into the woods, or out in nature
> walking around.

When I asked him why that was important, he replied: "Well, it's
the same reason as any goal is important. Anything you do in life

you have to have a goal or you don't succeed. It's just something to focus on."

For this mushroomer and others, even though the hobby is emotionally rewarding, it requires having a goal. Focus allows one to appreciate the beauty of nature by exploring its details. I once asked a mushroomer about those who claim to appreciate all of nature; he responded that "they look at things, but they don't see the individual details. They tend to see things as impressionist paintings. From a long way off it's one picture. I tend to get in to see the brush strokes and technique."

An inability to justify one's interest provokes suspicion:

> I used to go hunting with my father, then I decided what I really liked was walking in the woods, but you can't just go walking in the woods. People will wonder what you are up to. You need a focus for your walks.

The linguists Edward Sapir and Benjamin Whorf (and their Sapir-Whorf Hypothesis) recognized that people develop a rich vocabulary for objects, particularly corners of the natural world, that they consider culturally significant:[3] a finding applicable to cultures and subcultures alike. Without language and knowledge one may not even notice features of the natural world:

> I can't remember ever seeing a single mushroom in Kentucky, and yet I hiked the hills and spent a great deal of time in the country [as a child]. . . . I can't remember *one single mushroom*. I wonder how many morels I stumbled over.

> I do love to walk in the woods. I look more on the ground actually than I do up. I am more fascinated by what's going on in the ground, not like my brother-in-law. Now he looks down and says, "I never realized there was so much stuff growing on the ground."

Focusing involves choosing a corner of what has been opaque and making it transparent and meaningful. In the apt phrase of the philosopher Arthur Danto,[4] we participate in the transfiguration of the commonplace.

For novices interested in a corner of nature, and specifically for mushroomers, a first task is to identify their discoveries, distinguishing them from others of that class, so that everything is not simply a "mushroom." The act of distinguishing objects allows one to separate them by their meaning.[5]

Yet by itself the ability to distinguish is not sufficient for the establishment of meaning. These distinguishing features must be given significance. In this chapter I explore how this is achieved. I examine the use of metaphors to specify natural objects. Metaphors depend on temporarily equating one object with another that is outside its usual set. Under the rubric of metaphor I discuss three elements of the assigning of meaning: moral meaning, sensory and aesthetic meanings, and the limiting case of personification. I conclude with a brief discussion of how collectors discuss and interpret morel mushrooms, a highly marked edible species with a rich body of metaphorical constructions.

THE METAPHORS OF MUSHROOMS

In a language such as English that does not devote great attention to the sensual, it is not always easy to talk directly about objects. To do so we rely on concepts from one sensory realm to comment on another.[6] Often we are reduced to discussing objects in light of their metaphorical significance (the claim that A has a resemblance to B, and that this relationship is a meaningful one). Metaphors are pervasive in everyday life—in language and in thought and action. When we describe objects we do not refer to the whole of our imagining—or the whole of the object. Rather, we abstract some features, incorporating them into well-established cultural packages.

Our goal is to draw from one another similar evocations of objects. In the philosopher Arnold Isenberg's[7] terms, we strive "to induce a sameness of vision, of experienced content." We have talked and worked together, and so we understand the images that each speaker provides. Further, as George Herbert Mead[8] notes, we can identify with one another; thus we can call out in others attitudes similar to our own because of the power of our social relations.

As a result of their "tacit knowledge,"[9] people can identify objects that they have difficulty describing. We know many things that we cannot explain (the philosopher Ludwig Wittgenstein[10] gives the example of the sound of a clarinet). We frequently can neither explain nor define, a point made by Wittgenstein:

When we're asked, "What do the words 'red', 'blue', 'black', 'white' mean?" we can, of course, immediately point to things which have these colours,—but our ability to explain the meanings of these words goes no further![11]

We understand objects in terms of prototypes and family resemblances.[12] The ability to "know in context," to use external social worlds to explain internal ones, and the ability to compare present contexts with past ones permits understanding and appreciation of natural objects: objects without inherent cultural significance or human intent. These are innocent objects that we situate in our own schemas.

Because natural objects are not created in readily identifiable forms, metaphor becomes critical. Howard Kaye emphasizes this in *The Social Meaning of Modern Biology:*

> The phenomena of nature must be unpacked with words and symbols. Reality can be described and analyzed in a variety of ways, the choice of which can be influenced by a variety of factors—personal, scientific, and social. To speak of the "altruism" of the impalatable moths or of "genetic programming," "selfish genes," or aggressive "drives" is neither compulsory nor a careless use of language. Such conceptualizations are as rich in meaning and moral consequences as were "natural selection" and the "survival of the fittest" in the nineteenth century, because the biases and evaluations they conceal can influence our emotional, behavioral, and even political responses to the phenomena addressed. . . . What thus makes it possible for biologists to deduce . . . far-ranging implications from their scientific work is neither the logic of facts nor the illogic of naturalistic and genetic fallacies, but the guiding presence of metaphysical, moral, and social assumptions embedded in their scientific work.[13]

When we look at a fungus, what sense are we to make of it? A mushroom has a shape, a size, and a color, and each contributes to its meaning. Mushrooms have deep semiotic connections to myth:

> In many traditions essential semiotic oppositions are formulated with particular clarity through the use of mushrooms as a classifier, such oppositions as, for example, nature–culture, foreign (or collective)–native (or one's own), the profane–the sacred, feminine–masculine, the here and now, terrestrial–the not-here (celestial or subterranean), water–fire, etc.[14]

Whether or not one wishes to inflate the power of fungus to this extent, my observations suggest a wide range of meanings. Mushrooms are known as culturally mediated objects, revealed through metaphorical linkage. As Edward O. Wilson notes, it is culture that "transforms the snake into the serpent."[15]

Fieldguides are particularly salient in depicting the metaphorical substrate of natural objects, which they do in the guise of providing "objective" information from a pose of full knowledge. The writer's goal is ostensibly the "presentation of truth."[16] Most guides present descriptive statements about a set of mushrooms: knowledge that is designed to be culturally transparent. Consider an extract from the *Audubon Society Field Guide to North American Mushrooms* on "Slippery Jack" (*Suillus luteus*):

Slippery Jack
Suillus luteus (L. ex Fr.) S.F.G.
Boletaceae, Agaricales
Description: slimy, reddish- to yellowish-brown cap with white pores, becoming yellow, and purplish sheathlike ring on brown-dotted stalk.
Cap: 2–4-3/4" (5–12 cm) wide; round, becoming convex to flat; slimy, smooth; dark reddish- to yellow-brown.
Flesh: white, becoming yellowish.
Tubes: attached; whitish, pale yellow to olive-yellow.
Pores: yellow, becoming brown-dotted.
Stalk: 1-1/4–3-1/4" (3–8 cm) long, 3/8–1" (1–2.5 cm) thick; brown-dotted.
Veil: partial veil membranous, shiny, white; leaving a persistent, purplish-drab, sleevelike ring draping stalk.
Spores: 7–9 X 2.5–3 microns; elliptical, smooth. Spore print dull cinnamon.
Edibility: good, with caution.
Season: September–early December.
Habitat: on the ground, under Scots pine, red pine, and spruce.
Range: E. North America.
Look-alikes: *S. subluteus* has longer, more slender stalk and less pronounced ring. *S. cothurnatus* has brown, cigar-bandlike ring and grows mostly in South under loblolly and longleaf pines.
Comments: Although this is a favorite edible, it may cause transient diarrhea if the slime is not removed.[17]

Accompanying this description are a small ink drawing and a color photograph, which continue the illusion of transparency. Despite the claim of clarity and inevitability, this description, one of some 750 in this guide, reveals the ambiguous and metaphorical quality of natural description. In order to use the guide and understand the description, one must rely on a stock of background knowledge and personal experiences of having seen the mushroom previously (what Alfred Schutz[18] terms "recipe knowledge"). The description is insufficient for identification. To understand this passage is to understand the difficulty of a claim that nature is a simple, unmediated reality.

One is immediately struck by naming practices. The major American fieldguides (the Audubon fieldguide and the Peterson fieldguide) use "common" names as the primary label, even to the extent that the authors must *invent* names (hobbyists use Latin names for many mushrooms). This choice stems from the metaphorical linkage of mushroom collecting to birdwatching, in which a manageable number of avian species is awarded a set of consensually agreed upon common names. These names have become accepted through the institutionalization of naming practices by the American Ornithological Union. Given that there are more than a quarter million fungal species and no institutional naming practices, what works well for birders is a source of annoyance for mushroomers.

The Audubon guide uses not only Slippery Jack but shaggy parasol, dead man's fingers, coral mushrooms, and more esoteric names such as fat-footed clitocybe, ornate-stalked bolete, and jelly crep. The former are, indeed, common, but the latter are social constructions for a publisher that felt its volumes should be consistent: mushrooms are to be organized like birds. Yet calling something by a "common name" does not make that name common. In Peterson's guide the latter three mushrooms are named clubfoot funnelcap, goldstalk, and soft stumpfoot. Although each volume includes the scientific "Latin" name as a secondary identifier, novice mushroomers who rely upon these metaphorical constructions may be unable to communicate with those who rely on other texts. The Latin names are themselves folk names created by a scientific community. *Suillus luteus*, for instance, means "yellow pig." Perhaps the most dramatic example is the "stinkhorn," whose Latin name, *Phallus impudicus*, characterizes it better than its more circumspect English folk name.

The Audubon text employs the convention of linked Latin genus and species names (which together constitute the *scientific* name, with the wider genus capitalized and coming before the species, as if this book were authored by Fine gary). Following this is an abbreviation of the namer or namers and describers. As I discuss in Chapter 6, the scientific name of a mushroom species is potentially problematic, as mushroom species and even genera may change according to the outcomes of mycological debate, a circumstance that may be frustrating, comical, or satisfying to mushroomers. Following this, the mushroom family and order are listed. That we speak of family and order reminds us of the metaphorical linkage of categorization in the social world and the natural world. Yet even for species and genus, the question—not a simple one—is which objects "belong" together. Within the scientific community there are vigorous debates between those who are termed "splitters" and those who are termed "lumpers"—the latter see objects as alike, the former make distinctions among them. Species categories are constructed within the constraints of the scientific method; scientific practice determines scientific result, and in turn determines how amateurs understand nature.

The description of a class of mushrooms is inherently ambiguous owing to variation in what is labeled a species (perhaps because of habitat, weather, age, species variability, or disease). Species categories could be created that are oriented to macroscopic determination, although scientific practice, for most species, is ostensibly dependent on microscopic features. In practice, visual inspection—and sometimes smell, touch, or taste—is key to identification. We define objects by a few key elements, leading to an imagined gestalt. A complex of properties comes together to make a whole.[19] In the case of Slippery Jack, its slimy surface is its defining characteristic, leading to its description as "slippery." Throughout the description, variability is built into the identification. The mushroomer is told that the cap of the mushroom may be reddish to yellowish brown, the flesh is white to yellowish, the tubes are whitish to pale yellow to olive-yellow; the pores are white to yellow, becoming brown-dotted; and there is a "purplish"-drab, sleeve-like ring on the stalk. The spore print is a "dull cinnamon." The cap varies from two to five inches, the stalk from one to three inches high and three-eighths to one inch thick. The variability of this relatively easily identified mushroom is as important as its ideal color, shape, and size. Note the interpretive challenge of "-ish," the referent of "dull cinnamon" and "olive-yellow," and the shape of a "sleeve-like" ring. The description is filled with appeals to tacit knowledge, known by all but a "mycological dope."[20] Caps, rings, tubes, and veils are borrowed from cultural domains, flesh from human physiology, and spores and stalks from the plant world.

The assessment of edibility poses additional problems in that tastes vary and bodies respond differently. Some become ill from mushrooms that others consume avidly: a function of allergic reactions or different body chemistry. *Audubon* reports that Slippery Jack is "a favorite edible," but one that may cause diarrhea if not prepared correctly. Peterson's guide[21] labels it as "poisonous" (adding the iconic convention of a skull and crossbones), noting: "Although this species is edible for some people and is often rated as choice, recent reports confirm that it is toxic to other people. Remove slime layer and tubes before cooking." Another guide notes of the *Suillus* genus that "there are no poisonous U.S. species" and says simply that *luteus* is "edible, choice."[22]

Advice on edibility, as in the case of Slippery Jack, is variable, tied to legal liability and to local consumption practices. Discussions of edibility are often carefully and ambiguously worded, leaving interpretation to the reader. Fieldguides give the following advice on various species: "reported as edible," "edible, but not highly rated; often has a disagreeable acidic taste," "an excellent edible species when well cooked, for those who can tolerate it," "not recommended—some people eat it with impunity, but others experience mild poisoning," "poisonous to some people," "edible when young and fresh, but not recommended because of the difficulty of identifying this species reliably on the basis of field marks—need to use microscopic characters to confirm identification," and "unpalatable, but supposedly not toxic."[23] These reports of edibility and toxicity place considerable responsibility in the hands and the palates of collectors. Sometimes the mushroom is fine, other times toxic; for some it is edible, for others poisonous. As the toxic effects of mushrooms (as well as their culinary joys) are known by human ingestion, the attribution of satisfaction and illness is a serious concern.

This lengthy discussion of one description portrays ambiguity and metaphor in the formal depiction of a mushroom. Multiple metaphors are possible, as in this rich and evocative passage from Henry David Thoreau:[24]

> As I was going up the hill, I was surprised to see rising above the June grass, near a walnut, a whitish object, like a stone with a white top, or a skunk erect, for it was black below. It was an enormous toadstool, or fungus, a sharply conical parasol in the form of a sugar loaf, slightly turned up at the edges, which were rent half an inch for every inch or two . . . It was so delicate and fragile that its whole cap trembled at the least touch, and as I could not lay it down without injuring it, I was obliged to carry it home all the way in my hand, erect, while I paddled my boat with one hand. It was a wonder how its soft cone ever broke though the earth.

Thoreau's images of a stone, a skunk, a parasol, a sugar loaf, and a soft cone remind us of the wealth of imagery at the hands of a literary master.

Natural objects can be appreciated in terms of other natural objects, or by connecting mushrooms to manufactured objects. I noted above how both scientific and folk names provide this metaphorical structure, but metaphors also emerge in public discourse. A mushroom may be described as a lunar launcher (collared earthstar), a Pillsbury doughboy (giant puffball), a fairy castle (inky cap), toothpaste or spit (wolf's milk slime), jello (witch's butter), a can of worms (false morel), a bowling pin (purple-gilled *Laccaria*), bean sprouts (yellow coral), or a daffodil on steak (*Psathyrella* species). Metaphors on top of metaphors build the meaning of mushrooms. These examples demonstrate the range of mushroom colors and shapes, and the brilliance of the human imagination.

Sexual Metaphors

One dramatic metaphorical realm for the identification of mushrooms is sexuality. Any plant kingdom that includes *Phallus impudicus, Amanita vaginata, Nolanea mammosa,* and *Clitocybe nuda* demonstrates that human sexuality influences how we perceive nature.[25] The depiction of the erotic is a powerful, socially acceptable metaphorical trope, hard to escape. Given that science has traditionally been a male domain, most of these images are linked to male perceptions.

Many mushrooms do have recognizable phallic shapes.[26] The one that is best known for its sexual profile, however, is the "stinkhorn," or *Phallus impudicus*, a biologically sophisticated species[27] but a culturally problematic one. The mushroom is easily recognizable; shaped like an erect penis, it has a most disagreeable and potent odor. The immature mushroom is an egg that resembles a testicle. At one time these mushrooms were seen as evil and immoral: the devil's work. One Victorian woman recalls:

> [Aunt Etty] would sniff her way round the wood, pausing here and there, her nostrils twitching, when she caught a whiff of her prey; then at last, with a deadly pounce, she would fall upon her victim, and then poke his putrid carcass into her basket. At the end of the day's sport, the catch was brought back and burnt in the deepest secrecy on the drawing-room fire, with the door locked, *because of the morals of the maids.*[28]

One needn't be a devout Freudian to be struck by the imagery of poking carcasses into baskets. In 1929 a French cleric was almost killed when female devotees tried to drive the devil from him for growing "poisoned mushrooms of lascivious shapes and noxious odor."[29] Today the stinkhorn's odor is described as foul, fetid, putrid, vile, nauseating, and spermatic. Flies feast on the slime of the mushroom cap, adding to its reputation and spreading its spores.

Most contemporary mushroomers find the form of the stinkhorn amusing, and use the mushroom in sexual banter. The metaphorical link remains, but the discussion is sheathed in humor. On one trip, three middle-aged women were joking about photographing two stinkhorn eggs with a "fully erect" mature stinkhorn between them. One suggested that the photographer "should send the picture to *Hustler.*" The photographer called it "a little man," to which the third mushroomer responded: "It's a *big* man." They then began sharing dirty jokes. On another occasion Chuck told me about a prominent mushroomer who took pictures of stinkhorns with two little porcelain female hands fondling them. "In the middle of a slide show," Chuck informed me, "he'll put one or two of those in." Finally, in a discussion of a restaurant that is known for its wild mushroom dishes, the reviewer adds: "I hear there is even a large stinkhorn on view in the ladies room."[30]

This discourse speaks not only to the presence of community in the mycological world (Chapter 3), but also about the ways that metaphors can be transformed. Sexuality is perhaps the most dramatic way that metaphors can be used, but it is not the only means.

Mushrooms and Value

Natural objects exist to be. Their meanings are socially imposed. God works in mysterious, unknowable ways, and so, despite our own beliefs, we tend to ignore His purposes. We are faced with the divine task of placing things into categories, most dramatically in light of an evaluative dimension. Nature—both macrolandscapes and micro-ecologies—represents a moral order.[31] We inscribe our own judgments on a natural order.

Arrogant though the task may be, it comes readily. Naming is not enough; we need to establish the conditions of evaluation. Therefore, we readily and comfortably locate different species in our cognitive space: just as we hate mosquitos, fear bats, respect eagles, laugh at beavers, and love bear cubs. Birders are known to divide up the ornithological world into "good" and "bad" birds.[32] Often natural objects are judged on how they affect humans, with helpful things considered "good":

> Men ignore much of the living world except when it intrudes upon what they consider to be their own realm. When [spores grow] upon the very plants that feed them, men cannot afford to ignore their *fungus enemies;* but when a spore lands by chance on a bacteria-laden culture and shows itself capable of a mighty contest with germs, Fleming discovers penicillin. When a spore lands upon a precious manuscript, grows into a discolouring mould, and rots the paper, inspiration and the record of history are lost.[33]

Mushroomers build models of mushrooms on more than a simple dimension of worth.

As in most areas, a hierarchy of value is created in practice, although admittedly one may deviate from it. Central to this hierarchy is edibility, which is often translated into a related evaluation of good and bad. In this model, a "good" mushroom is one that you can eat, a "bad" one is toxic, inedible, or poisonous. It is common for new or marginal members to phrase their questions about edibility thus: "Is this a good one or a bad one?" On other occasions the link between goodness and edibility is contested. Commenting about a *Psathyrella epimyces,* Brian said, "This is a mushroom which grows on a mushroom [that is, a parasitic mushroom]. . . . We are very lucky, very fortunate to find these three meetings in a row. . . . This is good stuff." When one woman asked him if it was edible, Brian said that he didn't think so. But when the woman commented that it therefore must not be "good," Brian retorted: "It has its place in nature. It's good to see them. It's rare."

For Brian, the rarity of this *Psathyrella* trumps its inedibility. Indeed, qualities other than edibility may also affect mushrooms' value, including size, color, ease of identification, rarity, or novelty. During the presentation of mushrooms, Brian, the president, commented, "I think I'll save some of the fun ones for later." He chose to show tricholomas, which are generally not eaten, often not brightly colored, and difficult to identify to species. On a foray Dave told me that if you want to win a mushroom photo contest, you must submit a picture of a brightly colored mushroom. He said that you can't win with brown or white mushrooms. Later a woman asked Dave if he was interested in identifying a small duff-colored mushroom for her. He joked: "They've got to be big and colorful before I'm interested." Although he said this in a somewhat sarcastic way, to indicate that he knew it wasn't true, he didn't try to identify the mushroom.

As these instances suggest, color is deemed important; red, orange, and yellow mushrooms are privileged over those that are brown, gray, or white. The role of color was evident at one foray when Dave and Molly both found *Hygrophorus* species: Dave's were bright red and Molly's were white. Dave joked to Molly while they were identifying the mushrooms: "I'll take the brightly colored mushrooms any day." Molly responded: "The white ones were against a dark background. They just jumped out at you."

Molly justified how she found these mushrooms, for they are not justified in their own terms. Relative worth is evident when mushroomers compare mushrooms and have these evaluations validated by others:

> Human nature being what it is, each year we look forward to our first good mushroom crop, and dream about how good those first fresh fungi will taste. . . . In our area that means either morels or coprini

[shaggy manes?]. . . . The morels lasted only a very short time, but the lowly (and at first to us, delicious) coprini kept on producing. As other species began to make their appearance, the coprini we so welcomed at first, we began to ignore—and finally scorned. Our former love was no longer good enough, and we felt just a bit ashamed.[34]

In a similar vein, Leah told the club that she found a large number of dryad saddles in a park in Fridley (dryad saddles, though edible, are considered "tough," and so Leah was willing to share their location). She joked: "I'll pick these and trade for morels even up." The other club members laughed loudly.

VALUED MUSHROOMS

Some mushrooms are beloved and admired. Beyond the obsession with edibility and aesthetic qualities (discussed below), rarity and scientific interest matter as well. Some mushrooms are "good to think"[35] and, therefore, "good to find." When examining a *Hypomyces* (a parasitic mold) under the microscope, Brian noted : "It has a tremendous spore deposit. It looks like a lot of oil vases or jars under the microscope. It's really beautiful." In a lecture during the NAMA foray, Carl tried to get his audience interested in slime molds, his passion: "I'm here to win converts with the hope that we may tempt you to learn how to crawl on your navel and find all of these exceptionally interesting, subtle stages of acellular slime molds, photograph these for your pleasure." What others might find depressing, frightening, or troubling, mushroomers value: steady rain, steely skies, corn smut, slime mold, prickly ash, or root rot.

Perhaps the assignment of value is most dramatically evident in the respect that mushroomers have for their deadly foe, the genus *Amanita.* David Arora notes, "They never fail to attract attention and admiration . . . they are among the most beautiful and graceful of all fungi, the epitome of impeccability and elegance."[36] Because amanitas are large, often colorful, and shapely in stature, they meet most of the criteria for desirable mushrooms. For some, amanitas are the "ideal mushroom shape." Even the deadly poisonous quality of some species adds to their value ("such a beautiful thing and yet so deadly"). Mushroomers prize finding amanitas, and describe them as bright and cheery, beautiful, stately, as well as deadly. At one foray, an amanita (*Amanita mutabilis*) won the prize for the most beautiful mushroom collected. This genus contains desirable edibles (*Amanita caesarea),* deadly poisonous species *(Amanita phalloides),* and hallucinogens *(Amanita muscaria).* Mushroomers treasure eating the edible species of *Amanita* when they feel sufficiently confident. Since mushroomers are cautious about consuming amanitas, this genus challenges human ability, adding to the mushrooms' mystique:

> [Greg Wright's] major crusade is to clear the name of the *Amanita.* Most of us were taught to fear the whole genus, even though only a few species are dangerous. One of Wright's major triumphs was successfully challenging the reputation for lethality of *Amanita brunnescens.* Most of the field guides list it as poisonous, suspect, or unknown, but Wright has eaten it and gotten others to enjoy its asparaguslike flavor.[37]

An opinion leader, Wright is attempting, by example, to alter the moral worth of these mushrooms, which he feels have received a "bad rap."

DENIGRATED MUSHROOMS

Just as mushrooms may be valued, so may they be dismissed or disdained. Perhaps this is odd for those who claim to value all of nature. Yet just as weeds are plants that are out of place,[38] so are some mushrooms. Some mushrooms are booed, others are kicked, still others ignored, and others insultingly described as "yuck on a stick," "grunge," "garbage," or "junk." Just as birders speak of LBJs ("little brown jobbies"), rockhounds speak of "rock rubbish," and fishers speak of "trash fish," mushroomers have their own terms for mushrooms that are uninteresting. These species, typically small, drab, and hard to identify, are labeled as LBMs ("little brown mushrooms"). These mushrooms, difficult to identify, provide little satisfaction:

> I don't pay too much attention to [little brown mushrooms]. I see them, and I think some of them are kind of pretty where they are growing, and there generally are a whole lot of them around. Since they don't do anything, I don't see any point of pulling them up. You can't eat them, and even if you could eat them, you have to pick a bushel.

Perhaps the archetypal LBM genera are *Psathyrella* and *Inocybe,* which David Arora pungently describes:

> Few fleshy fungi have less to offer the average mushroom hunter (not to mention the average human being) than the Psathyrellas. They constitute an immense, monotonous, and metagrobolizing multitude

of dull whitish, buff, or brownish mushrooms. . . . Inocybes is a large, listless, and lackluster assemblage of malodorous brown mushrooms, of little interest to the average mushroom hunter except that many are poisonous. . . . They come in an endless, senseless procession of drab brown, sordid yellows, dismal grays, and wishy-washy whites. . . . Unravelling them is a tedious task. Its futility is exceeded only by its pointlessness.[39]

Mushroomers feel so strongly that they discourage colleagues from wasting time trying to identify small, dingy mushrooms. On forays not every mushroom is picked, even if that means that the species count, by which the success of the foray is judged, is limited. At one foray a mushroomer remarked when we found a group of (probable) mycenas: "Everyone looks at them and says, 'Oh, that's another of those mycenas. There's 250 species, and they all look alike.'" We did not try to identify the mushrooms. Or, as Molly explained: "There was a fellow who used to come in [to the club] with a lot of little stuff. We told him it was wood garbage. We don't have the books or chemicals to identify them. It's not worth the time."

Among the larger mushrooms, two that have low status are bracket fungi, or polypores, tough mushrooms that grow on wood, and *Russula,* a large, brightly colored genus that is hard to identify to species. Given that consuming and identifying mushrooms are the two main goals of collectors, both genera lack rewards. Although russulas and polypores are camera-worthy, their aesthetic properties are insufficient.

Bracket fungi. Most polypores are "woody" fungi with pores (not gills) like boletes. Many grow on live or decaying trees that are often shaped like shelves or brackets. Mushroomers shun them because of the difficulty of identifying them (particularly since few are included in fieldguides) and because their toughness makes most inedible.[40] In the Minnesota Mycological Society, only one member, Jay, had a special interest in brackets. He was teased and nicknamed "the polypore man." Brian said of Jay: "He has more experience with [bracket fungi] than I have, or want to!" Jay told me: "When I first joined, I would bring them in, and they'd all get thrown out at the end of the meeting, because all the gilled mushrooms were identified first." On a foray Tim told me: "Jay will never forgive me if I don't look at that polypore." He glanced at it very quickly, turned away, and added sarcastically, "OK, I've looked at it." He didn't pick it up or attempt to identify it.

For a few mushroomers, like Jay, polypores are considered a challenge, but for most collectors they are non-objects.[41] Their lack of importance gives rise to a moral evaluation that reminds us that not all natural objects are created equal.

Russulas. Whereas brackets are largely ignored and dismissed, the same cannot be said of russulas. They are the Rodney Dangerfields of the fungal kingdom, getting no respect, and sometimes are referred to as JARs (just another russula).[42] They are pretty and some are edible, but, being difficult to identify to species with certainty, they are treated poorly. One collector presents a merciless recipe:

> Collect as many Russulas as you can carry with a wheelbarrow if necessary. Don't bother to clean them. Just pop them into a kiln at 2,400 degrees F for 24 hours. Dump ashes into the garbage. Chalk up one good dead for the day.[43]

David Arora writes:

> Russulas are among the most maligned of all mushrooms. Even veteran mushroom hunters treat them mercilessly—throwing them over their shoulder or crushing them underfoot with disparaging remarks like, "Oh, it's just another *Russula*." . . . Try to resist the sharp temptation to mash, maim, and mutilate them.[44]

One feature of the *Russula* genus leads to this odd and brutal treatment: they are brittle and shatter easily, and are "tempting to the foot."[45] On one foray I watched a friend kicking russulas, or, as another called it, "playing football":

> People have developed very creative ways of using Russulas . . . when you are walking through the woods you can see Russulas that have been used to relieve stress . . . those are the ones that have been kicked. The rest of the Russulas you can see will have been already plucked and turned upside down and used as trail markers.[46]

They are sometimes known as "bammers" because they break into numerous pieces when thrown against a tree trunk. Indeed, throwing a russula against a tree is a primary means of identifying it to genus, making the difficult identification to species impossible. To the extent that adults believe they haven't removed the spores from the forest, they justify their "innocent" game.

Even those who defend russulas, often in a parodic vein, recognize the profound antipathy:

Karl Marx wrote . . . "The plains of Hindustan are strewn with the bleached bones of the weavers of Bengal" (sic). And so it is with our poor down-trodden Russulas. Just listen to how so called "mushroom lovers" malign this proletarian genus. Casting their broken bodies aside we mutter phrases like "garbage mushroom" with disgust. It sounds almost like "untouchable", or "outcast". Are not Russulas truly abundant even in drier months when the petit bourgeois genera are safely underground? Are they not toiling in mycorrhizal labors while capitalist [that is, parasitic] genera such as Honey Caps and Sulfur Shelf sponge off our forests? And are they not more colorful than the aristocratic Morchellas of spring? Yes, yes, and yes. Perhaps their inscrutability, their resistance to macroscopic identification are what give rise to such unprovoked antagonism.[47]

This clever pseudosocial-scientific analysis captures the socially con- structed nature of the dislike for these innocents. The author, a social science M.A. and well-liked club member, was teased about this arti- cle: his support of this oppressed genus, coupled with his esoteric display of a "Marxian" analysis, make him an easy target. The joking depended on a recognition that a love of russulas was as weird as the political theory behind the argument.

The size and color of this genus should permit us to use russulas for our benefit, but the difficulty that *we* have prevents our "accep- tance" of their value. Those few who are interested in these mush- rooms are treated with distinct suspicion. Dave commented sarcasti- cally about the owner of the inn at which we were staying on a foray: "This is the man who said if you find any russulas bring them in. Let's hope he doesn't come up with any mushroom specialties!"

Russulas more than most other species are made for humans to use for their own satisfaction. The game of morality that we play with this species, de-naturalizing it, makes it possible to treat these mush- rooms not as natural but as artificial, capable of being destroyed with- out guilt.

Mixed messages. Some mushrooms (morels, chanterelles) are in- variably seen as positive; others (bammers, brackets) are usually viewed negatively. Morality may not always be simple, however. Some mushrooms are desirable objects, but at a cost. Although I discussed amanitas in light of their positive evaluation, many fear these mush- rooms and keep their distance. They would feel no pain if amanitas became endangered. One person's meat is another's poison. Objects that in one domain are negative may be positive in another domain. Some "ugly" fungi are prime edibles ("tree ears"), whereas beautiful mushrooms (amanitas) may be deadly. Beauty is not the whole of moral evaluation. Ugly mushrooms may be prized. A collector explained: "They all have a place in nature. Even if they are ugly, they are beautiful for their function."

Consider dung fungus. Many mushrooms flourish in richly fertilized areas: dung can be a prime habitat. The repulsiveness of dung gives pungency to the encomiums to these mushrooms. One mushroomer writes of "the joy of dung":

> Spring and early summer are fine times to go dung searching. A balmy spring day spent browsing among the cattle can be a great tonic. And exciting, for there is always, lurking amongst the predictable inhabitants, a surprise, a misfit, something new and different. Let me assure you, there be many surprises among the dung-fungi.[48]

The negative images of dung are transformed metaphorically into positive images that enchant the mycological imagination:[49]

> The popular mind links coprophiles [dung fungus] with eeriness or ugliness or witchcraft; but can't we think of them more like worms metamorphosing into butterflies, or as chaos blooming into salvation?[50]

> A rich harvest [of mushrooms] may well await the man who cares to devote his leisure hours or his declining years to the study of stale dog dung.[51]

> Let us cheer for dung fungi!
> Dung fungi—unsung fungi!
> Never-touch-the-tongue fungi!
> Highstrung, ever-young fungi!
> Freely flung across the dung
> Freshly sprung with ho so gung!
> Stench a song so plainly sung![52]

That many dung fungi are hallucinogenic (such as *Psilocybe cubensis*) adds an additional appeal to the close examination of animal droppings, even for those who choose not to indulge in the consumption of this "sacred" comestible.

I do not argue that these moral evaluations are eternal or that they are universally shared. Some mushroomers appreciate russulas, are fearful of amanitas, and keep their distance from dung and all that grows nearby. I only suggest that the moral evaluation of leisure is used to invest the world with an emotional depth. These meanings extend the possibilities of thinking and feeling about objects in which others have little interest. This provides satisfaction and also builds a sense of community and cohesion, drawing symbolic boundaries from those with a "restricted code."[53] Leisure activities, and nature activities in particular, provide a wide array of knowledge and interpretations that are not shared outside a limited social world. Moral order contributes to this process; within this moral order are aesthetic interpretations and personification.

AESTHETIC IMAGES

All physical objects have sensory dimensions. We see, feel, smell, taste, and hear our world. To be "in nature" is to give oneself over to experience—ideally an experience of vividness and intensity. In the essayist Diane Ackerman's[54] view, the world is "sense-luscious." Our senses are crucial to this process. To experience the world is to connect emotionally and cognitively to things, and then to behave in accord with these feelings and thoughts. We cannot understand the world without reflecting on our senses. Ackerman asserts: "The senses don't just make sense of life in bold or subtle acts of clarity, they tear reality apart into vibrant morsels and reassemble them into a meaningful pattern."[55] The body converts experiences to a form that the brain can understand.[56]

It is perhaps odd to speak of natural objects as beautiful in that they were not *intended* as aesthetic (depending, of course, on one's view of the divine).[57] Some objects are "aesthetic by destination"—created to be appreciated for their sensory values, whereas others are "aesthetic by metamorphosis," with aesthetic qualities being read into the "thing."[58] An aesthetic object is no more than a piece cut from endless sequences of experience and self-consciously appreciated.[59] Yet naturalists reject this view of beauty as constructed, and hold to something closer to the nature writer Annie Dillard's[60] perspective that "beauty is something objectively performed." Since we can't depend on understanding the *intent* of the maker, we find beauty in the object (in either form or function)[61] or in the mind of the perceiver. These aesthetic standards develop from the appreciation of cultural objects.[62] Further, some argue[63] that our environmental attitudes derive from an aesthetic valuation of nature, a fundamentally cultural view.[64]

Mushrooms suggest the power of this process. Many find that mushrooms lack sensory and aesthetic significance. They are out of mind, and, hence, out of sight. For serious hobbyists, mushrooms are in sight and in mind. This appreciation of nature must be acquired, leading some to suggest that it is part of our moral education.[65] In the words of one mushroomer, we must discover that "lawns can be like mycological jewel boxes with resplendent rough stones awaiting the motivated seeker capable of transforming each into a brilliant discovery."[66] Borrowing our standards from cultural realms, it becomes easy to differentiate natural objects not only as good and bad, but as pretty and ugly. Some mushrooms, birds, mountains, and fish have more aesthetic worth than others.[67] On forays participants commonly call their colleagues to gape and gasp at a particularly "beautiful" specimen. One mushroomer made this explicit, asserting, "Aesthetics are really important to me—the aesthetics when they're really in prime condition . . . It's a developed love. The beauty comes from an understanding of fungi." Some mushroomers are so taken with the aesthetic quality of their quarry that they dry them or use them as potpourris.

The sensory range of mushrooms is astonishing. One writer remarks:

> The flavor and odor of mushrooms vary tremendously. Some smell like oysters or soap. Others have a woody smell. Their aromas may range from that of cod liver oil, bitter almonds or rotten fish to indescribably delightful heights. Their flavor covers the entire taste scale from that of oysters or veal to sweetbreads or kidneys.[68]

Mushrooms are said to feel like fine leather, dishrags, beef jerky, wax, styrofoam, or velvet. Tastes include bitterness, metallic taste, mud, butter, meat, chicken, oysters, chocolate, and eggplant. Smells, linked to taste, have more direct associations, including anise, apricot, almond, banana, black pepper, camphor, cedar wood, celery, chlorine, cinnamon, creosote, cucumber, clover, fish, garlic, grapefruit, green corn, maple syrup ("grind it up and put it on pancakes"), onion, paste, peach, pear, peas, potatoes, pumpkin, radish, resin, root beer, shrimp, soap, squash, sulfur, tobacco, urine ("the floor of a service station restroom"), and watermelon rind.[69] Although particular chemicals or molecular structures give mushrooms distinctive textures, tastes, and smells, interpretation depends on socialization.

Understanding and sharing aesthetic discourse is difficult because of the limitations of our sensory language.[70] We are left with metaphors, family resemblances, and shared experiences to categorize and appreciate these objects that do not easily fit into aesthetic niches. This is complicated by variations in mushrooms and in human standards of appreciation. Indeed, we may not know what the sensory meaning is until we are told what we should be looking for.[71] Jerry asked people in the lounge at our motel to smell a *Lactarius aquifluus* specimen. One man said that it smelled like buckwheat, another said that it smelled like celery seed; many couldn't tell. Once he announced that it was supposed to smell like maple syrup, the smell was evident.

The interpretation of smell (and taste) varies, especially prior to explanation, a fact to which novice wine tasters can attest. Although it is said that one can identify mushrooms by smell, one must first know what one is sniffing for before this technique is feasible. Some even suggest that one can *find* mushrooms by their smell—a dramatic privileging of a secondary sense. Mark told me that he once believed he could smell morels: "I thought I could smell them. I checked the wind, and there were some there." Some mushroomers contend that they can locate chanterelles because of their distinct apricot smell. On morel forays I have seen hunters sniff the air and then search visually for the mushrooms; they were correct on occasion.

The sensory quality of mushrooms (here, smell and taste) contributes to, but does not fully determine, whether a mushroom will be consumed. Fungi, such as truffles, that are endowed with aesthetic virtue are consumed and spoken of with reverence.

Magical truffles. Truffles are a dramatic example of the process by which the aesthetic qualities of an object are enshrined in images. Unlike most of the mushrooms I discuss, edible truffles are not hunted much in the United States (most American truffles are not prime edibles). Truffles are hunted in France and Italy, often by romanticized swine that are motivated by their musky odor.[72] The truffle is an acquired taste, despite its qualities as an aphrodisiac. Yet once the taste is acquired, metaphors give meaning to nearly inexpressible impressions:

> There they were. Big. The size of a man's fist. Black. Like the night sky. And with a thick powerful aroma. The aroma of overripe olives, of sweet old mother earth, of indulgence.[73]

> This gritty sphere exudes a flavor which seems to pervade all the peripheral areas of one's senses while coyly evading the center.[74]

> [Truffles are] some kind of ultimate taste sensation that ranked right up there with sex as the kind of mystical experience without which no life could be considered complete.[75]

After describing truffles as "earthy," "fungoid," "sweet," "nut-like," one author adds that they are "just ineffable."[76] The aesthetic quality of truffles cannot be expressed in direct or objective terms: truffles, like strong cheese, can only be appreciated by the experienced.

Eating tasteless mushrooms. It is surprising that, given the aesthetic rhetoric linked to some fungi, mushroomers will consume mushrooms that they do not think have very distinctive taste. Rarely are bitter or unpleasant mushrooms consumed, but relatively tasteless ones are. Some species have few distinctive qualities. After trying a *Strobilomyces*, Eliott told me that it tasted "kind of bland." He added, "You know, I read all these descriptions [of taste], [but] all I smell is mushroom. All I taste is mushroom." Although enthusiasts are supposed to differentiate among species, in practice comparative judgments are difficult. Mushroomers talk privately about not treasuring the taste of some prime edibles. Describing chanterelles, Janet commented: "They taste just like anything else that is fried in butter. They have a pleasant taste, but I think that comes from the butter and from the frying. I think that almost anything that's fried has good taste." Mushroomers joke about the lack of taste they find in some of the mushrooms they consume. One commented about *Peziza repanda* (a cup fungus): "Cut them into strips and you can put them into hot-and-sour soup. You can't taste them anyhow." Jerry joked: "You can barbecue cardboard, if you put enough sauce on it."

A club member asked about the taste of *Entoloma abortivum*. Brian commented: "They're good with hamburger and onions. The more hamburger and onions, the better." The other club members laughed, and Jerry added: "Most of these mushrooms don't have a real strong taste." Later Jerry said of *Tremella mesenterica* (a jelly fungus, witch's butter): "The Chinese roll it in sugar. It's edible, but it has no taste of its own. That's why they roll it in sugar." Jerry commented about *Hypomyces lactifluorum* (the lobster mushroom): "When they're fresh, they're crisp like a potato. I cooked them in butter, salt, and pepper. They tasted like butter, salt, and pepper." The other club members laughed. "It didn't have much taste. . . . You could do the same thing with cardboard or Kleenex, it would taste the same." It is not that everyone agrees with these evaluations, but together they raise the question, why eat mushrooms if they have no special taste? What is important in the "taste" of mushrooms is the means by which they are gathered, and the symbolic value of that collection, rather than taste per se. The taste of wild mushrooms derives in part from their "gatheredness"—the context of taste comes from the experience of the collector:

> *Barry:* The occasion on which I first had [morels] I remember very
> well. I was at the home of a very well known artist whose son had
> gathered them, and essentially [they tasted like] butter and garlic.
> *GAF:* They don't have a taste of their own?
> *Barry:* They have a quality. The quality is the gatheredness. That they
> are hand-produced products, although you can buy them at
> [gourmet groceries]. But these were things that were gathered. . . .
> I grow wild red currants in my backyard and make currant jelly
> and give it to my friends. My jelly is different. You can buy wild
> currant jelly at the supermarkets, but there is something about that
> hand-quality, that [it] is hand-gathered, prepared, preserved, and
> produced by individuals. . . . That's what I think about morel
> mushrooms. They are a special thing gathered by people and pre-
> sented; so, in that sense, they have a social and an aesthetic quality
> that's totally unrelated to taste.

The limitations of distinctive taste are overcome by the cultural meaning of hunting and gathering: a return to nature and a gift from the self.

THE PROBLEM OF PERSONIFICATION

Understanding nature depends on our recognition of similarity: it is like us, and we are like it. Just as we link nature to spirituality, so, too, we speak of "Mother Earth." We comprehend nature through our experience. We personify the world, interpreting the nonhuman in light of human characteristics.[77] Although some see personification as an affront to humans, giving human form to things, more often it is an affront to the natural object, which is characterized as human with its *otherness* erased. Yet despite the inadequacy of this process, personification provides a point of entry, taming the natural image to our values and providing for the possibility of a cultural link between humans and the wild. Personification has the virtue of generating support for "environmental" issues.

Role-taking presupposes that the target object is human in quality. As the philosopher Thomas Nagel[78] muses in his essay "What Is It Like to Be a Bat?" we ask what it would be like if we were bats (or fungi), rather than wondering what it is like for a bat to be a bat (or a fungus to be a fungus). To gain access to the core truths that nature supposedly supplies, we define nature as teaching wisdom and offering solace, anthropomorphizing it.[79] In attempting to understand the animal world, we see our own society reflected, as Marx noted about Darwin:

> It is remarkable how Darwin recognizes among beasts and plants, his English society with its division of labor, competition, opening up of new markets, "invention," and the Malthusian "struggle for existence." It is Hobbes' *bellum omnium contra omnes* [the war of all against all].[80]

The description of *Russulas* as proletarian shows that, as Darwin can draw upon Hobbes, others can rely upon Marx. Natural objects are given emotions, values, and character. Indeed, our interest in natural history can be justified morally and theologically because of its similarities to human *culture*.

Character

The attribution of *character* is central to the personification of wild objects. Literature is replete with noble lions, devoted dogs, and cunning foxes.[81] Every creature is given a character down to the "cheerful, humble" moss. Mushrooms have a more specialized public, but character issues are not absent. Given the rhetorical claim that character is a quality of all objects, an author can proclaim that "the sympathetic observer will soon notice that mushrooms have personalities—nuances of lifestyle that set them apart from their fungal brethren."[82] One can assert that mushrooms are concerned about privacy,[83] capable of going mad,[84] or have a "Dr. Jekyll–Mr. Hyde lifestyle."[85] A collector professes to revere mushrooms because he sees them as "anti-authoritarian":

> They are not subject to discipline. You can't grow them; very few of them are growable. They aren't subject to people control all that much. They are small and just pop up.

Another sees mushrooms as showing off. Tim told me that a professional mycologist commented about a species whose red mycelium is observable on top of logs: "She says she thinks *Coprinus radians* enjoys showing off its mycelium. It has no purpose." The fact that a trait has no botanically self-evident function permits this mycologist to draw upon the rhetoric of character. Function trumps character, but character remains a residual explanation.

Despite concern with the personality and motivation of mushrooms, mushroomers see character and personality adhering to species. One makes attributions not to a single specimen, but to the species as a whole.[86]

Gender

The assignment of gender to natural objects that reproduce asexually is close to character and personality. Botanically, mushrooms are neither male nor female. Yet often mushrooms are assigned gender. As Toporov notes in his semiotic analysis:

> It is hardly surprising that one of the most widespread motifs associated with mushrooms presupposes their division into *masculine* and *feminine*. In general terms this may be related to an opposition of types of mushrooms according to their external appearance; cf., on the one hand, mushrooms with a clearly expressed stem and cap-shaped top, and on the other, mushrooms without a stem or with a stem inseparable from the cap, and with a cap in the shape of a hollow depression.[87]

Toporov's claim depends on the structure of human reproductive organs. Although this is not totally wrong (witness the masculine *Phallus impudicus*), gender divisions are also social. Male mushrooms are bigger, stronger, and darker than female mushrooms. Boletes are prototypical male mushrooms. *Boletus edulis* is a large, "meaty" mushroom, known as "King Bolete." One mycological poet writes:

> Bold in the shade beneath the tree
> Boletus bears his shield of yellow,
> Blazoned with arrogant heraldry.[88]

Another comments in passing: "Ever Met a Boletus edulis You Didn't Like? Hard not to like the little fellows (or big fellows)."[89] In the *Boletus* family there is also *Suillus luteus,* or Slippery Jack, as well as Slippery Jill (*Suillus subluteus!*), but she is much less common. A third *Boletus* family member whose gender is emphasized by its popular name is the "old man of the woods" (*Strobilomyces floccopus*). This is a large mushroom with a knobby, scaly gray-black cap and blackish stalk. Its flesh is white, becoming reddish then black when exposed to the air:

> If dignity can be attributed to a mushroom, then the old man of the woods would get the "Most Dignified" award . . . Western collectors might want to attend an eastern foray sometime to meet in person the old man, a bolete with no peers west of the plains.[90]

The mature species is known as the "old man," and so mushroomers joke that if they find a young one (hard to find because it blends into the dark woods), "it would be a young boy." Another mycological poet captures this dignified, old man:

> Darkly knobbed with warts he stands
> Close to the ground. His cap, a coffee cup
> Drained of its brew; his mouth hangs open loosely. . . .
> No armor against foul weather
> His suit, threadbare and shaggy
> Wears thin. Black knight of fast
> Declining years, he has been vulnerable
> All his life.[91]

The old man represents age and gender in the minds of mushroomers, revealing the symbolic richness of botany.

Although female mushrooms include the "cup" fungi, in practice other mushrooms are so labeled. For example, many white mushrooms—those with white caps, stems, flesh, and spore prints—notably amanitas, are labeled female.[92] Amanitas are stem-and-cap mushrooms, but they also grow from a cup, which might cause Freudians to claim that they have female form. More significant, the mystery, whiteness, elegance, and perhaps the deadly quality of amanitas permit the labeling of the genus as female:

> The *Amanita* is ubiquitous, brazen, and feared. It beckons seductively and, as Odysseus was drawn to the dangerous cliffs of Scylla and Charybdis, as the charmed Orpheus was drawn to his lovely Eurydice, as Hansel and Gretel were drawn to the [witch's] gingerbread house, we too are drawn in our innocence to the *Amanita*.[93]
>
> ───────
>
> A lovely plain-dressing miz *Amanita breckonii*, known heretofore as a serious studious collegiate . . . was seen having a rollicking good time with her steady, *Monty Pine* (*P. radiata*, as he's known professionally). . . . And that reminds me that [*Amanita*] *ocreata* has her eye on a certain highly placed hyoomin [human] official.[94]

Jessie Keiko Saiki, the author of the tribute to the old man of the woods, also penned verse to *Amanita virosa*, death's angel:

> How sinister this mushroom's deception
> Luring with her immaculate
> Purity of presence.
> Death masquerades as virgin bride with
> Remnants of lace upon her cap
> And vestiges of veil around her neck.[95]

It is not that the old man of the woods will inevitably be male, or that the death angel will always be female, but that the traits that mushroomers define as constituting their identity are linked to cultural images. These mushrooms are not seen as being "biologically" male or female (although images of stinkhorns come close); rather, their cultural identity provides these roles. They have gender, but no sex. "Gender" is based on the social understanding of their physical reality and on a community that defines them as capable of being meaningfully personified.

Active Objects

Attributing human characteristics to objects is only part of the process by which we invest the world with magic. Humans are not merely beings but actors. As humans act, so do objects. The public recognizes this when discussing gurgling brooks or whispering pines. Mushrooms are said to hide from forayers:

> They're elusive little rascals. You have to walk slowly and quietly and spot them before they spot you, or they'll get up and run away from you.[96]

Or, alternatively, call to them:

> and all about me in various directions
> other mushrooms I can't yet see
> are singing to me, calling, calling,
> hoping I'll come over and look at them
> and pick them and take them
> home and cook them and eat them . . .[97]

Or, like the inky cap *(Coprinus)*, which liquifies into black spores, mushrooms are said to commit suicide.[98] Mushrooms may "mock" mushroomers, "spit juice" at them, or "come up and bite [them] on the leg."

If one imagines that mushrooms act, and thus identifies with them, then "killing" can be traumatic. One can almost hear the emotion, covered with a patina of amusement: Dave joked, "You can hear the mushrooms as they're pulled out of the ground"; and Howard commented, "I could almost buy the fact that the mushroom shivers in pain when you go down with the knife to get it. I don't necessarily buy into that but there are degrees of these things." That mushrooms act allows humans to feel empathy, and eventually create a relationship with them. One mycologist spoke of "empathy biology" in that he would attempt to "imagine what it's like being a fungus," which presumably aided his understanding of the function of biological mechanisms, as well as allowed him to appreciate his subject.

Knowing Mushrooms

Mushroomers talk and joke about knowing mushrooms. Perhaps this is odd, not only because of the surprising link between humans and nature (we also talk to our pets and house plants),[99] but because within a species mushrooms are interchangeable. Any dialogue with a mushroom is as a representative of its species. The relation depends not on a unique self, but on a species self.

Mushroomers talk about "meeting" mushrooms, noting "We had not met before"[100] when the species is unfamiliar. In identification, the question often is phrased "Who is it?" and not "What is it?" One professional mycologist noted: "You'll find new species, and old species in new surroundings. It's like a marvelous mix of old and new friends."[101] Amateurs report in a similar vein:

> Although the names of some interesting mushrooms and many "L.B.M.s" remained elusive we did make the acquaintance of numerous fungal friends. New members were introduced to long-time friends such as the Oyster Shelf, Shaggy Mane, and Sulphur Shelf.[102]

In creating a slide show, Burt removed many of the slides that he had taken, commenting: "It's like deciding which of your children to throw away." Brian added: "It's like a family portrait." This is dramatically evident when mushroomers discuss consumption. Typically the desire to consume takes precedence over images of cannibalism, except in joking. This is closest to the surface among professional mycologists:

> Some mycologists are chary of naming the edibles, for good reason. They may have spent so many hours at forays and mushroom shows putting name slips on specimens that it simply doesn't occur to them to *eat* mushrooms anymore, if it ever did. Or, to view it another way, if the little rascals provide you with a paycheck, eventually you may feel as though you're turning cannibal if you consume them. The mushrooms become almost like pets, or family.[103]

The relations between mushroomers and their objects are transient, but the reality that such rhetoric may be compellingly used suggests the power of creating meaning from matter.

Mushrooms R Us

By means of personification we allege that objects of nature are like people, and the reverse. The characteristics of people can be transferred to natural objects, and in turn people can be seen as natural objects. Although this is often done with a measure of levity, that it makes sense suggests that the connection is plausible.

To assume that natural objects are human involves transferring motivation and intent to them, as when in 1679 in London a woman and her canine partner were both hanged for an act of bestiality.[104] Less dramatically, mushroomers comment:

> Mushrooms are like people, in some ways. Now and then, they get confused, and show up when they aren't supposed to. Or, they're late, or early—or may not show up at all! . . . About the first fungus to appear in spring around here is *Urnula craterium;* when you see the first ones, you'll know the morels are yawning and getting ready.[105]

Sometimes mushrooms are said to incorporate humans, a symbiotic relationship based on the fungal property of decay:

> Nadya died in Mexico this past December a few weeks short of her 78th birthday. A devout atheist, she looked forward to no Great Foray in the sky. So let her moulder in the earth. Perhaps some day the atoms and molecules that constituted her will come back to us, components of fungi—say a morel or chanterelle—edible and delicious. But be not surprised if there is not an Amanita too.[106]

Just as mushrooms can be made human, so can humans be transformed—for a moment—into mushrooms. One writer notes: "Like fungi, we are parasites on plants, fungi, and animals; like fungi, we destroy and foul our environment—but our crop is the entire world, and like fungi, we now number in the billions."[107]

A mushroomer may describe his balding head as "glabrous" (that is, smooth). Another, when seeing a mushroom, comments that it is "too old to identify," and then jokes to supportive laughter, "We've got some members like that." Or a mushroomer may simply suggest that "there are several members of the mushroom society that *look* like mushrooms." With a little creativity, fungal descriptions can be made to apply to humans:

> [*Boletivorus clandestinus* and *Boletivorus brutalosipes* (clandestine and brutal bolete eater)] occur solitary to scattered in the woods, but always near roads. . . . The flesh is pallid, becoming blue when bruised and exuding a red latex when cut.[108]

Mushrooms, like other species, are occasionally named after scientists or others. When it was announced that an amanita was to be named after a well-known, beloved amateur (*Amanita ristichii*), one author presented a humorous description of the mushroom:

Medium-sized to large terrestrial fungi found mostly in woods. CAP white, shaggy, hairy, often covered with large red cloth wart which usually falls off upon passage through a doorway. GILLS double, opening and closing regularly, words of wisdom fall from them if the curious or interested are nearby. STALK central, slender, definitely not separable from cap without damage to entire organism, splitting just above mid-stipe into two arm-like appendages and below with two leg-like appendages. Usually mobile, more comparable to a myxomycete than to a basidiomycete in this characteristic.[109]

The description continues—perhaps tiresome in its preciousness to outsiders but delightful to those who know the mushroom and the man.

People do not confuse themselves with mushrooms, but some of them find these analogies meaningful. The linkage exposes the possibility that mushrooms and humans belong to the same universe of meaning. The natural world can be tamed, whereas human culture can be made wild. That those who are part of the scene find the linkage amusing means that shared assumptions are being upheld.

THE MOREL ORDER

The mushroom with the greatest cultural resonance is the morel (*Morchella*), a genus with approximately ten major species. This highly prized spring mushroom is a source of intense interest throughout its growing range. It is the "Cadillac" of mushrooms, an "elite mushroom." When I asked members of the Minnesota Mycological Society to name their favorite mushroom, 44 percent named the morel, with the chanterelle in second place with 11 percent.[110] The range of folk names given to the morel also speaks to its popularity: merkels, honeycomb mushrooms, hickory chicken, sponge mushrooms, and roons.

Festivals reflect the popularity of morels. Notable is the morel festival in Boyne City, Michigan, in mid-May.[111] Not to be outdone, the Minnesota state legislature, at the urging of the Minnesota Mycological Society, named the morel the state fungus, a decision that worried some club members, who were afraid of having outsiders pick "our" morels. Commercial pickers can make several hundred dollars a day during the few weeks that morels grow. I knew one couple who would take a week's vacation during late spring, spending more than forty hours a week in the woods. Catalogs offer products designed for the morel hunter, specialized cookbooks and fieldguides,[112] and even comic postcards depicting gigantic morels (one allegedly weighing ninety-two pounds!), much like the giant jackalopes cards found at rest areas along prairie highways.

Morels are linked to the divine, playfully but regularly:

> There is a theological theory that the forbidden fruit in the garden [of Eden] was in fact morel mushrooms, that the maker wanted to save the flavor (and knowledge) for himself, herself, or itself.[113]

> The morel is truly the food of the Gods. It is their exclusive food and it grows in the Elysian Fields in plenty; morels are rare among us mortals for the Gods only reluctantly and rarely bestow their blessings on man. We must be content with the crumbs from the tables of the Gods.[114]

The passion for morels provokes descriptions of odd behaviors—a shared madness, "the Captain Ahab in us."[115] Consider this mock-up of an advice column:

> Imagine my dismay when I saw a dog on our street eating morels as they came up underneath our neighbor's apple trees! What should I do?
> *This may be one of the few social situations where we can take a tip from the Burmese. Allow the offending canine to munch some mycological morsels, then offer him a bowl of white sauce seasoned with tarragon and dry white wine. After this, kill him—do it slowly—and roast him on a spit.*[116]

The shared understanding of the value of morels makes this grisly jest amusing and worth publishing in a mushrooming periodical. *Every-one* knows that hunters will do *anything* to preserve their morels. The symbolic centrality of morels as cultural objects gives a sacred quality to the hunt, and gives the right to provide sympathy to those who do not find any.[117] Morel hunting has greater emotional weight than other mushrooming:

> I wonder why morel hunting is so driven. I feel driven by it much more than other types of mushroom hunting, which is a pleasant stroll in the woods. It's *meshuggonah*.

Suddenly it is there in the shadows. A single, exquisite morel, almost six inches high, stands by itself boldly etched against the edge of the orchard. Awestruck at first, I am afraid to remove it. Perhaps it is the last morel in the world. Perhaps it will fall apart to my touch. Perhaps it is only an illusion after all. I step back, circle and, for a moment, admire the spectacle. Stooping then, I run my fingers gently along the surface of the cap, in and out of the grooves and hollows, down the long rubbery stem. Carefully carving the earth around the base, I remove the entire mushroom and place it with reverence in the basket.[118]

Is this nature's pornography or nature's piety? Such language is possible because it connects with images of controlled obsessions. The collective belief that this is an obsession bolsters the "shared madness" that mushroomers half-seriously feel characterizes them.

What is it about morel hunting that produces this discourse? If the woods are populated with natural friends, morels appear (and then quickly disappear) when few others are present. They represent the birth of spring and justify our emergence from artificial winter cocoons into the authentic world of nature. Morels provide a legitimating discourse and a focus for being away from the oppressive, deadly civilization that symbolizes winter.

Yet something is beyond this. As a morel hunter myself, I find it hard to know whether it is an objective reality or a socially constructed one that morels are damnably hard to find. Morels are tannish-gray mushrooms with light and dark patches that are easily camouflaged on the sun-dappled forest floor. I've looked unseeing at spots where morels were growing. As one writer described, "It was like looking for Easter eggs that nobody had put out."[119] I felt sure that morels were hiding. Perhaps it is the joy of finally being in the woods—a cultural joy—that makes mushroomers treasure the game of hide-and-seek with a challenging opponent. Brian joked at our spring foray about how difficult it is to pick morels: "Morels like to keep bad company, or at least protective company [in Minnesota, poison ivy, nettles, prickly ash]. Like having an Italian family around you. If you want it, you have to pay for it." Or as Mark explained: "Sometimes I could almost believe that the mushrooms make themselves invisible, except when they let you find them." He assured me that he believed this only symbolically.

Whereas hobbyists speak of collecting mushrooms, they invariably speak of "hunting morels." The inanimate is animated. One collects things but hunts animals. This quality is also evident when these "fleshy fungi" are spoken of in terms of an eroticism of being. Morels do vaguely resemble male organs, if not as precisely as the stinkhorn, and are simultaneously vulnerable—their symbolic richness is such that feminine themes seem appropriate:

> The morel is erotic. Because it will not be tamed. Because the morel is Spring itself.[120]

> One . . . photograph [of a morel] is a miscellany of nails, screws, pins, razor blades and a lone morel stuck plumb in the middle of all the metal, which nicely accentuates the fleshy, vulnerable, almost human quality of the mushroom.[121]

For others, sexuality is not as significant as the strategy inherent in the hunt. The divinity of nature is forgotten in the competition of the game:

> "The way I generally get mushrooms," he explained as we drove, "is to get my chainsaw running at the edge of the woods. I put it on the ground while it's still running so that the mushrooms think I'm cutting wood. I sneak up, pick off the lead mushroom, then round up the rest."[122]

> [Morels] almost always travelled in groups, he said, and one of the biggest thrills was trying to find where the captured morel's buddies were. If you made noises, he warned me, they would scurry away in the camouflage. With systematic stealth you had to comb the area, knowing they were nearby but not gonna go easily.[123]

These collectors "know" that they are kidding, but they also "know" that they are telling the truth.

If morels are so extraordinary ("their deliciousness exceeds normal limits of restraint"[124]; "steak and mushrooms, and you don't need the steak"), identifying their taste should be easy. After all, the purpose of hunting morels is to consume them. The problem is greater than the standard one of describing any foodstuff.[125] Morels taste like mushrooms, despite a distinctive texture. Mushroomers in my sample defined morels as "nutty," "chewy," "earthy," "woodsy," and "meaty."[126] Larry Lonik,[127] the author of *The Curious Morel: Mushroom Hunters'*

Recipes, Lore and Advice, surveyed morel hunters as to the taste of these delights. Among the responses were: "thinly sliced sirloin steak," "steamed, fresh clams," "chewy," "tender," "delicate," and "after a day in the woods, like gold." This last comment recognizes that the taste is linked to the gathered quality of these objects, as described above, and suggests that the aesthetic charms of morels may be as much in the mind as on the palate.

Part of the taste of wild morels comes from the mushroomer's belonging to the community of morel hunters, a world that excludes outsiders:

> No one has ever been able to describe to me what the morel tastes like. People just say they are "wonderful" or "like nothing else" while smiling knowingly as older girls do when asked by younger girls about love. But now that I have had my first taste, I can say that morels are tender, and they are sweet. . . . As a matter of fact, they are "wonderful" and taste "like nothing else." Just as they were described to me.[128]

Barry, the particularly thoughtful collector whom I quoted discussing the "gathered quality" of his morels and currants, explained that the taste of morels cannot be assigned to their "flavor" alone; the taste is socially situated:

> [Morels] have an aesthetic quality that is impervious to descripters. As a good cook, I'm also aware of when you serve a dinner, there's also impressions. And I think, in their own sense, morels provide an impression rather than a specific taste. . . . I know that morels served to me have been picked by those people, so there's a homeyness and personal aesthetic. It's not a particularly astounding distinctness. Morels are not the best thing to come along since sliced bread. They're different than mushrooms you buy in the supermarket, and you can now buy morels in the supermarket. The idea that someone has bought these adds a different dimension than those that are picked.

Morels stand apart as cultural objects. The meaning of the hunt, their value, and their taste emerge from their cultural placement. Morels are accorded a place that other prime edibles are not. As objects that have not been "manufactured," they are real and authentic. Although they grow according to their own schedule—and have an agency that humans cannot alter—morels are mediated, transformed into valued objects, whereas the other plants, fungi, and creatures nearby are ignored.

In this chapter I elaborated on the emotional, cognitive, and cultural meanings that naturalists give to nature, exploring how one corner of that world is filled with a richness of which most people are unaware. By examining the metaphorical construction of mushrooms and mushrooming, I have shown that even the most natural domains do not have inherent meaning. Rather, meanings are thrust upon them by cultural actors.

Fieldguides, ostensibly objective, depend on images and on the personal choices of their authors. No objective criteria of smell, taste, and edibility exist. Even size and color are so variable that choices must be made. In Chapter 6 I discuss the "problem" of speciation (what do we lump together and what do we split apart). In this chapter I noted that this is a practical problem for mushroomers who desire to know what to label mushrooms, what to think about them, and how to use them.

From this emerges the problem of evaluation. Rather than treating objects as separate and distinctive, we typify them, providing moral worth. Each object is seen as belonging to a species (and often as a member of a genus, such as russulas), and is interpreted in light of the typification of that species. This involves the establishment of worth, linked both to aesthetic judgments and to a robust process of personification.

Sharing
the Woods

I was obliged at last to come to the conclusion that the contemplation of nature alone is not sufficient to fill the human heart and mind.

—HENRY WALTER BATES[1]

It pleases us to believe that solitude is what we seek. We strive for a oneness with nature—to be part of the great Gaian design. Sometimes such isolation is desirable. Yet many who spend extensive periods in natural surroundings become homesick for civilization.[2] The writer Alex Shoumatoff notes of his several months passage down the rivers of South America:

> I began to feel the stir-craziness which the jungle, with its constant humidity, its apparent monotonous sameness, and its claustrophobic lack of open space, can impose. . . . I had wanted to "experience the jungle" as fully as I could, but try as I might, I could never stop the internal monologue . . . which had [nothing] to do with where I was. . . . As the trip wore on, the trappings of civilization became more important than they had ever been for me. Perhaps I fell back on them as a defense against the overwhelming wildness with which I was surrounded.[3]

The effects of isolation result not only from a lack of stimuli, but also from a lack of human contact. Without a social life, we suffer part of the fate of feral children.

Those who embrace nature typically have company. Sometimes they share the wild with "compartmentalized" friends,[4] with whom their limited relationships are based on a particular leisure pursuit, and sometimes with those with whom their ties are broader. One study of canoeists in the Quetico-Superior Wilderness area found that they *all* visited in groups.[5] One's social life is frequently brought to the wild. One canoeist remarked, "I wanted to find a nice secluded place where I could be with my friends and get away from it all"; another claimed, "I like to get away from people, the newspaper, and the radio, so I can be alone with my wife."[6] Stephen Trimble, a prominent naturalist, mused:

> My wife, Joanne, both enhances and distracts from what I see in nature alone. . . . In striving to articulate what we feel, how each of us reacts to the land, we use language earlier than I would alone to recreate the feel of light on sandstone or the smell of cliffrose. . . . Talking with the woman I love about the places we pass through makes the experiences warmer, simpler.[7]

Although one is away from casual acquaintances and instrumental tasks, being in nature often involves a personal, intimate relationship with little privacy. The forest is a social as well as a natural resource.

Mushroomers are not as removed from civilization as are backcountry hikers, and only rarely do they have days away from all social moorings, yet the reality of being alone with nature even for short periods of time can dull the pleasure that might otherwise be gained from the wild. Mushroomers relish sharing their experiences. They venture into nature in groups and then share the experience with others.

The mushroom quest typically has several stages: collecting, identifying, consuming, and narrating. Each depends on the existence of a vigorous social community. In this respect, mushrooming does not differ from other nature pursuits, including hunting and mountaineering.[8] A hunter who claimed to prefer the solitary quality of the field noted that often he cannot leave his "social self behind":

> There is conversation, which some companions cannot seem to help offering, about related things (dogs I once had, shots I made, things I saw, alibis I now offer), or even unrelated things. There is (and a tremendous amount of this) driving around—looking for particular spots, asking strangers for information, stopping for beer or cigarettes or candy bars, looking for game out the car window.[9]

Most mushroomers claimed to prefer the company of others. One noted that "it's very hard to enjoy mycology alone." Others were similarly social:

> I like going with at least one other person. Partly it's easier to search an area, and it's fellowship. They also have different insights too. It's more fun going out with other persons.

> I think it's fun to go in a group. You can chit chat and walk around, you see stuff and you draw their attention to it. Like when I camped out last year, that was when I found the stinkhorn with the skirt on it. I called them over even before I dug it out of the dirt because it was so pretty because of that lacy skirt on it.

Community in nature can be powerful—not because of the therapeutic force of trees, birds, or fungi, but because of the intimacy that being away with another can bring—cementing a relationship and building shared understanding:

> It occurred during one of the worst periods of my life. In less than three months my family and I were hit with an incredible series of calamities: serious illness, death, a miscarriage, the birth of a baby with congenital defects. For days the pain was so intense I was sure it would never go away. At other times, I felt numb. Then a friend called, asking if we could get together to hunt some mushrooms. . . . It was perfect—one of those cool, hushed, misty southern Appalachian days. The fruiting was meager for late July: *Lactarius, Collybias,* a few old chanterelles, lots of *Russulas.* But there were creeks to cross and mists dancing in the air, and plenty to smell and taste and look at and ponder and chuckle about. It wasn't the mushrooms that made the day so special, but the sharing of wonder with someone who loved them as much as I did. I wanted the day to go on and on, and I knew that night that I was going to be all right.[10]

This story is appropriate to share, is self-enhancing, and makes perfect sense to naturalists. It is not simply being in nature and not simply being with a friend that cures pain, but being in nature with a friend: sharing the experience with someone to whom it matters. We surmise that the two friends could not have had this catharsis in a coffee bar or a shopping mall.

From a shared focus, a community of friends develops: social actors who care for and about one another. Their cohesion comes from shared interests and is solidified through shared emotion. For many, part of the satisfaction of establishing a mushrooming community is the diversity of backgrounds that members bring to the group. An active mushroomer commented about attendees at the organization's foray:

> This has brought together so many different kinds. It's like Studs Terkel could come to a NAMA foray, and he would see all the people he interviews in books. You know it's *Working* there. Steel workers, doctors, artists, writers, engineers. Some very interesting people, you know, who do odd sorts of things. Where else can you find all these different sorts of people at once? I think when I first started going, it was for the mushrooms. I really was interested in the mushrooms, and after a while you start realizing that you're going for the people. I used to think that the people were just something that got between me and the mushrooms.

One becomes interested in the mushrooms, and fellow forayers are competitors, but in time sociability makes community worth pursuing. NAMA, like other social grous, sparks marriages, love affairs, and drinking buddies. Cohesion results from shared interests that are solidified into social ties.

Mushrooming groups attract people from a wide social net, but as this is a secondary social involvement,[11] these individuals typically do not meet outside their leisure activities. Members are encouraged to get to know one another, to "visit," and to develop friendships. One club president, dismayed at how few members she knew, asked everyone to wear nametags, noting that "our meetings somehow have not been so very conducive to extending or developing our friendships with one another (just with our fungal 'friends')."[12] One club fines members who forget their nametags. A shared focus must deepen to personal knowledge about participants to make an organization "feel" like a community. As noted in Chapter 1, mushroomers often do not discuss their backgrounds; their personas may be entirely linked to mushrooming.

This does not mean that no common core of interest and concern exists. But that concern is limited to mushrooming, unless (in the case of a major health crisis or the death of a partner) one's external self intrudes.

Personal linkages are created through sharing time. Organized forays serve a dual purpose. First, they "provision" leisure: the group sponsoring the foray provides resources (material, temporal, and informational) that permit members to accomplish instrumental goals of collecting and learning about mushrooms. Second, they provide a social situation in which acquaintanceships are built.

Forays vary widely in extent and participation. Local clubs often organize gatherings to hunt for and identify mushrooms at parks, preserves, or on private property. Smaller forays may last several hours. Unlike birds or fish, mushrooms do not care when they are picked, and forays need not be scheduled at dawn or dusk. Other forays last longer. The Minnesota club scheduled two weekend forays that several dozen members attended. Preparing dinner and evening entertainment builds a shared culture and strengthens social connections. In these small groups, mushroomers meet one another, learn their stories, and gain reputations.

A final set of forays are regional or national in scope. I attended three: one national foray, sponsored by the North American Mycological Society, held in West Virginia; a northeastern foray, held in New Jersey; and a midwestern foray, held in Illinois and attended primarily (although not exclusively) by professional mycologists. The first two forays had several hundred people in attendance, including professionals, whereas fewer than one hundred people attended the third foray. These forays lasted three to five days. Each morning and afternoon forays were organized to promising collecting sites. These events, like most conventions, bring together those who barely know one another and individuals who meet only at these gatherings. Participants renew acquaintanceships, updating one another on mycological (or personal) activities. The foray becomes, for a few days, "a big family." For a time, "the outside world of crime and politics disappears, and there is nothing but mushrooms."[13]

The ostensible goal of these gatherings is to identify mushrooms, and, in fact, much mycological knowledge is exchanged and experience is gained. An organizer explained: "The Northeastern Mycological Foray is all about the opportunity to eat, live, and breathe mushrooms for four days." One participant explained, "You can absorb more in three days than you can learn in a season [at club meetings]." Shared experiences in the woods, coupled with exposure to a wide array of mushrooms in the display room, are a potent source of knowledge. At the West Virginia foray, some 450 species were identified. At the weekend forays in Minnesota, approximately 100 species were identified, even without the aid of professional mycologists. Because of the weather, timing, and location, each foray was remembered for specific mushrooms, which were enshrined in jokes and stories. For instance, at the Smith Foray in Illinois, one participant joked, "If you randomly said *Entoloma* half the time, you'd be right." At another foray so many chanterelles (a prime edible) were found that leaders implored the forayers, half-jokingly, not to bring any back.

Forays are designed as social as well as mycological affairs. Participants photograph mushrooms and mushroomers, sometimes with the latter holding the former. At regional or national forays, souvenirs can be purchased (and gifts given, such as a totebag at the NAMA foray) that solidify one's memory of the event.[14] Mushrooms may be evanescent, but material tokens endure. The goal is to remember not only mushrooms but also the occasion itself. Social activities—lectures, tastings, poker games, banquets, jogging, drinking, and volleyball—build community and memory. One mushroomer recalled his first foray as "a great big party." The expressive culture matters as much as the instrumental culture.

Exploring the woods with a group underlines the social element of the experience:

> The figures cluster for a few minutes around one who is obviously their leader, then scatter like cockroaches from a stepped-on bathmat in a seventh-class hotel.[15]

The transitory, fragile nature of the community of mushroomers makes jokes about "getting lost" dramatic. Participants occasionally do lose their way. On one foray, an older woman was lost for several hours late on a cold afternoon. Yet the intensity of humorous responses in this community suggests that what is at stake is deeper than the pragmatic issue of keeping a group together. At the northeastern foray, Vic said of his foray leader, "He told us to stay close together, but we were a group of independent Yankees, and we went off our own way." He added that the foray leader and the four who went with him got lost: "This year the lost foray leader award goes to Leo Dahl. [Other members laugh.] He's not in attendance." One woman called out, "He's lost." The award comes with a year's supply of bread crumbs. On a local foray when we had lost Molly for a moment, Dave joked that "she is lying unconscious behind us." Brian said that she went on ahead, and Dave responded, "I was feeling guilty" (for not noticing that she had left). When Dave saw Molly again he joked, "We thought you were unconscious in the woods." This remark, though an expression of his guilt, is also a form of social control aimed at Molly. The continuity of community is evident in discussions of becoming lost, and also in continual references to the success of the foray, and what makes it memorable.

Although people attend forays for various reasons (identification, exercise, photography, consumption, friendship), the coming together and sense of affiliation are important. Even when mushroomers complain, as they routinely do, about the weather (too cold, hot, dry, or wet), the accommodations, the food, or the cost, their talk and memories serve to make the event satisfying.

Finding mushrooms with others makes the discovery particularly pleasurable. As Brian proclaims, "Besides the joy of finding them is the joy of sharing them." Despite the rhetoric of being with nature, the highpoint for many mushroomers is those occasions in which they are most crowded in the woods. The talk, at least as much as the communion with nature, builds collective memory at mushroom forays, birdwatching outings, mountain climbs, and other occasions where people gather to explore their natural surroundings.

THE COLLECTING URGE

When examining the activities of mushroomers, one finds oneself in three sequential worlds: collecting, identifying, and consuming. Although none of these activities is necessarily social, in each sociability enhances satisfaction.

In one sense, nothing could be more important for a mushroomer than gathering mushrooms. One does not merely find mushrooms, but actively creates the conditions under which collection occurs and interprets experience so that one is rewarded by searching, as well as by finding.[16]

Collection implies the selection, gathering, and display of objects[17] that are defined as significant within a culture.[18] A fair-sized literature now exists on collections, and mushrooming partially fits it. When one collects stamps or artwork, the permanent display of the object is important. In contrast, collections of morels or slime molds will be consumed or discarded within days, if not hours. Although some mushroomers create lists of mushrooms found or eaten (much like birders with their "big years" or "life lists,"[19] or climbers who engage in "peak bagging"),[20] and a few collect dried specimens (particularly amateurs who specialize in woody polypores), collecting has a different meaning in a transient world. Mushroomers collect without a collection; they gather without displaying; they find but do not keep.

This challenges a psychoanalytic model of collecting[21] which emphasizes that collectors wish to keep objects to prevent anxiety from separation and loss, avoiding despair and loneliness. Mushroomers in these terms are not real collectors but hunter-gatherers who are all too ready to discard their finds, sometimes even dumping them unceremoniously into the trash. Nor do mushroomers have an economic justification for collecting these objects that quickly become worthless.

A social scientific perspective is more relevant to mushroom collecting than is a psychoanalytic one. The anthropologists Brenda Danet and Tamar Katriel[22] depict two types of collectors: bureaucrats and connoisseurs. Although I see these as impulses rather than human types, the differentiation makes sense. Bureaucrats wish to find order among objects, striving for cognitive regularities.[23] They want to identify mushrooms to species. Connoisseurs are less cognitive, treasuring the aesthetic and emotional. They appreciate the beauty of the objects: mushrooms are valued for their form and taste. In these terms, mushroom "collectors" fit both categories: amateur mycologists fall into the former category, whereas mycophagists (pot hunters) and photographers are likely to be in the latter. Some mushroomers (and birdwatchers, rock hounds, butterfly collectors, and herpetologists) emphasize knowing nature (identification); others emphasize appreciating it (consumption or depiction); but few have an exclusive focus. Where mushroom collectors differ from "true" collectors is in the absence of desire for permanence: memory (and, perhaps, the photos that bolster memory) can be as potent as the objects themselves. When collections are situated within a community of narration (see Chapter 4), the remembrances have great power.

Collections are not random, but represent cultural stories. Collecting assigns "authenticity" to human activities. In our modern age (the eighteenth century on) we are driven to categorize and collect nature. Our attempt to name all of nature, and to observe and collect, represents a bid to achieve mastery through knowledge and narration. Collections provide a basis for storytelling that supports social values. Objects are the material from which tales are crafted. As one writer depicts Maxilla & Mandible, a Manhattan store specializing in natural objects: "Despite the avoidance of anthropomorphism, every specimen seems firmly fixed in some human story."[24] Even without an explicit story, the implicit line is that these objects are observed, selected, and identified by humans who appreciate the bounty and magnificence of nature.

Dividing motives into aesthetic goals and cognitive impulses misses the process of collecting, that is, searching and gathering. Central to the practice of naturework is that a collection results from a hunt. William Faulkner recognized that the hunt was as important as the kill:

> Most of anyone's life is a pursuit of something. . . . Always to learn something, to learn something of—not only to pursue but to overtake and then to have compassion not to destroy, to catch, to touch, and then let go because then tomorrow you can pursue again.[25]

Whatever happens with one's find, the finding justifies the effort. Collecting is not just a basis for narration but also a process of discovery:

> It's looking around for a little gem of beauty. Finding something small and precious in a large [world]. . . . The thrill of discovering. It's almost like gambling. You never know what you're going to find on the next square foot of ground. A lot of it is a personal challenge to spend the time looking.

> It's the search, which is the whole essence. . . . The search rather than the finding is what really interested me. . . . Being outside with a purpose.

The mushrooms collected indicate the success of the effort. As one collector notes, "If you have a basket, and you're out, you want to *fill* that basket. You don't want to put just one or two things in it." "Filling the basket" is self-validating.

In contrast to those who define collecting as display and holding, most mushroomers feel that understanding, appreciating, and gathering mushrooms constitute the core of the collection of nature.

The Art of Finding

Finding mushrooms (or snakes, minerals, or birds) is not a matter of "simply" looking. I recall my frustration when I first went birdwatching. My friend kept pointing to "invisible" birds. I trusted that they were in the trees *somewhere,* but I couldn't see them. I lacked a template for looking. Eventually I was reduced to nodding that I had observed the unseeable. Mushrooms are close at hand and don't move, so a mushroomer can force another to see them. Yet in the woods, ground covered with leaves, branches, plants, shade, and sunlight can make seeing a challenge. Too many other objects competing for attention can make us lose our focus. We search for things that are right there. As the philosopher Ludwig Wittgenstein proclaimed, "The aspects of things that are most important for us are hidden because of their simplicity and familiarity. (One is unable to notice something—because it is always before one's eyes.)"[26] One must train oneself to ignore distractions.[27]

Following from Wittgenstein, we don't see objects, but see them in context—in light of our templates (a "keying" of perception).[28] A mushroom (or any "hidden" object) must fit into a pattern:

> *GAF:* Do you think that mushroomers have a particular type of eyesight?
>
> *Tim:* It's not an eyesight; it's a mindset. If you just walk around with your head down, I swear you won't see anything. . . . There is always a little template that you carry in your mind; you try to fit the pattern into the mushroom after a while. It just grabs your attention if you're looking for morels or something.
>
> ------
>
> *Burt:* Others will tell you to look and you won't see anything. . . . I think you train your eyes and brain to pick them out.
>
> *Kathy:* Every spring you do the same thing. You have to train and you have to scan. Then when you find your first one, we still keep it with us in our bag. Then we look at the mushroom again and you actually imprint it on your brain.

When we search for natural objects, the template is often said to derive from a compatibility with nature: the organic being at one. To see is to belong to a nonhuman world, implying intuition that develops from natural appreciation, as when one mushroomer suggests that "the mushrooms are calling you":

I think it's learning to tune into nature and your subconscious. It's to reach into a realm where, if you go along with the idea that your subconscious sees everything, and your conscious mind picks up things here and there. . . . Developing this psychic sense of being able to feel these things are there.

This mushroomer emphasizes that this mystic sense doesn't apply to finding manmade objects, but is something that connects one to the universe. Although his view is not shared by all, it is sufficiently legitimate that he can express it to others without embarrassment. Seeing is linked to appreciating and valuing. This rhetoric helps to explain why those who do not appreciate mushrooms will notice only the most obvious or garish specimens. As Annie Dillard writes in *Pilgrim at Tinker Creek:*

> The herpetologist asks the native, "Are there snakes in that ravine?" "Nosir." And the herpetologist comes home with, yessir, three bags full. Are there butterflies on that mountain? Are the bluets in bloom, are there arrowheads here, or fossil shells in the shale?[29]

From this perspective, widely accepted by mushroomers, socialization is critical to discovery. Perhaps one associates microhabitats with places in which mushrooms were found in the past. Often one has a mystical, unexplainable feeling ("like a sixth sense")[30] that mushrooms are present:

> You're walking along the trail, and you get a feeling, "Well, look out here," and there's something there. Maybe hidden under leaves or something, but there's a mushroom there.

With nature as an authentic reality, a mystic connection seems plausible. Finding mushrooms is seen not so much as an extractive activity as one that demands being in close touch with the environment. These images of sympathetic discovery, accepted by many, derive from beliefs about nature that we have been taught and have persuaded ourselves and others to accept.

INDICATORS

Finding mushrooms depends on a semiotic understanding of the natural world. Natural objects are not found everywhere; indeed, they are found in the context of other natural objects. Some elements of the environment go together "causally." For instance, honey caps parasitize oaks—oaks provide an environment in which the mycelium of honey caps grows. Sometimes two species each find the same habitat hospitable, as the frequent cohabitation of morels and stinging nettles attests—with no known linkage between the two species. Finally, a symbiotic relationship may develop between two species, with each providing the conditions for the growth of the other. As this is not a biological treatise, the conditions of growth for mushrooms are not at issue; rather, what is important for mushroomers is belief in the existence of "indicators." Indicators serve—whatever their causal connection—as *environmental signs* of the presence of fungi. Just as the sociologist Thorolfur Thorlindsson[31] speaks of fishing boat captains reading the seas, mushroomers read the woods.

Two classes of indicators are central to mushrooming: temporal indicators and spatial indicators. The first set recognizes that mushrooms are not always present: they have their season. One might visit a spot on three consecutive weeks, and only on the second week will a particular species be found. Some of these temporal indicators are seasonal (such as the presence of species that develop simultaneously with the mushroom-growing cycle), and other indicators are causal (such as weather conditions that produce fruitings). Spatial indicators, too, can provide signs that are either closely or loosely connected with the spotting of mushrooms. So, for instance, one may believe that a particular species of tree provides the right habitat or that mushrooms will be growing directly in connection with other species. The existence of indicators, whatever their empirical validity, provides shared confidence and limits the hunt, suggesting when to avoid futile searches for mushrooms (one would be foolish to hunt morels in Minnesota in March or July).

Although morels are not the only mushrooms for which indicators are important, because of their cultural centrality and because until they appear there is no mycological reason to be in the woods, indicators tend to be particularly important for morels.

Temporal Indicators. In nature, most living things have their season. Butterflies are found at certain times of day and at certain times of the year. Birds have migration and feeding patterns. Some animals hunt in the evening; some sun themselves at noon. Even flowers (four o'clocks, morning glories, moonvines) have daily and monthly schedules. Mushrooms, though they do not appear and vanish as butterflies do, are seasonal, and are particularly dramatic in that they "pop up overnight," unpredictably, unexpectedly. Many a happy mycologist or anxious parent will gaze outdoors one morning to discover a lawn filled with fungi. An "empty" forest fills after a good rain.

Some temporal indicators occur annually. Minnesota morel season typically begins during the first week in May and lasts for about three weeks. In other areas morel fruitings are earlier or later, but the calendar (itself a sign of temperature changes and astronomical positioning) always provides a first sign of morel fruiting. More explicitly, cultural links are calendrical markings, such as Mother's Day or the opening day of trout season. Some indicators are tied to the concurrent growth of other plants. Morels are found "when apple trees blossom," "when the first asparagus spears are up," "when oak leaves are as big as squirrel ears," "when hepatica, arbutus, and white violets are blooming," "when May apples flower," "as dutchman's-breeches and trilliums are fading," "with the growth of cedar apple rust fungus," "when stinging nettles are four inches high," "the bloodroot is blooming," "the smelt are running," "wild plums are in bloom," "lilacs have started to show their color," "wild leeks are ready for picking," or "wood ticks are out." This list, compiled from numerous sources, could be expanded, but its richness demonstrates the range of changes within a natural environment. These indicators are not causal but indicate that natural processes may be simultaneous. One is a sign for another in a semiotic sense—a marker of change.

These indicators represent broad temporal changes, but they do not speak to the immediate and local processes that cause morels to appear. In a dry spring, nettles may bloom and ticks appear, but mushrooms will be absent. As a result, mushroomers look for those events that are perceived to *cause* mushroom fruiting. Some point to the warm spring rains or the first time the thermometer hits sixty-five degrees. Precipitation and changes in temperature are believed to provide the conditions for the growth of morels. Poetically:

> Warm nights and warmer rains that fall
> Are the surest May signs
> Of morels growing tall.[32]

In contrast, a mushroomer explained a poor morel season by saying that "it's the [weeklong] rain that [ended the season prematurely]." Another commented after a disappointing start to the season, "If we get a few more inches of rain, maybe they'll pop." Morel hunters are like farmers, always looking to the sky, never satisfied (three of the four years I conducted research conditions were considered poor). Unlike their secrecy about morel spots (see Chapter 5), mushroomers are voluble about temporal indicators, sharing interpretations, connecting the social to the natural. Linda Painter recounts:

> While discussing the scheduling of field trips this spring [someone asked]: "Would it be worth while to schedule one more trip for the following week?" Weather conditions and harvesting reports indicated that the season for the mushroom in question was over, and several members engaged in a lengthy discussion of temperature, weather, rain, and timing, the pros and cons of elevation locations, and explained this thoroughly and seriously. Another member added, after hearing all this discussion, "This is what makes mushroom hunting exciting."[33]

Temporal uncertainty drives morel hunters to search for signs of these treasures, minimizing the frustrations of returning from a hunt with only memories of sylvan glades.

Spatial Indicators. "Where?" is as potent a question as "When?". Spatial indicators may include large-scale physical features, such as old apple orchards, maple trees, oak, ash, spruce, pine, fir, elm, birch, aspen, willow, basswood, cottonwoods, swampy areas, golf courses, cement steps, open fields, deep grasses, river beds, cemeteries, roads, fence rows, hillsides, campgrounds, as far from civilization as possible, recently logged areas, burned-over areas, light snow, in the sun, and in the shade. Hope springs eternal. If each indicator were correct, one would have to beat morels off with a stick. Of course, no one believes that all indicators apply to one region, and many may result from wishful thinking or overgeneralization. That this range of habitats is named suggests a strong impulse to know. Anything is possible as long as it is based in experience and as long as someone is willing to listen.

These indicators apply to relatively large segments of the wild.

They may direct a mushroomer to a proper place, but they don't pin-point exactly where morels are found. Here microecology applies—knowledge of a more direct symbiotic relationship among natural objects depends on the experience of the human hunter. Some mushroomers believe that they can smell a patch of morels or others plants that grow with them:

> *Wilson:* At one time I thought I could smell them. Some people think you can. I discovered that I could not. What I discovered was something else that smelled like them. It was a bush of some sort.
> *GAF:* And the bush is around the morels?
> *Wilson:* Yes. Very pronounced smell. But I read where there are certain species that people feel they can smell.

Mushroomers become convinced that they can smell morels: "I think if you were given a big patch of morels, I think you can smell them." Like them, I forget those times I was wrong.

Beyond smell, Minnesota mushroomers believe that morels are found near prickly ash, leading them to dive into the thorns. Poison ivy and stinging nettles are also supposed to grow in proximity to morels. These folk beliefs give rise to the image, described in Chapter 2, of morels' keeping bad company, and suggest a pattern of exchange in which one must "pay" for these free treasures. "No pain, no gain" is transported from the cultural realm to the biological.

Dead elms (particularly those dead for three to five years) are sup-posed to be hospitable to the growth of morels. This belief leads to considerable joking about deliberately spreading Dutch Elm disease, just as the belief that morels are found in burned areas leads to jocular plans to set fires.

Few doubt the value of indicators. Mushroomers enter the woods with folk theories, but not finding morels does not alter those theories, which are not linked to actual probabilities; the presence of rare events is psychologically potent in preventing us from discarding sta-tistical connections.[34] One fellow mushroomer, a professor at the Uni-versity of Minnesota, was the only informant who doubted the valid-ity of indicators:

> I believe that mushrooms just occur. My personal experience is that when I intend to go looking, I don't find them. They just suddenly appear. . . . This morel weekend was a disaster this year, and nobody,

the leader, the town expert, knew the reason there weren't any morels this year. It was a local morel expert who said maybe it has something to do with the temperature this year. Warm very early, very heavy rain, but what these things mean, we don't know. . . . It's not a scientific thing.

Sufficient evidence is always available to make sense of the vagaries of mushrooms *after the fact*. Our causal explanations are grounded in perfect hindsight. We constitute the natural environment according to our theories of what belongs together (for example, warm rains and morels), but our evidence is not sufficiently compelling that we will be right with certainty. We develop folk theories about nature that are formulated and reformulated in action. Faced with uncertainty, inconsistency, and uniqueness, we attempt to provide ourselves with sufficient knowledge for solving practical problems. We think in terms of contingencies of cause and correlation. Perhaps these protoscientific hypotheses are correct, but we rely ultimately on what makes sense given cultural, not biological, knowledge.

THE EMOTIONS OF THE HUNT

Although walking in the woods might seem like a pleasant way to spend a few hours, nature is not easily controlled by humans, setting aside the large-scale changes that human presence has wrought. This lack of control leads to nature's generating a range of human emotions. In pursuit of their goal, naturalists will put up with unpleasant experiences.[35] The satisfaction of finding mushrooms outweighs, in some measure, the frustrations of an uncomfortable present, and eventually allows the mushroomer to reinterpret the experience positively.[36] Like the amateur astronomer who endures freezing cold,[37] mushroomers demonstrate their commitment to and their "love" of nature by suffering. One bears poison ivy, nettles, brambles, mud, ticks, chiggers, mosquitos. A mushroomer hunting morels in the backwoods withstood hypothermia, mosquitos, thorns, a broken-down car, and an abscessed tooth all in a week. Fortunately, he found seventy pounds of morels (worth $1,200). He said of his experience: "It wasn't all fun, but it was enjoyable."[38] The satisfaction was conceptual and economic; the lack of fun was immediate and personal.

The emotional response to mushrooming can vary depending on outcomes and experience:

Where's the sign that says "morel," I ask myself. I am tired of feeling at one with the earth. Bored with nature's wondrous acts, I want to find what I came for. My feet hurt and it isn't much fun anymore.[39]

> I guess the day that surpassed all others was when there were so many white chanterelles it began to irritate us to find them. . . . Then, as we were walking back to the car, completely satiated with the whole experience, we found that all these funny-feeling spots we kept stepping on were just more of them. We couldn't take a step without finding another one—memorable, but irritating![40]

These episodes were shared with other collectors, who participated in and supported the emotional experience. Each episode is set within a discourse that makes the emotions readable to others who were not present.

Because mushroomers set up ideal experiences (referred to as "treasure tales," discussed in Chapter 4), they are often annoyed when occasions do not live up to their expectations. This is evident when mushroomers complain about the vagaries of the weather. Because of these images of perfection (also found in other leisure worlds), mushroomers can express frustration and other emotions that contrast with what one might expect from participants in a voluntary leisure pursuit.

COLLECTING TOGETHER

Naturework is enriched when mushroomers bring their own community into the wild. Sociability helps the mushroomer to process the experience of nature. The essayist Vance Bourjaily recognizes this impulse toward community in hunting:

> [Leading] to neurosis and despair is the curious American abhorrence of doing things alone. Every man must have his buddy, and the relationship, in a well-established case of buddihood, is very nearly as complicated as marriage.[41]

A mountain climber made a similar point, in a more positive light:

> I myself go out there with the idea that I'm not actually going to enjoy it at the time, but I'm going to enjoy it afterward. I'm going to enjoy the experience I've had with my mates on the hill. If you get to the top, so much the better. But that's not the point.[42]

One's enthusiasm about the activity may draw others to join in. New recruits to the woods "either get caught up in it or decide that they can't stand it." Many hands permit a wider area to be searched, and sometimes lead to the assignment of specialized tasks:

> I personally pushed and prodded and dragged my dad and Scott through underbrush only a four-year-old (Scott) could crawl under. . . . "I see a mushroom, Scott! Go crawl under those bushes through the cobwebs and get it for mommy!" And, "I see one way up on that tree, dad, I can't reach it, try to jump up and grab it down!"[43]

This mushroomer writes with a self-deprecating charm, and her images of shared experience, though extreme, ring true:

> Sharing of experience may be, and often is, of a very simple nature, as when two good friends wander through a woodland in summer; one comes upon an exquisite wild orchid and calls to the other to share the sight. Even if there is nothing more, the simple process of sharing the experience greatly enhances its significance for each observer, but the experience itself remains nebulous and undefined.[44]

> I feel if there are new people and you find something interesting, you want to make sure they see it. If you go out there and you find morels, you want to make sure everybody has the opportunity to find some.

People typically spread out at a foray, but when a mushroomer finds an interesting fungus, she or he calls out, and others rapidly converge. Fellow forayers commonly are asked, "Are you finding anything?" or "How are you faring?" Some, particularly in small groups, share their finds, eroding competition.

Sharing the woods prevents dissatisfaction. As Molly explained at a foray, "If there are no mushrooms, we'll just sit around and yap"; others provide a safety net from boredom, danger, and discomfort.

ETIQUETTE IN THE WOODS

Sharing the woods may build community, but a danger exists. Searching for mushrooms may breed competition. In some sense finding mushrooms is a zero-sum game. The mushroom that I pick, you cannot. My filled basket suggests that I am a better collector than you. In activities that involve shared space and limited resources, participants must understand the "rules" that smooth transactions.

Despite claims to the contrary, mushrooming is often competitive: the competition is not only human vs. nature, but human vs. human.[45] Demonstrating that one has found the largest pile of mushrooms carries status. This is particularly evident in morel hunting, where the number or weight of morels is compared. Although this competition is "friendly," it is still significant; for example, one couple reported that seven years earlier they had found more morels than anyone else in the club (170 pounds!), a fact also reported in the club newsletter.

A joking culture legitimates "bragging rights" and simultaneously indicates social control. Mushroomers wish to reveal their prowess, but this may cause resentment or jealousy. The author of a "mushroom etiquette" column, Ms. Mushroom lectures:

> One should not overstate one's good fortune. No matter that one has an entire pickup load of Morels to process, one is permitted only to allude to having found a few, and to state that knowing one's friend might be wanting some, one would like to share. Not only does this induce in every acquaintance a warm feeling of friendship, but one appears beneficent while simultaneously retaining a goodly number of mushrooms for oneself.[46]

Some relationships may permit these teasing competitions:

> It was another friend, inquiring as to our success. I told him of the [one] *Verpa*. He said that he didn't wish to offend, but I might be interested to know that he, with a little help from a few of his friends, had picked three hundred and twenty-two (322) pounds of morels on Saturday and Sunday, and had done so not more than 25 miles from where we had found our solitary *Verpa*. "That's obscene," I said.[47]

This friend, prefacing his remarks with the wish not to offend, did indeed provide information that his friend was interested in, so interested that he could include this fact in a humorous narrative about his own skills and the variability of nature.

These bragging rights are legitimate, as people enjoy "telling the story. People like to make it seem as if they have had a great haul and probably because they did," even though exaggeration is not unknown. Needless to say, mushroomers are quick to point out that they themselves do not engage in this status display, often emphasizing that *they* do not count or weigh their finds. The couple described above with their 170 pounds emphasized that "we were counting [morels] for a while, then we started weighing them. Last year, we didn't even do that. We were very approximate." These stories require good listeners, a supportive community. Jealousy is a natural response, but one that must be tamed in the name of good fellowship.

The need to tame competition is even more evident in the woods. Here the zero-sum quality of the hunt is crystal clear. Either I pick the mushroom or she does. It goes in my basket or in his. An ethic of "finders, keepers" operates:

> Suddenly one person stopped, exclaiming, and turned to collect two obscure brownish morels in the shade of a rounded white granite rock. I stopped, too, and saw a morel almost under one of her feet. . . . In mushrooming . . . it was all right for me to collect that morel, and so I did.[48]

In practice, such "rules" are negotiated. That the author was a novice (and a journalist!) and the other mushroomer had just found a pair of morels surely made the author's immediate claim to the mushroom more appropriate. I suspect that in practice, the observer would wait quietly, if anxiously, for the other to move and then gain an unambiguous claim. To take a mushroom from another's personal space is a matter of delicacy; to find too many when searching with others is also questionable. One must balance one's own success with the need for harmonious relations:

> Should one encounter what is termed a "mushroom garden" while at a fellow mushroomer's side, it is considered ill form to sweep the entire contents of the garden into one's own basket. However, should one be confronted by a garden of 100 or so Morels while momentarily alone, one is permitted to gather the first 80 or so specimens before alerting one's bosom companion to the situation. It is wise to leave at least one or two fresh, non-rotten Morels among the remaining 20.[49]

The jocular tone of the advice only partially hides the tension between the goals of the hunt and the expressive needs of the community. One is competing not only with the woods, but also with other persons.

The image of brutal competition emerged when we found an oyster mushroom with a reddish stain. Jerry immediately joked that it was blood from mushroomers fighting over it. More serious are instances in which collectors race through the woods gathering all that they can (a common practice at competitive morel hunts, such as those at the Boyne City, Michigan, festival or among commercial pickers in the Pacific Northwest) without regard for either aesthetic appreciation or sociability: neither nature nor culture is enshrined. As in any social world, negative examples warn against improper behavior:

> I'm thinking in particular of the morel pickers who are going out with the idea that it's not just a hunt, it's a race. Fill a basket as quickly as possible. . . . There's an awful lot of greed involved in this. . . . You've got grownups acting like children in the woods. . . . If you grab all the mushrooms, that is in many places considered good form. . . . Some people go out of their way to share; they find a patch of mushrooms, and they call their friends in; they share. And other people would never say a word; they would pick every bloody mushroom. And they'll come back with a basket full of mushrooms, and, if on the way back home, they got a full basket and everybody else has little bits, too bad for those people.
>
> ——————
>
> I took some people out to this area that I had picked earlier, and I had left some puffballs to grow. And I had found them, and since I was bringing them to my puffballs, I had expected them to share them. They grabbed them and put them in their bags. And I thought, "I'm never taking you out again!" So, one of the etiquette things is to determine in advance how you are going to divide up the spoils.

These instances of greed are, in my experience, rare, and perhaps were exaggerated to make a point about the importance of community over collection. Yet the strain is evident over the degree to which one should give up personal rewards in order to build relations. Needless to say, this strain is not only a characteristic of naturework, but is evident in any situation (business, sexual intimacy, parenting) in which the maximization of one's own desires conflicts with other values.

The Identification Game

Once specimens are selected, mushroomers must interpret them. Mushrooms are meaningless until named. As Annie Dillard[50] remarks, following John Ruskin, seeing is a matter of verbalization. Knowing is crucial in building an appreciation for nature. Those unfamiliar with mushrooms cannot differentiate among them or make sense out of nonsense. One hobbyist explains, "If you're going to get an appreciation for this earth, I think you need to get to know things." Sharing the names of objects links one to the earth, and simultaneously to the community of naming. Perhaps this is part of the desire of naturalists to "enchant" the world with names: a connection that at least one mushroomer found appealing and linked metaphorically to the sacred quality of nature:

> The mushrooms are . . . placed on paper plates and brought before the presiding mycologists, who accept the offerings and perform the identification rites. At tables that sometimes resemble altars and at other times, checkout counters, the faithful line up and the chanting begins: *Russula brevipes, Pseudocolus schellenbergal, Hygrophorus eburneus*, variety *unicolor, ad astra per aspera, Te deum.* . . . The laying on of names is an old and complex ritual uttered in Latin and administered by those who descend from an ancient apostolic tradition.[51]

Identification provides the satisfaction of "understanding nature," but it does not come naturally from seeing and appreciating. Rather, identification is an application of legitimate knowledge, designed to produce a name.[52] Field identification is not a process of determining the truth so much as it is a process of providing a usable, satisfying answer; some name, even if uncertain, is better than none. Further, identification is set within a social context: categories have been set by human (scientists') choices and the tools of identification are created and authorized within a community. One learns about the mushrooms through socially produced materials, and the identification itself often occurs collectively. In the example above, one group brings its finds to a second group (specialists), which provides the identification.

CHALLENGE AND UNCERTAINTY

The mushroomer who is confronted with an object must narrow it from anything to one thing. Much categorization is unproblematic, and identifiers make quick work of many possible objects; for example, one can rapidly recognize that a mushroom is not a bus, bug, or begonia. Out of the millions of things that an object could be, it is quickly limited. We don't consider things out of their cognitive set. Even within the class of mushrooms, which sometimes overlaps with other sets, such as lichens or bolls, many genera are rapidly, thoughtlessly excluded: a morel is not going to be a polypore no matter how confused one is, just as carrots and peas are fundamentally distinct. If one cannot tell, one will not be making identifications. The subset of possible answers may not be entirely known (for example, some genera may be outside the experience of the identifier), but with tools of identification and the presence of others, that information should be available through shared or transactive memory.[53] The problem, then, is to link a natural object and a body of knowledge, a linkage that emerges in the form of a name.

Faced with ambiguity, we make an "effort after meaning,"[54] banishing ambiguity. Cognitive theorists have argued that to a point resolving uncertainty is satisfying. We treasure solving puzzles; cognitively we are "motivated tacticians":[55]

> The satisfaction is going out in the woods and seeing these mushrooms and being able to identify them. . . . It's so late in life; there's so much to know.

One mushroomer attempting to identify a rare mushroom (*Tylopilus*) told me, "Sometimes these things will drive you absolutely crazy. You want to throw them in the round bucket [trash]. I guess it's the challenge [that keeps you at it]."

The puzzlelike quality is apparent when everything falls into place, as in this partial identification:

> We were in the woods and found some mushrooms and identified them as *Leccinum aurantiacum,* I believe it was. In Phyllis Glick's book, she quotes Dr. Thiers as, "All of the boletes, even if they have red spores on them, are edible." [In fact, he is quoted as saying "most are safe."[56]] So I believed her. So [my wife] was sautéing them, and [said], "Hey, these things are turning black!" At the same time, I was reading the same thing in her book, "When these are fried, they turn black." That was one sure way of identifying them.

Like a crossword, nature provides clues that aid identification. Especially desirable are those species or genera that are identifiable by a singular sign(which in some cases may be transformed into a symbol with moral value). A mushroom may be known for this one feature; for example, smell is important for some mushrooms (such as *Lactarius aquifluus,* which smells like brown sugar or maple syrup), and taste is important for others (such as some russulas, with their hot, peppery flavor). Brittleness, staining, milk, a cup, fibrils, a slimy cap, a tough stem, a ball-and-socket connection of stem and cap, or gills free of the stem serve as markers. These clues allow the mushroomer to narrow the search for the correct identification.

Successful identification depends on overcoming three problems: relevance of categories, object variability, and interpretation of definitions.

Relevance of Categories. To identify a mushroom, one must know which clues to look for in any given case. Following Wittgenstein,[57] one must overcome "aspect blindness"—knowing which criteria are critical for identification. With a particular mushroom, the problem is not seeing but knowing what to look for. This assumes that one will *already* know enough about a mushroom and its possible identification to know which criteria will provide the information necessary for identification.

Object Variability. Mushrooms, like all objects, vary: not all specimens within a species are identical. This variability is particularly evident for objects that alter their appearance, those that are influenced by external conditions, and those with a genetic base. Specimens vary as a result of age, growing conditions, or genetic variability. In some species, this variability can be extensive. (Honey caps [*Armillaria mellea*] are known for the wide variability within the species in size, color, feel, smell, and taste, a reality that makes identifying this prime edible a challenge for novices.) In these cases of variability, one must rely on Wittgenstein's[58] concept of "family resemblances," identifying objects by fitting them into a set of categories, even though no single criterion characterizes every object.[59] Further, it becomes apparent when examining specimens found together that, though each may vary from an ideal type, variability "averages" itself out. The problem is not one of information, which is abundant, but one of interpretation.

Interpretation of Definitions. Finally, one depends on competence in applying the codes used for identification.[60] When a fieldguide describes a mushroom as dry, rounded, yellow, webbed, thin, powdered, or malodorous, each term must be interpreted. How yellow does a yellow mushroom need to be, how round, how dry? These terms themselves require a Wittgensteinian interpretive process. To identify mushrooms one must bracket the problematic meaning of these terms in light of consensus; that this is not always possible makes identification difficult.

To overcome the ambiguities and uncertainties of identification, many mushroomers rely on "keys": sequentially organized sets of clues developed by professional or "serious" mushroomers for use by those less expert. "Keys" are techniques that through a series of questions lead to a "proper" identification—assuming that one can interpret the question correctly, that the answers are correct, and that all relevant species are included (a problem if one stumbles upon a rare specimen). The amateur mycologist Maggie Rogers describes her use of keys, formalizing the more casual process of most identifiers and underlining the metaphorical resonance of the "key" for opening closed knowledge:

> I draw the specimen and write out that which helps me remember other characteristics. I am strict with myself about word meanings, for if I am careless in observation or in definition I could . . . "unlock a door to the wrong room," and not live to regret it. Botanical and mycological keys are designed to let us go from the known to the unknown, taking one clue at a time and moving forward (or sideways) toward our eventual destination, the identity of an unknown specimen. The identification is like a trip into an old, many doored mansion. The doors open into very different rooms. There are surprises in some ornate corners. Sometimes you are faced with long hallways of lookalike doors, waiting to be opened. Other times there is only one door, one decision, and moving from one opened door to the next is easy.[61]

Here the rules of the game are provided by others; one does not select the correct species, but only answers linked questions.

Although identification can be like solving a puzzle, the "right" answer is not always evident. The identification of a mushroom can be checked against others' judgments, but it cannot be measured against an absolute standard. Identifications have a penumbra of uncertainty. In other words, "identifying mushrooms is like playing a card game in which only the dealer knows the rules":[62]

> You start with an unidentified mushroom in hand, you spend several hours going through all your mushroom books and literature, and you end up being more confused about your mushroom than when you started.[63]

Between a half and a third of the mushrooms that are collected at a foray remain unidentified, and this is out of the sample of mushrooms that are considered interesting enough to be collected,[64] a recognition of "failure" that produces anxious joking:

> *Brian:* We found 105 species.
> *Jerry:* Unidentified. [They laugh]
> *Brian: Mostly* unidentified.
> *Dave:* In a good year there'd be two times as many we can't identify. . . . The identification committee was praying for drought.

The reality of uncertainty flies against the belief that with sufficient expertise everything is knowable, and that failure of identification is merely a lack of knowledge. This point was made explicitly in a newsletter from a small, newly established club:

> We in our club had the conviction that to the professional mycologist, easy identification of all fungi was a foregone conclusion, that with superior training, microscopes and other aids, it must be so easy. What brought this on, of course, is that this year we found [that] an unusual proportion of our new mushrooms were difficult to identify. We felt we were either lacking the will to make the necessary effort, or just didn't have the knowhow. How nice then it would be to have never-fail experts available. . . . We received a letter from a [professional mycologist who read a previous newsletter and] made it very clear that "easy and certain identification" of any and all fungi . . . just didn't happen. In fact he went on to point out that a substantial percentage were NEVER identified in the field, or at the identifying table. Further he was sure (with his knowledge of lab procedures) that a sizable number were never classified back at the lab. As a result, we do feel somewhat less stupid knowing this, but somehow let down. If this keeps up we will have to give up our belief in the tooth fairy too![65]

Most mushroomers are not as naive as this novice, but the legitimacy of identification depends on the belief that with enough work, identification is possible. Yet in practice perfection is not always essential. Sometimes, as in horseshoes, close is good enough.

IDENTIFICATION AS PRACTICAL ACCOMPLISHMENT

Most mushrooms are identified using field criteria: informal knowledge, based on past experience, perhaps coupled with a glance at a favorite fieldguide. I would be no more deliberate identifying a giant puffball, a sulfur shelf, an orange peel fungus, or a chanterelle than I would identifying an apple, blue jay, or piece of mica. Once learned, much identification is mundane. Although mushroomers are exhorted to take care identifying and to rely on keys, chemical reagents, scientific texts, and spore prints, they rarely do.[66] Microscopic analysis is almost unheard of except by professional mycologists, who themselves use these techniques only when attempting to identify a rare specimen or potential "new species." Identification is a practical matter, performed with the ease and confidence of the birdwatcher who makes a snap judgment of an object in flight a hundred yards away. We learn the standards for routine classification, and these interpretations are communally validated.

Common mushrooms are often identified in the field by sight, and uninteresting mushrooms are ignored, not brought to identification tables. As described in Chapter 2, some mushrooms, such as LBMs (little brown mushrooms) or russulas, have sufficiently little value that they are passed over. Indeed, one mushroomer joked, having found a patch of russulas, "Might as well not identify them right here."

Problematic cases include mushrooms that cannot be definitely identified by memory, but that are judged sufficiently interesting and capable of being known that identification is attempted. One mushroomer explained his technique for identification, which is a reasonable representation of what one *should* do:

> *GAF:* How do you go about identifying a mushroom?
> *Dave:* Well, that all depends. Usually if I know the genus, if it meets the genus characteristics, then I have an idea of the general stature types of what the mushroom is. If I can identify the genus right away, I will then go to a key in the book and try to key it through to a species. Unfortunately, that doesn't work most of the time. So then after that, I start by consulting the pictures and try to find something that matches. If a mushroom doesn't meet the genus and the stature type, then I start with the spore print and work through the key. I usually try to follow a key. . . . I try to avoid the pictures first, because they're just too easy to have something look like something else. After confusing myself for an hour or two with

different textbooks, and I find a picture that looks right, then I say, "Ah, maybe that's it."

This nicely captures the seriousness with which some mushroomers approach the problem of identification. Yet it also captures the need for a reasonable answer—the drive, despite one's initial confusion, to find a picture that "looks right" and make a decision. The identifier's choice causes no harm (other than being wrong) so long as the specimen is not consumed.

Mushrooming involves embracing the reality of uncertainty. Identification is satisfying, whereas giving up is frustrating. The practical question is how close to the "textbook" description a specimen must be before the identification is considered adequate. At a foray, Dave, Lin, and Jay were huddled together, attempting to identify a mushroom that they thought was a *Lactarius*, although it was too dried up to exude latex (or milk), a distinguishing feature of the species. Dave joked, going through a scientific volume on *Lactarius*, "Does one of those [species] say milkless?" After some discussion, the three decided that it was a *Lactarius lignyotus*. Jay joked, "It's as close to lignyotus as anything else. Let's see a show of hands. How many think it's as close to a lignyotus as anything else? How many think it's not as close to a lignyotus as anything else? The ayes have it. The vote is seven to three." Several onlookers commented that the specimen had no milk. Dave kidded, "With hormones, that could be corrected." Molly added, "That's a male *Lactarius*. That's why there's no milk."

How close to the target description must a mushroom be before it is called a match? In the example above, there was no possibility of improving the condition of the dried-up mushroom so as to make a better determination possible. Some label was better than none. Sometimes a wrong identification is acceptable. Dave said to Jay, who was struggling with an identification, "Let's just call it a *Lactarius* and no one will be the wiser. When I was taking over for Jerry [as the president of the club] when his car was hit, I said that *Agrocybe* has black spores [it has white spores], and no one complained."

The Minnesota club spends much of each meeting passing around mushroom specimens. The club president, along with the identification committee, which is composed of the more experienced mushroomers, has the responsibility of identifying mushrooms for club meetings. Unless *some* are identified, the meeting will be a failure, and

"bluffing" becomes essential. Confident identification is time-consuming, and communal demands encourage shortcuts. As one mycologist stated, "Who wants to measure ten spores [through a micro-
scope] and take an average? I just want to put a name on it quickly."
Accurate classification is constrained by demands for knowledge.

Knowing Species. As noted above, often we know without being able
to specify how;[67] we are imbued with tacit knowledge.[68] Seeing and
naming natural objects becomes routine. We know because we know.
A veteran mycologist explained:

> You were a bit short of your first birthday and quite unable to make
> use of a field guide to mammals when you learned the difference
> between the species cat and the species dog. To this day and without
> help from a field guide or a mammalogist you can instantly distin-
> guish a cat from a small short-haired dog with a longish tail.[69]

A honey cap, despite its variability, looks *exactly* like a honey cap. No
one but a true novice needs to look up inky caps, for their ink and
shape define them.

This supports the theory of expertise propounded by Herbert and
Stuart Dreyfus. The novice relies on the analysis of rule-based, con-
text-free information, closely linked to "facts" in authoritative guides.
In contrast, experts combine this information with situational knowledge, achieving intuitive expertise, treating guides as *guides.* They
note that "an expert's skill has become so much a part of him that he
need be no more aware of it than he is of his own body. . . . *When
things are proceeding normally, experts don't solve problems and don't
make decisions; they do what normally works.*"[70] Their intuition comes
from having solved problems; the solutions are part of how they see
the world. Objects are seen, not as a collection of traits, but as a
whole, a gestalt—inexpressible knowledge linked to experience.[71]
One mushroomer describes his ability to identify *Rozites caperata*
(the gypsy mushroom):

> I was at the foray at Cedar Creek and Leah came in with one, and it fit
> perfectly exactly to every description that I ever read or picture that I
> ever seen. I said, "That's the *Rozites caperata.*" And everyone said,
> "What? How do you know that?" Well, I can just tell. When I look at
> it I can see it right away. It's not just anything specific.

Others express similar confidence in their intuitive abilities, identifying without fieldguides or keys:

> Certain genera have that look about them or that stature about them. That comes from seeing a lot of species. That looks pretty much like a *Pholiota*. It comes from experience. It's just the way something looks.

The problem comes when intuition doesn't match the description, and choices are required.

Constructing Identifications. When intuition is enough, life is easy. The decision is made, and it stands. Creating meaning from ambiguous tests is a problem for both novices and experts, although they typically resolve the problem differently, owing to varying levels of expertise.

The novice relies upon the "authority of the text." As the sociologists John Law and Michael Lynch say of bird watching:

> Even after obtaining a "good look" at the bird in the field, repeated searching in the book reveals no description or illustration which appears to do the job. There are many possible reasons for this, but the beginning birdwatcher almost never concludes that she has discovered an uncommon species or that the book had omitted a common species. Rather, the novice typically accepts the authority of the text while attributing the trouble to her inexperience, problems in perspective, or to an atypical appearance of the particular individual or local variant of the species.[72]

Novice mushroomers, particularly those interested in consumption, are warned not to force mushrooms into categories; indeed, some Southeast Asians have been poisoned as a result of eating deadly mushrooms that "look like" edible mushrooms from home. Novices, myself included, attempt to identify species through a pictorial theory of representation:[73]

> [When I was a novice] my identification routine involved the venerable (though fallible) "leaf rapidly through a field guide until you find a picture which resembles exactly the specimen you are holding" technique.[74]

> My friends, and probably yours, tend toward "identification on the cheap," flipping through a field guide in search of the perfectly matching photo.[75]

With increasing expertise, the advanced beginner gains an idea of what the species might be; the danger is that not enough information is available to rule out other possibilities. One may decide in advance what the mushroom is, using a guide to confirm one's supposition. The authority of the text combines with the motivated interest of the identifier, and important information is ignored—a recipe for disaster. One beginner turned expert was comically candid in this regard:

> Then I found the Ceps. They were two little tiny ones but I was sure they matched the pictures I'd seen and one specimen I had observed at a Hudson Foray. I sliced them up and sautéed them but the first tiny bite was so terribly bitter that I could never have eaten enough to get sick. *Then* I noticed that Phyllis Glick says Tylopilus felleus is very similar to B. [Boletus] edulis but bitter. . . . [Another time] I found a chicken mushroom. Well it was small but maybe just starting to grow and it was on the ground but maybe growing from underground wood and it was more red-orange than sulphur-orange, but hey, no gills! What else could it be—so I ate it. No ill effects but since then I've seen Hypomyces lactifluorum [the lobster mushroom] and *that* is what I had found. The moral is: Don't force your identification to fit what you want it to be.[76]

Experts, by contrast, have the "right" to challenge and qualify descriptions found in texts. They are engaged in the social construction of nature by their authority to name. When identification cannot be determined from the guides and keys, a tension emerges between finding some "reasonable" explanation and giving up. Perhaps the description is "wrong" or the mushrooms are variable in such a way that they don't quite fit. In this sense, using one's intuition might be a reasonable strategy for understanding the natural world. For instance, Elliot was working on identifying a mushroom that just didn't fit the species that he thought it was. He said to his friend Matt, "I want to imagine lines on [the cap of the mushroom] so bad. . . . That's what the thing reminds me of for some reason." Matt commented, "You should be able to see that; it looks right for it. I just don't see them." They stared at the mushroom for an indication of lines, never suggesting that it might have been a new species. They finally quit, giving the specimen the name of the mushroom that it looked like. On another occasion, Stew and Claude were attempting to identify an old and dry polypore; eventually they came to a dead end. Stew said to Claude, "I don't know where we goofed. . . . It just bothers me that I can't get it. . . . Somehow the name *Polyporus elegans* comes to mind. Let's see the picture." They checked the picture and the description and decided that it was indeed *Polyporus elegans*. But the color of the cap was different from that in the key. Nevertheless, both accepted this identification deriving from Stew's "gut feeling."

This tension between the authority of the text and the identifier's authority of knowledge is also revealed in the jokes and sarcasm of identifiers when presented with a challenging specimen that they think they know, but that just doesn't fit the available descriptions. Identifiers realize that their claims do not make the identification correct, but the desire for a name is sufficiently strong that it overwhelms the need for absolute certainty. Thus when Clara and Burt were attempting to identify a green russula, Clara remarked in frustration, "There are just too many things which don't fit [the description of the species they thought it was]. It doesn't have a groove around the edge." Burt joked, "I can make a groove with my knife." Clara laughed. At one foray we attempted to identify the relatively few mushrooms we had found. We first looked at the *Volvariella*. The description said that the gills should have been pink, but these looked grayish brown. Jerry claimed that they were "sort of pink." Dave laughed, "Who are we trying to kid? That's not pink." Jerry joked back, "Let's get a hammer, so we can pound that square peg into a round hole." Next we examined a *Gymnopilus spectabilis*, which is known for its bitter taste. Jerry took a taste and made a terrible face when spitting it out: "Nailed that baby down. Nothing to this ID." Dave said of a *Psathyrella*: "If it's a *Psathyrella*, it's got to be a *candolleana*. It's the only one we know. Just like any red *Russula* is an *emetica*."

Mushrooms are fitted into those species of which identifiers are aware, no matter the effort. In the face of uncertainty, identification often involves applying labels that make sense given constraints of knowledge and technique. The natural order is adjusted to fit the need for classification.

Choosing Mushrooms. As noted, not every mushroom is selected for identification. Those that stand little likelihood of identification are ignored. Even though the process of keying an unknown mushroom is in theory educational, in practice it is frustrating to fail. One writer noted:

Genera stocked with myriads of look-alike brown mushrooms are generally avoided by the average amateur, who prefers identification by field characteristics if that is at all possible. Try striking up a conversation on *Crepidotus* at your next foray, or on the *Galerina* species other than *G. autumnalis* [a deadly poisonous species]. It can be safely wagered that it will be a brief discussion at best.[77]

Even genera with large mushrooms may be avoided if there are too many similar species or species that can be differentiated only by means of microscopic techniques, such as the seven hundred or so species of *Entoloma*, or the more than one hundred North American species of *Tricholoma*. In each genus a few species are known and eaten, but typically if the specimen doesn't fall into one of these species, it is ignored. As one professional mycologist confessed about entolomas, his specialty, "They all look alike." Despite their size and color, russulas are not identified. Molly once explained, "I couldn't even get Dr. [Alexander] Smith [a beloved field mycologist] to identify russulas for me!" These are *empty genera*. Even though they are filled with species, they are unknown and hence don't exist within the cultural world of mushrooming. In some genera, many mushroomers will not even eat edible mushrooms whose species they can identify, because there is too much uncertainty surrounding the genus. Mushroomers fear that the edible species may be confused with other, poisonous species for which the means of differentiation are unknown. One mushroomer aptly described mycenas as a "humility species." Even for experts the attempt to identify most mycenas only serves to convince them how little they know.[78] Humility species are the last to be identified, and the first to be discarded.

Mushrooms that are seen as particularly challenging and identifiable, such as amanitas, receive the bulk of attention at forays. Club members spent half an hour attempting to identify a brown amanita, debating whether it was *pantherina*, *rubescens*, or *brunnescens*. It didn't fit any description entirely. The consensus was that it was closest to *pantherina*, but the color was not exactly right. This large, well-preserved amanita was worth the time, whereas other mushrooms (for example, clitocybes) were ignored. In contrast, attempts to identify a cortinarius, despite its size and color, were derided. Dave commented about the *Cortinarius* specimens: "I think it's a lost cause." Jerry joked: "Why don't you identify them?" Dave joked back: "They're all mushrooms. . . . It's not a beginner's genus." Jay, a more serious identifier, joked: "It's hard even getting it to the subgenus. . . . I'll go back to birdwatching."

Whether or not a mushroom is meaningful depends on the choices of mushroomers. How much work is worth investing? The status hierarchy of natural objects is as real as that which characterizes the mushroomers. This hierarchy affects what is known, and, hence, what is seen. The "objective natural world" crumbles through human choices.

IDENTIFICATION AS COLLECTIVE WORK

At several points, I have indicated that mushroomers collectively discuss, decide, and negotiate what specimens are. When one is collecting on a foray or collecting with friends, the time for identification is accompanied by visiting and informal discussions. Typically mushrooms are brought to a central location, and collectors sit with their books trying to make sense of the objects, often collaborating with colleagues. The finder of the mushroom usually has first rights to attempt an identification, but others make suggestions and ask questions. Rarely are mushroomers so focused that they ignore the demands of sociability. A group may give advice on identifying difficult mushrooms, and novice mushroomers may check their conclusions with the more experienced. Some forays institutionalize this practice by inviting "guest mycologists." These notables serve as a court of last resort ("mycological gods") and as appreciators of all that is "good and rare."

Since each mushroomer has a stock of knowledge and experience, the collective wisdom is greater than that of any individual, and friends often work together. Molly told me that often she would know that she had seen a species in a fieldguide, but wouldn't be able to recall which guide: "A lot of times I'll look at Denise, and she'll look at me, and I'll say we saw it in a book. Which one?" The two had solved problems together and could draw on their shared understanding. The same was true for other mushroomers:

Mark: Those [mushrooms] are brick tops.
Jay: That's the wrong color for brick tops.
Jerry: They're flammulinas.

Mark: What's the difference from brick tops?
Jay: Brick tops have a smoky gill color.

Identification, particularly of nonroutine species, often involves "transactive memory,"[79] with others (especially "experts")[80] serving as a "transactive memory network" by which information can be efficiently accessed. The information found in minds and books must be mobilized for problems to be solved.

Identifiers are accountable for their judgments,[81] and others can fairly evaluate their claims. Yet when identifications are publicly disputed, tension and anger may result: the identification represents not only the mushroom, but the mushroomer—a judgment of competence that may cut to the core of identity.[82] Although mushroomers desire accurate identification, they are working within a social setting. On one occasion Molly became annoyed at Jerry and Dave for questioning her identifications at club meetings. She was a mainstay of the club's identification committee, which worked steadily on the mushrooms that were brought in. Dave and Jerry started jokingly calling themselves "the verification committee." They didn't identify mushrooms themselves, but they often disagreed publicly with Molly's judgments. At one point Molly was so annoyed that she stopped identifying specimens. Eventually Jerry and Dave recognized Molly's frustration. Jerry commented: "It must be hard to identify with jerks like us standing around." Dave said to me later: "Molly got really upset when I said we're the verification committee. I can't blame her."

Consuming Passions

Eating is a social passion, and deciding what to eat is a cultural choice. To eat wild food, we collect it (often in social settings), identify it (often with the counsel of others), and then consume it with friends and family. For most, though not all, consumption is the *raison d'être* of mushrooming.

For many novices, particularly those who wish to consume mushrooms, "the first question always is, 'Can you eat it?'" This attitude frustrates those who define themselves as nature enthusiasts or amateur scientists. Americans have recently recognized that wild mushrooms can be prestige goods, but the novice cannot tell objects of value from poisonous objects. As a result, clubs and guides urge novices to limit mushroom consumption to the "Foolproof Four," which are easily identifiable. (The list varies somewhat but usually includes sulphur shelves, morels, chanterelles, giant puffballs, or shaggy manes). Consumption provides a marker of knowledge. One self-deprecating foray participant, carrying a bag of boletes, made her desire for consumption explicit:

> I'm going to take these into the identification room, and say I'm not interested in any nonsense about what the name is. All I want to know is, is it edible? . . . I'll go to Hank and say, "Hank, don't say a word, except yes or no."

This view is also captured in doggerel:

> There are mushrooms that are pretty:
> There are mushrooms that are not.
> There are mushrooms that smell gorgeous,
> And some that stink a lot.
> There are mushrooms that are commonplace,
> And some that are incredible.
> But the mushrooms that attract me most
> Are the species labeled "edible."[83]

Although the sensory and aesthetic quality of mushrooms is certainly important for many collectors, the "gathered" quality is important as well: wild mushrooms are a gift from nature, and often they are consumed, even if not particularly appreciated. One mushroomer found sulphur shelves to be bitter, but added, "It's hard to leave [them] alone." Another, assuring me that she enjoyed eating mushrooms, added, "I really like the whole experience of finding them and eating them fresh. For some reason [eating] is not the major portion of the whole experience."

At first I was surprised that the vast majority of these mushroomers were not gourmets. At forays the lunches and dinners were thoroughly conventional. Mushroom preparations were often simple— there was no Duxelles avec Ris de Veau or Beef Wellington. Mushrooms were often sautéed in margarine, oil, or butter, with perhaps some onion, garlic, or shallots added. The claim was that wild mushrooms have a delicate taste that can easily be overpowered. In contrast, some preferred mushrooms in robust preparations such as cream soups, spaghetti sauce, or as pickled mushrooms. A dramatic example involved a controversy initiated when the book review editor of *Mushroom* objected to a recipe for "taco-flavored potatoes and mushrooms," in which the author suggested using matsutakes, mushrooms that sometimes sell for more than $100 a pound, in a dish with taco powder. When the author objected, he backed down, but noted that the taste of the matsutake "was scarcely discernable."[84] Although some mushroom cookbooks do include gourmet recipes, in my experience most mushroomers select more "mundane" preparations.

One mushroomer explained that he personally had no interest in gourmet food, and that "most of the people don't do anything interesting with mushrooms." When the club held a potluck dinner, the casseroles, soups, and quiches were similar to any average potluck dinner—with wild mushrooms added! Referring to honey caps, the club president suggested, "Fry them, or if you want to be real fancy, sauté them." A novice mushroomer noted that club members were different from the wine buffs he knew:

> [Mycologists] weren't overly zealous about mushrooms. . . . I couldn't imagine anyone at my table proposing a comparative tasting to judge the Craterellus cornucopioides [the horn of plenty]. In fact no one at the Fungus Feast judged anything. They didn't sniff at the Lentinus edodes or suggest the Cantharellus cibarius might be over the hill. They ate everything and enjoyed themselves.[85]

The comparison with wine tasting, an activity that requires extensive cultural capital, is apt: mushrooming is class-diverse, making it distinct from gourmet dining. Simplicity is the norm, as one mushroomer noted about a recipe for mushrooms and chicken breasts in Bearnaise sauce:

> It should be a pretty basic recipe, given the two major ingredients. But then comes the Bearnaise sauce. You got a couple hours to kill? Butter, tarragon, chervil, shallots, peppercorns, vinegar, white wine, double boiler, egg yolks, stir constantly . . . Or, on the other hand, you can stop by the market and pick up a package or two of Knorr's Bearnaise sauce mix. You got ten minutes?[86]

The two hours it takes to find the wild mushrooms are valued differently from the two hours it takes to prepare the sauce. The author would not consider it a fair compromise to hustle to the corner store to purchase some button mushrooms. Compromises with an aesthetic ideal are also evident in the realization that mushroom collectors are willing to consume "bugs" and "little crunchy black things," or the willingness of some more "liberal" tasters to risk diarrhea. One mushroomer indicated when encouraging club members to try multiceps (*Lycophyllum descastes,* the fried chicken mushroom): "For a taste of the exotic, who isn't willing to suffer an upset stomach?" One's relationship with nature is more important than maximizing a gustatory experience.

SOCIALIZING AND FOOD

Most mushroom societies organize occasions on which members gather to share dishes prepared from wild mushrooms. Allowing everyone a taste makes up for the variable levels of expertise and time spent collecting. The Minnesota club holds an annual banquet with other tastings at forays; the large Mycological Society of San Francisco has a culinary interest group that meets monthly.

A pleasure of consuming mushrooms is sharing them:

> With me, the mushrooms haven't tasted all that much different. Half of the enjoyment is circumstances when you're eating them. Like the reason I like chanterelles, I guess, right now, is last spring I was up north on a trip with some members of the Rovers Outing Club . . . and we were hiking this weekend near the Boundary Waters. I happened to find a bunch of chanterelles, so I was picking them and brought them back and cooked them up and the other people tried them.

Often one first tastes wild mushrooms with a more experienced mushroomer who shares his or her treasure. When consuming on their own, novices frequently insist upon having a more experienced mushroomer identify their find until they develop more confidence. Novices worry that even the Foolproof Four are not entirely foolproof until they learn those species that might possibly be confused.

Social pressure impels mushroomers to try even those mushrooms of which they are not certain. At club events novices taste many species that have been picked and identified by others. The novice cannot determine whether a given mushroom is poisonous (poisonings at tastings, though rare, are not unknown). Should the identifier be trusted? On most occasions pressure is sufficiently strong as to make it likely that the mushrooms will be eaten. Not eating a proffered mushroom could be taken as an affront. Such behavior would have to be justified, lest it be assumed that one mistrusts one's colleagues. Through their behavior, mushroomers attest that they accept the identifications of others, even though they may be personally unsure. This is particularly true when the mushroom in question is an "edible" amanita. At one club foray, a cook prepared a mushroom pâté using *Amanita fulva* and some russulas, identified by a knowledgeable club member. Both are edible, but neither is frequently eaten: the amanita because of its deadly genus mates and the russula because of the difficulty of identifying it to species. Many who ate the pâté had told me that they had no interest in eating amanitas, even if edible. Molly remarked later, "[The cook] wanted to make sure I tried that. I don't think that if I had found some, I would take it home to eat."

This concern comes through in jokes about "dangerous" mushrooms that are communally collected or consumed. At the national NAMA foray, some members were collecting *Amanita rubescens,* a "good" edible. One woman underlined the social character of the process, joking, "If I'm going to get *Amanita* poisoning, I can't think of a better group in which to get it." Likewise, it is a frequent, if tedious joke for someone to clutch his throat or stomach after eating prepared mushrooms. For their part, those who provide the mushrooms risk having their friends and family become ill, and attributing that illness to the mushrooms (and to the ignorance or malice of the preparer). Mark, who enjoyed serving wild mushrooms to his guests, worried about their physical reactions. He called his guests a few days after hosting a dinner party to find out how they were. He didn't explain his purpose, and joked that they thought he was fishing for compliments. He explained that one of his guests had become ill after eating morels, although he emphasized that this may have been a coincidence.

Mushroom consumption is social. Trust permits consumption but is never absolute. Yet if trust is absent, the fundamental sociability of the group is threatened and the range of nature to be consumed is limited.

The social organization of collecting, identifying, and consuming reminds us that naturework often is not a solitary pursuit. Even when one acts "alone," the doing depends upon social realities outside of the space and time of the activity. Immediate sociability is only a part of the social reality of life in a natural environment.

Mushrooming locations may be parks established by states or municipalities or private land to which the collector must gain access. Further, the occasions of collective collecting—forays—need to be socially organized. What is collected is also socially determined. Mushrooms do not have inherent meaning; their value is dependent on what we believe is important. I argue that collections depend upon cultural beliefs about the process of finding and seeing. Indicators provide a nice example of the centrality of a folk semiotics in nature-work. Collecting can be filled with emotion—joys and frustrations that depend upon expectations and experiences. When we are in the woods with others, rules of etiquette apply. What is right or wrong must be learned from one's subculture. Finally, sharing the woods and one's finds emphasizes the importance of the group as well as the self. The forest is an arena in which sociability is enacted.

The social aspect of collection extends beyond fungi and beyond the woods. All collectors—all selectors—cope with similar problems. In some venues, such as supermarkets, we operate individually, but often there are others at home to judge our choices; in other venues, such as purchasing a home, the selection process is more directly social. In each there are standards—perhaps inexplicable—that determine which features are noticed, which objects are selected, and what is left behind.

Once objects are collected, they must be invested with meaning through a process of identification: a human attempt to impose order. The structure of identification has been developed by a group of persons—called scientists, botanists, mycologists—whose determinations, as enshrined in textbooks and fieldguides, become the standard by which natural objects are known. From these rulebooks, important for the training of novices and as information resources for experts, identification is established. The formal procedures for identifying a mushroom specimen are quite different from the practice of identification, which involves intuition, a search for core clues, and a set of informal rules that determine how identifications should be done given constraints of time and effort. When normal procedures fail, mushroom species may be socially constructed. Given that identification frequently occurs in social settings, the relationships among mushroomers influence decision-making. The group serves to store collective knowledge that can be recreated when needed.

Mushrooming is thus similar to other activities in which decisions must be made about what is being confronted. Obvious parallels exist with other nature spheres—birding, butterfly collecting, and rock hounding—but this analysis also applies to realms of art criticism, jury decision-making, and evaluating grants, in which a group must reach consensus on an uncertain reality.

What is defined as food depends on the culture in which the consumption occurs. Organ meats are more acceptable in some cultures, mushrooms in others, and soil in still others. Most mushroomers value their consumption of these "wild" foods; they are free and authentic, nature's gift to the knowledgeable. The first goal of many novices, the first socialization requirement, is to learn what is edible, and, hence, books and clubs speak of the Foolproof Four. Next mushroomers make choices about how to prepare these objects—choices based on the culinary standards of the culture, class, and social location of the preparer.

Because mushrooms are often prepared, served, and consumed in social settings, the social dynamics involving presentation of self become important. People consume mushrooms based on trust; whether we eat at a restaurant or at home, we trust the cook not to poison us deliberately or accidentally. This trust becomes fundamental for cementing social relationships. It reminds us that much of our activity, from being driven somewhere to being operated on, requires that we place our lives in the hands of those we assume to have expertise.

Despite the image of being alone in the wild, naturework involves a series of socially significant relationships that makes the appreciation of nature possible. Nature cannot exist without the social.

Talking Wild

The climb is not over until the tale is told.

—RICHARD MITCHELL, *MOUNTAIN EXPERIENCE*[1]

To understand nature is to be able to talk about it.[2] We narrate our encounters in the wild, transforming our experiences so they fit the themes that make conversation flow. As satisfying as the activity may be, the "stories" heard and told are equally compelling. Having discussed how individuals and groups experience nature, I address discourse about the wild. I agree with those who suggest that memory (even collective memory) is not sufficient to create culture; performance is essential. Examining mountain climbers, the sociologist Richard Mitchell remarked:

> The meaning of mountaineering events emerges in the reflective discussion and debate that follow them. Debriefing is the occasion when one's private physical accomplishments become public social topics of interest. . . . The past event is reinterpreted, clarified, and judged.[3]

The climb is recounted; its meaning emerges from both the narratives about it and the responses to those narratives. Whether a particular account is "accurate and faithful" is less important than if it works as narrative, if it contributes to the lore of a group, building cohesion and personal satisfaction.

We narrate stories to process experience. Through talk, we create shared identification and rely on communal emotional reactions and a stock of commonsense knowledge that can be called out by others.[4] Nature not only consists of a set of beliefs, actions, and actors, but is fundamentally a *bundle of stories*. Participation in nature depends upon personal accounts that concretely assert the meaningful quality of one's activity. Participants are expected to maintain a stock of narratives that they can share with colleagues when appropriate; these narratives constitute the emotional resources and informal history of a group.

All groups develop narratives, accounts, and memories that are based upon and contribute to a shared understanding of their identity. I have previously termed these group traditions *idioculture,* which consists of a system of knowledge, beliefs, behaviors, and customs shared by members of an interacting group to which members can refer and that serve as the basis of further interaction.[5] Group members realize that, because they share experiences and accounts of those experiences, others will understand their meaning. This discourse constitutes a social reality. Meanings, borrowing from larger cultural systems, are locally generated, exemplifying the reality of strong social ties. Idioculture provides a shared past and a sense of continuity.

In a community, members are expected to listen sympathetically and supportively to colleagues whose remarks are seen as aligned with the group perspective. It is now customary to conceive of any string of action or talk as a "text"—a coordinated set of meanings aimed at specific or generic audiences. In creating texts, speakers develop symbolic productions, defined as discourse. Each performance has norms or expectations associated with its presentation. Within discourse, some talk is described as narrative, typically because of its storylike characteristics. Narrative talk presents events in overt or implicit chronological order with a recognizable set of dramatic personae.

Most of the narratives examined in the first section of this chapter might be broadly labeled *personal-experience stories.*[6] In a society that venerates individual experience, personal narratives are a central means of building community through sharing one's life story,[7] although this category may be expanded to include stories depicting others (second-order personal narratives). The accounts may reflect collective doings, or may refer to the actions of individuals made collective as a result of being shared. Related genres such as gossip and humorous anecdotes serve similar ends. These narratives simultaneously involve identity work for the individual, while building a sense of community so necessary in voluntary organizations.[8] In voluntary settings, participation is enthusiastic and narratives are highly motivated. Personal-experience stories allow individuals to fit into a group and shape the reactions of others.[9]

A "social world" consists of overlapping subworlds of interaction: family, work, neighborhood, and leisure. Individuals belong to several worlds sequentially and simultaneously, and each world has its own traditions. Because the boundaries of these social worlds may be indistinct, traditions can flow from one setting to another as individuals interact with others who belong to different social worlds, defining and redefining themselves in light of their interaction. Sharing personal experiences both expresses solidarity and builds boundaries.

Narratives distinguish mushroomers from outsiders who lack interest in their accounts and who would not be appreciative audiences. The differentiation of audience from non-audience recognizes that those outside the group boundaries—however permeable those boundaries—differ in behavior, attitudes, and knowledge from insiders.

The overlap among social worlds varies; multiple group membership, acquaintanceship ties, structural roles, and mass media diffusion permit, and in some cases encourage, the dissemination of information.[10] As the sociologist Tamotsu Shibutani remarked, "Culture areas are coterminous with communication channels."[11] Group narrations represent an "elaborated" (as opposed to a "restricted") code, meaning that the speaker has an extensive range of possibilities through which to organize meaning. Those with a restricted code have fewer alternatives. Although the linguist Basil Bernstein[12] speaks of these codes in light of language use, they can be extended to pools of knowledge or to cultural capital:[13] knowledge that one can use for status gains or for personal investment in communal life. Individuals have restricted codes for most social worlds; in only a few worlds of interest and involvement do these codes become elaborated.

BUILDING A WORLD OF TALK

Those who participate in leisure worlds enjoy sharing their experiences. This body of talk builds a community of knowledge, a basis for cultural elaboration in voluntary settings: "community work."[14] By incorporating the past into social life, participants develop a common focus.

People value thinking and talking about their pasts. Memories can sustain us:

> I took most of the Chanterelles back with me to Minnesota. Better still, I brought back the memories of two perfect weeks of mushroom hunting (which, unlike my dwindling supply of Chanterelles, can be shared without diminution). Both have sustained me through most of another Minnesota winter.[15]

Fond remembrances of shared interests build bridges.[16] Mushroom stories are not only "good to think" but also "good to talk." Happenings in the woods are considered *notable* events—appropriate topics for comments, reports, and anecdotes. As a result, groups provide venues in which such recall is possible, as is evident in this announcement in a mycological society newsletter:

> So you say you were unable to be there when we filled that pack basket with Oysters, or when the deer came up to eat out of our lunch bag, or when the very rare Amanita was collected. Well, fret not. Many highlites of the year have been preserved via the magic of Kodachrome, and we can all relive those moments on Friday . . . when we will have a wine and cheese social.[17]

Much time before, during, and after meetings is spent sharing experiences. The importance of stories in constructing group satisfaction is evident whenever members are reunited. The first meetings of the spring and fall at many mycological organizations are times of special fellowship, characterized by friendly and reciprocal inquisitions about personal experiences and which mushrooms have been found: a process of "updating."[18] The question, "How is the season going?" is a request for personal-experience narratives.

Amateur mushroomers belong to diverse social classes, ethnic backgrounds, and labor-market segments. When they begin to examine nature in a collective venue, they lack a shared culture. Stories establish a meaningful world that transcends differences of demography and latent culture.[19]

Much talk in any group focuses on the group's explicit interests. Personal narrative is a means of dealing with collective concerns.[20] In one sense, this is instrumental talk—talk aimed at the achievement of the group's formal goal. Yet frequently in voluntary groups the expressive and instrumental components of group life merge. Expressive concerns are instrumental in voluntary groups; talk is often as satisfying as the action itself. Talk is both the means of reaching the ends of naturework and, often, the end itself.

The themes of narratives can be classified in many ways. In examining three types of nature accounts, I have by no means exhausted the range of possible stories, although I suggest that the classes of stories I have selected are often found in the discourse of mushroomers as well as outside the world of nature. Specifically, I examine narratives that address transcending challenges *(war stories),*[21] failure and lack of control *(sad tales),* and successes that exceed expectations *(treasure tales).*[22] Each type of story draws out a central emotion that supports group affiliation,[23] permitting audiences to share the affect—what the sociologist Orrin Klapp[24] labels "emotional hitchhiking." The first type focuses on triumph, the second, anguish, and the third, joy—all feelings that are common in group life. Finally, I examine black humor in coping with the real and imagined danger of consuming mushrooms, negotiating risk and creating personae. I do not claim that these categories cover all talk found within folk communities, groups, and subcultures; however, in their meaningful and shared character they reflect the transformation of what is *outside* to what is *inside.* These stories strengthen inside bonds, while paying heed to the importance of the outside. In this chapter I take material that in other chapters might have described the content of naturework to examine the narration itself.[25]

War Stories

The war story is an account of how an activity, in this case mushrooming, gets done. It underlines those backstage elements that participants know to be true, but that are unknown to outsiders. War stories reflect the underside of activity, linked to commonsense knowledge, that permits the successful handling of challenging situations.[26] Central to the war story is the opposition in the account: having to deal with an "authentic reality," a nature that doesn't accommodate human desires. Coping with "wild" life is among the most dramatic of these warlike challenges:

> "Last year Ed Crozier came running over a ridge, and just over the other side was a black bear. Ed froze. The bear came toward him. Ed ran. He didn't stop until he was clear to Petosky. He flagged down a

car when he reached a road and the driver made him trade all his mushrooms for a ride back to Boyne City." Shaler paused and then added, "At least that's how Ed tells it."[27]

This printed tall tale is allegedly based on the oral account of another, who is reporting the personal experience of a third. We cannot—and perhaps do not care to—know how much of this account actually occurred. As a war story it presents a memorable encounter that speaks to the range of emotions that occur in the wild. The lack of control that the protagonist experiences in nature—running back to civilization—is contrasted by the mercantile avarice of those who are "civilized." The mushroom warrior is caught between the wild and the corrupt.

Numerous stories depict the suffering that mushroomers endure in pursuit of their goal. Suffering validates the desire for adventure:

> He told me about the side of morel hunting that wasn't all fun. He'd been lost (usually every year, he said sheepishly), caught in snowstorms, hypothermia-threatening cold rain, his vehicle stuck miles from civilization (another annual occurrence), walking 20 miles a day and finding nothing for weeks, mosquitoes, flies, swamps, thistle, thorns, spider webs, running out of gas and tearing off exhaust systems. He went north to a secret remote spot once, had a tooth abscess the first day, and stayed five sleepless, painful days and nights, sleeping (not sleeping, actually) in the back of a small car (the guy was six-foot-seven!). Fortunately, it was a mushroom-productive five days and he managed to preserve 70 pounds for the upcoming off-season. Unfortunately, though, the dried morels were destroyed—when his parents' house (where they were stored) burned down.[28]

For the purpose of creating identification, it doesn't matter if this dramatic account is factual. More important is that it provokes emotional reactions from audiences and colorfully exemplifies aspects of their own experience.

The bad times/good result combination characterizes many war stories (and differentiates them from other types of narrative). Suffering together and hearing of suffering builds solidarity and legitimates a narration:

> *Al:* Last spring we went looking for morels down in Northfield. My brother-in-law was along; he's seventy years old. It was raining. He

put on a big raincoat. We went mainly to pick mushrooms. We went out for about four hours picking them. We were just soaking wet.
Anne [his wife]: We picked forty-five pounds that afternoon.
Al: Anyway, my brother-in-law slipped and rolled right down the hill. He was really tumbling.

We went down by the Minnesota River and didn't take any bags with us because we'd never found anything before. So, we walked in the woods and there was a dead elm, and we see one morel, two morels, pretty soon, [we] see a hundred morels around that elm tree. [My wife had] just gotten her hair fixed that day. She had a jacket on over her blouse and the only thing she could do was take that jacket off and throw it on the ground, and we piled hundreds of morels in that jacket. We went through this prickly ash and her hair was a mess when we finally got out of there. She also was scratched up because she didn't have her jacket on. Talk about excitement!

Participants understand that what they are doing is irrational in that the potential risks may be greater than the benefits, certainly as understood by those outside this social world. Accounts of risky activities not only increase group status, but also cement relationships and collective identity. Narrators assume that only someone within the boundaries of the group can understand the emotional resonance of the talk: a key feature of cohesion. Many accounts are self-deprecating:

There were morels growing on ledges on cliffs. You'd be twenty feet off the ground on a seventy-degree slope, and there's a lot of ugly poison ivy and rocks, and all sorts of things to go through. God help you if you slipped. You wouldn't be worth putting back together again. We got two pounds off those ledges just because nobody else was dumb enough to go there. Then I think of the time I went to get an elm cap. They were growing on a log that had fallen on a fence in Stillwater. From the car it didn't seem so bad, but after crossing the road, I discovered that there was a large embankment and that mushroom was on a tree, over the fence, and I had to get more than seven feet off the ground over the tree to get it. I managed to get up there, and this tree split after I got the elm caps off. I dropped on the other side of the fence away from the car. That fence wasn't one of those fences you climb easily. It had the three strands of barbed wire over the top. I had a hard time getting out of there. It took about twenty minutes to get out. The car is running. Jean [his wife] and her mother are waiting for me. It's getting dark! That was fun. You've got to be a little crazy to go mushrooming.

The combination of "fun" (a view shared by appreciative audiences) and the recognition that others consider this behavior to be strange gives this account narrative power: it builds internal allegiance while drawing a boundary.

A common theme in mushroomers' stories is how they deal with or were dealt with by ignorant outsiders. Knowledge alone is not enough to differentiate members from nonmembers, but this knowledge is bolstered by a common set of attitudes that make the stories tellable. War stories that focus on boundaries often depict those who do not realize the value of the "treasures" on their lawns or trees, and who believe that the behavior of mushroomers is deviant or bizarre. Thus war stories, in addition to emphasizing the dangers of dealing with authentic nature, also underline subcultural knowledge that differentiates insiders from outsiders—what I describe as *boundary talk*.

Stories of mushroomers emphasize that the general public is unaware of the mushrooms that are easily available. In the following narrative told to a group of mushroomers, the different perspectives within the same setting are made evident through a double entendre. Beth described what happened when she and her husband, Don, were looking for morels:

> We were in this park crawling around on the ground searching for morels, when this young innocent thing came walking down the path, holding a paper bag and a book. Don thought she was out looking for morels, so he looks up and says to her, "Getting any?" This poor innocent looks shocked and starts to run. [Her audience laughs.]

The narrator and her audience recognize the alternate perspectives of the mushroomers and their "victim," engendering humor. It is precisely because this constitutes a war story (demonstrating behavior that is simultaneously harassing and communal) that the group appreciates it. Consider the following extended humorous narration, presented to an evening meeting at a regional foray:

> Our usual practice is to take back roads whenever we can and hunt for mushrooms as we go. We didn't get too far out of town on this little back road, dirt road. We came across this [bunch of sulphur

shelves]. Obviously we weren't prepared for it, so we went up to a house about a hundred and fifty feet up the road [laughter]; this is about eight o'clock on a Sunday morning [loud laughter]. A guy came to the door, bleary-eyed in slippers and a robe [laughter]: "What do you want?" "We'd like to borrow a ladder" [loud laughter]. He says, "What for?" [laughter] "We want to get a mushroom out of a tree" [loud laughter]. Well, he obviously wasn't awake yet, so he said there's one laying by the side of the house [laughter]. There was a step-ladder and we brought it back to the tree, and it wasn't tall enough [laughter]. So, we took it back and banged on the door again [loud laughter]. So he said, "I have an extension ladder in the cellar." So he quickly got dressed, and he opened up, and he gave us a single section of a ladder. At the same time we said, "By chance do you have a big knife?" [loud laughter]. 'Cause all we had was a penknife. So he got a butcher knife out of the kitchen [laughter]. And we chopped it off and he was interested enough to follow us [laughter]. I'm not sure what his wife was thinking. He stood on the road and watched. I put the ladder up against the tree. I climbed up and hacked off a bunch. . . . So we hacked the three bunches off of there, and gave a little bit to the fellow who helped us [loud laughter], and we told him it was very edible and how to prepare it—sauté it in butter and so forth, and brought his ladder back, gave him his knife back, and he went in the house with the mushroom [laughter]. As far as we know he's still living; his wife hasn't done away with him [laughter]. . . . That mushroom that we picked there weighed sixty-six pounds [oohs and ahs] minus the portion we gave up [laughter].

This marvelous performance has all the characteristics of a successful narrative: a plot, compelling characters who develop in the course of the narrative, and a rich meaning structure imbued with values and norms. The laughter that punctuated the account ratifies the shared understandings among the group. The collectors are painted as crazy yet resourceful. The husband is naively trusting. Obviously the story would not be told in this way if the mushroomers had been up to mischief (other versions might be told), but the tension derives from being able, for a moment at least, to place oneself in the position of the outsider. The oscillation of perspective between insider and outsider gives the narrative power. The figures make sense given the cultural logic of the activity.

A final category of war stories consists of the *times* that members have shared. One set is composed of tricks or pranks that members play on one another. For instance, the Minnesota club had a large number of younger males who were mostly in their thirties (Jay, Brian, Dave, Mark, and Jerry) and older women in their fifties and sixties (Leah, Beth, Molly, Helen, and Meg). A friendly sexual banter developed between the two groups. Jerry joked with Leah: "Want to see my stinkhorn?" On another occasion Molly joked with Jay: "You look too pretty to go out into the woods." Leah added: "He looks like a *Playgirl* centerfold." Later Jerry joked with Molly about playing strip poker. This reached its pinnacle on a memorable occasion—quickly entering into the club lore—when Dave stuck a zucchini in his pants. "The zucchini incident" was referred to several times during the next few years to demonstrate to new or peripheral members the friendly atmosphere of club forays. Another incident—also tied to the teasing relationship between the younger men and the older women—involved a trick that Jerry and Dave played on Beth and Molly at a foray. Beth and Molly were identifying mushrooms, and Jerry and Dave asked two new members to present a white clitocybe whose cap they had painted with purple food coloring.[29] Others (particularly the males) were sworn to secrecy. Not suspecting anything, Beth and Molly fruitlessly attempted to identify the mushroom for about a half an hour, as everyone stood around watching, making "helpful" suggestions about genus type. Eventually Jerry and Dave "noticed" that the mushroom looked "strange." Once it dawned on Beth and Molly that they were victims, Jerry and Dave admitted their joke. The purple clitocybe incident, fully recorded on slides, justified holding the foray at the same location annually because of how much "fun" was had. This episode was referred to for years in stories to new members and through collaborative narration. A few weeks after the incident, Howard told the club about it:

> *Howard:* We had a really peculiar specimen [laughter]. It looked like a purple clitocybe. I wish I had a tape recorder so I could have gotten them arguing about it. This is an award [giving Beth and Molly a gift] from Leah. It's a purple clitocybe award.
> *Beth:* It was actually blue.
> *Howard:* Dave was trying to keep his blue-stained hands in his pocket. Then he came out and made up another, and the wheels began to turn slowly.
> *Molly:* We almost killed him.

Brian showed slides of Dave painting the purple clitocybe, commenting: "Would you buy a used microscope from this man?" When Brian showed a slide of Beth and Molly looking at the mushroom, he noted: "The plot thickens. It's to their credit that they didn't put any label on it. It fooled them for a while." Molly said: "It was fun." The following year Dave joked that he didn't have the nerve to bring the food coloring to the national foray he attended. Jerry joked about putting food coloring in his reagents (chemical) kit "to make purple clitocybes." Later, when I asked Wilson which was his most memorable foray, He told me: "The one at Camp Sallie a couple of years ago, when Dave got food dyes and colored, I think it's a clitocybe, to fool Beth with identifying it. It stays in my mind as an enjoyable joke. We did have exceptional mushroom collecting that year too."

Whenever an usually colored mushroom was brought in (such as a "peach" morel or an orange pluteus), reference was made to its having been magically transformed by food coloring. This talk created shared experience at the same time that it described it. By validating that people can share times—personally and vicariously—narrative provides the basis for the belief that mushrooming is not solitary but social. Pranks, which create discomfort that becomes a comforting recognition of collective interest, provide the basis for war stories as compelling as the brambles and thickets of the woods.

Sad Tales

Sad tales invert the emotional resonance of war stories. In the latter, the protagonists overcome obstacles. In sad tales mushroom finds are somehow lost. What was there is now gone, or "like fishing. . . . you should have been here yesterday." Nature was prepared, society was not. These accounts are based on shared assumptions of natural bounty:

> It was a bittersweet experience. Bittersweet in that I found—in a place dear to my heart—a spot where there were these mushrooms and *they were all over the place!* But they were beyond the pale. They didn't go in the pail, either. What were they? *Boletus edulis* [a prime edible].[30]

> There was a fallen tree across the stream and it was just loaded with bushel baskets of *Pleurotus*. We took all we could carry, it was all we

could do. We didn't have enough baskets to gather them all, so we made a note of the place so that we could go back and reap another harvest. But the next storm washed the log away—the whole log, and all those *Pleurotus* with it.[31]

On occasion the disappointment can result from the intended or unintended actions of cultural actors. We deprive ourselves:

> Scotty [age four] wanted to carry some of the mushrooms but I was afraid his energetic prancing and bouncing would shake them apart so I carried them myself. I set the bag down on the trail to pick a specimen and Scott fell on the bag. Among the casualties was a very large and perfect specimen of Rozites caperata.[32]

> A small *Hericium erinaceus* (lion's mane) was found growing on the site of one found last spring. . . . This is very rare in our area. It was a perfect brown 4 inch diameter "pom-pom." I returned two days later to photograph it. Sadly, someone had ripped it from the scar on the oak tree and thrown it onto the ground.[33]

The sad story can also relate the loss of prime habitat, rather than particular specimens—frustration due to economic development over which one has no control, only sympathetic listeners:

> There was this spot by Chanhassen. It was a small place, about half a block. It got a shopping center on one end, homes all around the other side. We used to go there. We always ended up with maybe a hundred, two or three times a week that we would pick in this little dinky patch. We should've bought that piece because all of a sudden we went there one year, and they had built a drive-in bank there.

Whatever the cause, available treasures have been lost. These losses are cultural, resulting as they do from not collecting early enough, not being sufficiently careful, not knowing how to collect, or not preserving the wild. These narratives, responded to sympathetically, are similar to stories that fishers tell about "the one that got away," as if, in narrative, telling the story equals catching the fish.[34] The disappointment is made entertaining, and the sadness is assuaged by the satisfaction of the telling.

A related set of stories provides a more explicit cultural critique, describing crushed expectations when objects that *appear* to be mushrooms turn out to be something else on closer inspection: an artificial object stands in place of the natural one:

> I was out in the woods and I was looking and I saw what I thought was a perfect puffball. Before I examined it very closely, I called the family over. They came over and it turned out to be a weathered, plastic ball, which they've never forgiven me for. Again, my delight in finding this object, it was a small, plastic ball, looked *exactly* like the classic puffball, and it turned out to be a child's plastic ball.

Likewise, Jerry described the time he was driving down a highway, and he saw what appeared to be a giant puffball on the hill on someone's lawn. He stopped the car and climbed up the hill, and then found out that it was a painted rock.

Related to sad stories are the excuses that mushroomers give for not collecting mushrooms on occasion or for the whole season:

> Ask a disappointed hunter why his catch declined from last year, and they quickly offer a cornucopia of excuses: It's still too early in the season. Perhaps too late. There hasn't been enough rain. Or perhaps too much.[35]

These excuses call for support; collective sympathy connects the individual to the group. To share the story is to ratify the emotions that others experienced. These sad stories seem less about naturework than about the cultural and social expectations that individuals have of the natural environment. Sad tales remind us that sympathy is easier given than envy.

Treasure Tales and Fishermen's Lies

Treasure tales are in themselves self-validating. When confronting the wild, naturalists search for trophies to justify their activity.[36] By describing "finds," one demonstrates the rewards of the hobby and, implicitly, one's talent and good fortune. These narratives—structured like tall tales[37]—are entertaining for those with similar interests, and transform the teller into the center of attention and admiration. Perhaps memory magnifies the find, perhaps the exaggeration is a strategic decision involving self-presentation, or perhaps it is the right of the good storyteller; whichever applies, as with some fortunate fishers,[38] it is legitimate to doubt the story privately. As one mushroomer exaggerates: "Remember: all mushroom hunters lie";[39] or in the doggerel of another: "Early to bed/Early to rise/Hunt all day/Then tell lies." Thus when one meeting ended, Jerry, the president, announced: "We can visit now. That's one of the nice things to do. Swap lies about what you found and where you found it."

There are two types of treasure tales: those that are told as true (or plausible) and therefore are personal-experience narratives, and those that are told—in whole or in part—as tall tales, as legendary reports that, though harmless, are not to be taken literally. The stories that are told as plausible may *in fact* be true or false, but that does not affect how they are interpreted. The key feature of these texts is their entertainment value. Bragging is legitimized by its social context and is not seen as a character flaw. Some finds carry "bragging rights."[40] Before examining those stories that are legendary, I examine those that on their surface are credible.

NARRATING THE FIND

In elementary accounts, mushroomers simply note the size or amount of their finds: 700 pounds of morels, 2,500 morels in a day, 1,000 morels in a two-block area, 14 pounds of morels under a single tree, a 20-ounce, 17-1/2 inch tall morel, 80 pounds of chanterelles, chanterelles big as dinnerplates, 2,000 *Boletus edulis,* or a 35-pound hen of the woods. These accounts convey the excitement of the find and the rewards of mushrooming—like a Lotto jackpot or slot machine payout. In these accounts, however, the texture of the find is lost. As a result, the more memorable texts are longer and more detailed.

Some stories emphasize the aesthetic, whereas others detail the size or amount of the find. The former have an almost mystical, magical, other-worldly quality, stressing the authentic reality and aesthetic autonomy of nature[41]:

> I looked for [*Volvariella bombycina*] all my life. The mushroom grows on wood. Like an amanita as it grows from a volva, but it's pink-spored. It has free gills; it grows on wood. I have known about this mushroom and looked for it for years. I mean, there's a picture I have in my mind from Orson Miller's book, and I imagined walking up trails and finding it on trees. For years I imagined this thing. . . . I never found it. Last summer we were riding along on the road, my

wife, son, and I were riding along on the road, and as we passed a tree, I knew—I saw—I knew with absolute certainty that that's what it was. I said, "There's *Volvariella bombycina*," and she said, "You can't identify mushrooms at thirty-five miles an hour." So we went in town to get some groceries, and when we came back, I stopped and looked at it, and I went right home and got my camera. Photographed it, and that was exactly what it was, no doubt about it.

Ten . . . feet into the woods on a carpet of moss thick enough to give several inches with each footfall, I stopped short. Three intense white masses draped over fallen logs stunned me with their brilliance. I held my breath and recounted. I had found three of the much prized *Hericium abietis*, listed "edible and choice" in all the mushroom field guides. Each cluster was larger than my basket. My heart beat faster, my breath came shorter and quicker. I raced over to the closest one, knife ready. I knelt and cut between the log and the fairy mass, the sweet, heady fragrance rising up about me. Placing the delicate sculpture on my lap, I marveled at the weight of it. It felt like eight or ten pounds. As I carefully cut it in half to fit my basket, a branch five or six inches long clung to my hand. Gently I turned it this way and that, caught by its iridescence in the sunlight.[42]

[*Amanita*] Caesarea is not just uncommon, it is truly a beautiful specimen to behold. That bright reddish-orange cap emerging from a pure white egg, expanding quickly into a paler orange parasol is a sight I will never forget. Not always keeping up on my studies and seeing the Caesars first fully expanded, I didn't associate the egg state with the caesarea and was slightly embarrassed when coming across one, I thought it was a golf ball . . . golf balls everywhere in the middle of the woods! . . . After settling in, I went out for another quick walk little knowing that it would turn into a 'mystical journey to a land where Amanita caesarea ruled elegantly and profusely.' . . . We had truly found Caesar's Haven![43]

That mushrooms are aesthetic treasures gives these narratives power: the experience is "other-worldly." Other narratives, particularly stories of finding large numbers of valued but common mushrooms— notably morels—are accounts of mushrooms "out of time and place," away from cultural control. These mushrooms are not expected when and where they are found, even if they don't have the magical qualities of the rare mushrooms described above. Because of a shared desire for these species, the narratives are notable happenings, emphasizing the unexpected bounty of nature:

[My most memorable mushroom discovery was] finding a patch of morels on Memorial Day all by myself . . . my mother didn't want to stop, so I went back the next day, and they were there. I got one and a half shopping bags full at that spot. On my way to that spot, I picked about one pound of morels, and when I got to this one tree, there were morels everyplace I looked. I couldn't believe it. I cut so many morels that day, my knife actually started to get dull. It was raining and I'd go under a juniper to take a nap with the rain falling, in between cutting mushrooms. I was cold and wet, but there were morels and morels.

I was on my way to buy some oil barrels. . . . I got clear out to this barn and ranch. I went by and I saw these great big things [sulphur shelf mushrooms] growing on top of this stump. I turned around and went back, parked the darn truck and looked up there. The ditch was too deep, so I couldn't drive the truck in there and stand on top of it. So I thought I'd go up to these places, and borrow a ladder. So I knocked on this one door, and no one answered, so I went to this next one. A kid came to the door and talked to me through a screen door. He said, no, he didn't have a ladder. So I looked in the back of the truck and found this bunk bed ladder, and that was not nearly tall enough. First, I climbed up on this short stump, dragged the ladder after me, set it on top of the short stump and climbed up to the top of this tree. Here I am on top trying to get this thing off, and this fellow comes back from across the way in his truck. Finally, I guess he came over and said, "May I ask what you're doing?" So I said I am trying to clip [the mushrooms] off the tree. He asked, "Are you going to eat that?" "I'm going to try if I ever get it down." I brought that thing home, and I reconstructed it out here on my stump. It covered that whole big stump, about a foot around or something like that. I brought that thing in after I got done taking my pictures, then I weighed it, and I had fifteen pounds of sulphur shelf.

These texts gain richness by virtue of the fact that the find is unpredictable, out of time or place. Speakers often emphasize the one-time, special quality of the find; the following week or year, mushrooms have vanished:

I had a couple of grocery bags with me, and I counted them as I picked, and I picked 250 morels under four or five dead elm trees. And I went back the next year, and there was nothing there. And I went several times and there was nothing there, and there has never been anything there since. And I don't know how I lucked out that year.

The unpredictability of nature adds piquancy to these narratives.

Nature is filled with surprises: unexpected finds that cause a thrill. Some stories describe mushrooms that are found not in the wild but in the most cultural locations of all—in cracks in the built environment:

I remember . . . realizing that there were puffballs growing between Rarig Center, Wilson Library, and the parking lot [at the University of Minnesota]. A very small area. That was incredible. And I remember picking those and bringing them into the office and saying, "These are edible mushrooms," and people being totally astounded. And that was, you might say, almost a peak life experience.

One of the best morels I ever found was . . . in South Minneapolis in a cracked cement driveway. That was one of the best morels I've ever seen. It was simply growing up through a crack. . . . the largest and most perfect.

The surprise in these narratives involves the out-of-place character of the find; the possibility of nature's claiming, for the moment, a part of civilization.

TRUE LIES

Each account presented above is told "straight." Whatever the stories' actual truth, they are intended to be taken as a depiction of reality. Other tales, ostensibly similar, are presented through dramatic details as apocryphal "tall tales." These narratives exaggerate reality in an entertaining style characteristic of the "liar," and this storytelling device provides for wish fulfillment by the audience. Although they are allegedly personal-experience narratives, they are not treated as such. Shared desires are magnified by the narrator. Finding a giant mushroom (particularly a giant morel) is a basis for some tall tales, seemingly modeled on Paul Bunyan's exploits:

I have written elsewhere of the legendary *Morchella giganticus* (giant morel) and its strange disappearance in the early 1960s [the author reports having found a ninety-two pound morel]. Around here, these days, any morel weighing over a pound or two is cause for great excitement. However, if a person can get deep enough into an old woods. . . .

Last Spring the boy (Bud) and I had gone to Northern Minnesota to hunt with two old friends, sisters by the way, who really "know the woods." We had found some five-to-seven pounders and were snaking a bunch of them up a slope to where the truck was parked. The cable snagged for a second on a stump and when it let go I caught that flying mess of morels square in the face. The Doc is at a loss to explain it, but ever since even the thought of morels gives me a nervous tic. He says he's sure it will pass by next Spring, but for now it's best if I take it real easy on anything having to do with morels.[44]

One writer, noting tales about finding a sparassis (the cauliflower mushroom), contends that "tall tales about *Sparassis* fruitings are legendary, with reports of a single find weighing in at 50 or 60 pounds and filling a bushel basket, a wheelbarrow, and yes, even the better part of a pick-up truck!"[45]

Other tall tales and "lies" focus on the number of mushrooms found; for example, "*A. mellea* [the honey cap] was so plentiful it made some trails impassable."[46] Jerry told the club about collecting chanterelles: "I was pulling them up by the roots all the time and I got tendinitis. I had three grocery bags full up to the top." Brian joked about Jerry's "lie": "It was two before. It will be four." At another meeting, Molly brought Don's giant morels to the head table, where Jerry, the president, would be discussing the specimens that members found. Club members laughed when they saw the foot-tall mushrooms. Jerry joked: "You fillet them, don't you, Don?" Don responded: "You have one for breakfast and one for dinner."

Other narratives deal with the extraordinary size of mushrooms as well, joking that no mere knife is sufficient: "*Leccinum auranticum* is so thick around the house that some mornings I've got to get out the 4 x 4 and plow the driveway clear of the things before I can go to work."[47] In a similar vein, Jerry joked about going morel hunting with Dave: "Dave and I went to those morel farms. Pick your own. But you've got to pick the first one fast or they'll warn the others. They were so thick, we had to bale them." Don joked about finding a lot of morels: "I was thinking of getting a combine." Jerry claimed: "The big ones I got with my chain saw." Once, when describing meeting a collector who said that he had picked all the morels in the area, Harvey joked: "You chopped them down with a lawn mower, you got so many. You needed a grass catcher for them."

This talk weaves a magical fantasy, representing the world as collectors wish that it could be, if only for a moment. Narrators take the routine features of nature, in which few edible mushrooms are to be found, and enchant them. Stories transform a world that culture and rationality have systematically disenchanted.[48] Discourse has magic, communal properties: as a cultural form, it can make nature truly wild, and can lend it amazing properties in the face of the mundane. Through stories, autonomous, bountiful nature can compete against a sometimes dispiriting reality.

Joking and Risk Control

Humans have numerous ways of dealing with dangerous or painful thoughts. As Sigmund Freud and his psychoanalytic followers emphasize, we utilize defense mechanisms that include denial, repression, reaction formation, sublimation, and projection to protect ourselves from the implications of what we "really" think. Although Freud does not explicitly list humor as a defense mechanism for dealing with unacceptable thoughts, it is clearly implicated in *Jokes and Their Relationship to the Unconscious*. Freud writes, "A joke will allow us to exploit something ridiculous in our enemy which we could not on account of obstacles in the way, bring forward openly or consciously . . . the joke *will evade restrictions and open sources of pleasure that have become inaccessible.*"[49] Humor combines coping with threats, cognitive incongruity, and an attempt to postulate superiority. The ability of humor to deflect unpleasant thoughts is not merely a technique of individual psychology, but a property of self-conscious groups, organizations, and communities, requiring a social connection between performer and audience. Humor serves as a form of social control embedded in a group.[50]

Humor requires the joker to adopt a persona for the duration of the joke. This persona is typically performed before a sympathetic audience. In most instances the audience suspends the normal assumption that an individual "truly" believes whatever she or he says. Audiences permit speakers a "comic license." They implicitly assume that the joker is operating in a "humor frame" and that the connection of the remarks to the speaker's self is bracketed in most instances.[51] Humor—particularly tendentious humor—could, if taken seriously, rend the "good faith" and morality that actors routinely attribute to one another. For this reason, even when jokes prove not to be "funny," they are still recognized as jokes, letting interaction proceed harmoniously.[52] Humor has a fundamentally *dramaturgical* character that permits and often requires distancing of one's self from one's remarks. As a result, humor is differentiated from other forms of narrative, such as personal-experience stories.

Different groups face distinct threats that humor helps to transcend. In the case of mushroomers, concern over the expertise and competence of group members is central. Humor that addresses competence is in reality humor that centers on risk: coping with potential personal and communal danger. As many have noted, risk is not an objective reality;[53] rather, it is a collective construct.[54] Risk is not undesirable if we are confident that we can manage it.[55] Individuals and groups may control risk by processing it through talk. Yet this talk carries danger. Serious talk could become so persuasive by its focus on what *might* happen that participants might avoid those risks that had previously given them pleasure. Humor provides a means by which actors can address their fears while convincing themselves that it is manageable because they can joke about it: how can it be serious if they are laughing?

Joking about death is a defining feature of the humor of those who confront natural places. During my first weeks in the field, I was startled at jokes about dying from consuming mushrooms, although I later learned that similar themes are found in other communities of danger.[56] Humor about poisoning does not account for the majority of jokes told by mushroomers, but the sensitivity of the subject makes it a key topic.

Central to understanding poisoning humor is the reality that individuals differ in how much "risk" they desire (see Chapter 1). Some collectors are conservative in deciding which mushrooms to eat, whereas others are more liberal, willing to endure diarrhea for a new experience. For both the cautious and the daring, the possibility of poisoning is real, however close to the boundary of toxicity they explore. Although attitudes fall in a continuum, I divide mushroomers into "liberals" and "conservatives" in their consumption choices: these political terms, when used by mushroomers, do not necessarily correlate with national politics, but are linked to other social categories. In general, liberals tend to be younger than conservatives, and enter the hobby through other environmental activities, whereas conservatives often learn about mushrooms from relatives or within their ethnic groups. Many conservatives, at least in the Minnesota club, are women; men are more likely to be liberals and risk-takers. This of course maps on to the distinction between the younger men/older women division in the club discussed above, and, thus this banter is connected to issues of gender and sexuality. These groups recognize their differences and mediate them through humor, avoiding "serious" disagreements that might rend the fabric of the community. Since one's assertion of appropriate risk might be seen as arrogant, jokes clothe disagreements in good fellowship.

CONSERVATIVE HUMOR

Mushroomers who express fear of poisonous mushrooms reveal what others often consider excessive concern. Some of these collectors prefer not to *touch* lethal mushrooms for fear that contact alone might be toxic, because spores might either seep through their skin or be transferred to their mouths. Although the amount of toxins consumed in this way is clinically insignificant, and fears about these "dangers" relate more to cultural traditions of mycophobia and beliefs in "sympathetic magic" than to actual risk, they affect behavior. Mark worried about touching amanitas and galerinas (both deadly poisonous). He touched an amanita only with the edge of his knife, and then wiped the knife carefully. He didn't want any physical contact with it. When I touched a galerina on a foray, he told me: "Now you can't pick any mushrooms for the table." Given that these "conservative" mushroomers miss out on one of the main pleasures of the activity—eating mushrooms—they need to defend their position. They do this humorously, by chiding "liberals." Beth said of cooking honey caps: "Bring the water to a boil, then throw out the water" [because the poison found in the mushrooms when served raw might be in the water]. Dave, who was much more liberal than Beth, tells her: "I never did that and I never got sick." Beth joked, denigrating Dave's "rashness": "You're crazy anyhow, Dave." On another occasion, club members were discussing gyromitras (false morels), which some consider to be prime edibles and others consider to be toxic because of a small number of deaths associated with them, when the following exchange took place:

> *Brian:* They're considered poisonous. I think they're good.
>
> *Beth:* You might suggest that they not try them.
>
> *Brian (giving in):* I agree. I've tried them for my own benefit [others laugh]. My mother has eaten bushel baskets. I've tried them once. I'm not going to try them again.
>
> *Beth:* Their poison is cumulative. You can eat them for a long time and then you're dead. You have only one chance.
>
> *Nils:* They don't make you sick. They kill you. You can handle some sickness. You can't handle death. [laughter]

The problem for conservatives is that if they are wrong they have missed out on a treasure. The reality that others consume these mushrooms and survive is a challenge that humor must diffuse. As a result, conservatives present themselves as rational actors who have weighed the dangers and made a judgment, even though this rationality is contested by those who disagree. Conservatives argue that relatively few mushrooms can be identified with certainty and that consuming others is chancy. They reject trusting in "luck," and rely on certain knowledge. The presentation of their "rationality" results not in measured discussion but in banter. The issue is addressed, but the sense of community has not been breached because the remarks are "not taken seriously."

LIBERAL HUMOR

Some mushroom "liberals" make an enthusiastic case that so long as they avoid deadly mushrooms, the experience will be worth the risk. Life is filled with difficulties, and one learns from adversity. An aesthetic experience is not necessarily a pleasant experience. One mushroomer described his desire to try numerous species of mushrooms, even some that are allegedly dangerous:

> *Howard:* I eat mushrooms every year that I haven't eaten before, and the rule is that you don't eat a mushroom unless you are 100 percent sure. Yet I question 100 percent.
>
> *GAF:* Why would you want to try a possibly dangerous mushroom?

Howard: To see what it was like. To tell someone that this is what it was like, so they don't have to read it out of a book, because books aren't necessarily true. . . . I've put up with a lot of unpleasantness for the sake of the experience.

In order to defend themselves against the charge that they are suicidal or "crazy," these mushroomers rely on humor directed toward those who self-consciously avoid any mushroom that might carry risk. Although most of these liberals are confident in their abilities, and most do not consume mushrooms of which they are not *reasonably* certain, this attitude involves a measure of chance that conservatives reject.

Some liberals explicitly counter the belief that they should avoid anything potentially unpleasant or anything that they cannot exactly identify by bravely claiming that the effects of mushroom "poisoning" aren't so bad. Don told the club that eating *Verpa bohemica* makes some people temporarily lose coordination in their arms and legs. Kristi joked: "You just get a little spastic, so what?" The others laughed, and Don joked back: "I was there before I started." At another meeting Brian noted that *Psathyrella epimyces* may be mildly poisonous, and then joked: "It isn't going to be anything terrible. It's just going to be a little bit yucky. Eat them on a Friday, so you have all Saturday to recuperate."

Attributing illness to the mere touch of mushrooms is scorned by those who feel that such fastidiousness is unnecessary or even a neurotic manifestation of mycophobia. Sam joked to Jerry, the club president, about showing mushrooms to the club: "Be sure you can handle the amanitas first. It sparks conversation." Sam was referring to the time the previous year when the then president was criticized by some for holding an *Amanita* and then touching edible mushrooms. Deadly mushrooms were often passed around in a sealed plastic bag or glass jar. Another time Nanci said sarcastically as she ate potato chips on a foray: "I picked amanitas, and now I'm eating potato chips. Will I die?" These jokers adopt a persona (in the first, a deliberately provocative stance; in the second, a satirical portrait of a conservative), at the same time as they interact with others. Their colleagues recognize that they are not speaking in their own "voices" when making these remarks. Yet their orientations toward mushrooms are reflected in the selves that are portrayed in their humor. The selves that they project or imply are a joking transformation of real attitudes in the community, but because they are not "real persons," the jokes do not undermine friendships. The speakers are "just" joking.

Tension is possible either way. Humor creates a sympathetic "animator" who can satirize those too liberal and too conservative, revealing communal ambivalence. Mushroomers are drawn both ways: they are torn between wanting to consume as many different kinds of mushrooms as they can—attesting to their knowledge of mycology and their confidence in their powers of identification—and heeding the belief that a mushroom is not worth dying for.

Humor limits proper action, but in a social world like mushrooming, various targets of humor are possible. Since few define *themselves* as representing an extreme position, they can laugh at jokes that target both extreme attitudes toward risk—those whose desire for certainty is too great and those whose desire is not great enough. The humorist pokes fun at behavioral extremes and inflexibility,[57] and so the jokes can be enjoyed by all. These targets frequently do not recognize themselves as the butt of the joke, and even when they do, they are often not willing to confront the serious issue or do so only through a counter-remark.

DANGERS TO THE SELF

Since the likely victim of a mushroom poisoning is the person who picks and identifies the specimen, it is not surprising that much joking is about what could happen to him or her. Although few admit "seriously" that this is a major concern, their joking reflects underlying anxiety. They are ambivalent about consuming these other-worldly objects, against which many were warned vehemently as children. Mushroomers occasionally feign surprise at having survived after consuming mushrooms. At one of our forays, the owner of our lodge commented: "Someone [another customer] wants to know if anyone had died." Dave joked: "No one yet." Another time Jerry asked if anyone had eaten *Pluteus cervinus* [an edible mushroom that few eat]. One man said that he had barbecued some, and "I haven't died. . . . I may be a long-term victim." These concerns can be communal. An article in *Mycophile* announced: "According to latest reports, or lack of, all fungi-eating affectionados [sic] attending the January 22nd Survivors' Banquet did survive."[58] This surprise is most striking when it refers simply to touching mushrooms, as when Dane thanked the club for helping with his preadolescent son's school science project, for which he took second place: "He's outside playing, so he's still alive. He's still alive." At this the club members laughed politely.

Mushroomers suggest through "gallows humor" that they are continually at risk, and thus that they are both brave and foolish. By accepting these sentiments, members of the audience recognize that others experience the same dilemma.

Mushroomers recount their personal experiences, indicating either fear or foolishness, although by the time the story is told, they clearly have survived. For instance, Carl reported having eaten *Gyromitra esculenta* (the false morel): "I ate quite a few of them before I found out they were poisonous [big laugh from the audience]. I must admit I don't eat them anymore." Similarly, Art talked to the club about eating *Entoloma abortivum* (many entolomas are poisonous, but this mushroom is a good edible): "I left a few in the refrigerator for the rescue squad [laughter]. It's the only mushroom I've done that with." These mushroomers transform their dangerous actions for public entertainment. Sometimes they even banter about their own demise, as when Jerry held up some galerinas in front of the club, asking: "How many of you know if you can eat a galerina?" The club members laughed, and Sam joked: "You *can* eat them." Another club member added: "You won't survive, though." Jerry commented: "If you put too many of these in the pot, there won't be too many days thereafter."

This snippet underlines that becoming ill or dying from mushrooms is a real concern, even though it is insulated by humor. A similar theme is evident in warnings about the dangers of eating mushrooms ("When in doubt, throw it out"). The real-life consequences are potentially grim, but to avoid dealing with them the speaker uses humor or aesthetic imagery—establishing community and shared values without oppressive control. Art commented about a friend who was poisoned by a mushroom: "It turned him inside out. He was worshipping the porcelain goddess all night. He only ate a piece [of *Chlorophyllum molybdites*] the size of a pea." Another time, when the club placed Mr. Yuk stickers on the cards of mushrooms believed to be poisonous, Jerry joked: "You won't find these stickers in the woods." The most extreme example of this warning occurs when mushrooms are portrayed as predators out to kill mushroom hunters:

A chap from the hills of Carolina
Was buried last week in Elvina
After eating some Honeys
He began to feel funny
(He was attacked by a fall *Galerina*).[59]

This instance of gallows humor is strikingly different from the factional jokes described above. In those jokes the humor is directed at the beliefs and skills of individuals. These jokes focus on dangers from mushrooms themselves. Yet both represent attempts to police the boundaries of risk.

MURDER AND MUSHROOMS

As murder mysteries such as Dorothy Sayers's[60] *The Documents of the Case* remind us, humans consider fungi a deadly weapon.[61] The Roman emperor Claudius was allegedly poisoned by his wife.[62] More recently, in 1918, a French murderer induced a number of his friends to insure their lives with him as beneficiary, and then served them poisonous mushrooms.[63] Although mushroom murders are uncommon, jokes about such poisonings are not. On one foray Beth gave Sam a cup of tea, at which Sam joked: "It's not laced with any *Amanita*?" Beth retorted, "We tried." It is striking that good friends such as Beth and Sam can joke about her wanting to murder him, but such joking is permissible because they are good friends within a strong community. In the terms of the philosopher J. L. Austin,[64] the illocutionary force of the utterance (that is, its role as entertainment) is evident. The joking context permits the content of the remark to be disassociated from the self of the teller: the remark is taken as being told by a fictional persona.[65]

In most jokes mushroomers are the murderers rather than the victims. Perhaps this is because they are threatened by jokes that reveal their vulnerability; after all, mushroomers *are* in theory the potential victims of murder as a result of the trust they place in others.

Given American family roles, and the fact that it is often publicly more acceptable to claim that spouses hate rather than love each other, many jokes center around feeding deadly mushrooms to one's mate.[66] Again, the issue is the legitimate persona of the speaker; a loving persona is less permissible than an intolerant, hateful one because the former might be seen as self-aggrandizement. Such remarks speak metaphorically of the legitimation of violence in family life. Jerry once asked if anyone had eaten *Hericium erinaceus*. Bernie said that he had tried some: "I liked it. . . . My wife, however, got sick." Club members laughed, and Jerry joked: "Is that why you liked it? I've been trying to figure out how to get my wife to be a guinea pig. I've got to talk to you about it." Another time Ev asked whether a particular mushroom was edible. When told that it wasn't, he said: "You feed them to your wife when you get tired of paying alimony."

These mushroomers are willing to assume abhorrent roles in the name of fun, but also to express their fear. In addition to spouses, mushroomers often make other groups the symbolic target of poisonous mushrooms. Al said to a nonmushroomer about some deadly amanitas: "This is one you give bankers and lawyers, because it takes three days to kill them" (that is, death is slow and painful). Or after noting that several Southeast Asian immigrants had died from eating amanitas, which resemble edible Southeast Asian mushrooms, one informant joked: "To get rid of the Vietnamese, I think, Americans could have just imported all of the amanitas instead of Agent Orange." These jokers are not murderers, but through their joking they express improper and otherwise inexpressible sentiments—including racism and revolutionary class violence—that they don't "really" hold. These "cruel jokes"[67] are enacted in conversation. The joke content is insulated from the teller, so the unacceptable does not spill over to contaminate the self.

An equally focused example of humor is evident in jokes about having naive outsiders sample mushrooms to determine their edibility: to be "guinea pigs." On a club foray Harvey said: "I want to bring home some mushrooms. I have a neighbor girl who eats them and calls me in the morning [if she's not poisoned]. She thinks she's eating something out of my garden. I don't tell her." The others laughed, and Brian added: "Then you get a new neighbor girl [when she dies]." On a similar theme, Jerry joked about the birch polypore, which some books say is edible, but is tough, and, according to some, bitter: "I'd like to encourage someone else to try it and tell me." After saying this, he assured the other club members at the meeting that the mushroom was not poisonous. He added: "By the way, new members, if you join, you're guinea pigs for the first year." After the others laughed, he said: "Not so at all. Just joking." A related story concerning Dr. W. C. Coker circulated among graduate students at the University of North Carolina at Chapel Hill:

[Coker] is alleged to have been walking with one of the myriad nieces and nephews in the Coker family one fall afternoon when he stopped, picked up a mushroom, and gave it to the child to eat. After eating they continued the walk. Later he looked down at the child and asked how the child felt. The child responded, "I feel fine." Whereupon Dr. Coker said, "Good, we have another edible mushroom."[68]

These jokes reflect wish fulfillment as displayed in the comments of the "self-centered" humor persona. Club members want to taste as many specimens as they can, but they fear the experimentation. By suggesting that others should do the dirty work, they project their fantasies—having the best of both worlds. Their "mycophobic" reactions remain intact, while they maintain a "mycophilic" ideology. By being sadistic for a moment, they can deflect attention from possibly masochistic behavior. Participants play out internal debates in the realm of humor. This allows ambivalent meaning, because of the flexibility of the performance role and the support that comes when others respond similarly.

Through talk we understand nature and our place in it. We situate ourselves, and through our reactions to the talk of others we validate that placement: a linkage of self-announcements and acceptance. As folklorists have noted, contemporary discourse emphasizes personal narratives, humor, and informal dialogue.

Several goals are achieved through talk. Members build a culture together—a set of meanings that can be referred to during future interaction and that sets group members apart from outsiders, permitting them to recognize their common features. This is achieved through creating an idioculture—a group culture found in all groups, although it is more robust and supportive in some. Personal-experience stories, in particular, serve to link the self and the community.

The first group of personal-experience stories, which I have termed war stories, address overcoming obstacles. Whether the obstacles were overcome collectively or individually, the audience can appreciate and support the effort. Even if the sharing does not occur in the doing, the telling is shared. These stories can involve interaction with nature or the public, or recounting pranks (artificially created troubles) within the group. Satisfying endings are central to these stories.

The second group of personal-experience narratives are sad stories, which permit group members to process limits on satisfaction, such as the inability to collect mushroom treasures. The primary emotion is sympathy, deriving from the reality that the audience either has been or can imagine being in a similar situation. That narrative repertoires include sad stories, war stories, and treasure tales suggests that the sad stories recount not a record of failure but an immediate frustration that other treasures assuage. The stories are appropriately told within the emotional economy of the group.

The third class of personal-experience narratives are treasure tales. In these texts notable finds are discovered: finds that typically emphasize the remarkable and magical generosity of the natural environment. In these narratives tellers judge their audience, as fishermen do theirs. It is less important that the stories are true than that they are meaningful. Some narratives are told as remarkable but truthful occurrences. In other cases, the legendary character of the details sweeps the audience along; they put aside their skepticism in the name of entertainment and wish-fulfillment. In each instance, mushroomers, like others engaged in voluntary activities, enchant their world, making the mundane meaningful. Whether we are examining birders, book collectors, social movement activists, charity workers, or skiers, if the community matters and the activity is engaging, similar personal-experience stories will be shared.

Along with personal-experience narratives, humor plays a central role in mediating the anxieties and ambivalence of risky voluntary activity. The desire to eat and the desire to be safe conflict, and are addressed through humor. Just as risk is a cultural product, the performance of stories provides for its resolution and control.

The joking culture of mushroomers reveals that their fears about their activities have not been fully resolved. As a consequence, jokes are made both about dying from consuming mushrooms (external danger) and about being afraid to eat mushrooms (skill and certainty). The use of talk to harness risk and contain communal anxiety is not limited to mushroomers, but is evident in many dangerous and anxiety-provoking social situations.

Mushroomers, like all who joke, can rely on the remarkable flexibility of the performance of humor. Audiences are tolerant of the jokes of people they like and admire, and those whom they consider to be part of their community. As a result, the jokers can embrace various social roles with impunity and not get challenged when they do so. Performed joking permits the moral disengagement of the jocular persona from the "polite self." The world of mushroomers is similar to many social worlds in which sensitive subjects are communicated and mediated through humor. In order to communicate effectively, speakers and writers play at being characters who, if "serious," would be defined as morally reprehensible.

Humor permits jokers not only to share what might otherwise be kept hidden, but also to escape blame for their social naughtiness. That death and murder can be made a source of laughter is a remarkable tribute to the possibility of friendly communication. It is, further, a testimony to the power of normative constraints in that even when contradictory attitudes exist, both can be legitimately expressed. The bonds of affection are stronger than the topics that could rend these bonds. The flexibility of persona and audience gives voluntary communities their tensile strength in a world in which disputes sometimes lead to social disintegration.

Talk—anecdotes and humor—provides a basis for community, and provides those engaged in naturework with a template that tames activities in the wild, while simultaneously bolstering their magic and enchantment. By talking wild, and listening wild, we can simultaneously feel free and part of a community of vigor and care.

CHAPTER
FIVE

Organizing Naturalists

Americans of all ages, all stations in life, and all types of disposition are forever forming associations. There are not only commercial and industrial associations in which all take part, but others of a thousand different types—religious, moral, serious, futile, very general and very limited, immensely large and very minute.

—ALEXIS DE TOCQUEVILLE

From the time of Tocqueville, America has been described as a nation of joiners.[1] Our predilection for informal organizations has set us apart; indeed, it might be said that such groups are part of the "American way."[2] Although data demonstrating that Americans establish more or larger voluntary organizations than members of other Western societies are not readily available, little doubt exists that organizations characterize leisure activities, and nowhere more than in nature activities.

As Robert Stebbins[3] notes in his comparative analysis of leisure worlds, among the rewards of leisure involvement are sociable interaction and group accomplishment. Leisure groupings are "sociable organizations"[4] that provide resources and opportunities for reaching desired goals, either individual or collective. These organizations are a means of escape from the dilemmas of both ascriptive ties and radical individualism. In leisure groups one can share one's interests with like-minded others, producing a community of acquaintances—a smaller version of those communities that Robert Bellah and his colleagues term "lifestyle enclaves."[5]

The range of leisure groups is astounding. There are national and local organizations devoted to bells and buttons, cookie cutters, beer cans, bricks, spark plugs, postmarks, hat pins, Edsels, and Barbie dolls. In arenas that require specialized knowledge, such as those involving naturework, leisure organizations are particularly prominent. Within the realm of nature, there are clubs devoted to butterflies, orchids, nuts, minerals, bonsai, koi, caving, bass fishing, skiing, surfing, snakes, turtles, and particular species of cats, dogs, game, and flowers. These groups, large[6] or small, underline the importance of sociability. National organizations often provide the infrastructure through which local clubs organize and affiliate; local clubs support the national organization financially and through strong memberships. Whether or not clubs have face-to-face meetings, their newsletters provide a forum through which enthusiasts can communicate. The vast array of discussion groups on the Internet speaks to a similar desire to communicate with those who have like interests.

The vibrancy of "nature" clubs emphasizes that nature is processed through culture. Perhaps cultural groups are most important in taming and organizing that which is perceived as outside of culture. The environmental movement began in the mid-nineteenth century with the establishment of "sportsmen's clubs,"[7] social groupings that provided arenas for sociability. With the development of national sporting journals, the club idea caught hold, as clubs communicated[8] and leisure networks were established.[9] A desire for middle-class bonhomie merged with the desire to protect places in which fish and game could be conserved:

> Throughout this period (and afterward) [in the late nineteenth and early twentieth century] conservation groups were in large part social clubs. Members went on outings together, whether to hunt, to fish, to watch birds, or to sleep out under the stars. . . . Even when the Izaak Walton League sprang up in the Midwest in the 1920s, quickly gaining a membership many times larger than any of the other groups, its base was limited. A typical chapter, historian Stephen Fox has written, resembled "a Rotary Club that liked to go fishing."[10]

For many environmental organizations, such as the Audubon Society and the Sierra Club, the social aspects of the group and the provisioning of leisure were for much of their history at least as important as their political lobbying. The appreciation of nature as a collective arena for leisure provided the basis for its protection. This conservation ethic, which grew out of self-interest merged with public interest, led to an increase in awareness of the dangers posed to the American environment by uncontrolled growth and a base from which to fight for these beliefs. Many nature clubs, including mushroom societies, play at least a minor role in conserving the environment, no matter their opinions about more controversial issues:

> On May 3, NYMS proved that it does not lack a social conscience. Fairness demanded that we take not only morels but garbage from the woods. So we turned out five carloads strong to do our bit on NY-NJ Litter Clean-Up Day at Blauvelt State Park where we collected bags of bottles, cartons of cans and pails of pollutants, leaving the park nice and clean for the next invasion of careless picnickers and nocturnal partiers. In return, Blauvelt gave us a handful of LBM's.[11]

Although conserving the aesthetics of the park for their own enjoyment is little enough, it reminds us that environmental rhetoric is part of naturework. One can wonder whether the environmental damage from removing mushrooms outweighed the benefits from removing bottles.

Organizations are, at their heart, institutions through which the "interests" of participants are met. In the case of voluntary organizations with low exit costs—of which leisure organizations are a model—the satisfaction of these goals becomes crucial if the organization is to continue. In this chapter I explore ways in which voluntary organizations become strong; I also look at some threats to this strength. Specifically, I address the means by which organizations provide resources to members, the process by which organizations become internally differentiated, the threats to organizations that these political divisions cause, and the centrality of trust and secrecy in developing group cohesion. First, I discuss briefly how members are recruited to mushroom organizations, given the reality that one can collect mushrooms without organizational support.

RECRUITMENT

People generally become interested in a subject either through a personal relation, who serves as an activity role model (relational recruitment), or through exposure to an object or event that catches their attention (interest recruitment). Although the line is often hazy between these two categories (one can, after all, be fascinated by an object discovered with a significant other), the distinction is between a focus on the objects of interest and a focus on social rewards. In either instance the person recruited must feel that the activity might produce personal satisfaction. In other words, if one is consumed with work or leisure, another "interesting" topic will be only mildly appealing; the person lacks the temporal luxury of adding a new action domain. The new activity must be sufficiently compelling to displace other activities (mandatory activities, such as employment or family life, are often not easily displaced). Thus recruitment occurs in light of the possibility of involvement: there is a perceived time and place for the establishment of a new interest. The reverse happens, of course, when one severs one's ties with a leisure group; other activities may be seen as having greater weight, the activity itself may provide fewer rewards, or relational ties with group members may weaken. In either form of involvement, social organization is significant: in the former because of the other's position as interactant (or role model/ego ideal), and in the latter through the cultural construct of what constitutes interesting objects or activities.

Relational Recruitment

Parents have great significance in the lives of their children. They have the power to define which topics are interesting because of the trust their children place in them, because of their social control (taking children on outings), and because of their ability to provide resources (baskets, books, automobile travel). Of the Minnesota Mycological Society members who responded to my questionnaire, 22 percent said that they had picked mushrooms with their parents; for members of the North American Mycological Association, the comparable figure was 19 percent:

> My parents were from Czechoslovakia, so every picnic we went out
> on was a mushrooming foray. . . . My mother made wonderful dishes

with them, so there certainly was reason to find out [about mush-rooms].[12]

My dad always collected morels especially. They just called them mushrooms; morels you didn't hear back then. Every spring he used to go out looking for them, that's why we started looking. Finally we joined a club to find out where to look.

In other instances a friend or neighbor introduces the novice to the joys of mushrooms, an introduction that must be based on some measure of trust, given that most Americans are aware that some mushrooms are deadly:

One day when we arrived at our vacation cabin on the slopes of Mt. Hood we found our next door neighbors in our backyard. When they saw us they looked very sheepish. They explained that they were gathering mushrooms. We had seen the mushrooms before, but were afraid to eat them. The neighbors offered to show us the edible ones.[13]

My interest in mushrooms dates back to my experience in Scandinavia [as an exchange student] . . . particularly when I was seventeen, eighteen years old living in the south central part of Sweden going out with families and collecting mushrooms as part of early fall family activities . . . We spent a number of delightful fall afternoons collecting mushrooms and later on discovering and knowing that essentially the same type of mushrooms grow in Minnesota that grow in Sweden.

Interest Recruitment

For others, the mushrooms themselves are the lure. The objects may be dramatically impressive in their brightness, size, or beauty—all socially desirable markers. In the Introduction I recounted how a brilliant orange mushroom led Harry Knighton to found the North American Mycological Association. Other accounts are similar:

The experience of finding for the first time the exquisite Coral Fungus in the cool, moist woodlands of Sweden aroused the interest of Elias Fries to such a degree that he became one of the founders of mycological science.[14]

Long ago when I was an art student in New York I lived in a cabin in the woods. One morning early I stepped out on the porch and there were several beautiful, brilliant red mushrooms. I went to a library and got a book.[15]

In a similar vein, John told me that he became interested in mushrooms when he was living on a mountainside, and one day, "I picked up a scleroderma and cut it and it went from white to black, and I said, 'Whoa, *what* is going on. I should know about this.' Then when I came off the mountain I bought a book." Sometimes the presence of mushrooms is less romantic and more mundane, as in the case of the composer and mushroomer John Cage, then a starving artist:

> The first time I noticed mushrooms particularly was when I was in Carmel, California. I was about 21 and I had no money. . . . When I arrived in Carmel I noticed that the place was covered with a kind of mushroom. I took one to the library and compared it to an illustration in a book and satisfied myself that it was edible. I ate them for a week.[16]

Only later does one's interest in the object merge with an interest in others who share that fascination, as when the novice collector joins a mushroom club.

Some mushroomers become interested after berrying, collecting flowers, cooking gourmet foods, or the like.[17] A person, object, or event will still affect the recruitment, but the gap between previous interest and one's new one is not as wide. Whatever the path into a natural world, a relatively undifferentiated set of objects provides, over time, the opportunity for subtle distinctions, metaphors, and value judgments.

PROVISIONING THEORY

All behavior rests on an institutional and material base. An obdurate reality shapes events. As Richard Butsch[18] notes in his historical analysis of the development of the model airplane hobby, leisure is embedded within markets. To act we need resources and support structures. This recognizes the utility of applying resource mobilization theory[19] to the analysis of leisure organizations, and specifying how organizational, economic, and ecological realities direct the strategies and effectiveness of voluntary organizations. Leisure organizations, in this view, can be understood in light of the resources (personnel, finances, and communication) that permit them to operate within a social and institutional environment. Although ideas and personal motivations do matter, so do the material bases of power.

Like social movements, the site of much resource mobilization theory, leisure organizations are voluntary. As a result, they have the traditional problem of voluntary organizations: how to cement members to the collectivity,[20] a problem with which mandatory organizations, such as workplaces and schools, are less concerned. Resources are expected to lead to commitment, cohesion, and satisfaction. The "good" produced by movement organizations is typically a socially significant good, whereas leisure benefits are transient and personal. Leisure organizations have as their primary goal the provisioning of fun. A leisure activity that does not produce enjoyment is likely to have few adherents.[21] As one new club leader commented: "The first and foremost objective on my list is to have fun! . . . It's fun to be together and it's fun to learn new things. . . . I'm really looking forward to a year of putting the 'fun' in fungi . . . with *You!*"[22]

How is this fun generated? Unlike social movements and more instrumental organizations, resources in leisure groups are gathered for the use of members; they are deployed internally, rather than externally. Providing satisfactions to members is the organization's first priority. Nowhere is this more true than in nature organizations, in which access to private or hidden places is crucial, and in which the secrets of the wild must be provided in a social setting. The origins of many nature organizations ("sportsmen's clubs") can be traced to the desire to provide resources and facilities for leisure activity:[23]

> As early as the 1850's, city sportsmen united in informal associations to ensure the company of social equals. Hunting clubs soon appropriated the better shooting grounds on such famous waters as the Chesapeake Bay and Currituck Sound, offering collectively to members the sport and comfort which none singly could afford. By the end of the century, the hunting club's suburban equivalent, the "country club," developed from the same desire for an appropriately private, rural landscape.[24]

By the late nineteenth century, it was necessary for groups to provide nature. Nature was becoming scarce, and could be obtained only at a cost,[25] often through purchasing spaces of solitude.

Resources allow for the appreciation of nature and, by implication, all leisure activities. I have previously termed this approach "provisioning theory," recognizing that leisure organizations depend for their existence and their tensile strength on the ability to gather and distribute resources. Although these include material resources, they may also include knowledge and opportunities for interpersonal interaction and identity support. What is considered "fun" is not merely a function of hedonic preferences, but is socially contingent on organizational activity. Although individuals are free to engage in numerous leisure activities, that freedom is possible because others have laid the groundwork that facilitates these choices. In contrast, a lack of organizational opportunities constricts leisure options.[26]

What must a leisure group provide to its members in order to have fulfilled its purpose? Three elements seem crucial: (1) distribution of knowledge about the leisure activity; (2) opportunities for sociability; and (3) access to identity symbols. These components of leisure activity are evident in mushrooming, a world that some value because it demands little in the form of goods and services. As one participant asserts, writing for new members and contrasting mushrooming with hunting and fishing:

> You don't need expensive and complicated equipment, ammo, boats, baits, traps, or other supplies. A paper bag, wicker or plastic basket, a folding knife, whistle and compass (rain suit if raining). . . . You don't even need to travel to deep wilderness areas and set up campers.[27]

Although a basket, knife, and bag may be sufficient for the collection of mushrooms, they are not sufficient for "mushrooming."

Knowledge

Involvement in a leisure world presumes the existence of information that enables the competent doing of an activity. From where does that knowledge come? Much knowledge circulates throughout society; *some* information about many types of leisure is known widely, but this information, of course, contains gaps, stereotypes, and errors. Almost everyone knows that some mushrooms are poisonous, gourmets are aware that morels and chanterelles are delicious, and many have read that clubs or classes exist that train novices in collecting edible species. This information is acquired through friends, relatives, the media, and casual conversations.

The novice arrives with some knowledge and experience. Although this knowledge and experience may be necessary for initial involvement, it is not sufficient, and not seen as sufficient. One member reports:

> I had educated myself pretty well by looking through those [mushroom guide] books. But it was totally divorced from reality. So after joining the society, I suddenly absorbed all this personal experience that people had, and that's the main reason I joined—to find some people who had some concrete knowledge to draw from.

The recruit typically lacks the "member's knowledge" that permits the competent doing of the activity, according to subcultural standards. The challenge for the leisure organization is to provide the novice with knowledge to participate. Ideally, the information is provided conveniently and in an emotionally satisfying manner.

Many mushroomers learn about fungi through classes, which are often taught by self-proclaimed experts who lack a degree in mycology but have considerable field experience. Typically these classes are sponsored by an organization—a mushroom society, school, museum, government agency, or for-profit organization. Some classes last a few hours, others require several hours a week, and still others demand continual attendance for days or weeks at a distant venue. An advertisement for the Wild Mushroom Conference at Breitenbush Hot Springs in Oregon, published in the fall 1988 issue of *Mushroom* magazine, reveals the elaborateness of some of these gatherings:

> The conference is expressly designed for mushroomers interested in developing their identification skills and understanding of the taxonomy, cultivation, chemistry and ecology of mushrooms. Emphasis will be placed on edible, poisonous and psychoactive species. There will be comprehensive instruction in contemporary commercial and small scale cultivation practices for mushrooms including shiitake, oyster and wine-red stropharia. Workshops encourage a "hands-on" approach. Other topics include mushrooms in history and culture, mushroom photography and art, and medicinal possibilities and applications. Extensive forays will bring in many kinds of mushrooms from the Breitenbush forests and meadows. Plus the annual Wild Mushroom Cookout and Dance on Saturday! This year's faculty includes David Arora, Paul Przybylowicz, J. Q. Jacobs, Paul Stamets, Gary Lincoff, Mike Wells, Kent Polowski, Dr. Cal Seeba, Tom O'Dell and other scholars, cultivators and aficionados.

The cost of this fungal experience was $145 per person. Although this was an elaborate course, it underlines several features of leisure provisioning. First, it was sponsored by an established organization, in this case a resort. Second, the conference recruited a faculty of experts, several of whom were well known within the mycological community. By their presence, they represented privileged knowledge and validated the event's legitimacy. Third, the experience was structured to train mushroomers to improve their technical skills within their community of interest. Finally, the occasion was situated as a leisure pursuit, combining fun with the acquisition of knowledge: instrumental and expressive needs merged. In voluntary worlds, education is not an end in itself, but a means to increased satisfaction; the event should increase allegiance.

Courses do not emerge spontaneously; they are created by organizations serving as leisure entrepreneurs. Resources (capital and an organizational infrastructure sufficient for planning, marketing, and hiring personnel) and the credibility that the organization brings to the project are crucial. The possibility of educational experiences in leisure worlds, including those outside nature, indicates the desire for mastery. Aerobics classes and "fantasy" baseball camps reflect the same impulse, as do—within naturework—birding symposiums or mountaineering schools. In nature, with its hidden secrets, this demand for training seems particularly apparent. Students arrive with modest knowledge and an ambition to become "experts": to elaborate their restricted codes of knowledge.

The presence of others is not the only means by which individuals learn. Written resources are critical in many leisure communities.[28] Clubs, such as the Minnesota Mycological Society, maintain lending libraries. The Minnesota club has a library of more than sixty volumes; the club lends fieldguides to novices and provides discount prices on other guides. The club also prepared a twenty-page packet of information for new members. More written material is available through bookstores, both generalized and specialized. Specialized bookstores and mail-order marketing expand the possibilities for sales. Mushroom fieldguides are published each year,[29] and many hobbyists subscribe to *Mushroom, the Journal*, a quarterly with a circulation of approximately 2,000 that features articles on well-known hobbyists, mushroom forays, mushroom philately, evaluations of fieldguides, and advice on cultivation. The volumes advertised in one issue of *Mushroom* magazine included *Mycological Dictionary in Eight Languages; Celebrating the Wild Mushroom, A Passionate Quest; The Edible Mushroom: A Gourmet Cook's Guide; One Thousand American Fungi; The Audubon Society Field Guide to North American Mushrooms;* and *The Mushroom Cultivator.* Many amateurs regularly purchase books, sometimes spending hundreds of dollars annually. The existence of a recognizable, accessible, affluent leisure world encourages publishers to cater to this market.

Every leisure world has an associated resource base. Whereas some differences might be attributed to the particular needs of the leisure activity, others are a function of the resources to which leisure groups have access and the organizational structure that permits sharing of these resources. Those groups that have meetings, forays, and other face-to-face events have greater possibilities for gathering, transforming, and redistributing resources than those that rarely meet and have loose ties among participants. The social class and cultural capital of the participants have a considerable effect on access to resources as well. A well-established pursuit, such as birdwatching, with masses of committed participants has more resources and a more effective structure than a newer or smaller activity, such as observing snakes in the wild. Neither activity is inherently more satisfying than the other; a key distinction is the organizational base.

Sociability

To be sure, leisure is possible outside an organization. But participants may feel that they need structure.[30] People derive deep satisfaction from voluntary organizations . These groups provide not only information but also social arenas. The organization is responsible for the provisioning of community, a task that is difficult for the individual. Leisure organizations are in effect content-based "fraternal" organizations in which a communion of "brotherhood" develops.[31] Leisure organizations provide personal communities.[32]

Successful organizations provide staging arenas for friendship,[33] notably by furnishing the location for contact. Regular meetings are important for many groups in cementing members to the organization *and* to the activity. The provisioning of place contributes to allegiance. For instance, the Minnesota Mycological Society held weekly meetings four months annually at a local community center. When a voluntary association draws members from a large metropolitan area, the choice of location may be controversial, as it increases the cost of attendance for some, while minimizing it for others. One year the club contemplated moving to a more centralized location, but the plan was scuttled, in part, when it was learned that free parking would not be available. The costs were seen as outweighing the benefits.

Sufficient time at the meetings for informal talk is critical for member satisfaction. Leisure organizations rarely begin their sessions on time and the lights are not extinguished until long after the meeting ends. Meetings of the Minnesota Mycological Society did not begin until fifteen or twenty minutes after their scheduled time so that members could converse; after the meeting participants stayed and talked. For years the society had a postmeeting get-together at a local McDonalds, where core members gossiped, joked, and informally discussed club business. At times these gatherings became "official" meetings of the board, and they often lasted as long as the official meetings.

Other, festive occasions are set aside to provide a sense of community. The annual banquet, held in the winter, and the annual picnic, held in the summer, are two such occasions. In "successful" banquets, a restaurant, dining hall, or hotel provides a private room, tasty, modestly priced food of general appeal, and an area in which homemade mushroom dishes can be served. One year the hotel at which the banquet was held refused to permit members to bring in prepared food (perhaps especially mushrooms!), for fear of liability. That banquet did not promote the sociability of members and was judged a disappointment. Forays, as described in Chapter 3, are critical to enhancing member satisfaction and affiliation with the organization, and may involve considerable coordination. Forays, after all, transform mushroom collecting from individual activity to group work. For this to happen, those coordinating the foray must select a location, choose a date on which mushrooms are likely to be fruiting, secure permission from park authorities or private landowners, provide directions and maps to the location, and publicize the event. The foray chairman relies on locations that were successful in the past and adds to these places that members have had personal success visiting.

These decisions must be publicized weeks in advance, and so guessing the state of mushroom fruiting becomes a problem. With half a dozen forays scheduled in the fall, considerable time will be spent in group pursuits. If the club organizes an overnight foray, the price for room and board must be reasonable, according to implicit organizational standards, and the accommodations and cooking facilities must be adequate. Club members search for mushrooms and hope for fun, but someone in the organization must do the spadework so that a reasonable likelihood exists that they won't be disappointed.

Organizations and their leaders rely on members to generate sociability. To create these occasions, some individuals must take the responsibility, in order to permit others—for the moment—to be free riders. These workers receive esteem and deference. In many groups, it is expected that the position of sociability manager will rotate. Yet this remains a challenge for organizations, given members' tendency to demand benefits without responsibility. As a consequence, members are exhorted to participate ("this is your club . . . be an active member") and, once participating, are approached to "do their share." In a sense, the invitation to participate is part of a communal "bait-and-switch." One is told of the fun of participating, and then one's presence legitimates a request for involvement. These approaches are personal requests, hard to refuse when coming from friends and colleagues, and involve a rhetorical exhortation of the importance of making a voluntary "contribution."[34]

In turn, members look to organizations to ensure that they will enjoy one another's presence in locations that connect to their interest: they strive for *focused sociability*. Sociability is not pure friendship, but friendship can emerge because participants have something in common.

Identity Symbols

Leisure worlds incorporate styles and fashions that mark identity.[35] Those within the activity, on its edges, or on the outside may provide expressive symbols that reflect how participants wish to be known. Around each well-developed leisure world, vendors provide identity symbols—items that enhance one's sense of self.[36] Although these symbols are found in all leisure worlds, they seem most dramatic—because of their cultural and materialistic implications—when selected by actors who embrace naturework. The authenticity of the wild seems at first to conflict with the market, but in practice it is thoroughly congruent with it.

The identity symbols of leisure vary according to their potential markets. Some are limited, in practice if not in theory, to members of a particular leisure world. Who but a mushroomer would place the bumper sticker "I Brake for Fungi" on his car? Who but a mushroomer would wear a t-shirt with a pair of large morels on her chest? Other accouterments may have a wider audience: boots, work shirts, knives, baskets, or whistles. The more limited the artifact's market, the more likely are leisure participants to consider it central to their identity. Some high-quality items aimed at a general market (for example, fine knives or baskets) may also have status within a leisure world. Although the owner will not consider him- or herself more of a mushroomer by owning one, the quality of these items bestows meaning on the self.[37]

Artifacts of style are provided to leisure actors through three distinct types of vendors: organizational vendors, peripheral vendors, and mass vendors.

ORGANIZATIONAL VENDORS

Leisure organizations can provide identity symbols themselves, although most organizations are not manufacturers. They commission firms to produce the objects that they are responsible for marketing and selling. The organization serves as a resource broker. For instance, mushroom societies publish cookbooks that are typeset by printers. Clubs design and sell t-shirts, bandannas, sweatsuits, or hats that they provide through arrangements with other organizations.

PERIPHERAL VENDORS

Identity symbols can also be provided by groups or individuals familiar with a leisure subculture. For those leisure activities that attract members with considerable disposable income, small businesses arise on the periphery of the subculture, attempting to satisfy the desires of participants; these entrepreneurs know the needs of fellow enthusiasts and are attuned to changing styles and preferences. Many of them are closely linked to the activity, often as prominent members, and their status is transferred to their products.

Within the world of mushrooming, groups and individuals sell books, postcards, stationery, bumper stickers, and apparel, and organize tours. For instance, the former president of the Minnesota Mycological Society published a metaguide (a guide to the listing of mushrooms in a dozen fieldguides). He marketed his project through the mailing lists of the national organization and local clubs. A former winner of the NAMA photo contest printed several of her impressive photographs as postcards, selling them at forays and through *Mushroom* magazine. Several respected mushroomers organize overseas tours for colleagues. These actors choose to earn a profit, albeit a small one, from friends and acquaintances who are pleased to support them.

MASS VENDORS

The final source of products and services for a leisure subsociety is external enterprises.[38] Most products needed for naturework or other leisure activities can be purchased in locations catering to the general public. Although some products are designed primarily for members of the leisure world (for example, fieldguides), most are purchased by those outside it.[39] Sturdy rubber boots are desired by fishers as well as by mushroomers. A high-quality wicker basket can hold sewing, berries, or a picnic lunch, and is also an aesthetic object in its own right.

Manufacturers and distributors appeal to markets of various sizes. General merchandisers are disadvantaged in appealing to a subcultural market because they cannot efficiently target their audience and be aware of the audience's needs (for example, producing baskets with slots for knives, gloves, or guides). Nor can they gain customer loyalty from shared community identification. Yet these entrepreneurs have advantages of economy of scale and sophistication of production values that smaller and more focused firms lack.

That all worlds of nature activity are material worlds leads to recognition of the importance of organizational activity. In order to engage in virtually all forms of leisure, a wide array of resources must be coordinated. These include spatial, temporal, affective, and material concerns. Having fun and having access to resources are linked, even in the absence of an organizational structure. Organizations are, in leisure as elsewhere, efficient means by which resources can be provided. The role of organization in naturework emphasizes once again how dependent nature is on culture.

THE POLITICS OF ORGANIZATIONAL DIFFERENTIATION

Most leisure organizations are riven by divisions, often papered over, but evident when needs conflict. Often an organization serves as an umbrella for several distinct interests that overlap but do not entirely coincide. Some naturalists see the wild as a gymnasium, treasuring the exhilaration of exercise, whereas others see it as a theater, treasuring the exhilaration of aesthetic observation.[40] Some birders create lists, whereas others reject this goal in favor of photography.[41] Some fishers seek large fish (for example, bass), whereas others pursue difficult species (for example, trout).[42] Some climbers place bolts in the rocks to provide safety and permit more dangerous climbs; others see this as desecration.[43] Organizations must provide for each group, although what is legitimate and how much to provide may be grounds of contention. Nature is an arena in which different models of enjoyment are played out with the support of organizational resources.

In the mushroom club, the primary fault line[44] was between those who were pot hunters (or, more politely, if less commonly, *mycophagists*—those whose primary concern was edible mushrooms) and amateur mycologists, whose orientation was more explicitly scientific.[45] The growth of environmental education, which led younger members to embrace mushrooming, coupled with the expansion of science education (both in secondary schools and in colleges), legitimized the scientific study of mushrooms.[46] Younger, better-educated members competed for legitimacy against older members with less formal education. These differences were well recognized by club members:

> You have people who are dedicated scientists who want to know every single thing about mushrooms, and to be able to identify any mushroom that there is. They're willing to put a lot of time and energy into that. Others are interested in mushrooms, but more interested in finding only edibles and also interested in the social aspects, forays, picnics, and they don't want to go beyond that. . . . I think the ones that are more dedicated tend to group together because they have more interest than the pot hunters and those that are just social. . . . Most realize that there have to be both types of mushroomers. It's healthy for the club to have both kinds.

> I sort of split the club into two groups of people: those that are inter-
> ested in identifying mushrooms and those that are into a more pas-
> sive interest of eating mushrooms. The people interested in eating the
> more common mushrooms seem to be more similar in personality
> than those who are interested in identifying mushrooms. The more
> passive people are usually quite a lot alike. They're usually retired
> people. Lately we've been getting younger people. . . . [Mushroom-
> ing] is something they've chosen as an interest. It's part of their na-
> ture appreciation.

These divisions are not absolute, but as the second speaker noted, demographic differences exist. Interest in identification might best be conceptualized as a continuum, not a dichotomous category, al- though it is often characterized as a division.[47] Few lack any interest in the more spectacular specimens, and even the more serious reject examining "little brown mushrooms." Some older members are ac- tively interested in identifying mushrooms through their macro- scopic characteristics, but it is the younger, educated members who wish to explore the microscopic characteristics of mushrooms through scientific analysis (that is, microscopes and chemicals).

Although friendships develop between the two groups, differences are evident in how each group typifies the other. The amateur mycol- ogists deride the lack of interest of those whose primary concern is whether they can eat the mushrooms: "Some mushroom societies don't want to do anything except *eat*. If a mushroom isn't edible, they *step* on it."[48] For instance, Dave described a t-shirt with a picture of a pig and the caption "I don't care what it's called, just tell me if I can eat it." Tim asked him knowingly: "Who are you going to give that to?" It was understood that Dave would give it to a prominent pot hunter whom the two had previously joked about.

Among amateur mycologists, status differences emerge over who recalls the most Latin names or other esoteric information, a perspec- tive that threatens the identity of new members as competent nature- workers:

> What interests me, and disturbs me to some extent, is that the hierar-
> chy is based very largely on how many names that you know, and
> how many Latin words that you can pronounce, and I think there's a
> lot of competitiveness over this issue.

[At the NAMA foray] I enjoyed sort of learning about the mushroomers. Listening to them, watching them behave, just around a table. Who could put the name on it fastest, and who could put a name on it that nobody had ever heard before.

In my early days I wanted to be able to copy down mushroom names without continually interrupting a Mushroom Authority. . . . I was also motivated, I must confess, by a compelling desire not to be thought completely and irretrievably stupid. And so after years of uninterrupted diligence I have achieved a modest notoriety as a Local Mushroom Oracle, enabling me to satisfy a not-so-latent tendency to Show Off.[49]

Such status politics can undermine the moral legitimacy of the organization as an egalitarian and collective entity: being able to translate the obscurity of the natural world becomes a mark of authority. In turn, those who focus on edible mushrooms may scorn those whose interests are considered excessively scientific and who may be seen as looking down on others, missing the transcendent beauty or bounty of nature:

I personally think that the real scientific people think that the ordinary mushroomer is a moron. . . . There was one I talked to once, they were so into the *real* scientific stuff, they just didn't seem to have anything to say to me.

A serious situation [in the Seattle area] has arisen in which the various mushroom clubs have divided. The parent group in Seattle has become too technical in pursuing this study and only a limited few of its members can get much benefit from belonging, as the leaders are more interested in highly technical microscopic studies that more properly belong in University laboratories. . . . Some of the more knowledgeable people from other clubs are so far advanced that they live in a world of their own and cannot use common words to communicate with our people. . . . Most of our happy group only want to know one thing: "can you eat it?"[50]

We have gone out of our way to temper the club getting too scientific so it scares off the ordinary people who are coming and enjoying it, and who don't really identify mushrooms, but they bring mushrooms in and enjoy it. [The more scientific members] look down everybody's throats, and [say], "You can't use the common name, you have to use the Latin names," and that kind of stuff.

Their mark of competence is tied to who found the most and largest specimens.

The mere existence of segmentation does not suggest how the division enters into organizational politics. For a theme to penetrate group life it must be triggered by some event. At several points during my observation of the Minnesota Mycological Society the divisions between club segments became pronounced. This was the case at the end of the presidential term of a man who was more interested in the scientific study of mushrooms than were many in the group, and who was resented by several members for his interests and for what they defined as his autocratic style. An ironic effect of his perceived autocratic style was that more decisions were made through formally democratic procedures than was true before or since. For instance, both the board *and* the membership voted on all expenditures of club funds. This process, though constitutional, was not used the following year, when the president in office was trusted and therefore allowed to make more decisions with only informal consultation with the "right" members.

One active member described this "autocratic" president and his mentor, a former president:

> They had an idea how they wanted the club to be and were going to see to it that it was that way, no matter how much resistance was brought on by it. Howard was used to teaching high school classes, and that's how he treated his job at the society. That's not what the membership wanted. He taught it like a class. That isn't why people came there . . . When Brian came in, he pretty much took the same approach. He's a student of Howard. He knew an awful lot about mushrooms, but he didn't go through the right channels and alienated people.

Later this mushroomer—situated between the mycologists and the pot hunters, with links to each—became president and told the older members that he wouldn't try "to rock the boat. . . . I'd rather risk [new ideas] with you guys before I say it. Not that I have any radical ideas. The one thing I wanted to see was some harmony." For the first time in two years, the veteran members (called "The Old Guard") were treated as the elite, and they responded by complimenting their new leader.

The personal,[51] the demographic (younger men vs. older women), the economic (with older members unwilling to spend the club dues on projects), and the ideological were linked, and eventually led to a consensus against the amateur mycological approach. Although several events triggered the tension between the groups, including Brian's attempt to use club funds to purchase fieldguides for members[52] and to award prizes for a photography contest with separate categories for pictorial and scientific slides, the possibility of moving meetings to the Bell Museum of Natural History on the university campus served as a focus for conflict.

A staff member had invited the club to hold meetings at the museum, promising storage space for club equipment, the library, and organizational records, a larger meeting room, and access to the museum's microscopes. The meetings would be more centrally located, and the club would not have to end meetings at 9:00 P.M. The drawback was that members would have to pay for parking at the university. Although the proposal appeared reasonable, the idea triggered a storm of protest. For some, parking was the paramount issue. Others objected that Brian raised the proposal at a club meeting without taking it to the board. But the main objection appeared to be that holding the meetings at the museum would make them too scientific. This concern was provoked by Brian's comment that "there seem to be more and more people studying mushrooms in a more in-depth fashion." The image of the "microscope" became key. Roy, a conservative, older member, asserted: "This organization has been in existence for over eighty years, and its main purpose has been to look at and feel mushrooms. I don't know what we need with microscopes. This club serves its function . . . There's no reason to change it." Tim, a younger, scientifically oriented member, attempted to counter this, noting that "my microscope is one of my most useful possessions." An older woman responded curtly: "We're out of school," and an older man added: "We have speakers from the U [of Minnesota] who may know mushrooms from the microscope, but not by eye." Diane, a middle-aged member, contributed: "I think most of the people here might want to know if the mushroom is edible; they don't want to know about the spores." Another man added: "I want to know if I can go out to pick it and eat it." An older woman said of the university: "I hate going over there." Finally, Roy addressed Brian bitterly, overreacting: "You should start a club of your own, and if you get enough members, we can get together."

Although the club acts in an advisory capacity to the board, they voted 27-0 against the move, with the supporters, a minority, holding their fire. Eventually the board reaffirmed this decision, suggesting that a scientific "study group" could be organized. Some of the supporters of the move later joked that "'microscope' was a dirty word," that "the microscope kinda scares people," that some didn't like "just having [a microscope] in the same room," and that those who spoke the word would have to "wash their mouths out with soap," an image that emphasized the conservatism and age of the move's opponents. After the dispute was settled and a new president was in power, a study group was established, although it remained separate from the main meetings of the club. Several years later, however, club meetings did move to another location on the university campus.

This dispute, acrimonious at times, reminds us that the fight for control of resources can threaten leisure organizations. The division between the groups, originating simultaneously from different interests and social positions, was brought to the fore when club members confronted a decision that would alter the balance of power and control over resources. Fortunately, the election of a well-liked president acceptable to all saved the organization from major disharmony, permitting the focus to remain on nature—which all supposedly enjoyed equally—without consideration of disagreements and conflict. All leisure organizations have the potential to fail; they are expected to be fun, and when they are not, they are threatened. Thus the establishment of community becomes a prime goal of voluntary organizations.

GENERATING COHESION THROUGH SECRECY AND TRUST

As communitarians aver, participation in a voluntary organization encourages—perhaps demands—a sense of belonging. Within small-group research this "belongingness" or "we-ness" is labeled "group cohesion."[53] Although cohesion has numerous definitions, the standard views suggest that cohesion constitutes those forces that cause members to remain within a group[54] and/or to resist centrifugal forces.[55] Cohesion is an intervening variable between characteristics of group life and outcome variables, notably the success of the group (for example, survival of the group or stability of membership).[56] Cohesion is a property of social systems rather than individuals,[57] even though individuals experience the feelings of commitment on which this solidarity is based.[58] The group as an entity has power.[59] Cohesion is linked to a set of cultural processes that regulates group life, and it serves as a collective orientation that draws upon social relations and produces a group culture[60] that organizes interaction and encourages continued participation.[61] In the words of Cartwright and Zander in their classic formulation of group dynamics, cohesion is "the resultant of all the forces acting on all the members to remain in the group."[62]

Leisure groups, by virtue of the absence of force and moral compunction, are ideal organizations to examine how affiliation arises in the face of individual interest. If individual interest is privileged, the need for solidarity is diminished, except when it serves instrumental goals. Yet if this were true, voluntary groups would be far less stable than they are in practice. Groups in which members engage in dangerous leisure, such as the naturework involved in mushrooming, because of their subcultural character (that is, sharing tasks beyond the skills of most outsiders) and because of the need for mutual aid in achieving desired ends and avoiding tragic ones, are particularly likely to encourage communal affiliation. Status within the group and satisfaction from the activity flow from individual achievement.

All leisure worlds depend for their survival on providing egoistic satisfaction;[63] they are grounded in self-interest. Thus the paradox: how is voluntary organization possible, given the tension between solidarity and individualism? As the sociologist Erving Goffman famously remarked in his essay "Fun in Games":

> Games can be fun to play, and fun alone is the approved reason for playing them. The individual, in contrast to his treatment of "serious" activity, claims a right to complain about a game that does not pay its way in immediate pleasure and, whether the game is pleasurable or not, to plead a slight excuse, such as an indisposition of mood, for not participating.[64]

Yet in this passage Goffman ignores the relational context in which many games occur. Within leisure scenes an egoistic perspective is inextricably linked to a need for communal belonging. Relationships and social identity may be as important as the activity itself:[65] we often play without complaint even when "we don't feel like it." For a leisure group to remain stable, it must provide benefits that begin with and then transcend the activity for which individuals join. Many leisure activities can—once participants become knowledgeable—be performed outside the organizational order.[66] As a result, the activities by themselves do not necessarily bind actors to the group; other forces must provide that social glue.

One answer to the question of why people participate in leisure organizations is simple—they receive benefits that outweigh the costs of participation, and this ratio is better than that for nonparticipation. To some degree, this simple model is true. People do not participate in organizations unless they are "getting something out of it." But if this were the full extent of participation, one might expect leisure organizations to be fragile, and individuals to be neutral rather than emotionally committed to the group. Many leisure participants, particularly those who are active, have a long-term allegiance that transcends immediate benefits. The "groupness" of the scene is powerful,[67] and stabilizes the attachment of individuals, building cohesion.

In addition to the activities themselves, many enthusiasts treasure the company of others. They choose to belong to an organized group, even though they could engage in these activities by themselves or by developing private dyadic or group relationships. Yet "sociable organizations"[68] are valued—a group with common interests magnifies the pleasures derived from the doing of the activity. These individuals select a social setting that motivates them to rely upon, care about, and share with others. This leads to identity work[69] in which participants, through a sense of belonging, come to see themselves as characterized by the activity, rather than seeing the activity as merely something they do.

Generating cohesion in a social system that relies on individual interest demands a recognition of the interplay of integrating and centrifugal forces. To do this, I focus on two fundamental and seemingly oppositional forces, trust and secrecy, that often combine to create social integration, stabilize leisure organization, and provide a basis for communal allegiance.[70] Trust and secrecy operate through the regulation of information and the building of meaningful, extended relationships. An organization provides the environment within which relationships can flourish. This is particularly important in those risky activities that involve external dangers.[71] Although my analysis relates to all leisure groups, nature groups serve as particularly good exemplars of the process: nature, because it is seen as a dangerous, uncontrolled, and secret realm, requires some measure of trust in the advice of others, while simultaneously emphasizing the private communion of each person with the wild, a means through which social position within the group may be established.

To suggest that the combination of trust and secrecy provides the basis for the existence of voluntary organizations devoted to competitive risky activities is to recognize a profound irony: that the tension between attachment (trust) and competition (secrecy) builds social order. Both attachment and competition require an arena to flourish, and the leisure group provides this space.

What begins with the sharing or withholding of knowledge becomes, in time, a basis for the establishment of tight-knit social connections, linked both to status claims and to emotional ties. These connections, with their boundaries of legitimate information domains, create organizational stability. Voluntary allegiance depends on the existence of both a public and a private sphere. In an effective organization, expectations exist among members as to how much of their selves and knowledge to invest in the collective good, and how much to shelter. This play of persons and information constitutes the basis of collective attachment and personal satisfaction.

Trust

Cohesion depends on making the existence of the group *matter* to individuals, bolstering its voluntary character.[72] One fundamental way in which this process occurs is through the creation of a cocoon that protects individuals from the risks of the activity. Trust refers to an actor's belief that a person or collectivity will perform actions, including providing information, that will prove helpful or not detrimental, permitting the establishment of a relationship of cooperation.[73] Yet this perspective, with its emphasis on the cognitive, evaluative component of trust, is necessary but not sufficient. Interpretation is possible only within a world of cultural meanings, emotional responses, and social relations: a moral world that depends on what people ought to do, as well as what it is in their interest to do.[74] Although trust depends at first on information that is seen as protective, in time trust involves valuing the *relationship* in which trust is embedded, rather than simply the information that is acquired.[75] First the information is accepted—derived from organizationally validated sources—and subsequently the sources are themselves trusted,[76] transformed from being spokespersons for the group to being personal acquaintances. Reputation is an important feature of relationships of trust; those with good reputations are likely to receive information (if novices) and to be asked for information (if veterans).[77]

The means by which trust commits individuals to an organization is most obvious in the secret society, where the existence of one's membership must be held in confidence. The hidden relations among members constitute the power of the group; breaching this relation threatens the group's existence.[78]

Yet though secret societies represent a dramatic instance of the importance of investing confidence in others, such a connection is significant in any organization that provides information on which members rely. The sociologist Georg Simmel[79] notes that confidence is one of the most important synthetic forces within group life.[80] It is an intermediate position between knowledge and ignorance—neither of which requires the presence of others. Confidence is social, reflecting *trust* in another or a group of others, and emerges from the "objectification" of culture (that is, the segmentation of the self into specialized roles) and the growth of specialized knowledge, which we acquire by trusting others.

We judge and evaluate information provided within socially meaningful contexts. The social theorist Anthony Giddens[81] writes of a "moving world of normalcy," maintaining that trust is "the outcome of the routinized nature of an uneventful world" and that it creates a protective "cocoon" that makes the enactment of the social world and the emergence of meaning possible. The metaphor of a protective cocoon is important, especially for social activities, such as mushrooming, that are not routine. Trust is interactional, interpreted, and negotiated,[82] not fully determined or calculated. Because of its grounding in interaction, trust depends on facework; yet to the degree that it is institutionalized within an organization, it is also faceless—simultaneously fragile and robust, fluid and consequential.

The trust that participants place in others allows them to see the dangerous world as, if not routine, at least manageable.[83] Members depend on organizations—and those who compose the organizations—for relevant and protective information and for keeping that information sheltered from those outside who are deemed to have no right or competence to know. As trust in information becomes trust of persons, ties to the organization are strengthened,[84] leading to the potential for cooperation. Instrumental affiliation becomes emotional attachment.

Trust is established through rapport and identification, not merely through common interest or spatial co-presence. Trust, which originates in confidence in information provided by groups and individuals and builds on personal commitment to the group,[85] is translated into a "pure" relationship that, when generalized to the collectivity, produces organizational loyalty.[86] Trust anchors cohesion.

New members of an organization are pressured to show regard for others by heeding their advice, thus demonstrating that they are trustworthy. As a result, the establishment of trustworthiness becomes critical. One must be socialized to risk and to competence, and the organization must establish procedures—formal or implicit—by which trustworthiness is created. Finally, trust changes over time, from an emphasis on meaning to a more subtle connection to the identity of others and one's relations with them.

AWARDING TRUST

Trust is particularly important when external threats are present. Mycological organizations generate trust by supplying novices who find themselves in an uncertain environment with protective information. Mushroomers must learn how to avoid illness—and, in the extreme, death—from consuming "bad" mushrooms. As a consequence, the practical question of trust emerges early and dramatically. The first question that novices ask "experts" is, "Can I eat it?" (a blunter version of "What is this?"). Not all mushroomers make consumption their central reason for joining a club, but few lack interest in the question.[87] Mushroomers know that eating mushrooms is considered potentially dangerous, particularly given the publicity accorded the occasional death. Organizations provide both the resources to experience risk and the expertise to cope with it.[88]

Throughout organizational life, social pressure exists to award trust to members of the group, and this trust seems easily given. As noted in Chapter 3, novices taste many species of mushrooms at social events where the mushroom has been picked and identified by others. This poses a delicate problem of impression management for the novice who cannot personally ascertain whether the species identification is accurate. Should the (often unknown) identifier be trusted? Typically the social pressures are sufficiently strong to ensure consumption, however anxious it may be. Persons who refuse to eat mushrooms prepared by others at a foray or banquet must justify their behavior lest it be assumed that they don't trust their comrades: an affront that could disrupt social relations. They must attest through their behavior that they accept the identifications of others and the legitimacy of a community of competence, even though they may be unsure personally of the proper identification.[89] At one club foray, a fairly new member consumed a pâté made with—unbeknownst to her—some *Amanita fulva*, which are rarely eaten because of their deadly genus mates. She told me later that knowing about the amanitas wouldn't have made a difference: "I don't think it would have stopped me from eating it, because I really have a lot of confidence in the group. And I just have the feeling that nobody is deliberately mixing something up that hadn't been proved edible."

The absence of established personal relationships is a striking feature of this story, and emphasizes the extent to which novices place their trust in the organization: trust that has been established previously but is made relevant situationally. New members trust not just individual expertise but a system of expertise.[90] They are willing to consume potentially deadly mushrooms collected, identified, and cooked by strangers. Or, as a novice rock climber noted after an energetic climb: "I suddenly realized that I was putting my life in the hands of someone whose last name I didn't even know."[91]

As noted, the social psychological centrality of trust is evident in jokes that veteran mushroomers make about using new members as "guinea pigs":

The oath taken on induction [into the International Mushroom Pickers Society] indicates [members'] enthusiasm in the mycological pursuits: "I solemnly promise to cherish the brotherhood and good fellowship of my brother IMPS, even to the extent of willingness to serve as a mushroom taster of wild mushrooms for a probationary period of one year *without liability to our organization if rigor mortis sets in due to ingestion of nonedible fungi.*[92]

The demand for trust legitimates leisure organizations. To alleviate the concern about who should be trusted, organizations often establish roles that deserve trust, while maintaining the illusion that the organization as a whole is trustworthy.

MANAGING RISK

Socialization is essential to ensuring that members can be trusted. It is desired both by the participants, who voluntarily select this domain, and by organizational leaders. Only through expertise can one achieve the rewards that belonging entails. Yet once one is in the organization, how is competence socialized? It is risky to share one's activities and organizational identity with the untutored. A tension exists between teaching and shunning a novice. As a result, competence and trustworthiness may be hard to acquire, as experienced members may find it more rewarding to socialize with other experts, rather than serve as teachers of novices.

A set of social and normative pressures encourages voluntary instruction. In practice, expert members teach novices out of the belief that one should repay one's own socialization with the socialization of others (a form of generational justice, crucial to parenting as well), the satisfaction of creating shared interest, the status rewards of contact with those less knowledgeable, and the belief that by creating other experts, one's own community will be extended. In order for the novice to become an expert, he or she must spend time with experts; thus affiliation must develop, sometimes through collective events sponsored by the organization.

When mushrooms, particularly those with toxic counterparts, are to be consumed, providers may be limited to those whose trustworthiness has been validated. For instance, at the national foray, only a small number of experienced mushroomers were selected to pick edible amanitas (*Amanita rubescens*) for the tasting session, and these specimens, part of a family with deadly species, were carefully reviewed by a small identification committee, composed of even more experienced mushroomers.

For mushroomers the protection against danger[93] is social: new members are advised to join a club, take a course, foray with an experienced participant, or have another identify their mushrooms.[94] Novices are often encouraged to attend club meetings, lectures, and forays to gain practical information, simultaneously cementing their attachment to the group. Trust in information provided by the organization and in the members of that community provides a bulwark against danger.[95]

TRANSFORMING TRUST

An individual's experience of trust within a group is altered over time. The organization is transformed from an object of trust to an arena of trusting interactions. When joining an organization, most new members simultaneously express interest and ignorance. As a result, the first goal of membership is information, which is provided by group members. For novices, organizational legitimation is crucial to trust. The group awards status to some members (by role or reputation), and the new member trusts these individuals, perhaps not totally, nor without some anxiety. Without trust, the push to exit is high. Over time, trust becomes based in shared experience, and evaluation depends on topics on which the judge has some expertise. As one becomes more proficient, one develops standards of judgment to evaluate competence and award trust.

The novice at first assumes that "mere" membership bestows a "cloak of competence," in the same way that we give those with professional credentials the benefit of the doubt. Since novices rarely begin with highly dangerous or difficult activities,[96] the advice given, if in error, will likely be relatively inconsequential. For experienced members who engage in more risky activities, trust must be earned. As in work situations,[97] participants must decide if they can trust new colleagues; experienced members evaluate the developing competence of new members before accepting their advice and before developing long-term trusting relationships. One veteran explained:

> If someone I don't know really well comes up and offers me some mushrooms that he just picked, I know enough to know that I want to know what he picked. I know enough that I am not just going to eat anything that somebody hands me.

Testing occurs when experienced members judge whether they should trust novices. One mused: "When we first joined our club we were watched by the long-time members for interest and consistency."[98] Or in the words of another: "The society was filled with friendly people who shook my hand and welcomed me. Then they waited."[99]

The trust derives from the relationship, where "knowing well" and "judging highly" combine to establish a zone of trust. Trust gained can also become trust lost. Should one identify a poisonous mushroom as an edible species, others would remain suspicious until competence had specifically been demonstrated. In most situations, credibility is lost only once,[100] unless the mistake is defined as reasonable.

As one learns, trust that was originally based on organizational position begins to be based upon displayed competence. This change alters the role of the organization from a validator, or an object of trust, to an arena in which trusting relations are enacted and in which organizational interaction serves as its own reward.

Secrecy

Trust, directly connected to mutual support, contributes to cohesion. In general, the more trust, the greater the level of cohesion.[101] Secrecy is not as obviously implicated in the development of group feeling, because, on the surface, it separates individuals. Trust depends on a willingness to share knowledge and experience. Secrecy, like trust, is linked to information and to relationships, but it privileges information[102] and implies that relationships are competitive.[103] If trust is one of the prime synthetic forces of a social system, then secrecy, at first glance, is its analytic equivalent. Trust represents the mid-point between certainty and ignorance—the knowledge to recognize what constitutes legitimate information and who provides it. Secrecy, by contrast, represents the two end-points—keeping knowledge for oneself while keeping others ignorant.

Secrecy may be necessary for smoothing social order,[104] for managing impressions,[105] and for controlling individuals within a group.[106] Even though concealment of information can impose heavy burdens on social systems and individuals,[107] raising questions of ethics and participation, secrecy also protects valued resources. Secret societies represent the institutionalization of secrecy,[108] but in many organizations that are embedded in systems of internal or external competition, secrecy is endemic.[109] One can examine organizational secrecy under two conditions: when members of organizations keep information from those outside the organization (external secrecy),[110] and when they keep information from other members (internal secrecy). My concern is with the latter.

Secrecy is particularly evident in leisure worlds that operate in conditions of scarcity and competition. Despite the communal, subcultural features of leisure, and because of the potential scarceness and zero-sum quality of the quest, mushrooming, like other competitive subcultures,[111] has an air of secrecy. Competitive social worlds are structured so that few see a contradiction between protecting information and establishing close bonds. For mushroomers, resources are scarce and knowledge directly contributes to obtaining these resources. Under these circumstances transaction costs limit the information individuals voluntarily share, unless the relational context outweighs the value of keeping information private.

How can secrecy both divide and unify? How does the existence of a robust and recognized class of secrets within a group—"a community of secret holders"—permit, and even encourage, continued allegiance? Part of the answer involves what Beryl Bellman[112] terms "the paradox of secrecy." This is the fact that secrecy is constituted by the procedures by which secrets are communicated; in other words, the *telling* of secrets in "appropriate" contexts and relations defines secrecy. Secrecy is governed by implicit rules, and is, in this sense, normative. The telling of secrets on certain occasions builds community: with enough members privately communicating secrets, everyone becomes, in time, a secret holder, a secret giver, and a secret recipient. As with trust, information leads to the development of relationships. There is an economy of secrets, by virtue of their breach.

Not all secrets are transmitted. Community is built not only through the occasional spread of information, but also through its keeping. This depends on the assumption that, over time, all members will have secrets, and that none will be without the resources (for example, places to pick mushrooms) necessary to succeed. The underlying assumption is that mushrooming need *not* be a zero-sum game; whereas particular specimens may be picked only once, numerous unpicked mushrooms await energetic collectors.

As noted in Chapter 4, mushroomers describe their experiences in lengthy narratives, excluding relevant details, preventing others from gaining access to the same locales.[113] With all participants operating in this way, a community of secret holders can share triumphs and frustrations, as well as a sense of comradely competition. Relation-ships depend on the existence of privileged information.

Secrecy calls into question the assumption that all in the group have the interests of others at heart.[114] This centrifugal force is mediated in circumstances in which all participants keep secrets from others while sharing protective knowledge. This process has been observed in those occupations, such as commercial fishing, in which individu-als strive for scarce resources but require a general sharing of informa-tion to protect themselves.[115] The voluntary segregation of knowledge among all members of a collectivity preserves relationships. The drawing of boundaries around one's information preserve is expected, and the friendly competition that results is recognized as part of the satisfaction ("fun") of sharing an avocation with people about whom one cares.[116] The recognition of a paradoxical relationship between secrecy and sociability is evident in humor, which reveals ambiva-lence in hiding information in a group that defines itself as a commu-nity. For instance, Jerry, the club president, in adjourning a meeting at the end of morel season, joked: "Why don't you share your favorite spots now that the season is over. We'll put them on slips and next year give everyone a slip. Don't give any bum spots." Of course, noth-ing was done about either of the suggestions; spots were used by members from year to year. The president teased members about sharing, knowing that the absence of sharing made members inter-ested in one another's experiences and narratives.

Members propose an ethical justification for their secrecy, claiming that they enjoy finding mushrooms for themselves, as it provides a sense of personal accomplishment. As one commented:

> Something's worth as much trouble as it takes to get it. This is true of learning to find mushrooms. I've told people to do some searching, and have them put forth an effort so they'd appreciate more.

The assumption is that each member can or should discover mush-rooming spots; although locations are rarely shared, everyone finds mushrooms. This is not entirely true, particularly for new members who haven't found spots and may not even know where to look. As a result, most clubs sponsor forays that provide long-time members with the opportunity to identify and compare a wide range of mushrooms, as well as to socialize with friends, and that teach novices which habitats and natural indicators to look for, so they can develop their own "secrets." Novices quickly learn that, except on forays to public areas, they will not be given specific locations; rather, members share enough general information—about indicators of edible mushrooms—so that novices can discover mushroom spots themselves. Jokes socialize novices to group expectations. When one novice collector asked Jerry where he should go to find morels, Jerry responded: "In the woods." Then he seriously described indicators of morels, such as poison ivy, bed straw, and prickly ash. Once burned, the initiate learns to use similar mocking remarks (and helpful information) to train those who arrive later.

In some sense, finding mushrooms is ultimately a zero-sum game, even though the game can be expanded by the search for new spots. If you pick a patch of mushrooms, no one else can find that same patch, at least in that fruiting. You "own" your spots, particularly since many species appear annually in the same location.[117] They are valuable resources. Morel spots, in particular, are "owned" and are not shared or given lightly because of their scarcity, the short fruiting season, and their economic value. When I asked one mushroomer about his concept of secrecy, he referred specifically to his morel spots:

> [The morel grows] one particular time of the year for a very short time. It happens to be an edible and hard to find, and we work hard to find them. The reason you don't usually just give it to somebody else is the hours it took you to find it. I've put in some tough days.

To share the location of a cache of morels is to risk having the other person reach that location first the following year.

To maintain their spots, some collectors cover the stems of the mushrooms that they have picked with leaves, so that others will not learn that mushrooms grew in the area. Others, recognizing the game, look for piles of leaves as a sign that mushrooms may be underneath. One mushroomer explained that although he tells others the direction he finds morels (for example, "east of here," "way up north," "by the Mississippi"), he will not announce the county in which the mushrooms were found.

The value of secrecy is underlined in humorous attempts to get members to reveal the locations of their finds—particularly of morels.

Once Howard mentioned that he had found a lot of morels the day before. Another club member asked where, and Howard didn't answer at first, then joked that he had "morelitis," adding, "There is a temporary disease which we get called morelitis, which involves a temporary loss of hearing" (that is, when someone asks where you found morels). He explained that he was northeast of Forest Lake, but wouldn't be more specific. This discourse emphasizes shared understandings of mushroom etiquette. One must respect the informational preserve of another, as Helen and June indicated when talking at the national foray about picking morels. Helen (from Minnesota) told June (from Pennsylvania) that she found morels right across from her house. June asked: "Where do you live?" and they both laughed. On another occasion Jerry described a foray that he planned to lead near his summer home: "I won't take you to my favorite [chanterelle] spots, but I will take you to [my friend's] favorite spots."

This concern with respecting the locations of others is also expressed seriously when one is afraid that the person one is addressing might get the wrong idea about the nature of the questioning. On one foray Donna presented some very large sulfur shelves, a prime edible. Dave asked: "Where did you find these?" Then he quickly added: "On what kind of tree?" At the national foray, Mary (who visits Philadelphia often) asked John (from Philadelphia) where he finds mushrooms: "Where do you go outside Philadelphia? You don't have to tell me specifically. I'm just curious." John told her the small city near where he picks. The elaboration of these questions reflects motive talk—justifications and disclaimers—that ratifies shared assumptions about appropriate informational preserves. Without these accounts, the listener could assume the social incompetence of the questioner—either novice status or cultural marginality.

SHARING SECRETS

On occasion, secrecy is breached, underlining the legitimacy of secrecy in other circumstances. Mushroomers do—now and then—share their spots with others. This sharing indicates the boundaries of the normative character of secrecy. In some cases sharing otherwise secret information is a group policy, as when a mycological society schedules a foray to a public place.[118] But the private transmission of "held" information can also occur within a developed or developing relationship. Sharing information becomes linked to relationships.

This sharing reflects a special act of friendship, cementing a social tie, as when Mark told me that he didn't begrudge Jerry the 800–1,000 morels Jerry found on his father's property, because at the end of the previous season Jerry had told him about a morel spot he hadn't used. Mark made exchange explicit within the context of a relationship. He told me: "I must have found fifteen pounds of those things [matsutakes]. It was one of the best mushroom pickings of my life. It was like another world." After he told me he had given the spot to a friend, he added: "I returned an old debt. I had been picking his spots for a number of years."

Sometimes spots are given privately to new members who seem enthusiastic—a symbolic gesture of acceptance and an indication that they are judged to be committed to the activity. In addition, spots may be shared when a mushroomer decides that he or she is no longer interested in picking a particular species or when he or she plans to leave the community, revealing in the gift the "ownership" of the spot and the control over the resource. In the latter case one's mushroom spots are labeled a "legacy" or "heirloom"[119]—analogizing the leisure group to a family. The transfer of this knowledge involves the recipient's acknowledging the status of the giver. As noted, ideally such a gift should be reciprocated through some exchange, for example, the trade of a morel spot for a spot where hen of the woods mushrooms are found, or, in cases of status difference, an expression of respect. Occasionally a member will invite another to a favorite spot for companionship: a "gift" that implies reciprocity.

Belonging does not entitle members to all information; indeed, complete knowledge is outside the legitimate privileges of participation, despite ideals of trust and communion. It represents a tie that transcends organizational membership, albeit one that depends on the organization to give it meaning. On occasion the special relationship implied by the expression of private information may provoke mild friction among members. For example, Jerry told several members that he picked hen of the woods in Theodore Wirth Park. Jerry said that Dave "gave" him the trees one fall when Dave had stopped picking there. Harvey, an older man who lived near the park, was very interested, but when he asked Dave where he found the hen of the woods, Dave was noncommittal: "I just go around everywhere." Harvey tried to get him to be more specific, but Dave remained vague.

The legitimacy of withholding information allows relationships within the club to retain their power, and not be reduced to a homogenized sharing. In addition, limits exist as to how information can be used. Sometimes members give others "limited" access to spots that they themselves still use, as happens when one member is treated as a "guest"; the information that is learned from the invitation is "provisional" and should not be shared or used without permission. For example, Jerry told me that he was annoyed with Howard. He had shown Howard some of his chanterelle spots, and then the next week without telling him, Howard had visited those spots. This particularly annoyed Jerry because the spots were located on someone else's land: "I don't know why he did it. I asked him not to." The guest does not "own" and should not use the secret knowledge.

Expectations, related to the fair distribution of scarce resources, exist as to what information can be kept secret without affecting the trust that is embedded in the relationship. Sharing a secret exemplifies trust among members; for relationships to remain strong the secret must not be abused: personal information enters into a private relationship. In a stable, tight-knit organization a network of such relationships collectively ties members to one another in a complex web. If secrets are localized in a few dyads or small groups, fragmentation or cliques may result.

SOCIALIZATION TO SECRETS

Voluntary organizations face the problem of how to socialize novices to "moral" behavior. If new members wish to be seen as competent, they must learn what knowledge they should reveal to others; the location of their "spots" should remain closely guarded. This flies in the face of an ideology of communion which suggests that nothing should be held back from the "brotherhood." Many enthusiastic new members embrace this perspective, wishing to tell everyone about what they found *and* where they found it. As one mushroomer commented wistfully:

> At first I wanted to share information, but no one else did, so [my wife and I] stopped. It was kinda sad, but it was like putting pearls before swine.

Another described a personal experience that convinced her of the need for secrecy:

> I now practice the same form [of secrecy], which I did not at first . . .
> until I "learned better." I used to show anybody who was interested
> where and how to pick morels and other species . . . until one day I
> showed a person my *Pleurotus ostreatus* log . . . loaded . . . I wanted
> to get a photo of this before harvesting and the person knew this . . .
> but couldn't hold himself back long enough. He had cut off almost all
> the mushrooms before I had safely put the camera and lenses away—
> and the result was I got only a handful of mushrooms off "my own"
> (note I use a possessive phrase for a wild log) log.[120]

This mushroomer is sensitive to the irony of considering public land
"her own," but despite this recognition, she accepts the validity of secrecy, given the structure of the leisure world. Although some feel
that the need for secrecy is unfortunate, its practical value is widely
accepted.

Novices also desire to communicate their spots to prove their competence; in fact, it only announces their novice status, demonstrating
their ignorance of cultural scripts. At one meeting Jerry, the club president, asked if anyone knew any place the club might foray. A woman
in the audience responded: "I know a wonderful place for shaggy
manes . . . Literally thousands and thousands." Jerry joked: "I'll give
you my phone number [meaning he wanted to keep the information
for himself] . . . You don't have to give us your best foray spots." The
spot was not mentioned again. Ms. Mushroom addressed the delicate
issue of secrecy:

> When one returns from the hunt, it is bad form to tell anyone, even
> one's nearest and dearest, the precise location of a Real Find (should
> there be one). The location of a find may be offhandedly reported as
> somewhere within 60 miles of the precise spot.[121]

One should describe the find for the enjoyment of one's colleagues,
but provide little information as to its location. Novices must learn
not to share too much.

Secrecy seems to fly in the face of leisure community, and novices
must quickly recognize that the existence of secrecy does not suggest
the absence of interpersonal and collective concerns.

Leisure organizations help to tame nature, and thus create culture.
Students of leisure traditionally examine personal needs or the demo-
graphics of involvement. In contrast, I emphasize that much leisure

occurs in the context of organizations, and that these structures are undertheorized—in terms of how they gather and provide resources, how differentiation affects organizational decision-making, and how needs for communion and personal satisfaction affect organizational stability.

Dangers clearly exist in generalizing from a single organization, raising the degree to which this organization is similar to other voluntary organizations that support naturework, much less to other leisure activity. Still, this focus on the organizational reality underlines that nature does not stand alone. Although individuals could enter a forest with only their cultural templates (Chapter 1) or with a group (Chapter 3), the reality is that often they do so in the context of an organizational structure. They believe in the value of the organization to which they contribute both time and effort—populating the organization with officers, committee members, and other volunteers.

Although voluntary organizations often face a threat from a lack of formal social control, other features—sociability, expertise, and resources—strengthen bonds among members, and, more significantly, commit them to the organization *per se*. Disputes heed the reality that the organization matters to individuals, that it is worth fighting for. Even those who lose the argument remain members, suggesting that, as with the electorate generally, a loss is not equivalent to a termination of involvement. Leisure organizations provide a means by which interest is transformed to commitment.

In a study of MENSA, the organization for individuals with high IQs, the sociologist Howard Aldrich[122] proposed the existence of a class of groups he termed "sociable organizations." These organizations provide settings in which voluntary "communities of rapport" develop.[123] Groups that engage in serious leisure[124] are particularly inclined to form tight-knit organizations. We join these groups because we choose to. Unlike some voluntary organizations that depend on temporal commitments, in sociable organizations we select the amount of time we wish to spend without serious complications. They are "ungreedy" institutions.[125]

Just as Erving Goffman claimed that games must be fun, participation in a sociable organization must be rewarding over time; the lack of institutional rewards justifies disengagement. Participants' attitude toward the organization differs from that toward the activity itself, which typically has an elaborated rationale. The organization is seen as the means to the end of the activity. Few would suggest that one should continue to participate in a sociable organization that one did not enjoy. In theory the organization is tangential, whereas the activity is essential. How are these organizations that we have examined stabilized? How is group cohesion generated in the face of forces, such as the recognition of danger and secrecy, that militate against continued involvement in group life?

A group must generate trust so that individual members facing danger are literally willing to leave life-and-death decisions in the hands of colleagues (or in other leisure groups, willing to accept information that may be of economic or social consequence). Patterns of interaction create confidence that the other members of the organization (and the organization itself, as reflected in the leadership) share interests and operate to protect one another.[126] This trust is evident even though members compete, hiding information. The information that is hidden could be accessible to all members if they devoted sufficient time and effort; the information that is shared exemplifies the process, though not the outcomes, of successful performance (information on *where* to collect, not *how* and *what* to collect).

Secrecy, though appearing to be centrifugal, binds members together in friendly competition—an arena of fun, reflected in narrative. That others care about the successes and failures of their colleagues suggests that relationships are meaningful. Secrecy provides ground rules for this game, given scarcity and the possibility of effort. Being competitive implies incorporating knowledge and skills that differentiate oneself from others. Participants enjoy their competition and the secrecy that flows from it. Competition permits them to judge themselves against group standards, incorporating the experiences of others. The group trains the novice so that he or she can find collecting spots: a perspective on socialization that assumes that prime mushrooming locations are not scarce, and are limited only by the effort one exerts.

Given the importance of relationships and information preserves, trust in others and shielding of knowledge are compatible. The linkage between trust and secrecy supports group cohesion, while leaving room for personal investment. Collective spheres of knowledge are compatible with private information that in turn creates a satisfying

competitive culture among those who are perceived as sharing interests. The community of secrecy depends on the recognition of trusting relations and on the fact that others can be trusted not to hold
back information that might be protective.

Because mushrooming involves personal risk, trust is especially
important; however, in many, if not most, voluntary worlds (and
many nonvoluntary worlds as well), members rely on others for information that will protect them from costs and embarrassment. A
comparative analysis of dangerous and secure worlds may illuminate
how trust operates similarly and differently in groups. Likewise, the
types of secrecy found in competitive groups (for example, hiding resources or not sharing techniques) affects what information is shared.
Competition is not antithetical to group cohesion but provides a consensual grounding for the establishment of a status system—a basis
for competence on which status is built. Members become friends
over time, and though turnover occurs among peripheral members,
the stability of core members is impressive.[127]

To be sure, the relative influence of trust and secrecy varies among
groups. Groups based on competition and lacking dramatic consequences may give greater weight to secrecy than do groups in which
consequences are real and omnipresent. The relationships within a
group vary as a consequence of the salience of trust and secrecy, even
though each group may be a community grounded in personal commitment that is translated into group cohesion.

Ultimately, the dialectic between individual and group interest can
be resolved through the paradoxical compatibility of private action
and collective concern. Trust and secrecy are pervasive and necessary
features of social order; indeed, they are present in virtually every situation in which interactants care about the actions of others.

Beyond voluntary groups' facilitating dangerous leisure, this linkage of trust and competitive domains belongs to culturally valued
scripts. Open and closed awareness can coexist.[128] Customers often
do not share excessive change with cashiers, and cashiers may be
silent about items of poor quality; yet within their relationship they
expect and trust each other to avoid forgery, violence, gross harass-
ment, and claims of financial dishonesty. In family life, children and
parents are supposed to hide some doings, while ensuring that
their kin are able to pursue life, liberty, and happiness. Even the

relationship between mugger and victim, though filled with surprises and hidden knowledge, often follows a script that parties can trust. For interaction to proceed, trust must exist in its routine grounds, even though information may be withheld that permits parties to achieve their ends in the face of resource competition. Trust and secrecy—open and closed information systems—operate within the same social web.

Fungus and Its Publics

And plants, at whose names the verse feels loath,
Fill'd the place with a monstrous undergrowth,
Prickly and pulpous, and blistering and blue,
Livid, and starr'd with a lurid dew.
And agarics and fungi with mildew and mould,
Started like mist from the wet ground cold;
Pale, fleshy, as if of the decaying dead
With a spirit of growth had been animated.

—PERCY BYSSHE SHELLEY, "THE SENSITIVE PLANT"

No forest is an island. All leisure groups share the wild with those outside their communities. In pursuit of leisure, mushroomers frequently encounter two groups: the general public and professional mycologists. Each views nature (at least this corner of the natural environment) through a different lens.

Robert Stebbins,[1] in a profound analysis of the structure of leisure, argues that for many voluntary pursuits, a Professional-Amateur-Public (PAP) system exists. Stebbins spent fifteen years examining eight groups of amateurs, including those in the arts, the sciences, sports, and entertainment: classical musicians, thespians, archaeologists, astronomers, football players, baseball players, magicians, and stand-up comics. From these cases Stebbins finds regularities in the relationships among amateurs, related professionals, and publics. Stebbins also distinguishes among amateurs who are committed to "serious leisure" (amateur mycologists, modeling themselves on professionals), hobbyists (pot hunters), and career volunteers (volunteers at nature centers).

Stebbins is particularly interested in amateurs as an ideal type. In mushrooming the designation of amateur or hobbyist depends on whether one's focus is on identification (and publishing one's discoveries[2]—a professional concern) or consumption (a hobbyist concern). Many mushroomers include elements of both amateurism and hobbyism in their leisure. Because they wish to acquire knowledge, however, mushroomers interested in "serious leisure" are, by virtue of exploring a previously unknown natural world, protoscientists. To engage in serious leisure one must persevere; have a leisure "career"; diligently gain knowledge, training, or skills; identify with one's pursuit; search for durable benefits linked to the development of the self; and share a subculture.[3]

PUBLIC MYSTERIES

Mushroomers recognize that many outsiders judge their hobby as odd and deride their expertise. Many Americans are mycophobic;[4] they fear mushrooms and mock mushroomers' dangerous and obsessive behavior. Although interest in nature realms is faddish,[5] during my observation, the awakening of interest in the consumption of wild mushrooms, a trend of the 1990s,[6] was only beginning.

Mushroomers see the world as divided into mycophiles and mycophobes. Some understand the natural world well enough to appreciate its bounty, whereas others choose to remain ignorant. One writer stated:

> We mushroomers know there are two kinds of people in the world, mycophiles like ourselves, and otherwise perfectly fine people who, when shown a log full of oyster mushrooms exclaim with distaste: "You're going to eat *that?*"[7]

The psychedelic psychologist and philosopher Andrew Weil remarked: "How convenient it is . . . for mycophiles to collect mushrooms on the property of mycophobes."[8] Brian once joked that it is easy to pick mushrooms on other people's property, because "people think you are a crazed fool with a knife." One mushroomer who patiently let a psychedelic mushroom (*Gymnopilus spectabilis* or "big laughing gym") grow in New York City's Central Park mused that adolescents who spend thousands of dollars on drugs are unaware of the free treasures at hand. The limits of public knowledge of an opaque natural environment serve hobbyists' interests. The ignorance of most citizens both supports the identity of mushroomers and permits them to collect treasures. Yet being unable to share one's enthusiasm with others limits one's pleasure, as in this moving account of mother-daughter interaction:

> The young mycophobe insisted that her long, flimsy skirt and open sandals were not the proper attire for mushroom hunting and she complained mercilessly about the brambles and poison oak. But by early afternoon, her pores were soaked with sun and wine; she had shed her sandals and was flying through the fields. Laden with their lilac [blewit] harvest and heady with joy, mother and daughter staggered back to the car and headed for their final feast—dinner at the elegant restaurant run by Domaine Chandon. . . . [The] daughter pointed to the Cote de veau aux morilles, paying homage to her mother's long-ignored passion for morels. Her maternal visitor made no comment, reluctant to break the spell. . . . The dinner was beyond expectation, each bite eliciting breathless superlatives. Suddenly, when the waiter came to clear the table, our letter-writer gained a clear view of her daughter's plate which had been previously hidden by the vase of tulips. "What's the matter"? her daughter asked, noting the pained expression. Speechless, her mother could barely manage to point to the blackish mound piled neatly on the side of the plate. "Oh, is that all?" her daughter asked. "You know I hate mushrooms."[9]

For mushroomers this qualifies as a "sad tale," not merely an amusing anecdote. Yet those who attempt to spread their enthusiasm often repeat stories just like it.

The avid amateur must cope with the skepticism of a public that assumes any participant is "weird,"[10] a rejection made particularly potent because of the assumption of a death wish.[11] Many participants feel labeled; mushroomers see themselves as classified into "Genus: *Weird*."[12] One explained: "The rest of society considers us unusual and we have to make light of it":

Bridget: A lot of people who aren't interested in getting out, even friends of mine, say, "Oh, what are you going to get mushrooms for? I'd never taste any of those, or do anything like that."

GAF: What do you think the general public thinks about mushroomers?

Bridget: We're crazy! Even people I work with think I'm crazy for going out and picking mushrooms.

GAF: What have they said?

Bridget: "Oh, are you really going to eat that? I'd never do that!" They are critical, but they think I'm a little crazy anyway. Mostly just the people who aren't outdoorsy people to begin with.

GAF: How does your family feel about your mushrooming?

Bridget: My daughter thinks I'm crazy. "Why are you doing this?"

I immediately called my parents and told them [about my interest in mushrooms], and they thought this was far crazier than anything I had ever called them about [laugh]. . . . They're waiting for me to grow up and get through this phase. You don't know what it is to grow up in a mushroom-phobic family. . . . When I go home now I can bring any mushrooms I want . . . and cook any mushrooms I want, if I bring my own pots and pans [big laugh]. (taped transcript)

Mushroomers adopt this attitude as a defense. In the past I have jokingly referred to "Fine's Law of Shared Madness,"[13] whereby groups often present to observers and one another the knowing claim that they are "crazy," "mad," or "addicted." Those engaged in naturework cope with the lack of amenities and the thorns and brambles, cold and heat of an "authentic reality."[14] For mushroomers, this is given additional piquancy because of public reaction. Thus Don joked to me, an observer: "How do we shape up? We're pretty normal for being weird," at which the others laughed.

These subcultural accounts—often parodies of psychological or medical discourse—allege insanity of a kind, but carry the underlying message that the joys of the activity overwhelm what seems at first bizarre behavior (as one mushroomer put it, discovering mushrooming is "like falling in love"[15]):

MYCOSIS: A mental neurosis resulting from an over-enthusiastic interest in fungus life. Mycosis can be chronic but not fatal—as long as mycophagists watch their diets. Mycosis neurosis seems to cause a series of ailments, among them shortsightedness (although this is not proven, there does seem to be a high rate of accidents as mushroomers can't see beyond what's on the ground under their noses); late evenings spent over ID books; restless nights as one dreams about the "elusive mushroom"; then there's the compelling need to spend hours out in the woods on the Hunt; and the lower back pains caused by bending over picking mushrooms. Now, mycosis sufferers of America, is this all worth it????[16]

My name is Dianne, and I am a myco-maniac. I am married to Jerry, who is also a myco-maniac. . . . On a cold, rainy day in early spring or late fall you will find the myco-maniac wandering through the forest, shaking with cold and soaking wet and so excited at the promise of finding the first morel or the last *Armillaria ponderosa* [matsutake, now *Tricholoma magnivelare*] that he doesn't even notice the physical discomfort. A normal person would be sitting in a warm house, looking out the window with dismay at the dreary weather. . . . If you happen to know a MM please be kind and understanding. And be *careful*—the disease can be highly contagious.[17]

There has been increasing notice of a mood disorder amongst mycophiles. The condition, which has been noted for centuries, is known as involutional mushroomcholia. . . . In its most benign form the afflicted are quite obvious with their highly active verbalizing, socializing and foraging behavior. As for the beginner with the full syndrome of mushroom fever . . . there is no known effective treatment other than adaptation through continued exposure to mushroom hunting along with monthly group support through the society meetings.[18]

Having done a case study of the female amateur mycologist, I have arrived at the following conclusions:

1. Mushroom hunting is addictive. [As] with Cocaine, the hunter begins slowly, just daring to venture forth. As she becomes more comfortable, she attempts large amounts until finally she is uncontrollable. . . . By the end of the first year her refrigerator is stocked only with mushrooms. Her children are unfed. Her house smells of rotting fungi. And there are no glasses for drinking. They are all spread out on the diningroom table covering spore prints. . . .

4. Once you begin, you are committed for life. If you are prepared to eat, sleep, talk, walk and act like a mushroom, then you should consider mushroom hunting. . . . I, like many other daughters of mushroom hunters have been ill-fed, ignored, neglected and

abandoned. . . . [That] I discovered my new white pants covered with spore prints, however, makes it impossible for me to continue to suffer in silence.[19]

This fictionalized compulsion—with the mushroomer in the position of the Other—is amusingly portrayed in a personal narrative, which can be told because its audience recognizes both its likely factual falsity and its symbolic truth.

One member of a mushrooming club reported on a most unusual visiting day at her son's camp in New Hampshire:

> It was a beautiful place, set deep in the forest of mostly conifers, some hardwoods. I didn't get to see much of my son, but I've never seen so many mushrooms. . . . It was hard to keep my mind on what I was supposed to be there for and every once in a while, I would hear a voice, "mom, mom, where are you?" Later I was severely and justifiably admonished: "What," he said, "am I going to tell my friends when they ask me why my mother didn't come to visit."[20]

Of course, the public attitude is not only that the mushroomer is compulsive, but that the activity is profoundly dangerous and even that the quest for mushrooms is "evil." Emily Dickinson referred to mushrooms as nature's Judas Iscariot, and Arthur Conan Doyle saw mushrooms as reflecting disease:

> A sickly autumn shone upon the land. Wet and rotten leaves reeked and festered under the foul haze. The fields were spotted with monstrous fungi of a size and colour never matched before—scarlet and mauve and liver and black—it was as though the sick earth had burst into foul pustules. Mildew and lichen mottled the walls and with that filthy crop, death sprang also from the watersoaked earth.

Although others, including John Cage and Robert Penn Warren, have seen mushrooms as benign, the mistrust of mushrooms has deep roots.[21] Many parents warn their children about the danger of touching fungi:

> Willy Postma picked her first mushroom when she was 8 years old, on a bicycle tour near her home in Amsterdam. "It was beautiful," she says of the fly agaric (*Amanita muscaria*). But her father didn't think it was beautiful, and didn't even want her touching it. "Don't put your fingers in your mouth," he said, "or you'll die."[22]

"Don't touch the toadstools, they're poisonous," my mother would warn me, and then make me wash my hands. That year, or perhaps the next, men came on horseback to search for an old woman who'd become lost in the woods. . . . She had been collecting mushrooms in a wicker basket and failed to return the night before. "Probably ate a poison mushroom and died," my father muttered sadly as they rode off.[23]

Mushroom magazine abstracted an article that counsels parents to have their children play "Stamp That Mushroom." Children compete to see who can stomp on the largest number of new mushrooms each morning, reducing potential poisoning and the following year's mushroom crop.[24] Even the august *New York Times* editorial writers, normally passionate about natural pursuits, make an exception in the case of wild mushrooms:

You can cash in your chips by eating an Amanita "toadstool" by mistake. So when the autumn leaves, in purples, reds and yellows, skate gently down and cover all the brown and red and orange mushrooms—greenish "death cap," creamy "poison pie," and white "destroying angel," as well as the luscious vermillion and golden chanterelles that are so good to eat—we feel some relief. Certain risks, decisions and ways of living high and dangerously have been postponed until next spring.[25]

Some might find it odd that nature enthusiasts couldn't tell a golden chanterelle from a white destroying angel, since the two are totally different in size, shape, and color, but such is the fear of wild knowledge. This fear is shared with mushroomers:

[A friend] said, "I worried about you all summer." When the mushroom season was over, she said, "Oh, I don't have to worry about you anymore." But when I told her that I had put some [mushrooms] in the freezer, she said, "Oh, for god sake!"

I remember talking to my officemate, who was totally afraid and scared [of some mushrooms he had picked]. I mean, seeing these objects and saying, "You better not eat those." . . . [My family was] frankly fearful. And I remember joking with my mother at the time, saying, "Listen, when I was a kid I had to eat all sorts of strange things that you said were OK, like okra and eggplant, and so forth, and I trusted you and won't you trust me now?" Absolutely not.

On a visit to a friend in California, Meg planned to eat some inky caps, which are easily identifiable. The friend, who was going to work, told her: "I'll give you my number at work so you can tell 911." These comments, along with laws against trespassing and government restrictions on mushroom picking, remind us that for a large segment of the public mushrooming is "morally controversial leisure,"[26] a position that it shares with hunting, parachuting, and other pursuits that allegedly are cruel or dangerous. Mushroomers do what they can to counter this view, and many clubs sponsor "fungus fairs" that expose the public to the diversity of fungus as well as to the sponsoring organization. Feature writers and television reporters sometimes contact mushroom societies and, in the stories that result, present a favorable, if cautious, portrayal of them.

One local triumph for mushroomers was the Minnesota state legislature's naming the morel the state mushroom, even though the legislators had to endure ridicule as a result. Minnesota is apparently the only state with a state mushroom; the state legislature of Pennsylvania explicitly decided against such a symbol. Public awareness does not necessarily imply public support.

SELLING THE WOODS: THE MUSHROOM WARS

With the increase in consumption of wild mushrooms in the United States and the long-standing desire for certain species in Japan (matsutakes) and Europe (chanterelles), the broadest—and most controversial—linkage between mushroomers and their public involves the commercial sale of mushrooms: transforming one's private preserve into a factory producing "luxury goods" for outsiders. During the past decade, commercial picking and "overpick" have been seen as a social issue—at least within this leisure world. Mushroomers wonder whether the day will come when so many mushrooms have been picked that the future supply of fungi is jeopardized. Will overpick affect the mycelium of mushrooms? Will the decisions of individuals combine to destroy the community?

The last decade and a half has been difficult for the Pacific Northwest. The recessions of the early 1980s and early 1990s hit hard, and they were coupled with the downsizing of defense industries and restrictions on timber companies. For much of the period unemployment was high. Asian immigrants also settled in the region, creating further employment pressures. These economic strains were tied to the growth of an international economy and an increasing interest in exotic edibles. Local residents scoured the woods for chanterelles and matsutakes to ship—canned or dried—to Europe and Asia. The image of hired hands (often Asian immigrants) harvesting American forests for Japanese and German elites, perhaps permanently altering the environment through overpick, is profoundly threatening.[27] It remains unclear whether any significant, lasting environmental damage is being done, but considerable heat has been generated. With the growth of wild mushroom sales,[28] these issues will remain salient until commercial morel, chanterelle, matsutake, and truffle farming is feasible.

In contrast to Washington and Oregon, the debate in California focuses on private entrepreneurs—naturalists themselves—who pick mushrooms and sell them to restaurants or gourmet shops, "turning traitor" to the ideology of nature as a sacred space separate from commerce. This represents a classic instance of the construction of a social problem, with all sides using their own perspectives as they define the situation. The problem is not objectively constituted but subjectively established through a set of moral concerns.[29] As often occurs, debate merges self-interest with ideological beliefs, using salient images to persuade. As one mushroomer joked: "The way I think about it, is to prohibit everybody collecting mushrooms except me."[30] But the issue is about more than which mushroomers will benefit; it is also about the relations among pickers, their public, and the wild. What rights does the public have to use nature?

Little systematic evidence exists that the ecosystem, certainly in the United States, has been damaged by the excessive harvesting of mushrooms; some species "prefer" disturbed areas. Yet it seems plausible that tromping in the woods and raking mushrooms should—over time—alter the ecological balance. The argument fits a "cultural logic," even if the primary support is anecdotal. The image of overpick has come to have symbolic significance for the debate over picking mushrooms, as similar concerns earlier motivated restrictions on hunting and fishing.[31] Some state parks and national forests are now closed to the collection of all fungi, regulations that are, in practice, only sporadically enforced. Restrictions on the activity of mushroomers seem to be growing, as the danger of overpick increasingly seems plausible, even in the absence of definitive evidence.

Although the Minnesota club did not debate this issue (large-scale commercial picking is not a problem in that state), mushroomers in California, Washington, and Oregon were divided by it. A knowledgeable observer of West Coast clubs explained:

> People who were friends now are hardly speaking. Marty Cruse won election [to the presidency of the Mycological Society of San Francisco], because he said we cannot allow this woman [his opponent] to become president of the club because she is violently opposed to the commercial collection of mushrooms, and she is going to tear this club apart, because people are going to leave the club because there are so many people involved in, in one way or another, either picking the mushrooms or buying them in the marketplace.

The North American Mycological Association, which serves a diverse membership, chose not to take a position, but only "to study the problem."[32] One NAMA officer explained:

> NAMA has stayed out of that controversy, and I'm hoping that it won't require any sort of national position, although we do have people interested in somehow organizing licensing, and there's a lot of opposition to that.

Aside from the desire to unite the organization, members feared that any regulation might apply to all amateurs.[33] If nature is to be preserved in order to protect the environment—the heart of the critics' argument—could this position be generalized to all pickers? How does one protect nature from only the "bad guys?" Were only large, foreign corporations involved, without the presence of American entrepreneurs committed to mushrooming, the debate would surely have been more one-sided. The issue is about not just which mushroomers will benefit, but also the proper linkage of humans, woods, and markets.

Ideologies and experiences provide a schema for proposing solutions to environmental management. The debate about commercial harvesting of wild mushrooms can be understood in light of the three alternative templates of how human actors should treat the wild: protecting, embracing, or using it. Each suggests a different orientation as to how the woods should be treated and how they should be linked to economic realities.

Protecting the Wild

Those who object to the commercial collection of mushrooms argue that mushrooms must be "protected" from commercial picking: both mushroom species and the woods themselves (through ecological links) are harmed by large-scale collecting. One Sierra Club member proclaimed that to permit *any* collecting amounts to "opening a Pandora's box," asserting that "the environment . . . is nobody's to touch."[34]

Nature in this view is vulnerable rather than robust, legitimating a need for protection. Of course, how much change constitutes *change,* and what kinds of changes are desired, are disputed within the community. Some mushroomers feel strongly about the "destruction" of the woods:

> "It's a crime!" I hear an angry voice behind me. A timid-looking woman from Seattle who has been quiet for most of the evening is engaged in heated debate with a group of people gathered around her. "They're depleting the forests. They're raping the land. Do you know that a single company last season collected over 210 tons of chanterelles? A single company!" "Overpicking causes fruiting failure," somebody else adds, "In Europe they've had to regulate the days, hours, and numbers of people who pick mushrooms. And that can happen here if we're not careful." Others add their voices: "Mushrooms nourish trees. Without them, there is ecological holocaust."[35]

Rape! Holocaust! These critics are exercised about powerful dangers. The label *overpick*[36] similarly represents real danger:

> When the role of the "lowly" fungus is properly understood, it is clear that their existence, no matter which species, is absolutely necessary for maintaining the health of the forest. Pickers picking for the "fast-buck" do not always take proper care for the habitat of the mushroom (or its edibility). . . . What many do not realize is the delicate balance of the forest eco-system.[37]

This rhetoric involves claims of extinction and habitat protection, as when a mushroomer implausibly defines his area as "one of the last ecological niches for the wild chanterelle in the northern hemisphere," and arises from the speaker's seeing "my own chanterelle patches devastated."[38] That ecological destruction is often not recognized until *after* the damage has been done makes the claim more compelling. As the environmentalist Karel Deller recounts: "In this country, fishing, hunting game and logging are all controlled, but sometimes only after major environmental damage has occurred. Remember the American Bison, the sardines of Monterey, [and] the Passenger Pigeon."[39] The image of habitat loss makes a powerful argument for protection.

Embracing the Wild

To embrace nature is to appreciate the purity of the other, not to desecrate it. One belongs to a community and does not exploit that community. This argument suggests that the values that are brought into collecting could contaminate the romantic oneness of the world. When commercial mushrooming is grounded in greed—when collectors are not at one with the ecosystem—it is wrong. These arguments enshrine the amateur and his or her "loving" relationship with the forest as central to forest management.[40] "Overpick" depicts the excesses of those who care little about the moral effects of their actions.

From this perspective commercial collecting suggests a lack of moral balance. Nature is not treated with respect. The mushroomer is a stakeholder in the ecological system. Mushroomers object to those "who wish to take advantage of a delightful hobby for personal greed and gain."[41]

The morality of amateur mushrooming depends on a belief in oneness with nature. The commercial harvesting of chanterelles and matsutakes dispels the illusion of oneness, drawing a dividing line between "right" and "wrong":

> We enjoy mushrooming because it is a way . . . to enjoy nature in an unexploitable way. Somehow the idea of commercializing this pastime is unacceptable.[42]

> You don't want your activity to turn into a big commercial venture, and there are people who . . . are very sensitive about it, and they want to see mushrooms kept out of the arena of money. Mushrooming is a pure activity. It has nothing whatever to do with making a

buck. They don't want to see people turn into buck makers, 'cause that will degrade mushrooms for everyone.

This argument is distinct from the protectionist view in that it addresses not how commercial mushrooming affects ecosystems, but how it affects the relationship of naturalists and the wild. For those with the luxury of keeping their leisure noncommercial and unsullied, the woods should be temples, not markets.

Using the Wild

Whereas those opposed to commercialization connect the "problem of overpick" to the rhetorical division between altruistic "white hats" and greedy "black hats,"[43] harvesters and their supporters reject this imagery, denying the existence of a problem. They define themselves as naturalists, and have developed their own altruistic justifications. They claim that their actions differ little, except in scale, from those of the purest amateurs, who also use the forest from self-interest. They provide a service to those otherwise without access to the wild: the elderly, the handicapped, and the busy. Commercial collectors *mediate* nature.

Commercial collectors embrace a conservation ethic, grounded in stewardship:[44]

> Larry Stickney, the portly ex-president of the [Mycological Society of San Francisco], announces, "I can find no commandment that says"—he pauses—"thou shalt not pick and sell wild mushrooms." "Once a mushroom drops its spores"—another voice joins in—"its only job is to be picked and eaten." "Sounds to me more like a problem of etiquette," suggests Gary Lincoff . . . president of the North American Mycological Association . . . "than a problem of ecology."[45]

One mushroom collector, noting the division between commercial distributors and amateurs, suggested that, within limits, nature is for humans to use:

> [Mushrooming] is not a passive use of nature, but it's not something that nature can't handle. We have the right to use nature . . . It's not the same as scouring. There are limits. . . . It's a public good. . . . You have a right to use [land to pick mushrooms], but you don't have the right to abuse it.

Commercial harvesting permits mushroomers to appreciate the wild for personal benefit, aligning work with leisure. One writer asserted: "It is a way to capitalize on our own mushroom lore, our knowledge of habitat, and our initiative to bring in a little extra bakshish [money]."[46] An entrepreneur explained: "I want to make part of my living from collecting and selling mushrooms while respecting nature and earning the respect of my peers."[47]

These hunters also legitimate their actions with an explicitly humanistic rhetoric of social justice, claiming that they provide goods for those without access, "sharing a wonderful, unique experience with a lot of people who would never find [mushrooms]." They are not greedy but generous. A commercial collector reminded his critics:

> Four or five people get a chance to enjoy wild mushrooms for every pound I collect. Far more people in the U.S. have savored these wild fruits in the last five years through commercial collection than through mycological society-sponsored collection. I'd remind hobbyists that *all* the people in the U.S. who pay taxes are supporting the parks and public lands where wild mushrooms are found in astounding quantities. The general public has a right to taste wild mushrooms too, and the most available route is through the work of commercial collectors like me. I think too many of the critics of commercial collecting are motivated by selfish interest, i.e., keeping the goodies for themselves and their friends. They want their private preserve funded with public money.[48]

Another wrote: "One day when I can perhaps no longer go out and gather my own, I want to assure would-be suppliers the freedom to engage in the business of providing them for me as some are now doing for others."[49] These collectors suggest that selling mushrooms is linked to an equitable distribution of public resources. The woods belong to everyone through the mediation of the commercial collector.

The "problem" of overpick is constituted through social actors who draw upon a set of schemas that aligns them with the environment, and through these schemas they organize the experience of nature. Protecting nature, embracing nature, and using nature are models for thinking about and constructing environmental problems—connecting one's experience to the wild. Which schemas are emphasized is a consequence of individual histories, social place-ment, and situated features of effective rhetoric. But in every case the response is mediated through both idealized images of the environ-ment and personal desires.

The Battle over Licensing

The debate over commercial collecting often is played out in the arena of governmental intervention. Should limits be placed on what one can do with one's finds? Should collecting be unlimited? As noted, in some parks and forest lands, particularly on the West Coast, limits exist as to where and when mushrooms can be picked; some parks limit the number of pounds one can pick, others require per-mits, and still others ban picking altogether.[50] Health departments are now considering whether restrictions or quality controls should be placed on mushrooms to be sold. Amateurs have increasingly orga-nized themselves as political actors in these disputes.[51] If mushrooms are a "social good," then agents of state control may be obligated to regulate them, and mushroomers want a say in this process that af-fects their leisure directly.

Although I imagined that there would be sizable opposition to all control, I discovered that a substantial minority of the Minnesota club (47 percent) believed that "the government should regulate those who sell mushrooms." (I assume that the figure would be lower if the issue were regulating those who pick mushrooms.) In the national NAMA sample, 74 percent supported government regulation of mushroom sales.[52] Regulations to control the sale of wild mushrooms have been established in Berkeley, California,[53] and have been considered both by the Food and Drug Administration and by the state of Washington.

Those who oppose regulations argue that no social problem ex-ists—consumers, after all, have not be poisoned by wild mushrooms. This is coupled with a libertarian hostility to regulation, and the claim that establishing a system of control would be a bureaucratic nightmare. On the latter issue, one opponent asks:

> What constitutes a "properly qualified specialist?" Who would over-see the training, testing and licensing of such persons, including periodic "refresher" courses? What would be the cost of administering the program? Of obtaining the licenses? How would the regulations

affect the prices and availability of wild mushrooms? What safeguards would exist against corruption, favoritism and bureaucratic overkill? What kind of penalties are envisioned for violations of the regulations? Who would administer them? Would there be a means of appeal?[54]

After raising this litany of questions, the author concludes that no need has been demonstrated for such measures. It is easier to set up regulations requiring permits for collecting than to create a bureaucratic infrastructure to judge which specimens can be sold.

The absence of "blood on the floor" has never prevented social-problem entrepreneurs from making a case for regulation. The absence of deceased diners leads proponents of regulation to speak of hypothetical terrors, using "near tragedies" as grounds for action.

Perhaps the most potent argument is that sellers and buyers are not sufficiently competent to protect consumers. The following "horror tales" exemplify the claimed dangers in a "free" market in which expertise is absent:

> An unknown person . . . asked for help identifying a bagful of what he was "certain" were chanterelle mushrooms. He intended on setting up a roadside stand and selling them to passersby. Upon examination of the contents of a plastic bag, Martin informed the person that there was not one chanterelle in the collection, he had a mixed bag of mostly Russulas and a hodge-podge of miscellaneous species in mostly poor condition.[55]

In a similar vein, Brian told the club that a Twin Cities hotel served lobster mushroom in their dishes, but did not have anyone on staff with the expertise to judge the mushrooms purchased.[56] He noted ruefully: "So when you get yourself poisoned, you can chalk it up to French cuisine." The death of a prominent Washington, D.C., chef from consuming poisonous mushrooms that he had picked was used to argue that the public needs to be protected.

This debate suggests that if natural objects are to be used, they must first be judged by experts, and thus culturally tamed. Those who argue that few wild mushrooms should be sold set the standards high, often bootstrapping an environmental ethic with their concern for public health. Others are more likely to assume that collectors are competent. Regulation of the sale of agricultural products (for example, beef) and wild meat (for example, game) suggests that "natural" objects routinely require inspection—as much because of mistrust of human judgments and decisions as because of a perceived danger from the object itself. Wild mushrooms, potentially poisonous, and wild mushroomers, potentially incompetent, are targets for the protective power of state control.

AMATEURS AND PROFESSIONALS

Amateur status has advantages and disadvantages. Amateurs act out of love. Yet enthusiasm often conflicts with technical competence that may overwhelm passionate advantages. If one doesn't find leisure satisfying, why bother? Exit costs are minimal. Because of differing structures of professional work and amateur leisure, the standards for competence in each differ.[57]

Whereas mushroomers know much more than their publics, standing above them are professional mycologists whose expertise, in some domains, brooks little dispute. Amateurs inhabit the world of forests, whereas professionals are found in laboratories. Amateurs depend on their wits, whereas professionals need technology (for example, computers and electronic microscopes) and techniques (for example, using chemical reagents and herbarium collections). Members of the two groups rarely meet except at forays and at club meetings, where the professionals are invited guests.[58] Most amateurs have little interest in the writings of professionals, unless those professionals write fieldguides (for example, Alexander Smith, Orson Miller, Nancy Smith Weber, and Kent McKnight). Within mycology those interested in taxonomy and morphology (and those who study large, fleshy fungi) have more to share with amateurs than do those interested in plant pathology or cell structures.

Professional mycologists, separated from the world of amateurs, are situated within their own social world: applied or university science. As members of a "discipline," mycologists are treated by some colleagues the way that amateurs are treated by some of their public: they are tarred for having focused on an odd, trivial, and unpleasant corner of the world. As the writer Sara Ann Friedman explains:

> In the scientific world, professional mycologists are the bit players while astrophysicists and microbiologists are the superstars. As a

science, at least in this country, the study of fungi still receives some of the contempt that fungi themselves have suffered over the centuries.[59]

At the time of my research, no American university had a Department of Mycology; mycologists were housed in biology, botany, or plant pathology departments. Within mycology, I was told that those who study the taxonomy of large fleshy fungi (the concern of serious amateurs)[60] have particularly low standing, and jobs for their students at major teaching institutions are rare. Perhaps their scholarship is perceived as being too close to work that any committed amateur could achieve with sufficient effort. This drives some mycologists to more esoteric ("scientific") topics, and drives others to the arms of amateurs, who revere them as "gods"—in contrast with their colleagues, who deride their work as pointless. This further separates amateurs from professional scientists, as real scientists gain status by the elaboration of technique.[61]

Although I did not conduct a survey, I was surprised by the small number of professional mycologists I met who chose their field on the basis of an adolescent fascination with mushrooms. Most mycologists found their specialties through an interest in biology, with the chance connection with a mentor or the opportunity for research support. One respected mycologist specializing in boletes, a choice edible, has eaten only one, which he described as "worse than eating oysters."[62] A pair of professional mycologists tell a similar story:

> A mycologist was carrying away a box of chanterelles after the collection was duly recorded on the species list by the official recorder. Just as he was about to dump the specimens into the growing pile of excess mushrooms, a small, wiry woman from New York City rushed up to him and demanded to know what he was going to do with those mushrooms. After being told, the woman indignantly asked, "How could you do that to such delicious mushrooms?" Whereupon she immediately whisked the box away from the man and retreated to a bench underneath a large tree, where she patiently sorted and cleaned all of the mushrooms. After drying the mushrooms, she took them back to the city with her, where it is rumored that she is still enjoying the fruits discarded by the chagrined mycologist.[63]

Despite their different goals, a link remains between amateurs and professionals.

Amateur Support

The primary way in which amateurs aid professionals is through collections and field observations. A mycologist interested in a particular species informs amateurs of this interest, and uses them as eyes and hands. Because this requires advanced knowledge (professionals would not need help in collecting common species), only a few serious amateurs participate in these long-distance collaborations. Those who do take part speak proudly of their work.[64] One mushroomer aptly described amateurs:

> The amateurs have lots of enthusiasm and go lots of places, get out and collect, and the more well-informed bring in interesting things to pros. Pros get a chance to look at material they may never get a chance to see, and there's a common bond.

Amateurs at regional or national forays provide specimens for professionals to study. At forays specimens are found almost by chance—participants collect whatever happens to be fruiting and defined as interesting. As noted, though occasionally a previously unidentified mushroom is collected, few professionals leave with intriguing fungi. Yet the idea that "you've got so many pairs of eyes going so many places" is compelling. In theory, the amateurs do "the dirty work" of mycology; all they ask in exchange is a set of names for the more obscure of these gifts.

Amateurs also engage in projects that contribute to knowledge but may not be suitably scientific for professionals. One mycologist joked when I asked what amateurs could do for him: "They can get sick on poisonous mushrooms," recognizing that much of our knowledge of toxicity derives from personal experience. A professional noted:

> Contributions amateurs have made and can make are very valuable, and [are ones] that no one else can make by [collecting] information about seasonal occurrence, about edibility, and about all sorts of things about cooking mushrooms, and about the folklore of mushrooms, and about the uses and the medical significance of mushrooms. I think [amateurs are] some of the real authorities on the drug uses of mushrooms. . . . They can also provide obscure information. If you're giving a speech and you want to know if anyone ever has eaten a stinkhorn egg, someone almost always has, and you can find out how it tastes without having to [taste] it.

Professionals are unlikely to define these topics as within their domain, but the topics nevertheless contribute to knowledge.

Finally, amateurs provide support, esteem, and friendship (and, sometimes, room and board) for professionals who engage in field collecting.[65] Amateurs represent a steadfast support network for professionals.[66] According to one professional, "Amateurs can increase the popular support for scientific studies of all kinds. Scientists of all stripes are not the most economically popular people in the world. They don't get much support, and amateurs are very important in increasing this kind of support." Although mycologists have not used this resource, support for the space program and the Hubble telescope by amateur astronomers was effective in convincing legislators that these programs had a public.

Professional Support

Just as amateurs can help the professional's quest for information, the professional provides information and support to the amateur. I have mentioned how fieldguides abetted the development of this leisure pursuit. More generally, the amateur wants the professional to teach— to mediate a scientific discourse of nature so that the narrative is clear. The lectures of professionals at forays, when successful, are humorous and not burdened with detail. If a little knowledge is dangerous, a lot is tedious. The problem of inviting a guest mycologist (or Great Man) is recounted by a droll foray chair:

> In addition to rubbing shoulders with a live famous mycologist, forayers generally expect a lecture about some absorbing topic. In your early negotiations with the guest mycologist, he may proudly propose speaking on "Observations on the Inhibitory Action of Hydrolyzed Agar and Increasing Potencies of Enzymes Produced by Aspergillus Niger." You are then called upon to suggest discreetly that a more general topic, such as "The Mushroom and How to Find It" might prove more entertaining. A whole lot more. An amicable compromise usually results in a nice short title such as "Cortinarius" or "Boletes" or whatever agaricale interests the guest mycologist at this stage of his career.[67]

The professional should provide information that is protective (from danger), useful (for edibility), and notable (for retelling). Professionals wish to educate amateurs—teaching them about cell structure, use of reagents or magnification, or apparently "insignificant" fungi—but they must do this in a context that invites even the most naive of questions. Summer workshops and lectures at forays and meetings serve this purpose, and occasionally provide supplementary income for the underpaid academic.

The few professional mycologists who treasure the company of amateurs and are willing to teach them (and even admit that they learn from them)—professors like Alex Smith, Harry Thiers, and Dan Stuntz[68]—are revered by amateurs. For instance, one amateur described taking a course with Thiers as "not unlike taking piano lessons from Paderewski."[69] Another treasured attending a professional foray, describing it as "going into the woods with a lot of morels with a very small basket"; that is, being exposed to more information than he could ever retain.

On rare occasions direct collaboration occurs between professional and amateur,[70] bolstering the self-image of the amateur. One serious amateur, who has contributed to mycology, described himself as a "semi-pro mycologist . . . comparable to semi-pro ball players whom Murphy's Bar & Grill pays five bucks a game and all the beer they can drink."[71] Another serious amateur, an expert on amanitas and an official mushroom identifier at forays, considered himself a "long-distance graduate student" and was honored by a professional co-authorship.[72]

At its best, the relationship between amateur and professional is symbiotic ("mycorrhizal"); each depends on the other in a mutually beneficial connection. Each is, in a sense, a public for the other.

The Limits of Allegiance

Despite their rapport, amateurs and professionals have different goals, levels of expertise, and perspectives, which can lead to conflict. Amateurs wish and expect professionals to be omniscient and continually willing to serve their needs, especially at forays, to which they are invited as paid or subsidized guests. This transforms the autonomous professional into a service worker.

Although professionals are given great status, this status comes at a cost. Mushroomers speak of the relationship between professionals and amateurs as that of "gods and goons." The amateur goon brings his or her finds ("sacrifices") to the mycological god to name and bless, and allows him to skim off the rare ones for later study. Amateurs may feel awed and ashamed of their ignorance, as well as frustrated by the fact that the god removes the best mushrooms for personal study. They may feel that though they have learned the name of the mushrooms, they have not learned how to identify them in the absence of the expert; nor have they learned how science operates. Professionals in turn feel that they are being used as naming machines, without recognition of their scholarly depth, what one professional labeled "vulturism." The phrase "god and goons" suggests that neither group is defined as fully human.

This relationship is complicated by the type of knowledge that most mycologists have. Although there are (or were) a few whose knowledge of fungi is broad, most professionals are more limited in their expertise, particularly without the aid of their equipment. Ignorance and disputed answers are common:

> When I give up on books and go to the experts at a foray, the real fun begins: each one comes up with a different name for my solitary mushroom, followed by a dubious "maybe . . . I'd have to study it"— and I walk away with my ignorance, feeling blissfully like an expert.[73]

> It's self-defeating to make an absolute determination that if you have a "Dr." in front of your name, everything you say is right, and, if you don't, whatever you say is not right. That's obviously not true. If you stick around for more than twenty minutes, you will find out that you may get a more satisfactory answer sometimes from a person who . . . may not be a professional than you might get from someone who is very narrowly trained in one of the very specialized areas. . . . A professional is really kind of threatened when asked to look at things like medicinal properties of mushrooms and edibility of mushrooms, because those are not the things that get him professional recognition. Also, professionals are not necessarily going to be generalists, because they can't always be accurate outside their field.

One professional joked: "I'm so specialized, I can recognize a genus in the field, *maybe*." Another noted that although he specializes in amanitas, "when it comes to inocybes or boletes, I'm just as much an amateur as anyone else."

Even within a professional's specialty he or she may have gaps in knowledge. An expert on *Pyrenomycetes,* a group of minute fungi, including Dutch Elm Disease fungus, commented at a workshop: "Any aspect you want to know about, we don't know about. . . . If you want to make a contribution to science, *Pyrenomycetes* are a perfect group, because there has been so little work done on them."

Professionals are annoyed when amateurs give them too much authority, as this forces them to engage in self-deprecation, claiming that they are only guessing or that they frequently misidentify mushrooms. They are also annoyed when several professionals are given the same species to identify. One professional described an experience as a new Ph.D.:

> One guy gave me [a russula, his specialty], and I said I didn't know what it was. He had peeled it, and he pasted on the peel of another species. I'm lucky I said I didn't know. There would have been no end of it if I said I knew what it was.

Another professional described the status games that he feels some amateurs play in an attempt to embarrass professionals:

> Yesterday somebody was cornering me about *Laccaria trullisata.* There were two collections out on the table, and were they the same one or weren't they the same one? I don't want to deal with that. Within ten minutes of leaving [the foray] nobody in this place will give a good hoot whether one of those were *ochropurpurea* and the other was *trullisata.* I get nothing but hassle if I get in the middle of that, because if I say this is *ochropurpurea,* somebody's going to say, "Oh, no, how can that be? Look at the bottom of it, it's obviously too long. It's got sand on it. It must be *trullisata*" [said in a sarcastic voice]. But if I say it's *trullisata,* somebody else will say to me, "How can that be? It's got purple gills, it must be *ochropurpurea.*" So I get nothing but hassle coming out of that.

This mycologist fantasized about attending a foray after all the mushrooms have been collected and all the amateurs have left. He joked that the amateurs wish to "handcuff" him to the identification table. Not all professionals are so dramatic about the relations between professionals and amateurs, but both groups recognize that they have different goals: they are two interest groups, dependent on each other, uneasily sharing a space. For amateur mushroomers, professionals validate their leisure and provide information, but they exist in a different universe of talk, except when professionals deign to address amateurs on their terms. That amateurs don't understand how researchers work makes these ties amicable but prickly. These distinct visions permit each group to develop rhetoric to insulate it from the stereotypes of the other.

THE POWER OF NAMES

What is the point of traipsing through the woods if you don't know what you see? Although there might be an aesthetic thrill (I admire some flowers or birds of which I am ignorant), the richness of the experience is linked to knowing what things are: meaning must be anchored in signs that are taken as "real." Indeed, this mirrors in some measure the situation in which we find ourselves in society: a world too often composed of strangers, who, through knowledge, can become friends. Perhaps we should not press this metaphor too far, but only recognize that social competence and confidence depend on our ability to name things. But how?

Birders have life relatively easy in that a set of common names has been established for birds. As there are only some 800 "native" American species, a shared consensus on proper names has developed, although identification is more complex in tropical rain forests.[74] The estimated number of mushroom species varies widely, but one respected guide[75] includes more than 2,000, by no means naming all North American species. One estimate is that more than 1,500,000 species of fungi exist, but only 75,000 species have been classified[76] in 6,600 genera.[77] Although not all of these species are "mushrooms" and many are microscopic molds, the numbers do pose a challenge for mushroomers, and contribute to a dual system of nomenclature: common names and scientific (Latin) names.

The Challenge of Common Names

If the value of names within a community is that they facilitate communication, it would appear that naming tied to routine language practices would be desirable. Surely common names are easier for a novice to recall than "two-dollar scientific names." Why learn a new (or old) language just to share information? Wouldn't it be better to refer to common names such as morels or chanterelles? Of course, for these genera, anglicized Latin names (*Morchella* and *Cantharellus*) work well, particularly when one is not concerned with differentiating species (for *Morchella: conica, deliciosa, esculenta,* and so on). Puffballs, stinkhorns, lobsters, inkies, milkies, sulphur shelves, oysters, parasols, or cauliflower mushrooms refer to specific species or genera, and are unlikely to cause confusion. In practice, when referring to prime edibles, mushroomers typically use common names. These names are readily recalled and used. Even the more scientific amateurs typically depend on these common names, although they may rely upon scientific nomenclature in identification.

Many find common names linked to the object:

You can always relate the common name to the type of mushrooms. Like a shaggy mane, you right away know it's got a shaggy top on it. Inky caps, you know very well it's going to turn black. Honeycaps. It looks just like honey on the cap. Very easy to identify. Puffballs. It's right there.

If you're new to a NAMA foray and you don't speak Latin, you're going to be hearing a lot of Latin. . . . But you have to understand that the Latin you're hearing is a form of prayer [laughter]. It's a two-part prayer. The first part is "God, I hope I'm pronouncing it correctly," and the second part is, "I hope it's close [to the right species]."

But though common names *are* central for edible mushrooms (and a few other notables), identification of species at forays and club meetings depends upon scientific nomenclature with its hard-to-pronounce names, seemingly arbitrary changes, and pseudo-Latin constructions (for example, *Lactarius kauffmanii, Trichoglossum hirsutum,* or *Pseudomerulius curtisii*).[78] This leads some amateurs to wish for a set of common names:

I think the common mushroom people can rise and move to standardize all mushroom names. The use of common names and words is vital to clear communication and that is why we have dictionaries. . . . The names that are difficult to spell and pronounce are unscientific since they do not provide simplification and clarification, which are goals of all science. We need to standardize the common, genus and species names of mushrooms.[79]

Mycologists should consider taking a page from the bird people and set up a national committee for the purpose of compiling a list of suitable names. The subject is emotion laden, but persons of good will should be able to come up with reasonable suggestions without spilling too much blood.[80]

The problem for the widespread adoption of common names is threefold; though none is insurmountable given enough effort, they are significant when taken together. First, sharing names with professional scientists is self-enhancing for serious amateur hobbyists. Sharing a language with professionals separates them from those who are interested only in edibility. Second, some common names vary by region or by group. Although these localisms may indicate a "regional environmental literacy,"[81] they do not enhance communication among collectors, as when "morels" are known as "merkles," "sponges," or "roons." Third, given the large number of mushroom species, many mushrooms do not have common names that are in use. Even such a prime edible as *Boletus edulis* is usually referred to not as King Bolete, cepe, or porcini, but as *Boletus edulis*. The insistence of some field-guide publishers, notably the Audubon Society[82] and Peterson's, that their expert authors create "common" (folk?) names leads to sarcasm. Kent McKnight, the author of Peterson's guide, joked at a NAMA foray:

> A rose by any other name would smell as sweet, but I don't know anything that would create as much stink as discussing names for mushrooms. [He notes that his editors forced him to create common names.] All editors assume their readers are so dumb that they wouldn't understand Latin names.

Or consider the following mock dialogue:

> *1st Mushroomer:* Great field trip! What did you find?
> *2nd Mushroomer:* Some nice fresh Sooty Heads, a couple of Rusty Hoods, and a big Pea Rock. I see you came up with some Red Riders and a lovely He Goat.
> *1st Mushroomer:* What you really have are Streaky Grey Trichs, Brown Dunce Caps, and a big Dye Maker's False Puffball. I don't know about Red Riders and He Goats—you mean my Plums and Custards and this Pungent Cort?

3rd Mushroomer: Great collections, but you're talking about Streaked Tricholomas, Common Cone Heads, a Dead Man's Foot, Variegated Mops, and a Lilac Conifer Cortinarius.

2nd Mushroomer: You want to argue with a guru like Kent McKnight?

1st Mushroomer: Sure, with this Audubon Guide in my hand.

3rd Mushroomer [using Arora]: You're both using obsolete nomenclature!

Latin Man: Let us not spoil a foray with unseemly quarreling. Your finds, in order of their appearance in this fable . . . are *Tricholoma portentosum, Conocybe tenera, Pisolithus tinctorius, Tricholomopsis rutilans* and *Cortinarius traganus.*[83]

Of course, if Latin Man returned to the querulous trio a decade later, he might argue with himself, since Latin names change. Further, if this were all that were found, the foray would be anything but great, given the absence of an easily recognizable collection of bright, edible mushrooms. The marginality of the species leads to the absence of consensual common names. Perhaps a committee could create a list of names around which there would be permanent consensus—avoiding excessive metaphorical fancy (he goats) or excessive verbiage (lilac conifer cortinarius).[84] Whether these would truly become folk names or merely another expert system imposed on natural objects is an open question.[85]

For those who favor them, scientific names have the virtue of providing a seemingly unambiguous connection between sign and object. For those species with several competing regional or local common names, a single set of names has value. Further, as common names vary from language to language, formal names avoid the challenges of translation. Any set of syllables can be learned with enough exposure—the problem is not the length of the Latin name (*Hypsizygus* has only four syllables, whereas *unambiguous* has five), but the fact that we cannot relate these syllables to other "common" words and, for a time, will not have heard the term frequently enough to incorporate it into our vocabulary.

In addition, the phrase "common name" is misleading when talking about little-known objects. For many species, common names simply do not exist; their creation is arbitrary and not collaborative. These might be English names, but they are not names used in practice. As one amateur jokes, "You can look up the common names in your favorite books," suggesting that the common names are just as hard to memorize as the scientific names that their use is supposed to avoid. The fact that mushrooms have not been treated as acceptable food has limited the number of names necessary. The term *champignon* has been known in France from the fourteenth century (originally referring to the field mushroom, *Agaricus campestris,* but extending to all fungi), and *mousseron* (referring originally to *Lyophyllum georgii*) from the twelfth century (becoming *mushroom* in English by 1563, referring to all fleshy fungi).[86] Most other terms for mushrooms, particularly in English, are recent coinages. Popular discourse has a restricted code as applied to mushrooms. To rely upon common names is to rely upon a specialized expert system, although one that requires an expertise different from that required for Latin binomials.

The Challenge of Change

If only the world would stand still, perhaps we could catch up. Name changes bedevil amateurs (and some professionals). The forest is a moving target, filled with objects whose labels do not last. Indeed, the rate of change of scientific names has been increasing, perhaps as a consequence of increasing numbers of mycologists or more subtle equipment for distinguishing differences. In the next section I discuss how this occurs from a scientific standpoint; here I examine its effect on amateurs.

Although some amateurs profess to appreciate name changes (feeling that they are witnessing scientific progress) and dismiss critics as "insecure," frustration is more common. Consider the blewit, a common edible that has gone by the names *Clitocybe nuda, Lepista nuda, Tricholoma nudum, Tricholoma personatum,* and *Rhodophyllus nudus.* We have sympathy for the mushroomer who wrote: "It is sometimes easier to find them near shaded paths and open woods than in mushroom field guides."[87] Although this is an extreme example, many mushrooms, remaining the same, have been reclassified; others, once changed, have reverted to the previously discredited name when a new argument persuades the scientific community (and their representatives at the International Congress on Biological Nomenclature). These changes, particularly given the claim that Latin names are preferred because they are unambiguous, can lead to intense frustration:

[Reclassification is] a pain. They do that with birds too. What is the point? If they are going to have a Latin name because that is universal, then why do they change it? If it is universally known, then all of a sudden, why does it have to have a completely different name?

This amateur sees classification as an artificial system, behind which can stand (if professionals wish) a phylogenetic organization, but believes that names themselves should not be used for purposes of classification. Stability is more important than a scientific naming practice grounded in *truth*. Common names represent this artificial system. Given the artificial nature of these names, amateurs express annoyance, joking or not, with changes that they link to the status games of professionals:

I muse that even the shifting Mississippi bottom cannot compare to the capricious sins visited upon the amateur mycologist by the nomenclaturist. A river boat captain merely battles floods, drought, sunken trees, rocks and loose women. The amateur mycologist must instead constantly seek order and immutability in the face of overwhelming odds—i.e., the professional mycologist's Quest for Immortality.[88]

I bought Orson Miller's *Mushrooms of North America*. . . . What a shock! I felt I had just stepped out of a time capsule, into a strange new world, a Lewis Carroll world of unfamiliar generic names: Melanoleuca, Leucopaxillus, Tricholomopsis, Flammulina—some 30 or more. Psalliota was now Agaricus. *Volvaria* had an added syllable, becoming the cumbersome *Volvariella, Lepiota morgani* was now *Chlorophyllum molybdites*. Even the honey mushroom did not escape the new name epidemic. It appears it had developed a very bad stutter, and was now *Armillariella mellea*. . . . I finally learned to live with this upheaval, but never completely forgave Orson for what he had done to my blewits, nudum and irinum. Clitocybe? You must be kidding![89]

One guy, who I just thought was an amateur and he was naming things right and left . . . *Pouzarella nodospora*. Now in the three years I had been studying mushrooms, I'd never come across the name *Pouzarella*. I would have remembered it if I had come across it. It was something out of the blue, and I said, "Come on, where did you find that name," and he said, "I made it up." So I assumed he was being straight with me, and he had made it up on the spot. That's Sam Mazzer from Kent State. In fact, he had studied the *Entoloma* mushrooms, and he had decided that this mushroom was not an entoloma, that it was a separate genus, and he decided it was a pouzarella. When I found that out, I was thinking, "Well, I'll give up mushrooming now because these young turks are going to begin to put new names on all these mushrooms."

The effect of these changes is to provide humorous repartee for amateurs and to distinguish the two groups, which have different goals. The names that are chosen and the taxonomy on which they are based affect our view of nature. The nature historian David Scofield Wilson puts the matter directly, noting that "if you call a thrush a robin it never protests. On the other hand, if you call a bison a buffalo, you presuppose its potential for domestication."[90] Given the reluctance of some amateurs to eat any amanitas, the placement of a mushroom into the *Amanita* genus influences whether it will be consumed—even though it remains as tasty as before. Likewise, when a mushroom that is widely known as poisonous is reclassified, the "new" mushroom may not be defined as poisonous. The head of NAMA's committee on poisoning reports with respect to the change of *Lepiota morgani* to *Chlorophyllum molybdites*: "changes in nomenclature may involve hazard."[91] One may search in vain for a description of edibility or toxicity. Amateurs joke that names are changed just to confuse them, enshrining the artificiality of taxonomy:

> I suppose you're wondering, that if they've moved the *Dentinum* species into *Hydnum*, what's happened to the *Hydnum* species such as *Hydnum imbricatum*? Even if you *weren't* wondering, you can rest easy in the knowledge that they are safe and sound in the genus *Sarcordon!* . . . Now we know what mycologists do when they aren't tramping around in the woods. . . . Maybe it's nature's way of keeping us confused, uncertain what to pick, and what to eat.[92]

> Leah: I didn't find any *Dentinum repandum*.
> Jerry: That's because they changed the name. [laughter]
> GAF: They were all recalled. [Everyone laughs. Jerry enjoyed my joke so much that he repeated it twice.]

Jerry commented about the change of name of the elm cap from *Pleurotus ulmarius* to *Hypsizygus tessulatus*: "[The professionals] thought it was too easy. Just because they changed the name doesn't mean you can't eat it." The others laughed, and he continued: "The mushrooms haven't changed a bit. Just the name."

Although amateurs understand the justification for taxonomic change and are sympathetic to scientific demands, each change emphasizes the status and power of professionals, leading to a desire to wrest control over nature from those who seem not to appreciate its authenticity and who wish to fit mushrooms into cultural categories. Scientists claim that they are not as autonomous as amateurs suggest, but operate under rules and conventions of their own creation.

Constructing Taxonomies

On those remote pages it is written that animals are divided into (a) those that belong to the Emperor, (b) embalmed ones, (c) those that are trained, (d) suckling pigs, (e) mermaids, (f) fabulous ones, (g) stray dogs, (h) those that are included in this classification, (i) those that tremble as if they were mad, (j) innumerable ones, (k) those drawn with a very fine camel's hair brush, (l) others, (m) those that have just broken a flower vase, (n) those that resemble flies from a distance.[93]

This imaginary taxonomy, created by Jorge Luis Borges, was supposedly taken from an ancient Chinese encyclopedia entitled the *Celestial Emporium of Benevolent Knowledge*. Its impossibility reminds us how we struggle to find meaning in the world—a psychological process of categorization, grounded on cognitive economy and a perceived correspondence with the world "out there."[94] Science requires not just "objective knowledge" but also "organization."[95] For Adam to name "every beast of the field, and every fowl of the air" as God brought them to him, shows that Adam could recognize *patterns* of categorization, so that whatever Adam said "*was* the name" (Genesis 2:19). Taxonomy is ultimately opinion: a "scientific art intended to bring order."[96] It is, perhaps, the taming of disorder that makes scientific puzzles joyous. The spouse of a prominent mycologist reported her husband's nightmare:

When St. Peter opened the gates of paradise to him and heard that the new guest was a mycologist, he took him to a wonderful forest with uncountable mushrooms, all neatly labeled and identified.

When Rolf [Singer] protested that there were some misdetermina-
tions according to his modern taxonomy, St. Peter admonished him
that all these labels had been written by the Creator himself, and thus
there could not be any misdetermination and everything was already
done to perfection. So how was Rolf supposed to spend his time during Eternity? Fortunately he woke up.[97]

Ultimately, the decision of when the difference is sufficiently great to
call for a new subspecies, species, or genus is human.[98] How can one
determine what constitutes a natural other? Species are assumed to
have a basis in fact,[99] but, if this is so, how should this reality be determined?

Several models of speciation have been proposed.[100] The first is the
Field Species Concept, which depends on the macroscopic sensory
categorization of objects: mushrooms that look, feel, taste, and smell
the "same" are the same species. Although this model can be challenged on several grounds as labeling on the basis of human senses
rather than on biological categories, it serves the amateur well *in situ*
and appears to be the grounding on which professionals as "natural
actors" operate.[101] The second model is the Morphological Species
Concept, which uses both macroscopic and microscopic characteristics, including chemical analysis. In addition to the human sensory
apparatus, the reports of human-created equipment (the extension
of human senses) constitute the reality of species.[102] Computerized
analysis of mushroom characteristics from scanning electronic microscopes provides the reality of species difference, even though human senses cannot determine difference without the aid of these machines. The third model, the Biological Species Concept, uses mating
incompatibility to define speciation: those who breed together are
within the same species, given morphological similarity. Finally, the
Phylogenetic Species Concept recognizes that compatible species
may show substantial genetic divergence, and so genetic similarity
must be added to the mix, along with sensory characteristics, equipment reports, and mating compatibility. This extends the morphological concept, as the genetic evaluation is based on equipment read-
ings, but includes dimensions that are not considered morphological,
"physical" features.

According to the status structure of the sciences, those who work with the more complicated (and expensive) equipment or experiments have more status, grants, and contracts. This leads to the relatively lower status for morphological identification (termed alpha taxonomy) versus genetic analysis, tissue culture analysis, and scanning electronic microscopes (beta taxonomy).[103] According to one informant, the former is "art," the latter "science." The amateur depends on Alphas, often older taxonomists who are retiring and expiring (or Betas willing to play at being Alphas for a weekend).

Another distinction, crosscutting the difference between Alphas and Betas, is that between Lumpers and Splitters, a distinction that seems firmly grounded in aesthetics. Just as some critics (and some art worlds) prefer complex and highly differentiated objects, others prefer simplicity and unity. Given the differences in how species (and genera) might be defined, one's aesthetic preferences, swaddled in theory, affect taxonomic debates. Some prefer to lump species in large genera (permitting considerable variation within a species); others prefer to split species and genus on dimensions that others consider unimportant.[104] Amateurs prefer Lumpers, who provide them with fewer categories and greater ease in identifying their finds. Yet at present, Lumpers seem in retreat,[105] as the new toys of the scientific enterprise permit an increased ability to "see" differences.

The existence of distinct models reminds us that what constitutes a species is not self-evident, and is determined by our "rules" of metacategorization. As Bruno Latour and Steve Woolgar[106] emphasize, all scientific models produce socially constructed information, but equipment makes "all traces of production . . . extremely difficult to detect." The machine appears to generate reality. One professional explained:

> The guy who is doing science is the guy who goes back and finds the original specimen on which that name was based. He orders it from the herbarium in Sweden, and now he looks at it under the microscope, and whatever other way he can, and he looks at his under the microscope in every way he can, so at least he's comparing his to a known entity. That's at least more scientific than simply saying, "Well, that's what this is." So that person is doing science. The other people who are doing science are the people who are taking the fungi, the mushrooms, and experimenting with them, manipulating them in some way.

The sensory evaluation of the natural object has been eliminated from science. The very object that constitutes nature as an authentic realm has been erased, making biology thoroughly and insistently cultural, limited only by human mechanical ingenuity.

Species concepts followed one another chronologically. Owing to the shortage of mycologists, however, many mushrooms are understood only through field and morphological analysis. Yet as professional mycologists begin attacking species (and species complexes, such as honey mushrooms, or *Armillariella mellea*), using criteria by which amateurs cannot make field distinctions, the pressure to develop a "nonscientific" system of identification will increase. One leading amateur notes:

> It should be the amateur who creates a taxonomy that the amateur can use. After all, taxonomy is not science. It is an art form that can be constructed to reflect the current state of scientific knowledge— but there is no taxonomic imperative. We are free to create a taxonomy that works for us. . . . Mushroom hunting is just too much *fun* to leave all the naming (in the literature and at forays) to the professionals and the advanced amateurs.[107]

The issue is not naming *per se* (Latin vs. common names), but the deeper issue of the criteria for classification decisions. One young professional explained that when he created a new genus of *Austroboletus,* "I caught literal hell . . . because it relied on SEM [scanning electron microscope] characteristics." Given changes in the process of identification, it is fair to ask whether amateurs will continue to accept scientific taxonomic discourse or develop an alternative system.

Naming Practices in a Social World

If we accept the givenness of the scientific name, the question becomes how these names come about. Science is a rivalrous community of interests:[108]

> I ask [mycologist Kent McKnight] how many species of morels there are. "That's difficult to answer," he says. "In France, fifty. Here, maybe five or six." "More morels in France?" I wonder. "No," he answers, "more mycologists working on them."[109]

> Alex Smith [a prominent professional] was at that foray along with Snell and Dick. Snell was the bolete man for the Northeast, and

Esther Dick was, I guess, his secretary at one point and became his wife. They wrote this beautiful book on the boletes of the Northeast. Anyway, Alex named all the boletes, and Snell and Dick went all along the tables, and they scratched out the names [on the labels], and they put in their names, because they had different generic concepts, and then I saw Alex walking by . . . scratching out those names and putting his names back in. . . . There was a personal element involved in it. Whose name was going to prevail?

One professional told me about a mushroom that he labeled *Tylopilus conicus:* "I think that it belongs in a new genus. [Rolf] Singer [a prominent mycologist] doesn't like [my idea]. I published it, but he [sank] it. He thinks it's *Fistulina conicus.* . . . There are no rules for setting out what is a genus. It's terribly subjective. After a while ego worms its way into it." Add to this the status that a young Ph.D. gains from demonstrating that a genus or species should be split or placed in a new category, an increasingly subtle differentiation resulting from more sophisticated equipment, and one recognizes the politics of science.

The regulatory control of naming becomes important. The formal system of accepting or rejecting names occurs through the International Biological Congress, first called in 1905 in Vienna to legislate some semblance of order in an increasingly fractious and diverse scientific community. Some method of social control is necessary to prevent "nomenclatural vagrants":[110] the answer is policing through the community of scientists.[111] Several "filtering" principles for taxonomy were enunciated at this and subsequent congresses and published in the International Code of Botanical Nomenclature.[112] Legitimate names must be "published" in the literature (printed matter distributed to botanical institutions); the specimens must be "typed"—dried and stored in an herbarium; the names must be "legitimate"—not ambiguous, superfluous, or a homonym of any other taxon; and they must have "priority"—the same object or group cannot have been named previously.[113] Finally, there is the principle of "conservation," which permits the congress to reject an otherwise legitimate name, preserving an illegitimate one, if the change is seen to have considerable disadvantages. Behind all this naming is the question of scientific proof for speciation: evidence that the community of scientists determines by vote. Although seemingly objective, the process may be political, as when Europeans vote as a block against their American colleagues. Ken Harrison, a prominent North American mycologist, indicated:

> A recent international nomenclature conference has ruled (6 to 5) that the genus *Dentinum* is no more. Instead we revert to the appellation *Hydnum* which is preferred by the European mycologists who made up the majority at the conference. North Americans like *Dentinum* but the conference was in Australia and not many North Americans were there.[114]

The assumption of objective (if transitory) naming practices suggests that we have improved from Adam in our techniques and the size of our deliberative bodies, but not in the need to choose. Debates within the Congress establish the new name and may, at times, override the power of American scientific consensus, which sometimes produces changes in nomenclature before the next International Congress sorts out taxonomic challenges.

The Dynamics of Discovery

By one estimate, one thousand fungal species are "discovered" each year. Although many are microscopic organisms, enough large fungi are named, including those found in American woods, that mycology seems a good home for one who wishes to shape the world. Imagine sharing with Adam the naming of a previously unknown object, something of which particle physicists and ornithologists[115] can only dream. Ken Harrison, a senior mycologist, noting that he had named twenty-five species, added: "That's one of the things that keeps you interested. . . . It keeps you young."[116]

The choice of what to name a natural object provides the namer with power, even if the name selected does not describe the mushroom in question:

> [Nancy Smith] Weber is quoted on the advantages and disadvantages of a girl following her father into his profession. "I think Dad [Alexander Smith] encouraged it a little bit, because there are several species that are named after me." One is *Brauniellula nancyae,* a dull yellowish fungus that resembles a misshapen button mushroom. "It looks like a gouty toe," says Weber. "It's one of the ugliest little mushrooms you've ever laid eyes on, but it's mine."[117]

Elliot, a professional mycologist, joked about a mushroom that he thought should be a new species:

> Maybe one of these days I'll write it up. . . . There's not a name out there that fits. I think I'll call it *Xantherconia pennsylvanicum* and make my employers [a Pennsylvania university] happy.

Related to the problem of naming is determining that what has been found has not been described before: that the object is not "known" to science. One mycological text notes that "probably less than one in two 'new' fungi are in fact previously undescribed."[118] For a set of specimens to be described as *previously unknown,* the stated and unstated conventions of the discipline must be followed.[119] The mushroom finder does not name it; that right belongs to the person who determines that it is a separate species and publishes that notice.

During my research I observed the beginning stages by which a new species was "discovered" (that is, described in a scientific publication).[120] At the 1984 Northeastern Mycological Foray, held at Glassboro State College (its name now changed to Rowan College) in Glassboro, New Jersey, several pale charcoal/brownish gray bolete specimens were collected whose flesh stained reddish-orange when cut.[121] Prof. C. B. Wolfe, a specialist on boletes from the Biology Department of Pennsylvania State University, Mont Alto campus, took an interest in those specimens that he could not easily identify. He subsequently involved a colleague and friend, Roy E. Halling of the New York Botanical Garden. Three years later additional specimens were collected in Southeastern Louisiana. I was present when Wolfe began analyzing the specimens and followed his investigation. I subsequently met him at another foray and corresponded with him.

After five years the article describing the new species was published in *Mycologia,* the leading American mycology journal ("*Tylopilus Griseocarneus,* a New Species from the North American Atlantic and Gulf Coastal Plain"). The brief article (fewer than five pages) has a formulaic quality: (1) title (fourteen words), (2) authors and affiliations, (3) abstract (thirty-seven words), (4) key words (five), (5) a brief discussion of the circumstances of collection, (6) a formal Latin description, (7) an expanded scientific description (in English, but filled with technical terms), (8) seven drawings of the microscopic features of *Tylopilus griseocarneus,* rendering the complicated microscopic material suitable for presentation, (9) a black-and-white photograph of three specimens (one revealing the cap, and the other two the tubes and stalk), (10) a coded description of the specimens, (11) a brief discussion of the habitat and distribution,[122] (12) a discussion of differences with possibly similar species, (13) acknowledgments (to the organizers of the two forays at which these mushrooms were discovered, to a person who lent specimens of a related species, to two persons "for their generous assistance with the Latin diagnosis,"[123] and by the junior author to the NSF for grant no. BSR-860024, (13) a fifteen-item bibliography, and (14) the date on which the article was accepted for publication (December 11, 1988). Much could be made of the typographical conventions of this literature (bold, italics, capitalization), the conventions of writing, drawing, and photography, as well as the glossy paper stock on which this journal was printed. These features contribute to the creation of science as a legitimate, serious, stable discourse. The reality that for mycology the mushroom does not exist until it is published emphasizes that the publication of documentary evidence is central to scientific knowledge.[124]

Yet if science relies on documents, a social process precedes the creation of those documents. I was struck that early in the process of identification, Wolfe had an intuitive sense that the specimen probably belonged to a new species, that it didn't fit with the *Strobilomyces* genus, where it might most obviously be placed because of its gray-black cap and the staining of its flesh from gray to peach/reddish orange. Yet the shape of its spores and the reticulation of its stalk seemed wrong. As the bolete specialist at the foray, Wolfe was expected to identify the boletes that were brought in. His presence gave him the right to pluck out this interesting specimen for further analysis. Interestingly, a second bolete was collected that didn't fit, but in that case, although Wolfe spent some time working on a precise identification, he did not take it to his laboratory for further tests. He labeled it as a *Boletus pseudosensibilis,* commenting, "It's good enough for me," and was done with it. Whether this second mushroom that didn't fit was a new species we will never know, but it reminds us that discovery depends on time and inclination. Wolfe had a specimen that intuitively seemed like a new species, so this second specimen that didn't produce the same reaction was ignored.

As he examined the mushroom, Wolfe justified his interest to a colleague, modestly claiming a sphere of knowledge: "These people just found a little gray thing. It was in an area I knew something about. That was nice." His colleague wondered: "Maybe this will be a new species," to which Wolfe responded: "That would be wishful thinking." At that stage in the investigation, modesty was important. The mushroom was small and gray; the possibility of its being a new species was "wishful thinking." Yet from the beginning the working hypothesis was that it was what it seemed: a new species. At first they attempted to eliminate alternative hypotheses, particularly that it would be in the *Strobilomyces* genus or a black tylopilus. In our taped conversations Wolfe held an internal dialogue:

> [Speaking of *Strobilomyces floccopus,* the old man of the woods, a black bolete with warts and flesh that stains reddish, then black] This specimen here approaches it in having some very reduced mounds on the cap. . . . I bet this is a species of *Strobilomyces,* sure enough. But I don't think . . . perhaps it's not. . . . It's almost as if the cap has lost the ability to produce those warts. But the cap has a convoluted surface, often times like a grain . . . the convolutions of a grain. . . . But nothing with warts. . . . Everything is perfect for *Strobilomyces.* I think that's surely what this has to be. I bet this is a species that simply hasn't been described. Perhaps. I'd like to be so bold as to think that it hasn't been. . . . More than likely it will never make a spore print, and that will make things much more difficult [eventually one specimen makes a pink print]. . . . Sometimes they just won't print and that's what makes things even more difficult. . . . We got plenty of spores . . . and they're all smooth [unlike the spores of *Strobilomyces*]. . . . This thing right here I don't know what's going to happen to it; it perhaps is going to be described as maybe new . . . and then again maybe it will not.

As noted, Wolfe invited a colleague, Roy Halling, "to collectively write it up." Halling, a respected senior mycologist and friend of Wolfe's, might have held potential mycological critics at bay. When I asked Wolfe why Halling was collaborating, he joked: "Just for the hell of it. I think it will be fun. We probably will come up with a better species example. If you go out on a limb, take as many people [as possible] out there with you." For a newly tenured associate professor, the desire to avoid looking foolish may be as powerful a motivation as the desire to advance one's career with single-authored articles.

Together, Halling and Wolfe continued the dialogue:

Halling [commenting about Austroboletus subflavidus*]:* That stipe is so distinctive, one would know it immediately.
Wolfe [laughing]: One would think that about this little bizarre creature sitting over here.
Halling: This black fellow?
Wolfe: You know what this is?
Halling: I don't know what it is.
Wolfe: I'll tell you what I'll do . . .
Halling: Is this a tylopilus?
Wolfe: I'm not sure. I don't think so. Read [my notes on] what happens to tissues on injury there.
Halling: That sounds like a strobilomyces.
Wolfe: 'Cause tissues go to pinkish-orange.
Halling: No, no, tissues go orange to black.
Wolfe: Tissues go from orange to a dark gray. . . . The tissue is strictly pallid, very pallid, then it goes to orange, then it goes to this color.
Halling: That's just like *Strobilomyces.*
Wolfe: Uh-huh. Singer describes a *Strobilomyces velutipes* . . . but they don't talk about a smooth cap. The reticulated apex of the stipe might be, you know, OK for *Strobilomyces.*
Halling: Traditional veil.
Wolfe: No.
Halling: If you look at this mature thing, it's got pinkish tubes.
Wolfe: Pinkish-orange, yeah. It's just not *Strobilomyces* tubes. . . .
Halling: This isn't a strobilomyces. . . . Nothing describes this one.
Wolfe: Absolutely nothing.

This dialogue continued for hours, with the two men using chemical reagents, hand lenses, and microscopes. They sometimes included other mycologists and graduate students, with each giving advice, but no one found a published species that sufficiently matched the specimen (especially the combination of smooth spores and bruising). Later, when I asked about the identification, Wolfe explained with some self-mockery: "We're on the verge of a great discovery." Later he added: "We've ruled out everything that it might be. . . . It has all of the characteristics of *Strobilomyces* except the spores are elongated [instead of having a tooth-edge]. . . . I think we know instinctively that this is something new." He added that it might be a new genus, but said that he had already elevated two subgenera to genus level, and "I got a lot of flak for that. . . . I kinda hate to create a new genus." Perhaps because of disciplinary politics, when the final determination was made, it was placed in *Tylopilus* and not a new genus. Given the potential criticism, the specimens were not sufficiently different from what Wolfe and Halling imagined was the *Tylopilus* ideal type. This process continued after the foray, as they sent to herbaria for similar specimens that they wished to check, deciding to examine "all black boletes described from the world before describing this one as new."[125] Because of Wolfe's tenacity, the world has a "new" natural object.

Choices are involved in the process of discovery. If the mushroom is to be "discovered," it must be written up in a conventional form and appropriately named. This inscription depends upon an elaborate dialogue—internal and external—with significant others. An object that is wild has been tamed and entered into scientific culture. It need hardly be remarked that it isn't the mushroom that has changed, but only our knowledge of it. The next stage in the process is the authors' publicity: "You got to get people out there to know you, so you start blasting the world with reprints whether they want them or not, you send them. That's the way the game is played." Perhaps if it is found by others the species will eventually be incorporated into fieldguides. The boundary between professional science and amateur leisure is porous. Amateurs provided the specimens for Wolfe and Halling to discover *their* mushroom and on which they receive raises, promotions, and esteem; in turn the discovery of this interesting mushroom that changes color while one watches increases amateurs' satisfaction with their naturework. Both science and leisure depend upon collective engagement: whether in the woods or in the lab, one shares space with friends and colleagues and is judged by them.

In this chapter I examined those who are linked to amateur mushroom collecting—publics and professionals—drawing upon Robert Stebbins's Professional-Amateur-Public model. The public and the professional have perspectives on mushrooms that are different from those of amateurs. Although professionals are more likely to create finely grained differentiations than are amateurs, they have less differentiated "moral" values. Expressing moral judgments about mushrooms is seen as "not professional." A thicket of jargon seals professionals from their emotions and aesthetics. This means not that these are absent, but that they can be spoken only in the cracks of discourse. It is clear from the "discovery" of a new species that these mycologists are having great fun solving their puzzles. Although they may not collect for the pot, the lab table represents, in some ways, their pot. They are as fascinated and as mystified as amateurs are by those objects that the forests and fields provide. Like hobbyists, they are engaged in taming, in making the natural order cultural.

Given that their decisions, particularly regarding naming practices, impact amateurs, professionals are both esteemed and demeaned. Amateurs want names that they can *use*. Most are unconcerned with the metaphorical models of evolution that mycologists construct. Changes in metaphor (scientific theory) frustrate them, as they are not participants in that world of theory and may be ignorant of it. Thus name changes for the amateur are decontextualized. They seem idiosyncratic and arbitrary, matters of status games rather than the aesthetics of theory. Fortunately, those amateurs who are least interested in scientific theories (pot hunters) are in least need of them: popular species typically have stable common names.

The relationship between amateurs and professionals depends on each group's providing for the other's needs: amateurs provide specimens and professionals provide education and status validation. Through the institution of the foray, these needs are met adequately, if not perfectly.

The relationship between the amateur and the public is of a different order. The public is ignorant of amateur concerns, and often reveals amusing fear, ignorance, or curiosity. Members of the public play the part of the naïf or fool in the stories of hobbyists. Only when the public has control of those arenas to which the amateur wishes access does conflict emerge. Mushrooms are dangerous, but not until the victim makes an active choice to eat them, and so many adopt a "live and let live" attitude toward these monstrous fungi.

The overlap between public and amateur occurs when mushrooms are sold to the public, potentially affecting the purity of the woods. Although members of the public are the ones potentially "endangered" and may be those who have the responsibility of guarding ecosystems, the debate also pits amateur against amateur, reminding us that, as in Chapter 5, a leisure world can be a highly charged political world. What one does in and with the woods may affect others; the whole social world potentially has a stake in how nature is used.

The world of the mushroomer, small though it is, reverberates through other arenas and institutions. Mushrooms are a lens through which we can view society.

CHAPTER SEVEN

Naturework and the
Taming of the Wild

There is no nature. By this I do not repeat the claim made by Bill Mc-
Kibben[1] in *The End of Nature* that because of human impact on our
planet, a pristine environment can no longer be found. That impact
is surely evident, but it is only part of my argument. My claim is
broader, deeper, and more subversive—both to environmentalists
and to developers: to conservers, protectors, and organicists alike. To
understand and to be in "nature" *in every way* involves drawing upon
social understanding. My point is not that stones, fish, and flowers
have been affected by society, but that we who interpret them have
been. We cannot see the wild with fresh eyes. Human senses have been
fully socialized. Natural objects do exist; natural processes have consequences, but they must be interpreted to be made meaningful.

Environmental ethics depend on human values. For instance, our
attitude toward extinction not only is a human choice—is having
more species a public good?—but also depends on the existence of
the idea of *species* (a construct created by human naturalists) and of
survival rights (a construct created by human political theorists).
When we are romantic, we are cultural; if we believe in a utilitarian
logic, we are cultural; if we protect rights, we are cultural; if we believe that species may promote our survival, we are cultural. We decide that a beaver dam is not the same class of object as a human dam.

By examining the odd and esoteric world of mushrooming, I have attempted to explore the claim that all understanding of nature is fundamentally cultural. By analyzing a social world in microscopic detail in its empirical richness, I hope that I have permitted the reader—whether knowledgeable of fungi or not—to appreciate the specifics of how humans develop systems of value. Although on the surface this may seem to have little to do with the debates among environmental theorists, I have attempted to describe how people "in practice" shared their lives with nature, and with one another in pursuit of natural experience. Mushrooming, despite its uniqueness, serves as a means by which we can understand other realms of naturework. Other studies are needed to confirm, dispute, and expand my analysis, but fungal doings are a place to begin to understand how nature is known through culture.

In the Introduction I outlined three distinctive, though overlapping, perspectives on the relations between humans and their natural environment: a protectionist view, an organic view, and a humanist view. These models, in practice, are resources employed to justify our behaviors and to make sense of an otherwise ambiguous context. Human beings are not conditioned to act upon consciously created, rigorously logical, philosophically sophisticated moral systems. Typically we do what we wish, although our wishes are shaped by immediate desires, long-standing preferences, and ideas of the just and proper. This helps explain why most of us are sensitive to environmental issues at some times and not at others. For instance, I am convinced that I have no compelling argument against animal rights, and, as a consequence, I no longer wear fur or own pets. I talk about the animal rights movement as a serious concern, not as a bizarre jape. Yet my immediate ire permits me to slap mosquitos and smash roaches. My desire for pleasure lets me eat veal—limited only by egocentric concerns about cholesterol—and wear comfortable leather shoes. I suppress the recognition of my hypocrisy, and I realize that in time I may change, to support either my moral convictions or my personal pleasure.

My motive is not to point to personal contradictions, but to recognize that much of our nature doings have this quality of being situated rather than rigorously philosophical. We are influenced by beliefs, but we can also shape and massage those beliefs—or ignore them—to permit us to act.

BEING IN NATURE

To desire to be in nature in a voluntary, leisure capacity is to embrace a particular cultural model of nature—a desire for nature's virtues to rub off on the self. Being in nature is pleasurable—it will not always be "comfortable," but it is ultimately comforting, rewarding, or self-enhancing. Part of this satisfaction develops out of a model of opposition, of distinction between that world and "civilization." For many, being away, and then being at one with nature, are desirable. The sharp dichotomy between these two "worlds" is part of our logic and our environmental ethics. Even those who see the world as an organic unity cannot escape the realization that city and country are different kinds of places with a wider gap of meaning than that between a forest and a desert.

The appreciation of nature is linked to our perspectives on the world in which we reside. Indeed, the act of collecting and identifying rare and unseen objects can be seen as a metaphor for identity in a mass society. The importance of determining the name of a mushroom individualizes the otherwise anonymous object. Eating mushrooms further connects our selves to the particular objects of nature, now properly identified. Particularizing the world is a powerful means by which we can hold off forces of alienation.

Part of the compelling charm of nature is that it is an "authentic reality." In seeing nature in this way, we express a willingness to embrace the lack of control, indeed, even to embrace the danger of nature. To kill all the poisonous snakes or bears in a wilderness area might—according to one way of looking at things—be a desired end; yet it is a policy that few embrace. One comes to the wilderness to find a way to coexist with this danger. If poisonous mushrooms did not exist, one imagines, mycology would be far less appealing: there would be no challenge, no need for knowledge or concern. The forest would be a supermarket. For mushroomers amanitas contribute as much as chanterelles. Culture is to be made safe, whereas nature is permitted to be a risky reality. The irony is that forests may well be tamer than some corners of civilization.

The distinction between nature and culture places the human actor in an awkward situation: we are the representatives of the civilization from which we wish to escape. Our mere presence civilizes the wild, which is precisely what we wish to avoid. Even those who are not searching for wilderness far distant from civilization are still in the woods because they are different. We attempt to respect this "other," while remaining comforted by its otherness. Whether we are humanists, protectionists, or organicists, the segregation of these other spaces is critical. We attempt—within the limits of our desires to use nature—to erase our civilized selves. But our own needs—perhaps the "need" to carry a picnic lunch, a six-pack of beer, or a basket to collect natural objects—remind us that our presence in nature is connected with its use value. To be sure, the impact on nature differs according to one's activity, but even a step kills plants or insects, and a breath alters the ratio of oxygen and carbon dioxide in an ecosystem. The self can never be totally erased, and so battles occur over where lines should be drawn. Typically lines are drawn to include *our* preferred activities, excluding *theirs*. Most mushroomers are not overly concerned with limits on deer hunting, just as many birdwatchers are not troubled about those parks that no longer permit mushrooming. Battles over whether to permit snowmobiles in wilderness areas often center around the question of proper use, as judged through one's own personal choices. The issue is not conscious hypocrisy, but rather the fact that one's own chosen behaviors seem to provide a "reasonable" standard by which all should live. Subjective decisions can easily be seen as an absolute standard.

MEANINGFUL MUSHROOMS

One of the more remarkable human properties is the ability to transform anything into a symbol. Dust can stand for a slovenly housekeeper, a pimple stands for puberty, and a bud stands for religious rebirth. The world is the richest text that we own. I discovered this depth of meaning in my travels with mushroomers, and in my own socialization to the significance of fungi. As I noted in Chapter 2, the range of meanings that can be attached to these growths is remarkable and striking. A white growth is recognized for its deadly beauty, a red growth is to be kicked and stomped, a golden one is to be treasured as a choice edible, and a brown one is ignored. For those who have not been socialized to the meaning of this corner of the natural world, this differentiation may seem curious, if not bizarre. All mushrooms are "toadstools," even if species of mushrooms are no more similar than the proverbial apples and oranges that we are warned not to lump.

No one knows everything. The choice of which corners of our world we choose to explore—whether natural or cultural—depends on our desire for *expertise,* coupled with a temporal space that a specific interest can fill. We select a focal concern that drives us. This selection may be a function of personal links—strong or weak ties—or a result of being impressed by an object and having the time and the resources to follow through on that interest. The fact that nature is regarded as a "good place to be" means that objects within this broad surround are often seen as desirable scenes on which to build expertise.

Of course, seeing objects is insufficient; one must also learn how to talk about them. Because of linguistic limitations, we are left with the need to identify objects in light of their metaphorical relations to other, often human-made, objects. Good-bad, beautiful-ugly, tasty-disgusting come tripping to our lips and our minds. I contend that a similar process of differentiation occurs in all collecting worlds. It is not only that we see objects as belonging to different categories, recognizing that others belong together, but that we define these categories as inherently meaningful. We differentiate them on various moral and aesthetic dimensions. This applies to birders, fishers, rockhounds, as well as hobbyists outside of a natural realm, such as stamp or antique collectors.

The personification of these natural objects is perhaps the most dramatic example of the technique by which nature is made cultural. That this process occurs easily in mushrooming—and elsewhere—reminds us just how cultural are our thoughts, no matter how far from civilization we choose to be. The argument is not, of course, that all mushroomers at all times will use these metaphors, but rather that they *make sense* to collectors. Human character is a metaphorical model that we use to make sense of the wild. An object (or a class of objects, such as a species) is like a person and can be known in a similar manner. Man is the measure of all things.

SHARING THE WOODS

Interpreting the natural environment in light of cultural concepts is only part of the process by which we claim that nature is cultural. The romantic imagery of "man in nature" is of the lone individual tramping through the back country—the image of the heroic hermit who only occasionally returns to the human world to bring an account of personal experience. Although some people do visit the wild by themselves, more common are joint excursions: couples, families, friends, and affinity groups. The woods and fields can easily be transformed into social spaces, arenas in which treasured human interaction occurs. To be alone with nature for too long can be distinctively oppressive, insufficient to "fill the human heart and mind." We often bring our social world with us—not merely cultural objects, such as books, knives, baskets, and lunch, but significant others.

Each realm of naturework has social characteristics. For mushrooming I sliced the activity into three components: collection, identification, and consumption. Each depends in considerable measure on the mushroomer's ability to get along. As collectors we operate both as competitors and as teammates. Finding mushrooms is desirable both as a mark of status and because edible mushrooms are valuable in their own right. Further, the collection of edible mushrooms (like other objects) is a zero-sum game in that what one finds others will be unable to discover.

The act of finding is not transparent, but depends on a range of knowledge provided through socialization and experience. If I wished to find morels in November, I could look compulsively without success. I must learn what others have learned previously. Even at the proper moment I must select sites carefully, choosing areas with elms and apples and ignoring pine forests. Other species grow in different microclimates, and this information is socially generated and distributed.

Once found, an object must be interpreted. To pick it, I must have realized at a distance that it was a "mushroom," not a leaf or a stone. Much identification of mushrooms, as with person perception and object identification generally, comes easily. I don't need a visual template to recognize my children. But other objects do not call out to identifiers, and must be examined with the aid of keys and guides, which are culturally produced and distributed.

More significant is the fact that much identification occurs in a social environment. Identification becomes negotiation. Because there is no objective reading of a mushroom (an ideal type may reside in an herbarium somewhere—or may not), we decide at some point that a belief that we have arrived at is good enough for our purposes. We construct the boundaries of species and how objects fit into these categories. For those mushrooms that are seen as especially interesting or unusual, the identifier may rely upon the advice of a community, just as birdwatchers ask others to make sense of their momentary glance at an object whose defining characteristics do not remain still for careful consideration.

Because we dislike ambiguity, we force objects into categories—a technique that is particularly comforting when no harm will transpire from a choice made in haste or without sufficient experience: better to be confidently wrong than honestly uncertain. The techniques that we utilize to identify mushrooms are social, dependent on human choices as sedimented in fieldguides and texts and as emergent from interaction. Identification is a practical accomplishment, as is so much certainty in science, political policy, and elsewhere.

Finally, we consume our finds. This consumption depends on a "reasonable" certainty of what we found and our confidence in the consequences of consumption. If a mushroom may cause an upset stomach, we must decide whether we are willing to suffer that potential consequence in our desire for the *idea* of consuming wild and free food. Further, when mushrooms are consumed with others, confidence in the identifications of others is essential. There are no federal mushroom inspectors, and even though a species of mushroom may be edible, a particular mushroom may be contaminated or a particular eater may be allergic. This reminds us of the degree of faith we assign to all of those—personal acquaintances or corporate entities—who provide us with sustenance.

TALKING WILD

To know nature is to be able to talk about it. Frequently doing is made meaningful because of our conversations. The climb is not over until the tale is told; the foray does not end until the narrative does. Any human activity can be profitably recognized as constituting a *bundle of stories*. The spoken and written accounts that collectively demonstrate that actors have a common interest are a crucial component of group life.

The desire to satisfy an attentive audience suggests the reality of shared values and concerns. Talk (and listening) is a community-building activity. Like all worlds of talk, it falls into several genres. I divided narratives into war stories, sad tales, and treasure tales, but this does not exhaust all possible genres of talk. Not all nature activities have the identical set of story types, but in all arenas, the personal experiences of participants make for dramatic narratives. Actors select events that others will consider notable, and transform them so that others will find them compelling. That these are typically narrated as personal-experience stories means that the teller has the right to vouch for the validity of the happenings, and, not coincidentally, to alter them without being charged with impropriety. A body of printed material (for example, *Mushroom* magazine and club newsletters) provides for dissemination of these stories in other than an oral register.

Other accounts of happenings contribute to a group's culture. Most groups develop a store of memorable events, such as the incident of the purple clitocybe described in Chapter 3. Having shared the experience—or at least having shared the repeated telling—participants feel that they belong to a group of significance, a group in which events are memorable and worthy of being recalled. That many of these accounts deal with the interpretation of nature makes it evident that nature is a resource to be shaped for establishing group feeling.

In similar fashion, humor is used to define one's attitude toward nature and toward the group in which one is embedded. A witty remark can easily become a form of social control, delineating the boundaries between what is acceptable and what is not: a feature of all group life. That this need not be accepted is evident in the humorous jockeying between those who have a conservative set of attitudes toward the consumption of mushroom species and those whose attitudes are more liberal. The ability to joke about those things that cannot be directly discussed is evident in bantering about dying from and killing by poisonous mushrooms. The reality of naturework is transposed into a discourse to which participants respond, and they ratify it through laughter, joking responses, and further conversation. Talk can be seen as the taming of natural experience to fit collective models.

ORGANIZING NATURALISTS

Perhaps the archetypal form of group life is the organization, which reflects individuals' desire to shape their surroundings and make them regular and routine through the assignment of tasks and responsibilities. Although organizations dot the leisure landscape, in no area of leisure are they more prominent than in naturework. Organized naturalists gain advantages not available to those who remain isolated. The irony of the need to create social organization to confront the wild is not lost.

A key feature of all organizations that are designed to meet the needs of participants is the collection, coordination, and distribution of resources, what I label provisioning theory. Voluntary leisure organizations are models for this type of organization. Although examining a single organization is not sufficient for developing an adequate theory, my case study of the Minnesota Mycological Society reveals the importance of provisioning resources in nature worlds. Collective leisure is possible only because some group can provide the conditions under which it can be performed, physically and psychologically. Whether what is provided is knowledge, sociability, or identity symbols, the organization is an efficient means to make available desired events and objects.

With resources come the possibility of a power struggle. To the extent that resources are limited in availability (for example, the selection of a space and time to meet), controversy may result in those organizations in which participants have different visions about what they hope to gain and what the organization should provide. In the case of the Minnesota club, demographic, ideological, and personal considerations combined to produce a (temporary) breach in the fabric of the organization. Differing visions split those oriented to a scientific amateur mycology from those more interested in collecting mushrooms for consumption, even though few participants had no interest in either identification or consumption. With the defeat of a proposal to move the club meetings to a natural history museum and the election of a new president, acceptable to all, the club restored harmony. Although this was a unique circumstance, it points to the tension that voluntary organizations may face as an umbrella for those with differing conceptions of the activity and differing sets of social relations. Most groups are subject to disruption if circumstances facilitate disagreement and if resources are limited.

Perhaps the major task for a leisure group, achievable partially through providing resources and partly through building friendships, is the creation of cohesion. Sharing is key to creating cohesion, in part because it builds trust and creates a dense network of favors. By establishing relations of trust—beginning in sharing knowledge and extending to the sharing of relationships—people feel ties to other members, and, more significantly, to the organization as a whole. For mushrooming, involving as it does some measure of risk in coping with an authentic nature, social relationships are powerful as a bulwark against poisoning.

If trust were all that were involved, the analysis would be straightforward. Yet within mushrooming and other activities that have a zero-sum quality, secrecy is also part of organizational life. In the collection of morels, it is understood that club members will refuse to let others know the locations of their successes. Novices are rapidly socialized to this secrecy; they are taught that secrecy need not rend the fabric of allegiance to the organization, because in time all will have secrets. The group is tied together, in part, as a "community of secrets." Similar processes occur in other collecting hobbies, in which members compete actively with one another in finding objects; this competition demands that some critical information be held in abeyance.

It is easy to conceive of community as consisting of maximum sharing, but this model stands against the possibility of a competitive community. Members care about one another—and under some circumstances do share—but part of this caring is the willingness to listen to treasure tales about great finds. Since nature is seen as authentic and outside of human control, the symbolic resonance of these finds is particularly intense.

FUNGUS AND ITS PUBLICS

Naturework does not stand by itself, enveloped by its own community, but has connections beyond its borders. Robert Stebbins[2] speaks of the Professional-Amateur-Public (PAP) system. By this he refers to those leisure worlds in which the participants do, more or less, what a set of professionals do, and have a public that is interested in their activity. Those who play organized softball are amateurs, as are thespians of community theater. Stebbins nicely describes the ideal-typical form of amateurism, and how these actors both mimic and differ from professionals. Mushroomers—particularly those who are most committed, *amateur mycologists*—fall within Stebbins's model.

They emphasize the consumption of their finds more than do professionals and emphasize less the "scientific" (that is, microscopic) identification of mushroom specimens. Some amateurs still contribute to the professional literature by discovering new species and fitting them in taxonomic schemes. Many mushroomers do not have this commitment, and would be considered hobbyists, not amateurs, in Stebbins's model.

My concern, in contrast to Stebbins's, is not to provide an ideal type of amateurs but to examine how mushroomers deal with those around them. The reality of boundaries applies to all leisure activity. Specifically, I examine how mushroomers relate to their public, a largely ignorant public, more characterized by fear than by curiosity; how they relate to markets and those who are involved in the commercial gathering of mushrooms; and finally, how they relate to the activities of professionals.

Accounts of dealings with an ignorant and unappreciative public are part of many social worlds. Because of the mystical, mysterious, and evil connotations of mushrooms, this fear is greater in the world of the mushroomer, leading parents to overreact when their children place mushrooms in their mouths or even touch mushrooms. The community of knowledge that mushroomers share, making this realm of nature comprehensible, permits them to interpret this boundary with outsiders as central to who they are. External ignorance helps build a shared togetherness.

Commercial mushroom picking produces controversy in a world with limited resources. Does collecting mushrooms for profit affect the sacred quality of nature, transforming the forest into a factory? Perhaps this objection is based only upon self-interest, but it is typically phrased in light of a moral appeal. If nature is a special realm, set apart from civilization, isn't commercial work in this world sacrilege?

Although I did not spend many hours with professionals, I do address the question, central to a sociology of knowledge, of how a professional decides that an object is a new species—what in practice constitutes sufficient differentiation to embrace Adam's chore of naming the unnamed world. How do boundaries come to be set between things? No objective criteria exist as to when an object is sufficiently different from another that it deserves a new category; as a result, a set of conventions have developed in science that serve as guides to

decision-making, although in practice these guidelines are negotiated. The relationship between professional taxonomists and amateur
mycologists demonstrates the similarities between the two groups,
whereas this division is magnified when professionals are contrasted
with pot hunters. Ultimately, relations are defined by worlds of practice: whether there is a sufficient overlap that the two groups can
communicate, or, if not, whether there are realms in which each
group serves the needs of the other (picking specimens vs. the quick
identification of those specimens). Respect and labor are traded for
community and knowledge: a process applicable to many professions
with potentially overlapping domains of action and expertise.[3]

BY NATURE

Throughout this book I have argued that there is no nature separate
from culture; this is the more modest version of the line with which
I began this chapter. We humans enjoy our time in nature—it is
meaningful, emotionally satisfying, cognitively rich, behaviorally challenging, socially significant, and can even be understood in light of
spiritual development. It is this process of attributing meaning to the
environment that I have termed naturework: taking the particulars of
the world we confront, and giving them moral and social weight.

It has long been asserted that the critical question in sociological
theory is, How is social order possible? One response is that we work
at it. We not only experience the world but arrange and value it.
Much of this occurs through socialization: we are taught what to believe and what to feel. But this claim takes us only so far. We don't remember all that we are taught, and, as parents and teachers ruefully
recognize, we may reject or transform that which we learn. Although
this power of transformation is present in all human arenas, it has
particular force when we discuss nature. Nature is seen to have an autonomy and authority. Yet this perspective is cultural, both when we
discuss philosophical issues of nature generally and when we discuss
particular fungi.

The dramatic change in attitudes toward nature over the past two
generations indicates powerfully that attitudes are more than what we
have been taught. We shape these socializing messages, shifting
through a set of claims made by moral entrepreneurs, some of which

connect effectively with cultural themes that have great resonance. Further, we appreciate nature through our immediate circumstances, interpreting the world through the scenes that we confront. Thus it is possible simultaneously to be vehemently "environmental" and profoundly supportive of development and human usage. Our social location and immediate desires combine to affect the implications of our naturework: an argument that applies with equal force to the understanding of other circumstances and organizational worlds.

The argument that I propound—that nature is a social construction—has the potential to undermine environmental policy. If the wild is a social construction, isn't asphalt as potentially ennobling as soil? Such would be a misreading of my beliefs. Although on some absolute level, there may be no more moral worth in soil than in asphalt, the choices that we make have the potential to reverberate because of the reality of natural processes. Take an extreme case. If we uprooted all green plants and trees, we would learn quickly of these real and dire consequences. Although we debate the magnitude of the effects of acid rain and other pollutants, surely there is *some* point at which consequences will be noticeable.

A separate argument suggests another reason for concern for the wild. Collective aesthetic judgments matter. In nations that are governed through a democratic and representative system, the judgments of the people do count, and majorities have the right to enforce their judgments, even while we zealously protect minority rights. Property rights have long been seen as an arena in which majorities have some measure of control over individual property (the right of eminent domain is enshrined in the Fifth Amendment to the Bill of Rights). Although there are practical and ethical limits on the rights of majorities to define proper land use, the legitimacy of governments to make environmental decisions (zoning, the establishment of parks, curtailment of pollution, protection of endangered species) is well established, even in the absence of definitive scientific proof. A democratic society can legitimately enforce its values, no matter if the basis for these decisions are preferences rather than certain threats.

Perhaps in absolute terms there is no correct way in which nature should be used, conserved, preserved, or held. Yet to say this is *not* to say that we should or can avoid making cultural choices. Political decisions are legitimate for determining public policy, even though we cannot suggest that they are eternal or universal. Preserving the environment can be justified scientifically or politically. The fact that nature is cultural legitimates, not diminishes, our policy choices. We cannot and must not rely on scientists to control our decisions, even though we learn from their insight. To recognize that nature is cultural is to accept our responsibility as beings whose impact on the world will be great, whatever choices we make. Each perspective on nature recognizes the fateful quality of human decisions. Because we are cultural beings, we must recognize the inescapable necessity to make collective choices, for these choices are what environmental ethics entail.

Notes

INTRODUCTION

1. Gregory Stone and Marvin J. Taves, "Research into the Human Element in Wilderness Use," *Proceedings, Society of American Foresters* (1956), p. 26.
2. Clarence J. Glacken, *Traces on the Rhodian Shore* (Berkeley: University of California Press, 1964).
3. Kirkpatrick Sale, *The Green Revolution: The American Environmental Movement, 1962–1992* (New York: Hill and Wang, 1993); Philip Shabecoff, *A Fierce Green Fire: The American Environmental Movement* (New York: Hill and Wang, 1993).
4. Sale, *The Green Revolution,* p. 77, estimates that by 1990 there were 12,000 local and regional environmental groups, along with 325 organizations of national standing.
5. Christopher D. Stone, *Should Trees Have Standing? Toward Legal Rights for Natural Objects* (Los Altos, Calif.: W. Kaufmann, 1974).
6. Murray Bookchin, *The Ecology of Freedom* (Palo Alto: Cheshire, 1982).
7. Arne Naess, "The Shallow and the Deep, Long-Range Ecology Movement: A Summary," *Inquiry,* 16 (1973): 95; Bill Devall and George Sessions, *Deep Ecology* (Layton, Utah: Gibbs M. Smith, 1985).
8. Ariel Salleh, "Deeper Than Deep Ecology: The Ecofeminist Connection," *Environmental Ethics,* 6 (1984): 339–345.
9. Edward Tenner, "Warning: Nature May Be Hazardous to Your Health," *Harvard Magazine* (Sept.–Oct. 1987): 36.

10. Bennett Berger, *The Making of a Counterculture* (Berkeley: University of California Press, 1981).

11. Ann Swidler, "Ideology in Action," *American Sociological Review,* 51 (1986): 273–286.

12. Joseph Cohen, "About Steaks Liking to Be Eaten," *Symbolic Interaction,* 12 (1989): 191–213; Gary Alan Fine and Lazaros Christophorides, "Dirty Birds, Filthy Immigrants, and the English Sparrow War: Metaphorical Linkage in Constructing Social Problems," *Social Problems,* 14 (1991): 375–393; Andrew J. Weigert, "Transverse Interaction: A Pragmatic Perspective on Environment as Other," *Symbolic Interaction,* 14 (1991): 353–363; Thomas Greider and Loraine Garkovich, "Landscapes: The Social Construction of Nature and the Environment," *Rural Sociology,* 59 (1994): 1–24.

13. George Herbert Mead, *Mind, Self, and Society* (Chicago: University of Chicago Press, 1934), pp. 154–156.

14. Loic J. D. Wacquant, "The Pugilistic Point of View: How Boxers Think and Feel about Their Trade," *Theory and Society,* 24 (1995): 489–535.

15. Andrew J. Weigert, "Lawns of Weeds: Status in Opposition to Life," *American Sociologist,* 25 (1994): 80–96; George Herbert Mead, *Selected Writings* (Indianapolis: Bobbs-Merrill, 1964), p. 366.

16. Gary Alan Fine and Kent Sandstrom, "Ideology in Action: A Pragmatic Approach to a Contested Concept," *Sociological Theory,* 11 (1993): 21–38.

17. Niklas Luhmann, *Ecological Communication* (Chicago: University of Chicago Press, 1989), p. 112; Shelton Ungar, "The Rise and (Relative) Decline of Global Warming as a Social Problem," *Sociological Quarterly,* 33 (1992): 483–501.

18. Anthony Giddens, *Modernity and Self-Identity* (Stanford: Stanford University Press, 1991).

19. Neil Evernden, *The Social Creation of Nature* (Baltimore: Johns Hopkins University Press, 1992), p. 20.

20. Arthur A. Ekirch, Jr., *Man and Nature in America* (New York: Columbia University Press, 1963), p. 3.

21. David S. Wilson, *In the Presence of Nature* (Amherst: University of Massachusetts Press, 1978), p. 14.

22. Linda Smircich and Charles Stubbart, "Strategic Management in an Enacted World," *Academy of Management Review,* 10 (1985): 724–736.

23. Alston Chase, *Playing God in Yellowstone* (San Diego: Harcourt Brace Jovanovich, 1987); Theodore R. Catton, "Glacier Bay National Monument, the Tlingit, and the Artifice of Wilderness," *Northern Review,* 11 (1993): 56–82.

24. John Prest, *The Garden of Eden: The Botanic Garden and the Recreation of Paradise* (New Haven: Yale University Press, 1981).

25. Peter R. Grahame, "Narration, Sightings, and Science in Whale Watching: A Study in the Social Organization of Popular Nature Experiences," *Bentley College Working Paper Series,* no. 93–021 (1993), pp. 1–17; Peter J. Schmitt, *Back to Nature: The Arcadian Myth in Urban America* (New York: Oxford University Press, 1969).

26. *Oxford English Dictionary* (compact, second ed.) (Oxford: Clarendon, 1991), p. 1150.

27. Raymond Williams, *Problems in Materialism and Culture* (London: Verso, 1980), p. 67.

28. Bill McKibben, *The End of Nature* (New York: Random House, 1989), p. 64.

29. Ulrich Beck, *Ecological Politics in an Age of Risk* (Cambridge, England: Polity, 1995), p. 38.

30. Roderick Frazier Nash, *Wilderness and the American Mind,* 3rd ed. (New Haven: Yale University Press, 1982).

31. Walter Truett Anderson, *To Govern Evolution: Further Adventures of the Political Animal* (San Diego: Harcourt Brace Jovanovich, 1987), pp. 9, 347.

32. Robert Pogue Harrison, *Forests: The Shadow of Civilization* (Chicago: University of Chicago Press, 1992), p. ix.

33. Kate Soper, *What Is Nature?* (Oxford: Blackwell, 1995).

34. Riley E. Dunlap and William R. Catton, Jr., "Struggling with Human Exceptionalism: The Rise, Decline, and Revitalization of Environmental Sociology," *American Sociologist,* 25 (1994): 5–30.

35. Evernden, *The Social Creation of Nature,* p. 15.

36. John A. Livingston, *The Fallacy of Wildlife Conservation* (Toronto: McClelland and Stewart, 1981), p. 69; Alexander Wilson, *The Culture of Nature* (Cambridge, Mass.: Blackwell, 1992), p. 13.

37. Donna Lee King, *Doing Their Share to Save the Planet: Children and Environmental Crisis* (New Brunswick: Rutgers University Press, 1995).

38. Thomas McNamee, *Nature First: Keeping Our Wild Places and Wild Creatures Free* (Boulder, Colo.: Robert Rinehart, 1987), p. 8.

39. Livingston, *Fallacy,* pp. 116–117.

40. Williams, *Problems,* p. 70.

41. Irene Diamond and Gloria Feman Orenstein, eds., *Reweaving the World: The Emergence of Ecofeminism* (San Francisco: Sierra Club Books, 1990), pp. xi–xii.

42. Daniel J. Kevles, "Greens in America," *New York Review of Books,* Oct. 6, 1994, pp. 35–40; quotation from p. 39.

43. Tom Regan, *The Case for Animal Rights* (Berkeley: University of California Press, 1983).

44. Christopher Manes, *Green Rage: Radical Environmentalism and the Unmaking of Civilization* (Boston: Little Brown, 1990), p. 248.

45. Mark Sagoff, "Fact and Value in Ecological Science," *Environmental Ethics*, 7 (1985): 99–116; quotation from p. 99.

46. Charles T. Rubin, *The Green Crusade: Rethinking the Roots of Environmentalism* (New York: Free Press, 1994), p. 10.

47. Joseph L. Sax, *Mountains without Handrails: Reflections on the National Parks* (Ann Arbor: University of Michigan Press, 1980), pp. 2, 14.

48. Paul W. Taylor, *Respect for Nature* (Princeton: Princeton University Press, 1986), presents a particularly chilling view, suggesting that

> the preservation of the human species may not be a good. . . . It seems quite clear that in the contemporary world the extinction of the species *Homo sapiens* would be beneficial to the Earth's Community of Life as a whole. . . . And if we were to take the standpoint of that Life Community and give voice to its true interest, the ending of the human epoch on Earth would most likely be greeted with a hearty "Good riddance!" (pp. 12, 114, 115)

49. Barry Commoner, *The Closing Circle: Nature, Man, and Technology* (New York: Knopf, 1972), p. 41; *contra* Andrew Ross, *The Chicago Gangster Theory of Life: Nature's Debt to Society* (New York: Verso, 1994), p. 271.

50. J. Baird Callicott, "Animal Liberation: A Triangular Affair," *Environmental Ethics*, 2 (1980): 311–338; quotation from p. 311; Regan, *The Case*.

51. Quoted in Roderick Frazier Nash, *The Rights of Nature* (Madison: University of Wisconsin Press, 1989), p. 4, and McKibben, *End of Nature*, p. 180.

52. Alasdair MacIntyre, *After Virtue* (Notre Dame: Notre Dame University Press, 1984).

53. Manes, *Green Rage*, p. 37.

54. Elizabeth Dodson Gray, *Why the Green Nigger?* (Wellesley, Mass.: Roundtable Press, 1979).

55. Nash, *Rights of Nature*, p. 13.

56. Stone, *Should Trees Have Standing?*

57. Tom Wolfe, *Radical Chic and Mau-Mauing the Flak Catchers* (New York: Farrar, Straus, and Giroux, 1971).

58. Devall and Sessions, *Deep Ecology*, p. 66.

59. Frederick Ferre, "Moderation, Morals, and Meat," *Inquiry*, 29 (1986): 391–406; quotation from p. 391.

60. Anderson, *To Govern Evolution*, p. 346.

61. Robert H. Nelson, "Unoriginal Sin: The Judeo-Christian Roots of Eco-theology," *Policy Review*, 53 (Summer 1990): 52–59; quotation from p. 57.

62. J. E. Lovelock, *Gaia: A New Look at Life on Earth* (Oxford: Oxford University Press, 1979).

63. McKibben, *End of Nature*, p. 64.

64. Donald Worster, *Nature's Economy: A History of Ecological Ideas* (San Francisco: Sierra Club Books, 1985).

65. See Holmes Rolston, *Environmental Ethics* (Philadelphia: Temple University Press, 1988), p. 23.

66. Nash, *Wilderness and the American Mind*, p. 24.

67. Bruce Ames, the creator of the Ames Test, which alerted scientists and consumers to chemical dangers, finds natural pesticides in cabbage, broccoli, lettuce, spinach, figs, red wine, cocoa powder, and black pepper, among other foods. Nature, he suggests, is a mix of protective and toxic elements. John Tierney, "Not to Worry," *Hippocrates* (Jan./Feb. 1988): 29–38.

68. Ron Arnold, *Ecology Wars: Environmentalism as if People Mattered* (Bellevue, Wash.: Free Enterprise Press, 1993), p. 35.

69. Ross, *Chicago Gangster Theory*, pp. 12–13.

70. Quoted in Rolston, *Environmental Ethics*, p. 33.

71. Ibid.

72. Robert Gottlieb, *Forcing the Spring: The Transformation of the American Environmental Movement* (Washington: Island Press, 1993), pp. 316–317; Arnold, *Ecology Wars*, 1993.

73. Livingston, *Fallacy*, p. 17.

74. Sax, *Mountains without Handrails*, p. 1.

75. Kevles, "Greens in America," p. 35.

76. For example, Frederick Buttel, "Sociology and the Environment: The Winding Road toward Human Ecology," *International Social Science Journal*, 109 (1986): 337–356; Shirley Bradway Laska, "Environmental Sociology and the State of the Discipline," *Social Forces*, 72 (1993): 1–71; Dunlap and Catton, "Struggling with Human Exceptionalism."

77. D. E. Morrison and Riley E. Dunlap, "Environmentalism and Elitism: A Conceptual and Empirical Analysis," *Environmental Management*, 10 (1986): 581–589; Frederick H. Buttel and William L. Flinn, "Social Class and Mass Environmental Beliefs: A Reconsideration," *Environment and Behavior*, 10 (1978): 433–450.

78. Riley E. Dunlap and Angela Mertig, "The Evolution of the U.S. Environmental Movement from 1970 to 1990," in Riley E. Dunlap and Angela Mertig, eds., *American Environmentalism: The U.S. Environmental*

Movement, 1970–1990 (Philadelphia: Taylor and Francis, 1992), pp. 1–10; Klaus Eder, "The Rise of Counter-culture Movements against Modernity: Nature as a New Field of Class Struggle," *Theory, Culture, and Society,* 7 (1990): 21–47.

79. Robert Bullard, *Dumping in Dixie: Race, Class, and Environmental Quality* (Boulder: Westview, 1990); Bonnie Erikson, "Secret Societies and Social Structure," *Social Forces,* 80 (1976): 188–210; Harvey Molotch, "Oil in Santa Barbara and Power in America," *Sociological Inquiry,* 40 (1970): 131–144.

80. William R. Catton, Jr., *Overshoot: The Ecological Basis for Evolutionary Change* (Urbana: University of Illinois Press, 1980).

81. William R. Catton and Riley E. Dunlap, "A New Ecological Paradigm for Post-Exuberant Sociology," *American Behavioral Scientist,* 24 (1978): 15–47.

82. Stanley Milgram, "The Experience of Living in Cities," *Science,* 167 (1970): 1461–1468.

83. Fungi are a special sort of "plant" in that they lack the green pigment chlorophyll of flowering plants, and lack recognizable leaves, stems, and roots (Harold J. Brodie, *Fungi: Delight of Curiosity* [Toronto: University of Toronto Press, 1978], p. 124). They fit awkwardly (and, to some, not at all) in the Plant Kingdom. For my purposes I gingerly classify fungi as plants.

84. Arnold Arluke and Clinton R. Sanders, *Regarding Animals* (Philadelphia: Temple University Press, 1996).

85. Herman Schmalenbach, *On Society and Experience* (Chicago: University of Chicago Press, 1977); Kevin Hetherington, "The Contemporary Significance of Schmalenbach's Concept of the Bund," *Sociological Review,* 42 (1994): 1–25.

86. Burton R. Clark, *The Distinctive College* (Chicago: Aldine, 1970); Joanne Martin, Sim Sitkin, and M. Boehm, "Founders and the Elusiveness of a Cultural Legacy," in P. Frost, L. Moore, M. Louis, C. Lundberg, and J. Martin, eds., *Organizational Culture* (Beverly Hills: Sage, 1985), pp. 99–124.

87. Harry Knighton, "NAMA History and the People Who Made It," in *NAMA XXV* (n.p.: North American Mycological Association, 1985), pp. 1–7; quotation from p. 3.

88. Ibid., p. 1.

89. William Harlan Hale, "Every Man an Ambassador," *Reporter,* March 21, 1957, pp. 18–22; quotation from p. 18.

90. Sara Ann Friedman, *Celebrating the Wild Mushroom* (New York: Dodd, Mead, 1986).

91. There is only one mushroom club in the Twin Cities area. I felt that it would be disingenuous to create a pseudonym that would not shield the identity of the group as a whole. Following standard ethnographic practice, I use pseudonyms for individuals, except when referring to authors of published materials or public figures.

92. The Identification Committee is an informal group composed of those members with expertise in identifying mushrooming and who enjoy doing so. They sit in the rear of the room and name the mushrooms other members bring.

93. This is most notable in terms of psychoactive mushrooms. The most popular genus, *Psilocybe,* does not grow in great numbers in Minnesota. Observations in the South or parts of the Pacific Coast would reveal much greater interest in—and controversy about—these mushrooms.

94. G. J. Binding, *Mushrooms: Nature's Major Protein Food* (New York: Baronet, 1979), pp. 9–10; W. P. K. Findlay, *Fungi: Folklore, Fiction and Fact* (Eureka, Calif.: Mad River Press, 1982), p. 6; John Ramsbottom, *Poisonous Fungi* (London: Penguin, 1945).

95. Friedman, *Celebrating,* p. 30; R. Gordon Wasson, *Soma: Divine Mushroom of Immortality* (New York: Harcourt Brace Jovanovich, 1968).

96. Findlay, *Fungi,* pp. 85–87; Wasson, *Soma;* R. Gordon Wasson and Valentina Pavlovna Wasson, *Mushrooms, Russia and History* (New York: Pantheon, 1957).

97. R. T. Roalfe and F. W. Roalfe, *The Romance of the Fungus World* (London: Chapman and Hall, 1925).

98. Lucy Kavaler, *Mushrooms, Molds, and Miracles: The Strange Realm of Fungi* (New York: John Day, 1965), p. 52.

99. Ibid., p. 34; G. C. Ainsworth, *Introduction to the History of Mycology* (Cambridge, England: Cambridge University Press, 1976), p. 13.

100. Judith Tankard and M. Schaechter, eds., *The Boston Club from 1895 to 1976: A Small Celebration* (Cambridge, Mass.: Boston Mycological Club, 1976); Ainsworth, *Introduction,* p. 284.

101. W. P. K. Findlay, *Wayside and Woodland Fungi* (London: Frederick Warne and Co., 1967), p. 14; David Arora, *Mushrooms Demystified* (Berkeley: Ten Speed Press, 1979), p. 2.

102. Lenin was a collector of mushrooms (Anne Dow, "Russia Musha," *Capital Mushrooms,* 5 [Sept.–Oct. 1984]: 13–14), as is Lech Walesa.

103. Don H. Coombs, "McKnight Field Guide Offers Paintings and Drawings," *Mushroom,* 5 (Summer 1987): 9–11; quotation from p. 10.

104. John M. Roberts, Frederick Koenig, and Richard B. Stark, "Judged Display: A Consideration of a Craft Show," *Journal of Leisure Research,* 1 (1969): 163–179; quotation from p. 177.

105. Samuel R. Rosen, *A Judge Judges Mushrooms* (Nashville, Ind.: Highlander Press, 1982), p. 16.

106. As a point of comparison, a national survey of attitudes and behaviors toward wildlife found that approximately 25 percent of the sample reported birdwatching in the past two years, but on the basis of equipment used and ability to identify birds, only about 3 percent of the sample were "committed" birders (Stephen R. Kellert, "Birdwatching in American Society," *Leisure Sciences,* 7 [1980]: 343–360; quotation from pp. 346–347.

107. There was no significant difference in religious affiliation for those who picked mushrooms, but those who ate mushrooms were significantly more likely to be Catholic—a surrogate variable for ethnicity (Chi Square = 5.0, $p < .05$).

108. The respondents to my questionnaire from the Minnesota Mycological Society revealed a group that was almost equally divided between men (52 percent, as opposed to 58 percent of the random sample) and women. More than half had graduated from college (51 percent, compared with 42 percent of the random sample), and nearly one-fifth (18.6 percent) had a graduate degree. Most members of the Minnesota Mycological Society were married (66.2 percent, with 12.3 percent widowed; 12.3 percent single; and 9.2 percent divorced). Politically the group was evenly split, with 33.3 percent describing themselves as conservative, 32.5 percent as moderate, and 34.1 percent as liberal. In this mid-1980s survey, 35.1 percent of mushroomers had incomes of more than $40,000. Although the income range was wide, they were generally affluent. The age distribution revealed a bimodal trend with few young mushroomers under thirty (2.4 percent), many in their thirties and forties (21.0 percent and 21.8 percent respectively), relatively few in their fifties (14.5 percent), and many in their sixties and seventies (29.0 percent and 11.3 percent respectively). The questionnaires from NAMA revealed a sample that was largely male (66 percent) and college-educated (80 percent). Many had graduate degrees (46 percent). Sixty-seven percent were married, and the group as a whole was slightly more liberal politically than the Minnesota group (27 percent conservative, 33 percent moderate, 41 percent liberal). Forty-four percent had incomes of more than $40,000. The bimodal distribution was not as evident as in the Minnesota club, with the modal age in the sixties (twenties: 4 percent; thirties: 17 percent; forties: 12 percent; fifties: 23 percent; sixties: 30 percent; seventies and older: 15 percent). The NAMA sample was somewhat older, wealthier, more male, and better educated than the Minnesota sample.

From observation and the analysis of the Minnesota questionnaire, the most active members of the two largest groups differ in social and cultural background. The younger group was liberal, well-educated, more likely to be male, and many claimed that they entered mushrooming from an interest in nature; the older group was conservative, less affluent, and more likely to be female. Although not true for all of this group, many were introduced to mushrooming through their family or ethnic group. Many were older women. These generalizations should not obscure the impressive diversity of the group in class and gender. The occupations of members were widely diverse, although more participants than expected by chance were upper middle class. Race was another matter. Of the approximately 230 participants at the national NAMA foray, only 1 was African-American: an invited professional mycologist from Howard University. Few participants were Hispanic or Asian.

109. "The Psychology of Mushroomers," *Mycophile*, 30 (Sept.–Oct. 1989): 3.
110. David Snow and Leon Anderson, "Identity Work among the Homeless: The Verbal Construction and Avowal of Personal Identities," *American Journal of Sociology*, 92 (1987): 1336–1371.
111. Richard J. Mitchell, *Mountain Experience* (Chicago: University of Chicago Press, 1983), p. 72.
112. Gary Alan Fine, "Small Groups and Culture Creation," *American Sociological Review*, 44 (1979): 733–745; Gary Alan Fine, "The Manson Family: The Folklore Traditions of a Small Group," *Journal of the Folklore Institute*, 19 (1982): 47–60; Gary Alan Fine, *With the Boys: Little League Baseball and Preadolescent Behavior* (Chicago: University of Chicago Press, 1987).
113. Alexis De Toqueville, *Democracy in America*, ed. J. P. Mayer (Garden City, N.Y.: Anchor, 1969); Edward Banfield, *The Moral Basis of a Backward Society* (Glencoe, Ill.: Free Press, 1958); Hale, "Every Man."
114. Howard Aldrich, "The Sociable Organization: A Case Study of Mensa and Some Propositions," *Sociology and Social Research*, 55 (1971): 429–441.
115. John F. Rieger, *American Sportsmen and the Origin of Conservation*, rev. ed. (Norman: University of Oklahoma Press, 1986); Lynn Barber, *The Heyday of Natural History* (Garden City, N.Y.: Doubleday, 1980).

I. BEING IN NATURE

1. John A. Livingston, *The Fallacy of Wildlife Conservation* (Toronto: McClelland and Stewart, 1981), p. 11.

2. My usage of Latin names proves no barrier to serious mushroom collectors, who are mystified by my social scientific references. Academics will find the reverse trouble. Everyone knows *Hypsizygus tessulatus* and Mihalyi Csikszentmihalyi.

3. Edmund Burke, *A Philosophical Enquiry into the Origin of Our Ideas of the Sublime* (London: R. and J. Dodsley, 1758), p. 57.

4. Stephen R. Kellert, "Birdwatching in American Society," *Leisure Sciences,* 7 (1984): 343–360.

5. T. Whelan, "Ecotourism and Its Role in Sustainable Development," in *Nature Tourism: Managing for the Environment* (Washington, D.C.: Island Press, 1991); Peter R. Grahame, "'This Is Not Sea World': Spectacle and Insight in Nature Tourism," unpublished manuscript, 1993; Alexander Wilson, *The Culture of Nature* (Cambridge, Mass.: Blackwell, 1992), pp. 19–51.

6. David S. Wilson, *In the Presence of Nature* (Amherst: University of Massachusetts Press, 1978), p. 1.

7. Gary Alan Fine, "Justifying Fun: Or, Why We Do Not Teach 'Exotic Dance' in High School," *Play and Culture,* 4 (1991): 87–99.

8. Norm Strung, "The Greening," *Mushroom,* 1 (Fall 1983): 17–18; quotation from p. 17.

9. In discussing angling, George Will ("The Democracy of Angling," *Newsweek,* Aug. 19, 1985, p. 72) enthuses:

> Fishing, properly approached, is like the political philosophy of a civilized society: it is less a creed than a climate of opinion. Fishing is a way of life resembling what the incomparable Aristotle considered the best regime. That is, it combines democratic and aristocratic elements. . . . Fishing, like the classics, teaches patience, humility and the joy of life.

Like political pundits, the competent fisher needs a line to hook the unwary.

10. Bill McKibben, *The End of Nature* (New York: Random House, 1989), p. 55.

11. Holmes Rolston, *Environmental Ethics* (Philadelphia: Temple University Press, 1988), p. 15.

12. Hal Borland, no title, *New York Times,* 1964 (no date), p. 7.

13. Thomas McNamee, *Nature First: Keeping Our Wild Places and Wild Creatures Free* (Boulder, Colo.: Robert Rinehart, 1987), p. 9.

14. Roderick Frazier Nash, *Wilderness and the American Mind* (New Haven: Yale University Press, 1967), p. 1.

15. Simon Schama, *Landscape and Memory* (New York: Knopf, 1995), p. vii.

16. Harriet Ritvo, *The Animal Estate* (Cambridge, Mass.: Harvard University Press, 1987), p. 3; Catherine A. Lutz and Jane L. Collins, *Reading National Geographic* (Chicago: University of Chicago Press, 1993), p. 260.

17. Stephen Fox, *The American Conservation Movement: John Muir and His Legacy* (Madison: University of Wisconsin Press, 1981), p. 201.

18. Nash, *Wilderness*, p. 141.

19. Vance Bourjaily, *The Unnatural Enemy* (New York: Dial, 1963), p. 15.

20. Rachel Kaplan, "Wilderness Perception and Psychological Benefits: An Analysis of a Continuing Program," *Leisure Sciences*, 6 (1984): 286–287; Rachel Kaplan and Stephen Kaplan, *The Experience of Nature: A Psychological Perspective* (Cambridge, England: Cambridge University Press, 1989), p. 175. A dramatic example of the restorative properties of nature is evident in the justification for nudism in natural surroundings as involving, according to the American League for Physical Culture, the "cultivation of physical, moral, and social health through exercise and life under natural conditions" (Jane Stern and Michael Stern, "Decent Exposure," *New Yorker*, March 19, 1990, pp. 73–98; quotation from p. 83).

21. Gary Paul Nabhan and Stephen Trimble, *The Geography of Childhood: Why Children Need Wild Places* (Boston: Beacon Press, 1994), pp. xv, 26.

22. Nash, *Wilderness*, p. 232.

23. Jonas Frykman and Orvar Lofgren, *Culture Builders* (New Brunswick: Rutgers University Press, 1987), p. 86.

24. Kaplan and Kaplan, *Experience of Nature*, p. 1.

25. Charles R. Simpson, "The Wilderness in American Capitalism: The Sacralization of Nature," *International Journal of Politics, Culture, and Society*, 5 (1992): 555–576; quotation from p. 559.

26. Paul Gruchow, *The Necessity of Empty Places* (New York: St. Martin's, 1988), p. 12.

27. Alex Inkeles, *Exploring Individual Modernity* (New York: Columbia University Press, 1983).

28. Edward O. Wilson, *Biophilia* (Cambridge, Mass.: Harvard University Press, 1984), p. 118.

29. Fox, *American Conservation Movement*, p. 229.

30. Maggie Rogers, "In the Spring," *Mushroom*, 3 (Spring 1985): 12–14; quotation from p. 13.

31. Heinz-Günter Vester, "Adventure as a Form of Leisure," *Journal of Leisure Research*, 6 (1987): 237–249.

32. Frykman and Lofgren, *Culture Builders*, p. 86.

33. Maggie Rogers, "Going Out in the Fall," *Mushroom,* 2 (Fall 1984): 17–19; quotation from p. 17.

34. Richard Elias, "The Psychology of Mushroomers—A Reprise," *Mycophile,* 31 (Jan.–Feb. 1990): 1–8; quotations from pp. 1, 8.

35. Walt Sturgeon, "Here Come the Morels!" *Mushroom,* 3 (Spring 1985): 5–8; quotation from p. 8.

36. Maggie Rogers, "Deciding When to Go Out for the First Time," *Mushroom,* 2 (Spring 1984): 6–7; quotation from p. 6.

37. Samuel Ristich, "Get Outdoors Now," *Mushroom,* 3 (Winter 1984–1985): 5–8; quotation from p. 5.

38. Gary Thomas, "Stalking the Wild Morel," *Outsider Highlights,* reprinted in *IMA Newsletter* (Illinois Mycological Association Newsletter), Feb. 1984, pp. 3–5; quotation from p. 5.

39. Maggie Rogers, "Foraying With NAMA," *Mushroom,* 1 (Fall 1983): 43–45; quotation from p. 45.

40. Ms. Mushroom, "Etiquette," *Mushroom,* 2 (Summer 1984): 28–29; quotation from p. 28.

41. John Schaaf, "Biting Cassowaries," *Mycena News,* 33 (Sept. 1983): 37.

42. Patrick Stout, "Foray Softly," *IMA Newsletter* (Illinois Mycological Society Newsletter), Nov. 1982, p. 2.

43. David Arora, *Mushrooms Demystified* (Berkeley: Ten Speed Press, 1979) p. 12.

44. Larry Stickney, "Mushroom Vagabonding," *Mushroom,* 2 (Winter 1983–1984): 27–28.

45. Sheila Burnford, *The Fields of Noon* (Boston: Little Brown, 1964), p. 43.

46. Erazim Kohak, *The Embers and the Stars* (Chicago: University of Chicago Press, 1984), p. 6.

47. John F. Rieger, *American Sportsmen and the Origin of Conservation,* rev. ed. (Norman: University of Oklahoma Press, 1986), p. 35.

48. Sara Ann Friedman and W. K. Williams, "The Endless Foray Goes to L.A.," *New York Mycological Society Newsletter,* 7 (Spring 1984): 1–2; quotation from p. 1.

49. Rolston, *Environmental Ethics,* p. 16.

50. David Robbins, "Sport, Hegemony, and the Middle Class: The Victorian Mountaineers," *Theory, Culture, and Society,* 4 (1987): 579–601; quotation from p. 593.

51. John P. Hewitt, "Stalking the Wild Identity," unpublished manuscript, 1984.

52. Bill Bakaitis, "Reflections on the Northeastern Foray," *Mid-Hudson Mycological Association Newsletter,* 1 (Oct. 1983–1984): 1–2; quotation from p. 1.

53. Bourjaily, *Unnatural Enemy,* p. 28.

54. Gary Alan Fine, "Wild Life: Authenticity and the Human Experience of 'Natural' Places," in Carolyn Ellis and Michael G. Flaherty, eds., *Investigating Subjectivity* (Newbury Park: Sage, 1992), pp. 156–175; quotation from pp. 171–173.

55. Mihalyi Csikszentmihalyi, *Beyond Boredom and Anxiety* (San Francisco: Jossey-Bass, 1975), p. 172.

56. Stanford Lyman and Marvin Scott, *A Sociology of the Absurd* (New York: General Hall, 1989), p. 52; Georg Simmel, *Georg Simmel, 1858–1918: A Collection of Essays, with Translations and a Bibliography,* ed. Kurt Wolfe (Columbus: Ohio State University Press, 1959), p. 243.

57. The temporal quality of nature is also seasonal. Most Americans, particularly those in the temperate zone, are more "cultural" in the winter. Being in nature, as noted above, is connected to a sense of comfort that reduced temperatures diminish.

58. Lynn Barber, *The Heyday of Natural History* (Garden City, N.Y.: Doubleday, 1980), pp. 17–26; T. M. Luhrmann, *Persuasions of the Witch's Craft* (Cambridge, Mass.: Harvard University Press, 1989), pp. 46–47.

59. James A. Swan, *In Defense of Hunting* (New York: Harper Collins, 1995), p. 18.

60. Alston Chase, *Playing God in Yellowstone* (San Diego: Harcourt Brace Jovanovich, 1987), p. 300.

61. Rolston, *Environmental Ethics,* p. 25.

62. Samuel A. Rosen, *A Judge Judges Mushrooms* (Nashville, Ind.: Highlander Press, 1982), p. 25.

63. Chase, *Playing God,* p. 301; Arthur A. Ekirch, Jr., *Man and Nature in America* (New York: Columbia University Press, 1963), p. 14.

64. "Hymn to the Morel," *Mycelium,* 6 (April 1980): 2–4; quotation from pp. 3–4.

65. Simpson, "Wilderness," p. 566.

66. Peter Canby, "Of Men and Morels," in Peter Leach and Anne Mikkelsen, eds., *Malfred Ferndock's Morel Cookbook* (Denison, Minn.: Ferndock, 1986), pp. 66–74; quotation from p. 74.

67. Travis Dinoff, "Letter from Andrew Weil," *Spore Print,* 113 (Feb. 1984): 8–10; quotation from p. 10.

68. R. Gordon Wasson, *Soma: Divine Mushroom of Immortality* (New York: Harcourt Brace Jovanovich, 1968), p. 3.

69. Max Weber, "Science as a Vocation," in Hans H. Gerth and C. Wright Mills, eds., *From Max Weber* (New York: Oxford University Press, 1946).

70. In previous generations birders were more likely to have a direct effect—sometimes shooting birds or collecting eggs or nests. Audubon

shot most of the birds he painted, and several specimens in the Harvard birdskin collection were prepared by Henry David Thoreau (Don Stap, *A Bird without a Name* [New York: Knopf, 1990], p. 94). These traditions have since bowed to ideological pressures.

71. Bill Devall and Joseph Harry, "Who Hates Whom in the Great Outdoors: The Impact of Recreational Specialization and Technologies of Play," *Leisure Science,* 4 (1981): 399–418.

72. Natural objects may have different moral standings. Mosquitos provide a test for many naturalists. Even many birdwatchers would not mind the destruction of starlings or sparrows. One mushroom collector told me that he didn't feel bad about "overpicking" honey caps, because they are "virulent rotters of wood."

73. This is similar to hunters who deliberately do not shoot all the birds in a covey, saving some to breed for next year (Stuart Marks, *Southern Hunting in Black and White: Nature, History, and Ritual in a Carolina Community* [Princeton: Princeton University Press, 1991], p. 176), and those who run bass tournaments in which all fish must be released (Richard Hummel and Gary S. Foster, "A Sporting Chance: Relationships between Technological Change and Concepts of Fair Play in Fishing," *Journal of Leisure Research,* 18 [1986]: 40–52; quotation from p. 48).

74. "Mushroom Conservation: Is It Needed?" *Mycofile* (Newsletter of the Vancouver Mycological Society), April 1984, pp. 6–7; quotation from p. 7.

75. Wallace Kaufman, "Tree Oysters," *Coltsfoot,* 4 (Nov./Dec. 1983): 7–9; quotation from pp. 8–9.

76. Linda Painter, Personal communication, 1984.

77. "Morel Harvesters: Plea to Preserve the Environment," *Mush Rumor* (Snohomish County Mycological Society), March/April 1984, pp. 5–6; quotation from p. 5.

78. Schaaf, "Biting Cassowaries," p. 37.

79. "Mushroom Conservation," p. 6.

80. Bill Freedman and Louise Freedman, "Letter to the Editor," *Mycena News,* 32 (April 1983): 21.

81. When examining fishing in "A Sporting Chance," p. 48, Hummel and Foster distinguish between two models of contest. In the first, the fisher is contesting with the fish (an elitist version); in the second, the contest is with other fishers (a democratic version).

82. Some years in the United States no mushroom fatalities are reported. Although some serious poisonings occur (90 percent of mushroom fatalities in the United States are from *Amanita* species; see Walt Sturgeon,

"Vagabonding," *Mushroom,* 2 [Summer 1984]: 26–27; quotation from p. 27), most who eat deadly mushrooms can now be saved, despite lasting liver damage. One estimate of annual reports of mushroom poisoning places the figure at around 350 ("Beware the Wild Mushroom," *The Mycofile,* 26 [Nov./Dec. 1985]: 3, although many are too minor to be reported. Most "poisonings" are minor, involving an upset stomach or vomiting. In my Minnesota sample, 14.7 percent reported having been made ill by mushrooms, but only two hospitalizations were reported. No deaths of club members are recounted in the organizational lore. Most mushroom "poisonings" involve ingestion of mushrooms by children, and subsequent panicked reactions by worried parents (Denis Benjamin, "Who Gets Poisoned?" *Mycophile,* 30 [1989]: 2, Mar/Apr).

83. Jan Kuthan, "Fall in Czechoslovakia: It's the Main Season for Real Pickers," *Mushroom,* 4 (Fall 1986): 31–32; quotation from p. 31.

84. Georg Simmel, *On Individuality and Social Forms* (Chicago: University of Chicago Press, 1971).

85. Cited in J. A. Walter, "Death as Recreation: Armchair Mountaineering," *Leisure Studies,* 3 (1984): 67–76; quotation from p. 71.

86. Vester, "Adventure as a Form of Leisure"; Michael Balint, *Thrills and Regressions* (New York: International Universities Press, 1959); Jennifer Hunt, "Divers' Accounts of Normal Risk," *Symbolic Interaction,* 18 (1995): 439–462.

87. Michael J. Apter, *The Dangerous Edge: The Psychology of Excitement* (New York: Free Press, 1992).

88. Norbert Elias and Eric Dunning, *Quest for Excitement* (Oxford: Blackwell, 1986), p. 106.

89. Fox, *American Conservation Movement,* p. 338.

90. Linda Painter, personal communication, 1984.

91. Sara Ann Friedman, *Celebrating the Wild Mushroom* (New York: Dodd, Mead, 1986), p. 71.

92. One collector even professes satisfaction in eating a poisonous mushroom, causing two days of delirium, diarrhea, and vomiting. He reports: "I'm glad I did because it humbled me. It taught me to be careful, to be discerning, to learn more" (Simon Kelly quoted in David Arora, *All That the Rain Promises and More . . .* [Berkeley: Ten Speed Press, 1991], p. 41).

93. Serge Schmemann, "'Overpick': A Sore Subject in Russia," *Mushroom,* 4 (Winter 1985–1986): 15.

94. An interesting case is that of *Gyromitra esculenta.* This "false morel" is a prime edible in Europe. In America, a dozen deaths have been attributed

to it over the years (it is said to contain a chemical found in rocket fuel). Yet many American mushroomers have consumed it with relish, and some still do, even though most are now more cautious.

95. Jeff Donaghue, "Eat Russulas in '86! (A Challenge)," *Toadstool Review* (Minnesota Mycological Society), 11 (Dec. 1986): 2.

96. Lorelei Norvell, "A Romp through Lepiota," *Mushroom,* 5 (Winter 1986–1987): 14–16; quotation from p. 15.

97. Friedman, *Celebrating,* p. 137.

98. Emily Johnson, "Caesars by the Dozens," in *NAMA XXV* (n.p.: North American Mycological Society, 1985), pp. 23–27; quotation from p. 23.

99. Emil F. Guba, *Wild Mushrooms—Food and Poison* (Waltham, Mass.: Emil F. Guba, 1970), p. 6.

100. Denis Benjamin, "Types of Mushroom Poisonings," *Mycophile,* 31 (Jan./Feb. 1990): 2–3; quotation from p. 2.

101. A. Tversky and D. Kahneman, "Judgement under Uncertainty: Heuristics and Biases," *Science,* 185 (1974): 1124–1131.

102. Ida Geary, "Hunting the Wild Morels," *California Magazine* (May 1982), p. 72.

103. Andrew Weigert, "Transverse Interaction: A Pragmatic Perspective on Environment as Other," *Symbolic Interaction,* 14 (1991): 353–363.

2. MEANINGFUL MUSHROOMS

1. Ralph Waldo Emerson, "Man the Reformer," in *Essays and Lectures by Ralph Waldo Emerson* (New York: Library of America, 1983), p. 149.

2. Hobson Bryan, "Leisure Value Systems and Recreational Specialization: The Case of Trout Fishermen," *Journal of Leisure Research,* 9 (1977): 174–187.

3. Jonas Frykman and Orvar Lofgren, *Culture Builders* (New Brunswick: Rutgers University Press, 1987), p. 45.

4. Arthur C. Danto, *The Transfiguration of the Commonplace* (Cambridge, Mass.: Harvard University Press, 1981).

5. Gregory Stone, "Personal Acts," *Symbolic Interaction,* 1 (1977): 2–19.

6. Diane Ackerman, *A Natural History of the Senses* (New York: Random House, 1990), p. 9.

7. Arnold Isenberg, "Critical Communication," in William Elton, ed., *Aesthetics and Language* (Oxford: Basil Blackwell, 1954), pp. 131–146; quotation from p. 138.

8. George Herbert Mead, *Selected Writings* (Indianapolis: Bobbs-Merrill, 1964), pp. 147–148.

9. Michael Polanyi, *Personal Knowledge* (Chicago: University of Chicago Press, 1958).

10. Ludwig Wittgenstein, *Philosophical Investigations,* 2d ed., trans. G. E. M. Anscombe (New York: Macmillan, 1958), p. 36.

11. Ludwig Wittgenstein, *Remarks on Color,* ed. G. E. M. Anscombe, trans. Linda L. McAllister and Margarete Schattle (Berkeley: University of California Press, 1978), p. 11.

12. George Lakoff and Mark Johnson, *Metaphors We Live By* (Chicago: University of Chicago Press, 1980), p. 71.

13. Howard L. Kaye, *The Social Meaning of Modern Biology* (New Haven: Yale University Press, 1986), p. 6.

14. V. N. Toporov, "On the Semiotics of the Mythological Conceptions about Mushrooms," *Semiotica,* 53–54 (1985): 295–357; quotation from p. 295.

15. Edward O. Wilson, *Biophilia* (Cambridge, Mass.: Harvard University Press, 1984), p. 100.

16. Francis-Noël Thomas and Mark Turner, *Clear and Simple as the Truth: Writing Classic Prose* (Princeton: Princeton University Press, 1994), p. 116.

17. Gary Lincoff, *Audobon Society Field Guide to North American Mushrooms* (New York: Knopf, 1981), pp. 586–587.

18. Alfred Schutz, *Collected Works,* vol. I, ed. Maurice Natanson (The Hague: Martinus Nijhoff, 1967).

19. Lakoff and Johnson, *Metaphors,* p. 71.

20. Harold Garfinkel, *Studies in Ethnomethodology* (Englewood Cliffs, N.J.: Prentice-Hall, 1967).

21. Kent H. McKnight and Vera B. McKnight, *A Field Guide to Mushrooms* (Boston: Houghton Mifflin, 1987), p. 117.

22. Phyllis G. Glick, *The Mushroom Trail Guide* (New York: Holt, Rinehart and Winston, 1979), p. 180.

23. McKnight and McKnight, *Field Guide.*

24. Henry David Thoreau, "Mushrooms in Literature," *Spores Afield* (Nov. 1984), p. 4.

25. The connection of mountains with women's breasts suggests the same (male) fascination. We know of the Grand Tetons. Less well known are Nippletop in New York, Squaw Tit in Oregon, and the Jane Russell Peaks in New Hampshire (Don Nilsen and Aileen Nilsen, "Humor, Language, and Sex Roles in American Culture," *International Journal of the Sociology of Language,* 65 [1987]: 67–78, p. 73).

26. Because of their odor and taste, some mushrooms, notably truffles, have been claimed to be aphrodisiacs (or steroidal sex attractants). Truffles, remarked the nineteenth-century gourmet Brillat-Savarin, make "women more tender and men more agreeable" (Anne Dow, "Your Own Truffle Trees?" *Mushroom,* 2 [Summer 1984]: 11–14;

quotation from p. 12), a perspective backed by scientific evidence. One mushroomer noted: "Watch for Chanel #6 to come out made from mushrooms!" (Bob Burrell, "What the Scientists Are Doing With Mushrooms," *Ohio Spore Print* [May–June 1982], p. 6).

27. David Arora, *Mushrooms Demystified* (Berkeley: Ten Speed Press, 1979), p. 561.

28. Gwen Raverat, *Period Piece: A Cambridge Childhood* (London: Faber and Faber, 1952), pp. 135–136.

29. "A Theory about Stinkhorns," *Newsletter Parkside Mycological Club* (Autumn 1982), p. 2. Reprinted from the *New York Times*, Feb. 24, 1929.

30. Gary Lincoff, "Joe's Restaurant: A Review," *New York Mycological Society Newsletter,* 6 (Summer 1982): 4–5; quotation from p. 4.

31. Sharon Zukin, *Landscapes of Power* (Berkeley: University of California Press, 1991), p. 18; Frykman and Lofgren, *Culture Builders,* p. 58; Michael Mayerfield Bell, *Childerly: Nature and Morality in a Country Village* (Chicago: University of Chicago Press, 1994).

32. Peter J. Schmitt, *Back to Nature: The Arcadian Myth in Urban America* (New York: Oxford University Press, 1969), p. 37; Gary Alan Fine and Lazaros Christophorides, "Dirty Birds, Filthy Immigrants, and the English Sparrow War: Metaphorical Linkage in Constructing Social Problems," *Symbolic Interaction,* 14 (1991): 375–393.

33. Harold Brodie, *Fungi: Delight of Curiosity* (Toronto: University of Toronto Press, 1978), p. 22.

34. *The Ink Cap,* Northwest Wisconsin Mycological Society, vol. 1, no. 2, pp. 1–4.

35. Claude Levi-Strauss, *The Savage Mind* (Chicago: University of Chicago Press, 1962).

36. Arora, *Mushrooms Demystified,* pp. 228–229.

37. Sara Ann Friedman, *Celebrating the Wild Mushroom* (New York: Dodd, Mead, 1986), p. 72.

38. Andrew J. Weigert, "Lawns of Weeds: Status in Opposition to Life," *American Sociologist,* 25 (1994): 80–96.

39. Arora, *Mushrooms Demystified,* pp. 325, 347.

40. Ibid., p. 441.

41. Walt Sturgeon, "Perusing Polypores—An Area of Great Nomenclatural Change," *Mushroom,* 13 (Spring 1995): 20–21; quotation from p. 21.

42. Mike Wells, "Get Chanterelles, One Way or Another," *Mushroom,* 4 (Fall 1986): 25.

43. Doug Schlink, "Russula Recipe," *Toadstool Review* (Minnesota Mycological Society) 11 (Dec. 1986): 2.

44. Arora, *Mushrooms Demystified,* pp. 75–76.

45. Wells, "Get Chanterelles," p. 25.
46. "The Russula Family," *Mush Rumor* (Snohomish County Mycological Society), June–August 1984, p. 2.
47. Jeff Donaghue, "Eat Russulas in '86! (A Challenge)," *Toadstool Review* (Minnesota Mycological Society), 11 (June 1986): 2.
48. Paul Kroeger, "The Joy of Dung," *Mycelium* (Mycological Society of Toronto), Nov.–Dec. 1982, pp. 14–17; quotation from pp. 14 and 16.
49. Bud Schwartz, "The Pilobolus Story," *Mushroom,* 12 (Spring 1994): 7–8.
50. John Minot, "Coprophiles," *Mycolog,* 8 (Sept. 1981): 1–2; quotation from p. 1.
51. R W. G. Dennis, cited in Jeff Donaghue, "Winter Activities," *Toadstool Review* (Minnesota Mycological Society), 11 (Dec. 1986): 3.
52. R. C. Summerbell, "Ode to Dung Fungi," *Mycelium* (April/May/June 1983), p. 3.
53. Basil Bernstein, *Class, Codes and Control* (New York: Schocken, 1971).
54. Ackerman, *History of the Senses,* p. xv.
55. Ibid., p. xvii.
56. Ibid., p. 307.
57. Eugene Hargrove, "The Foundations of Wildlife Protection Attitudes," in Eugene Hargrove, ed., *The Animal-Rights/Environmental Ethics Debate* (Albany: SUNY Press, 1992), pp. 151–183; quotation from p. 170.
58. Brenda Danet and Tamar Katriel, "No Two Alike: Play and Aesthetics in Collecting," *Play and Culture,* 2 (1989): 253–277.
59. Georg Simmel, *George Simmel, 1858–1918: A Collection of Essays, with Translations and a Bibliography,* ed. Kurt Wolfe (Columbus: Ohio State University Press, 1959), p. 245.
60. Anne Dillard, *Pilgrim at Tinker Creek* (New York: Harper and Row, 1974), p. 106.
61. Brodie, *Fungi,* p. 32.
62. J. Baird Callicott, "Animal Liberation: A Triangular Affair," *Environmental Ethics,* 2 (1983): 346–347.
63. Hargrove, "Foundations of Wildlife Protection Attitudes," p. 153; Holmes Rolston III, *Environmental Ethics* (Philadelphia: Temple University Press, 1988), p. 10.
64. Hargrove ("Foundations of Wildlife Protection Attitudes") suggests that this developed in the nineteenth century, when natural scientists developed an aesthetic interest in nature as a result of their close association with landscape artists and poets.
65. Alexander Wilson, *The Culture of Nature* (Cambridge, Mass.: Blackwell, 1992), p. 55; Callicott, "Animal Liberation," p. 348.

66. Samuel Ristich, "Phenology," *Mushroom,* 2 (Summer 1984): 32–35; quotation from p. 35.

67. John Hewitt, "Stalking the Wild Identity," unpublished manuscript, 1984.

68. Samuel R. Rosen, *A Judge Judges Mushrooms* (Nashville, Ind.: Highlander Press, 1982), p. 41.

69. Gary Alan Fine, field notes; Greg Wright, "The Nose Knows! Identifying Mushrooms By Odors," *Mycena News,* 35 (January 1986): 4–6; Walt Sturgeon, "Add a Dimension by Bringing Your Nose into Play," *Mushroom,* 5 (Summer 1987): 25–27; "Mushrooms With Odors," *Toadstool Review,* 6 (October 1981): 2.

70. Gary Alan Fine, "Wittgenstein's Kitchen: Sharing Meaning in Restaurant Work," *Theory and Society,* 24 (1995): 245–269.

71. Adrienne Lehrer, *Wine and Conversation* (Bloomington: Indiana University Press, 1983).

72. A. B. Marin, L. M. Libbey, and M. E. Morgan, "Truffles: On the Scent of Buried Treasure," *McIlvainea,* 6 (1984): 34–38; quotation from p. 34.

73. Bob Kasper, "Truffles Are Here!" *Mushroom,* 2 (Summer 1984): 15.

74. Maggie Rogers, "Joe's Cookbook Teaches Lovingly," *Mushroom,* 4 (Fall 1986): 39.

75. Harley Barnhart, "Truffling Along," *Mushroom,* 3 (Summer 1985): 8–13; quotation from p. 8.

76. Ibid., p. 12.

77. Neil Evernden, *The Social Creation of Nature* (Baltimore: Johns Hopkins University Press, 1992), p. 53; Vicki Hearne, *Adam's Task: Calling Animals by Name* (New York: Knopf, 1987), p. 6.

78. Thomas Nagel, "What Is It Like to Be a Bat?" *Philosophical Review,* 83 (1974): 435–450; quotations from p. 435 and p. 439.

79. David Robbins, "Sport, Hegemony, and the Middle Class: The Victorian Mountaineers," *Theory, Culture, and Society,* 4 (1987): 579–601; quotation from p. 591.

80. Quoted in Stephen Jay Gould, "Pussycats and the Owl," *New York Review of Books,* March 3, 1988, pp. 7–10; quotation from p. 7.

81. Boria Sax, *The Parliament of Animals* (New York: Pace University Press, 1992), p. 3.

82. Kerry T. Givens, "The Joy of Mushroom Watching," *Maturity* (August–September 1987): 53–58; quotation from p. 56.

83. Lorelei Novell, "You Can Rise Above Morels to All the Rainbow Colors," *Mushroom,* 5 (Spring 1987): 13–15; quotation from p. 13.

84. Friedman, *Celebrating,* p. 92.

85. Ellen O'Brien, "Once a Year, a Shared Love of Fungi Mushrooms," *Philadelphia Inquirer,* New Jersey/Metro, Aug. 18, 1984, pp. B1–B2; quotation from p. B1.

86. This contrasts with the attitudes of pet owners who attribute character to the individual animal (Arnold Arluke and Clinton R. Sanders, *Regarding Animals* [Philadelphia: Temple University Press, 1996]).

87. Toporov, "Mythological Conceptions about Mushrooms," pp. 300–301.

88. Margaret Wallace, "Mushroom Hunter," *Fungus-Amungus Review* (Dec.–Jan. 1984–1985): p. 2.

89. "Cultural Mushrooms," *Capital Mushroomers* (Sept.–Oct. 1983): 6.

90. Walt Sturgeon, "It's a Beauty Contest," *Mushroom,* 6 (Winter 1987–1988): 5–6; quotation from p. 5.

91. Jessie Keiko Saiki, "Hypal Harmonies: Old Man of the Woods (*Strobilomyces floccupus*)," *Wisconsin Mycological Society Newsletter,* 1 (Fall 1983): 7.

92. *Lepiota,* another largely white genus with white spore prints, are often seen as female. One mushroomer contrasts them with their family mate, *Agaricus. Agaricus* with a brown spore print are seen as masculine; *Lepiota,* more delicate, with a white spore print are female. Another mushroomer uses the female pronouns "she" and "her" in describing *Lepiota,* calling them tidy, quiet, and pristine (Lorelei Norvell, "A Romp through Lepiota," *Mushroom,* 5 [Winter 1986–1987]: 14–16; quotation from pp. 14–15).

93. Friedman, *Celebrating,* p. 43.

94. Margaret Shane, "Call Me Maggie," *Mycena News,* 33 (February 1983): 5 and 8; quotation from p. 8.

95. Jessie Keiko Saiki, "Death's Angel (*Amanita virosa*)," *Wisconsin Mycological Society Newsletter,* 1 (Spring 1983): 5.

96. Maggie Rogers, "Keeping Up," *Mushroom,* 3 (Winter 1984–1985): 30–33; quotation from p. 31.

97. Wilbur Snowshoe, "Collecting Moments," *Mycelium,* 6 (Nov.–Dec. 1980): 3.

98. Jennifer Mueller Wettlaufer, "Coprinus: The Suidice," *Mycological Society of America Newsletter,* 35 (June 1, 1984): 7.

99. We also talk to manmade objects, such as cars and computers—those objects with which we feel we interact. A case in point is how ventriloquists treat their "figures": "Watch a vent put his dummy down and you'll see that he never just throws him on a table or into a trunk. He almost always sets him down gently, in a chair" (Cullen Murphy, "Hey, Let Me Outta Here!" *Atlantic Monthly* [August 1989], pp. 62–71; quotation from p. 67).

100. Maggie Rogers, "Keys," *Mushroom,* 2 (Spring 1984): 22–25; quotation from p. 22.

101. Susan Metzler, "Foraying Texas: In the Big Thicket," *Mushroom,* 4 (Fall 1986): 29–30; quotation from p. 29.

102. Pat Leacock, "Looking Back at 1986 and Looking Forward to 1987," *Toadstool Review,* 11 (Dec. 1986): 4.

103. Maggie Rogers, "The Top 30," *Mushroom,* 2 (Fall 1984): 45.

104. Harriet Ritvo, *The Animal Estate* (Cambridge, Mass.: Harvard University Press, 1987), p. 1.

105. "Spring Fungi—Morels and What Else?" *Arkansas Fungi,* 4 (Jan.–Feb. 1985): 3–4; quotation from p. 3.

106. Jim Snodgrass, "Nadya Sadoba Gardiner Letteney (1906–1983)," *New York Mycological Society Newsletter,* 8 (Spring–Summer 1984): 10.

107. Maggie Rogers, "Keeping Up," *Mushroom,* 5 (Summer 1987): 32–34; quotation from p. 33.

108. Rogers, "Keys," pp. 22–23.

109. Maggie Rogers, "Now There's Sam Ristichii," *Mushroom,* 5 (Summer 1987): 27.

110. The NAMA survey response was more diverse, with thirty-five mushrooms named as favorites. Morels were chosen by 22 percent of respondents; boletes (especially *Boletus edulis*) were second, with 12 percent.

111. Jim Silbar, "In Addition to All the Hoopla, Boyne City Really Has Mushrooms," *Mushroom,* 2 (Spring 1984): 9; Larry Lonik, *The Curious Morel* (Royal Oak, Mich.: RKT Publishing, 1984).

112. Peter Leach and Anne Mikkelsen, eds., *Malfred Ferndock's Morel Cookbook* (Dennison, Minn.: Ferndock Publishing, 1986); Paul Chelgren, Jerry Petermeier, and John Ratzloff, *Roon: A Tribute to Morel Mushrooms* (Long Lake, Minn.: Cabin Publishing, 1985); Lonik, *The Curious Morel,* 1984.

113. Justin Isherwood, "The Morelist," in Leach and Mikkelsen, eds., *Morel Cookbook,* pp. 36–38; quotation from p. 37.

114. Art Conrad, "Dry Land Spongers," *Farm Quarterly* (Spring 1958): 135–138; quotation from p. 138.

115. Friedman, *Celebrating,* p. 14.

116. Don H. Coombs, " 'Rot Nots' Is Back on Its Irregular Publication Schedule," *Mushroom,* 6 (Winter 1987–1988): 27–28; quotation from p. 28.

117. Melanie Ball, "Morel/Wild Plant Hunt," *Mycelial Mat,* 7 (April/June 1983): 1.

118. Sara Ann Friedman, "Morels, May Apples, and the Meaning of Life," *Mushroom,* 4 (Spring 1986): 5–9; quotation from p. 9.

119. Ida Geary, "Hunting the Wild Morels," *California Magazine* (May 1982): 72.

120. Friedman, "Morels, May Apples," p. 5.

121. Gary Lincoff, "*Roon* Serves to Whet the Appetite," *Mushroom,* 4 (Winter 1985–1986): 37.

122. Peter Canby, "Of Men and Morels," in Leach and Mikkelsen, eds., *Morel Cookbook*, pp. 66–74; quotation from p. 67.
123. Lonik, *Curious Morel*, pp. 4–5.
124. Tom Robbins, "Another Roadside Attraction," in Leach and Mikkelson, eds., *Morel Cookbook*, pp. 89–95; quotation from p. 94.
125. Fine, "Wittgenstein's Kitchen," pp. 245–269.
126. I asked respondents to the Minnesota and NAMA survey to describe the taste of morels in an open-ended question. "Nutty" was the most common description (24 percent and 22 percent, respectively), with chewy (21 percent, 19 percent), earthy (14 percent, 9 percent), woodsy (8 percent, 9 percent), and meaty (8 percent, 14 percent) following. These make sense to mushroomers, particularly the characterizations "earthy" and "woodsy," which connect to the morel's natural, gathered quality.
127. Lonik, *Curious Morel*, p. 16.
128. Geary, "Hunting the Wild Morels," p. 72.

3. SHARING THE WOODS

1. Don Stap, *A Bird without a Name* (New York: Knopf, 1990), p. 167.
2. Ibid., p. 168.
3. Alex Shoumatoff, *The Rivers Amazon* (San Francisco: Sierra Club Books, 1986), p. 162.
4. John Rosecrance, "Racetrack Buddy Relations: Compartmentalized and Satisfying," *Journal of Social and Personal Relationships,* 3 (1986): 441–456.
5. Gregory Stone and Marvin J. Taves, "Research into the Human Element in Wilderness Use," *Proceedings, Society of American Foresters* (1956), pp. 26–32; quotation from p. 28.
6. Ibid., p. 29.
7. Gary Paul Nabhan and Stephen Trimble, *The Geography of Childhood: Why Children Need Wild Places* (Boston: Beacon Press, 1994), pp. 162–163.
8. Richard Mitchell, Jr., *Mountain Experience* (Chicago: University of Chicago Press, 1983), p. xiii; A. Alverez, "Feeding the Rat," *New Yorker,* April 18, 1988, pp. 89–115; quotation from p. 93.
9. Vance Bourjaily, *The Unnatural Enemy* (New York: Dial, 1963), p. 14.
10. Teresa Ray, "The Sharing of Wonder," *Mushroom,* 6 (Fall 1988): 20.
11. Roland Warren, *The Community in America,* 2d ed. (Chicago: Rand McNally, 1972).
12. Liz Farwell, "From the President," *Illinois Mycological Association Newsletter* (Jan.–Feb. 1983), p. 2.

13. Sara Ann Friedman, *Celebrating the Wild Mushroom* (New York: Dodd, Mead, 1986), p. 172.

14. At the NAMA foray attendees were upset that only fifty t-shirts were printed; the organizers had to take orders for a second printing.

15. Dorothy Brown, Christel Goetz, Maggie Rogers, and Dorothy Westfall, "Mushrooming in the Pacifc Northwest," in *NAMA XXV* (n.p.: North American Mycological Association, 1985), pp. 29–35; quotation from p. 30.

16. Joseph Sax, *Mountains without Handrails: Reflections on the National Parks* (Ann Arbor: University of Michigan Press, 1980), pp. 26–28.

17. Werner Muensterberger, *Collecting: An Unruly Passion* (Princeton: Princeton University Press, 1994), p. 4.

18. James Clifford, *The Predicament of Culture* (Cambridge, Mass.: Harvard University Press, 1988), p. 220.

19. Stu Stuller, "Birding by the Numbers," *Atlantic Monthly* (May 1989), pp. 88–94.

20. Mitchell, *Mountain Experience.*

21. Muensterberger, *Collecting,* pp. 16, 48.

22. Brenda Danet and Tamar Katriel, "No Two Alike: Play and Aesthetics in Collecting," *Play and Culture,* 2 (1989): 253–277.

23. Susan Stewart, *On Longing: Narratives of the Miniatures, the Gigantic, the Souvenir, the Collector* (Baltimore: Johns Hopkins University Press, 1984).

24. "All That's Left," *New Yorker,* October 30, 1989, pp. 35–36; quotation from p. 35.

25. Stuart Marks, *Southern Hunting in Black and White: Nature, History, and Ritual in a Carolina Community* (Princeton: Princeton University Press, 1991), p. 3.

26. Ludwig Wittgenstein, *Remarks on Color,* ed. G. E. M. Anscombe, trans. Linda L. McAllister and Margarete Schattle (Berkeley: University of California Press, 1958), p. 50.

27. Annie Dillard, in *Pilgrim at Tinker Creek* (New York: Harper and Row, 1974), p. 18, writes, "I once spent a full three minutes looking at a bullfrog that was so unexpectedly large I couldn't see it even though a dozen enthusiastic campers were shouting directions."

28. Gregory Bateson, "The Message 'This is Play,'" in Bertram Schaffner, ed., *Group Processes* (New York: Josiah Macy, Jr., Foundation, 1955), pp. 145–242; Jurgen Ruesch and Gregory Bateson, *Communication: The Matrix of Society* (New York: Norton, 1951).

29. Dillard, *Pilgrim,* p. 18.

30. Muensterberger, *Collecting*, p. 147.
31. Thorolfur Thorlindsson, "Skipper Science: A Note on the Epistemology of Practice and the Nature of Expertise," *Sociological Quarterly*, 35 (1994): 328–346.
32. Ron Schara, "Always Look Twice," in Peter Leach and Anne Mikkelssen, eds., *Malfred Ferndock's Morel Cookbook* (Dennison, Minn.: Ferndock Publishing, 1986), p. 29.
33. Linda Painter, personal communication, 1984.
34. A. Tversky and D. Kahneman. "Judgment under Uncertainty: Heuristics and Biases," *Science*, 185 (1974): 1124–1131.
35. Sax, *Mountains*, p. 30.
36. Terence R. Mitchell and Leigh Thompson, "A Theory of Temporal Adjustments: Rosy Prospection and Rosy Retrospection," *Advances in Managerial Cognition and Organizational Information Processing*, 5 (1994): 85–114.
37. Robert A. Stebbins, "Science Amators?: Rewards and Costs in Amateur Astronomy and Archeology," *Journal of Leisure Research*, 13 (1981): 289–304; quotation from p. 295.
38. Larry Lonik, *The Curious Morel* (Royal Oak, Mich.: RKT Publishing, 1984), p. 6.
39. Sara Ann Friedman, "Morels, May Apples, and the Meaning of Life," *Mushroom*, 4 (Spring 1986): 5–9; quotation from p. 7.
40. Lester Hardy, "Completely Satisfied," *Mushroom*, 6 (Fall 1988): 20.
41. Bourjaily, *Unnatural Enemy*, p. 13.
42. Alvarez, "Feeding," p. 105.
43. Linda Painter, no title, *Mush Rumor* (December 1985), pp. 1–2; quotation from p. 1.
44. Harold J. Brodie, *Fungi: Delight of Curiosity* (Toronto: University of Toronto Press, 1978), p. ix.
45. See Richard Hummer and Gary S. Foster, "A Sporting Chance: Relationships between Technological Change and Concepts of Fair Play in Fishing," *Journal of Leisure Research*, 18 (1986): 40–52; Bourjaily, *Unnatural Enemy*, p. 12; Stuller, "Birding"; Mitchell, *Mountain Experience*, p. 113, on fishers, hunters, birders, and climbers, respectively.
46. Ms. Mushroom, "Etiquette," *Mushroom*, 3 (Summer 1984): 28–29; quotation from p. 29.
47. Mike Wells, "One Verpa," *Mushroom*, 4 (Summer 1986): 28–29; quotation from p. 28.
48. Ida Geary, "Hunting the Wild Morels," *California Magazine* (May 1982), p. 72.

49. Ms. Mushroom, "Etiquette," p. 28.

50. Dillard, *Pilgrim*, p. 30.

51. Friedman, *Celebrating*, p. 96.

52. John Law and Michael Lynch, "Lists, Field Guides and the Descriptive Organization of Seeing Birdwatching as an Exemplary Observational Activity," *Human Studies*, 11 (1988): 271–303; quotation from p. 273.

53. Daniel M. Wegner, "Transactive Memory: A Contemporary Analysis of the Group Mind," in B. Mullen and George Goethals, eds., *Theories of Group Behavior* (New York: Springer-Verlag, 1987), pp. 185–208.

54. Gordon Allport and Leo G. Postman, *The Psychology of Rumor* (New York: Holt, 1947).

55. Susan T. Fiske and Shelley E. Taylor, *Social Cognition*, 2d ed. (New York: McGraw-Hill, 1991).

56. Phyllis G. Glick, *The Mushroom Trail Guide* (New York: Holt, Rinehart and Winston, 1979), p. 174.

57. Ludwig Wittgenstein, *Philosophical Investigations*, 2d ed., trans. G. E. M. Anscombe (New York: Macmillan, 1958).

58. Ibid.

59. Those mushrooms that look precisely like their pictures and descriptions in a guide are referred to as "textbook." As Denise says of a *Paxillus atrotomentosus*: "Did you ever see anything more textbook."

60. Leslie Prosterman, *Ordinary Life, Festival Days: Aesthetics in the Midwestern County Fair* (Washington: Smithsonian Institution Press, 1995), p. 124.

61. Maggie Rogers, "Keys," *Mushroom*, 2 (Spring 1984): 22–25; quotation from p. 22.

62. Friedman, *Celebrating*, p. 51.

63. "April Meeting," *Spore Print* (newsletter of Los Angeles Mycological Society), May 1984, pp. 4–6; quotation from p. 5.

64. Some suggest that this refers to the primitive state of mushroom taxonomy (Ibid., p. 5), but even if each one of the estimated 250,000 fungal species were known and listed (!), judging the presence of traits would still make identification problematic. Sometimes having too many choices increases the difficulty of identification. Jerry commented that identifying mushrooms from a scientific book increased the difficulty of identification: "The better the book, the harder it is to get it down to species."

65. no title, *Ink Cap* (Northwest Wisconsin Mycological Society), no date, pp. 1–4; quotation from pp. 2–3.

66. Spore prints are important for identification, but are, in practice, rarely taken. At one club meeting Jerry challenged the Identification

Committee about a mushroom that appeared to be a lepiota growing on wood:

> *Jerry:* I'm buying for anyone at McDonalds who can identify this one.
> *Molly:* What's the spore color?
> *Jerry:* We don't know.
> *Molly:* That's not fair.
> *Jerry:* You do it all the time.

Eventually Laurel labeled it an *Armillaria* species, not previously found in the Midwest. Who knew if Laurel was correct, but she got her milkshake.

67. Richard J. Sclafani, "Artworks, Art Theory and the Artworld," *Theoryia,* 39 (1979): 18–34.
68. Michael Polanyi, *Personal Knowledge* (Chicago: University of Chicago Press, 1958).
69. Walter Litten, "Beyond Identification," *McIlvainea,* 7 (1985): 14–16; quotation from p. 14.
70. Hubert L. Dreyfus and Stuart E. Dreyfus, *Mind over Machine* (New York: Free Press, 1986), pp. 30–31.
71. Prosterman, *Ordinary Life,* p. 84.
72. Law and Lynch, "Lists," p. 296.
73. Ibid., p. 285.
74. Lorelei Norvell, "A Romp through Lepiota," *Mushroom,* 5 (Winter 1986–1987): 14–16.
75. Don H. Coombs, "Arora Field Guide Goes National," *Mushroom,* 5 (Spring 1987): 7–9; quotation from p. 7.
76. Brad Benn, "BWCA Mushrooms through an Amateur's Eye," *Toadstool Review,* 3 (September 1986): 3.
77. Walt Sturgeon, "Some Mushrooms Have More Appeal Than Others," *Mushroom,* 6 (Fall 1988): 22–24; quotation from p. 22.
78. Within each genus, exceptions exist. *Mycena haematopus* (the bleeding mycena, which "bleeds dark red when cut") is "easy to identify. It's almost like asking its name."
79. Wegner, "Transactive Memory."
80. The impetus to serve as an identification specialist for a particular genus or family demonstrates this process. Each member does not need knowledge to identify each specimen. For instance, Jay provides information about polypores for the group.
81. Law and Lynch, "Lists," p. 297; Stuller, "Birding," p. 92.
82. Not surprisingly, status is associated with the number of species that one can identify (Friedman, *Celebrating,* p. 45). Experts must show

tact in their comments to novices, as in this apocryphal story about a veteran's lack of sensitivity:

> Usually when people come up and ask if something is edible, you look at each one, and say, "This one is good, this one is not edible, and this is what it is." Generally there is a manner about how you do this, so as to encourage the person to go out and get more, and do it better. I was just pulling them out of [a novice's] basket until finally she was reduced to tears, because she hadn't picked anything that was good, and I made some crack . . . that "you couldn't have picked worse mushrooms if you'd tried," and then turned away from her and walked away.

83. Donald Goetz, no title, *Mush Rumors,* 22 (Aug.–Oct. 1982): 5.
84. Harley Barnhart, "First Knock It and Try It," *Mushroom,* 12 (Spring 1994): 4.
85. Brad Benn, "News from All Over," *Toadstool Review,* 13 (October 1988): 1.
86. Mike Wells, "Selected Edibles," *Mushroom,* 4 (Spring 1986): 28–30; quotation from p. 29.

4. TALKING WILD

1. Richard Mitchell, *Mountain Experience* (Chicago: University of Chicago Press, 1983), p. 72.
2. This argument applies more broadly. One comes to know a society when one is able to joke with members, or to understand a family when one can gossip.
3. Mitchell, *Mountain,* p. 72.
4. Elizabeth W. McNulty, "Generating Common Sense Knowledge among Police Officers," *Symbolic Interaction,* 17 (1994): 281–294.
5. Gary Alan Fine, *With the Boys: Little League Baseball and Preadolescent Behavior* (Chicago: University of Chicago Press, 1987), p. 125.
6. Personal-experience stories were first emphasized in the 1970s. Although some folklorists such as C. W. von Sydow discussed similar generic forms, the category took root with the publication of a special issue of the *Journal of the Folklore Institute* in 1977 on personal narrative. This issue provided a marker that personal-experience stories were a major folklore genre.
7. Erving Goffman, *Frame Analysis* (Cambridge, Mass.: Harvard University Press, 1974), pp. 503–516.
8. The emphasis on personal storytelling by self-help groups such as Alcoholics Anonymous is a characteristic of movements aimed at the

reconstruction of individual identity. In leisure groups, too, story-telling may be central to the individual's self-conception and public role.

9. William Hugh Jansen, "The Esoteric-Exoteric Factor in Folklore," *Fabula*, 2 (1959): 205–211.

10. Gary Alan Fine and Sherryl Kleinman, "Rethinking Subculture: An Interactionist Analysis," *American Journal of Sociology*, 85 (1979): 1–20.

11. Tamotsu Shibutani, "Reference Groups as Perspectives," *American Journal of Sociology*, 60 (1955): 562–569; quotation from p. 566.

12. Basil Bernstein, *Class, Codes and Control* (New York: Schocken, 1971), pp. 76–80.

13. Pierre Bourdieu, *Distinction* (Cambridge, Mass.: Harvard University Press, 1984).

14. Gary Alan Fine, "Community and Boundary: Personal Experience Stories of Mushroom Collectors," *Journal of Folklore Research*, 24 (1987): 223–240; quotation from p. 228.

15. Bruce Auerbach, "Reminiscences: Mushroom Hunting in the Pacific Northwest," *Toadstool Review*, 10 (April 1985): 2–3; quotation from p. 3.

16. Fred Davis, *Yearning for Yesterday* (New York: Free Press, 1979).

17. "Reminder," *Mid-Hudson Mycological Association Newsletter* (1983), p. 6.

18. Sally Yerkovich, "Gossiping as a Way of Speaking," *Journal of Communication*, 27 (1976): 192–196.

19. Howard S. Becker and Blanche Geer, "Latent Culture: A Note on the Theory of Latent Social Roles," *Administrative Science Quarterly*, 5 (1960): 304–313.

20. Susan Kalčik, "'Like Ann's Gynecologist or the Time I Was Almost Raped': Personal Narratives in Women's Rap Groups," *Journal of American Folklore*, 88 (1975): 3–11.

21. See also Jennifer Hunt, "Divers' Accounts of Normal Risk," *Symbolic Interaction*, 18 (1995): 439–462.

22. In analyzing discourse in social movements, I have described *horror stories* (or *atrocity stories* [Robert Dingwall, "'Atrocity Stories' and Professional Relationships," *Sociology of Work and Occupations*, 4 (1977): 371–396]) and *happy endings* (Gary Alan Fine, "Public Narration and Group Culture: Discerning Discourse in Social Movements," in Hank Johnson and Bert Klandermans, eds., *Social Movements* (Minneapolis: University of Minnesota Press, 1995), pp. 127–143). In the former, affronts to the narrator are detailed, leading to greater commitment. In the latter stories, related to treasure tales, the narratives reaffirm the value of the movement in achieving political and personal ends.

23. Dingwall, "Atrocity Stories," p. 381.

24. Orrin Klapp, *Inflation of Symbols: Loss of Values in American Culture* (New Brunswick: Transction Press, 1991), p. 78.

25. Some of this material derives from my interviews with mushroomers. Although the interviews were informal, the discourse was different from what one would find when mushroom collectors speak to friends and colleagues. Other narratives are from second-order accounts: written stories or written accounts of the oral accounts of others. The development of written channels (such as newsletters and magazines) may be important for transforming group activity into a subculture with a generally accepted code of conduct and thought, as happened with sportsmen in the early 1870s (John Rieger, *American Sportsmen and the Origin of Conservation,* rev. ed. [Norman: University of Oklahoma Press, 1986], p. 22). Since my concern is not the microtechniques of narration, I feel that these sources are legitimate.

26. McNulty, "Generating Common Sense," p. 283.

27. Peter Canby, "Of Men and Morels," in Peter Leach and Anne Mikkelsen, eds., *Malfred Ferndock's Morel Cookbook* (Denison, Minn.: Ferndock, 1986), pp. 66–74; quotation from p. 70.

28. Larry Lonik, *The Curious Morel* (Royal Oak, Mich.: RKT Publishing, 1984), pp. 5–6.

29. It was a common practice at forays for mushroomers to bring in objects for "identification" that had some resemblance to mushrooms, such as a doorknob, plastic hedgehog, or a styrofoam mushroom.

30. Scott Anderson, "Baring My Breast," *Mushroom,* 6 (Fall 1988): 19–20; quotation from p. 19.

31. Jane Maranghi, "The Whole Log—," *Mushroom,* 6 (Fall 1988): 19.

32. Linda Painter, no title, *Mush Rumor* (Snohomish County Mycological Society), December 1985, pp. 1–2; quotation from p. 2.

33. Bill Freedman, "A Sad Story," *Mycena News,* 44 (October 1994): 6.

34. These stories are told about other activities in which there is a shortage of prized resources, as when editors talk about manuscripts that "got away" (Douglas Mitchell, "First Person," *Sunday Chicago Tribune Magazine,* June 22, 1986, p. 30), or when poker players discuss "bad beats"—hands they should have won, but didn't (A. Alverez, "No Limit," *New Yorker,* August 7, 1994, pp. 56–63; quotation from p. 56).

35. Sara Ann Friedman, *Celebrating the Wild Mushroom* (New York: Dodd, Mead, 1986), p. 14.

36. Aldo Leopold, *A Sand County Almanac with Essays on Conservation from Round River* (New York: Oxford University Press, 1966), p. 284.

37. Richard M. Dorson, "Folktale Performers," in Richard M. Dorson, ed., *The Handbook of American Folklore* (Bloomington, Ind.: Indiana University Press, 1983), pp. 287–300; quotation from p. 290.

38. Timothy Cochrane, "Place, People, and Folklore: An Isle Royale Case Study," *Western Folklore,* 46 (1987): 1–20.

39. Lonik, *Curious Morel,* p. 16.

40. Large or beautiful mushrooms are often dried and kept as trophies, much like fish or animal heads. (One collector, upon finding a large mushroom, turned to me and said: "That's for over the fireplace"). More commonly photographs serve as keepsakes of a remarkable find. Some clubs use their slide libraries as repositories for "trophies."

41. The argument, of course, is not that there are not "finds" of cultural objects (for example, rare stamps or books; see Brenda Danet and Tamar Katriel, "No Two Alike: Play and Aesthetics in Collecting," *Play and Culture,* 2 [1989]: 253–277), but that the finding and appreciating process is particularly evident when engaging in naturework because of the presumed autonomy of the realm of nature.

42. Darby Morrell, "Finding Hericium Abietis," *Mushroom,* 2 (Fall 1984): 37.

43. M. E. Bobersky, "Caesars by the Dozens: A Postscript," *Ohio Spore Print* (March/April 1984): 5.

44. Malfred Ferndock, "Foreword," in Leach and Mikkelsen, *Morel Cookbook,* pp. 11–12.

45. "Fun with Sparassis," *Mycena News,* 42 (March 1992): 1. See also Lorelei Norvell, "Sparassis," *Mushroom,* 5 (Fall 1987): 26–28; quotation from p. 27.

46. Muff, "8th Annual Cain Foray," *Mycelium* (Nov.–Dec. 1982): 8.

47. Ron Sutcliffe, "A Serious Case of Underpick—Alaska Mushrooming," *Mushroom,* 5 (Winter 1986–1987): 11, 13.

48. Max Weber, "Science as a Vocation," in Hans H. Gerth and C. Wright Mills, eds., *From Max Weber* (New York: Oxford University Press, 1946), pp. 128–156; quotation from p. 155.

49. Sigmund Freud, *Jokes and Their Relationship to the Unconscious* (New York: Norton, 1960 [1905]), p. 103.

50. Chris Powell and George E. C. Patton, *Humor in Society: Resistance and Control* (New York: St. Martin's Press, 1988); Rose L. Coser, "Laughter among Colleagues," *Psychiatry,* 23 (1960): 81–89.

51. Goffman, *Frame Analysis,* pp. 87–92; Gary Alan Fine, "Humorous Interaction and the Social Construction of Meaning," *Studies in Symbolic Interaction,* 5 (1984): 83–101.

52. Joan Emerson, "Negotiating the Serious Impact of Humor," *Sociometry,* 32 (1969): 169–181.

53. James F. Short, Jr., "The Social Fabric at Risk: Toward the Social Transformation of Risk Analysis," *American Sociological Review,* 49 (1984): 711–725; Lee Clarke, *Acceptable Risk?: Making Decisions in a Toxic Environment* (Berkeley: University of California Press, 1989).

54. Mary Douglas and Aaron Wildavsky, *Risk and Culture* (Berkeley: University of California Press, 1982), pp. 186–198.

55. Mihalyi Csikszentmihalyi, *Beyond Boredom and Anxiety* (San Francisco: Jossey-Bass, 1975).

56. Mitchell, *Mountain;* Robert McCarl, "Smokejumper Initiation: Ritualized Communication in a Modern Occupation," *Journal of American Folklore,* 89 (1976): 49–66.

57. Henri Bergson, *Laughter: An Essay on the Meaning of the Comic* (New York: Macmillian, 1911).

58. "The Survivor's Banquet," *Mycofile* (Vancouver Mycological Society), Fall 1983, p. 4.

59. "Clean Limerick," *Ohio Spore Print* (Nov./Dec. 1982): 7.

60. Dorothy Sayers, *The Documents of the Case* (New York: Harper and Row, 1937).

61. Mushrooms can be used for suicide as well. One active collector told me that on three occasions she had been asked about committing suicide by eating *Amanita virosa.* A man who overheard joked: "It saves on medical bills."

62. Friedman, *Celebrating.*

63. Lucy Kavaler, *Mushrooms, Molds, and Miracles: The Strange Realm of Fungi* (New York: John Day, 1965), p. 42; W. P. K. Findlay, *Fungi: Folklore, Fiction and Fact* (Eureka, Calif.: Mad River Press, 1982), p. 79.

64. J. L. Austin, *How to Do Things with Words* (Cambridge, Mass.: Harvard University Press, 1975).

65. Goffman, *Frame Analysis,* p. 522.

66. The classic joke, heard perhaps a dozen times during the research, and known to nonmushroomers as well, speaks directly to this issue:

> There is [a joke] about the seventy-year-old man who is getting married to a twenty-year-old chick. She knows it's his fourth marriage, and on their wedding night she asked him what happened to the first wife. He said she died from eating poisonous mushrooms. She asked what happened to the second wife. She died from eating poisonous mushrooms. So, she said, "I suppose the third one did too, huh?" "No, she died from a fractured skull." "What caused that?" "She wouldn't eat her mushrooms."

In my observation, it is always the wife who is the victim; men have both access to knowledge and the physical force to back it up.

67. Alan Dundes, "The Dead Baby Joke Cycle," *Western Folklore,* 38 (1979): 245–257; Simon Bronner, "What's Grosser Than Gross," *Midwestern Journal of Language and Folklore,* 11 (1985): 39–49.

68. Michael R. Tansey and Donald J. Niederpruem, "Mycological Teaching Humor," unpublished manuscript, 1977, p. 2.

5. ORGANIZING NATURALISTS

1. Edward Banfield, *The Moral Basis of a Backward Society* (Glencoe, Ill.: Free Press, 1958).

2. Until adequate comparative data are available, one should be cautious about accepting this belief in American exceptionalism too readily. One might be impressed by the 1,800-member North American Mycological Association and its 77 affiliated local clubs until one learned that the mushroom society in Prague in Czechoslovakia had 5,000 members (Emil Lang, "The NAMA Foray to Czechoslovakia," *New York Mycological Society,* 8 [Winter 1984]: 12–14), and that 14 mycological societies with 2,000 members existed in Slovenia and Croatia (Emil Lang, "NAMA Foray to Austria and Yugoslovia," *New York Mycological Society Newsletter,* 5 [Summer 1981]: 12–14). A British survey found 315 leisure groups in a suburban area of Bristol, England; see Peter Hoggett and J. Bishop, *Organizing around Enthusiasms* (London: Comedia, 1986), p. 6.

3. Robert A. Stebbins, *Amateurs, Professionals, and Serious Leisure* (Montreal: McGill-Queen's University Press, 1992), pp. 94–95.

4. Howard Aldrich, "The Sociable Organization: A Case Study of Mensa and Some Propositions," *Sociology and Social Research,* 55 (1971): 429–441.

5. Robert Bellah, Richard Madsen, William M. Sullivan, Ann Swidler, and Steven Tipton, *Habits of the Heart: Individualism and Commitment in American Life* (Berkeley: University of California Press, 1985), pp. 71–75.

6. B.A.S.S., the largest fishing organization in the world, has more than 400,000 members. The real giant in the world of "leisure" organizations is the National Rifle Association (NRA), the bulk of whose members utilize guns in their encounters with nature. For a leisure organization to have as much clout as the NRA does is a remarkable testimony to the importance of leisure in the lives of Americans.

7. John F. Rieger, *American Sportsmen and the Origin of Conservation,* rev. ed. (Norman: University of Oklahoma Press, 1986), p. 39.

8. Ibid., p. 40.

9. Grace Seiberling with Carolyn Bloore, *Amateurs, Photography, and the Mid-Victorian Imagination* (Chicago: University of Chicago Press, 1986).

10. Jim O'Brien, "Environmentalism as a Mass Movement: Historical Notes," *Radical America,* 17 (1983): 7–27; quotaton from p. 11.

11. "The Morel Majority," *New York Mycological Society Newsletter,* 5 (March–May 1981): 2–3.

12. John Covach, quoted in Maggie Rogers, "Going Out in the Fall," *Mushroom,* 2 (Fall 1984): 17–19; quotation from p. 18.

13. Donald Goetz, "Reindeer Mushrooms Still in Good Taste," *Mushroom,* 2 (Summer 1984): 5.

14. Harold J. Brodie, *Fungi: Delight of Curiosity* (Toronto: University of Toronto Press, 1978), p. 45.

15. Charles Barrows, quoted in Rogers, "Going Out," p. 14.

16. Quoted in Sara Ann Friedman, "Cage on Mushrooms / Music/ Poetry / Food / Life and Other Chance Operations," *New York Mycological Society Newsletter,* 8 (Winter 1984): 5–8; quotation from p. 5.

17. Recruitment through interest transfer is relatively easy, and is found through leisure, as when miniature wargamers pick up on fantasy games (Gary Alan Fine, *Shared Fantasy: Role-Playing Games as Social Worlds* [Chicago: University of Chicago Press, 1983]), or when chess players try playing "shogi" or "go."

18. Richard Butsch, "The Commodification of Leisure: The Case of the Model Airplane Hobby and Industry," *Qualitative Sociology,* 7 (1984): 217–235; quotation from p. 217.

19. J. Craig Jenkins, "Resource Mobilization Theory and the Study of Social Movements," *Annual Review of Sociology,* 9 (1983): 527–573; John D. McCarthy and Mayer Zald, "Resource Mobilization and Social Movements," *American Journal of Sociology,* 82 (1977): 1212–1242.

20. Mancur Olsen, *The Logic of Collective Action* (Cambridge, Mass.: Harvard University Press, 1971); John C. Turner with Michael A. Hogg, Penelope J. Oakes, Stephen D. Reicher, and Margaret S. Wetherell, *Rediscovering the Social Group: A Self-Categorization Theory* (Oxford: Basil Blackwell, 1987).

21. Erving Goffman, *Encounters* (Indianapolis: Bobbs-Merrill, 1961), p. 17.

22. Steve Langston, no title, *Toadstool Review* (Newsletter of the Minnesota Mycological Society), 9 (April 1984): 4.

23. Aldo Leopold, *A Sand County Almanac with Essays on Conservation from Round River* (New York: Oxford University Press, 1966), p. 283.

24. Peter Schmitt, *Back to Nature: The Arcadian Myth in Urban America* (New York: Oxford University Press, 1969), p. 11.

25. Charles R. Simpson, "The Wilderness in American Capitalism: The Sacralization of Nature," *International Journal of Politics, Culture and Society*, 5 (1992): 555–576; quotation from p. 568.

26. The existence of the Minnesota Mycological Society increases the likelihood that people will engage in mushrooming. The club makes itself available to the media and sponsors exhibits at the local natural history museum. Contrast this with the sorry state of butterfly collecting. There is no Lepidopterist Society in Minnesota, and thus the media do not report on this hobby. According to the membership lists of the Lepidopterist Society of America and the North American Mycological Association, the former has a lower proportion of Minnesotans than expected by chance, whereas the latter has a higher proportion. One cannot definitively attribute patterns of membership in a national organization or newspaper coverage to the existence of a local organization, but it provides prima-facie evidence.

27. "Welcome to All New Members," *Mush Rumor* (Snohomish County Mycological Society), Sept./Oct. 1984, p. 3.

28. David Robbins, "Sport, Hegemony, and the Middle Class: The Victorian Mountaineers," *Theory, Culture, and Society*, 4 (1987): 579–601; quotation from p. 584.

29. A 1993 "Guide to the Guides" published in *Mushroom* describes 31 fieldguides, 25 of which are primarily North American in focus (Harley Barnhart, "How 31 Field Guides Measure Up," *Mushroom*, 11 [Spring 1993]: 5–18).

30. Robert A. Stebbins, *Amateurs* (Beverly Hills: Sage, 1979).

31. Herman Schmalenbach, *On Society and Experience* (Chicago: University of Chicago Press, 1977).

32. William R. Burch, Jr., "The Social Circles of Leisure: Competing Explanations," *Journal of Leisure Research*, 1 (1969): 25–47.

33. Hoggett and Bishop, *Organizing*, p. 32.

34. Lee M. Muggli, in "My First NAMA Foray," *Toadstool Review*, 9 (December 1984): 4–5, recalls how one mycological society officer relied upon popular motivational belief to increase group participation:

> Someone said the membership of an organization is made up of four bones. There are the wishbones, who spend all their time wishing somebody else would do all the work. There are the jawbones, who do all the talking but very little else. Next come the knuckle bones, who knock everything anyone else tries to do. And finally, there are the backbones who get the load and do the work. In the past, most of the work of the Society has been done by a very small [percentage] of the members. While they may enjoy doing it, I'm sure they

would welcome any offer of help. I would like to encourage new and old members alike to become more involved. (p. 5)

35. Dick Hebdige, *Subculture: The Meaning of Style* (London: Methuen, 1979).
36. Jeffrey Nash, "What's in a Face? The English Bulldog as 'Human Nature,'" unpublished manuscript, 1988.
37. Baskets provide a good example of the self-defining quality of tools and artifacts, at least for some experienced collectors. Maggie Rogers, in "Baskets," *Mushroom*, 4 (Winter 1985–1986): 16–20, recounted:

> I noticed that you could tell a lot about the mushroomer even before the first question ("Finding any?") by checking out the basket—its design, wear and tear, and tidiness. Mushroomers feel about their baskets the way sharpshooters feel about their rifles, woodcarvers their knives, photographers about their favorite cameras. Carefully selected, a good basket is like an old wicker fishing creel: perhaps smelly, stained with the catches of decades, reflecting the habits of its owner, a bit battered, but a treasured companion. (p. 19)

38. Hoggett and Bishop, *Organizing*, pp. 80–81.
39. The provisioning of identity symbols may be particularly problematic in "morally controversial leisure" (A. D. Olmsted, "Morally Controversial Leisure: The Social World of Gun Collectors," *Symbolic Interaction*, 11 [1988]: 277–287), in which the issue of identity display is delicate. For instance, gun collecting is sufficiently controversial that identity symbols may be available only in specialized locations, often tied directly to organizational or peripheral vendors.
40. Holmes Rolston, *Environmental Ethics* (Philadelphia: Temple University Press, 1988), p. 8.
41. Stu Stuller, "Birding by the Numbers," *Atlantic* (May 1989), pp. 88–94; quotation from p. 92.
42. Richard Hummel and Gary S. Foster, "A Sporting Chance: Relationships between Technological Change and Concepts of Fair Play in Fishing," *Journal of Leisure Research*, 18 (1986): 40–52; quotation from p. 43.
43. Lori Holyfield, "Risk Talk: Identity Transformation among Climbers," unpublished manuscript, 1994.
44. Other clubs have divisions between those who search for psychoactive mushrooms and those who reject them. Perhaps because the Minnesota climate is not conducive to psychoactives, this was not an issue. Also, there was no conflict between cultivators and pickers, or between those who picked commercially and those who collected for pleasure

(see Chapter 6), because of the small number of serious cultivators and the absence of commercial pickers.

45. Members of the Minnesota club with a college degree were more likely to classify themselves as "amateur mycologists" than were those who did not have a college degree (Chi-Square = 2.86, df = 1, $p < .1$). A slight but insignificant relationship exists between considering oneself an amateur mycologist and being under fifty years of age; one reason that this correlation was not stronger was that new, younger members did not use this term to describe themselves.

46. In hunting, a similar division was found between "sportsmen," who were said to appreciate and understand their quarry, and perhaps treasure "the hunt," and those "pot" or "meat" hunters who kill for the thrill of killing, to fill their stomachs, or to sell what they shot (Rieger, *American Sportsmen,* p. 31).

47. When I attended the NAMA foray, some told me that they felt that the vast majority of attendees were pot hunters, whereas others told me that most were amateur mycologists. Typically, I was told this to indicate that the speaker was in the minority. Presumably each group used different criteria for categorization.

    Attitudes may change over time as participants become more knowledgeable, desiring to emulate those with the most expertise (Hummel and Foster, "Sporting Chance," p. 42). For instance, Molly told me that at one time her primary interest was collecting edible mushrooms, but now her interest is in identification. Someone else mused: "Originally I went to find out . . . if I could eat [mushrooms]. Once I got there, [they] intrigued me."

48. Maggie Rogers, "Foraying with NAMA," *Mushroom,* 1 (Fall 1983): 43–45; quotation from p. 45.

49. Lorelei Novell, "Sparassis," *Mushroom,* 5 (Fall 1987): 26–28; quotation from p. 26.

50. John D. Parker, personal communication, 1983.

51. Some criticism was particularly harsh. One member joked: "I should get a gun and shoot him." Brian's critics recalled the time after his election when, as an ironic statement, he wrote "El Presidente" on his name tag, which they took to reveal his dictatorial ambitions. Anger was also directed against Brian's predecessor, with one member raging that he should be kicked out of the club so that he couldn't call himself "Past President."

52. One long-time member made the ideological implications clear, commenting: "I think that new members try to learn too many mushrooms in a year. I think that a book like this [the Audubon guide] will do

more to confuse them. I think they should learn five new mushrooms in the spring and five new mushrooms in the fall each year."

53. Rosabeth Moss Kanter, in *Commitment and Community: Communes and Utopias in Sociological Perspectives* (Cambridge, Mass.: Harvard University Press, 1972), presents a model of individual "commitment," grounded in an analysis of nineteenth century communes. The model distinguishes among continuance, cohesion, and control, important processes evident in voluntary total institutions. The social psychological literature on "cohesion" typically conflates the first two, sometimes incorporating the third—emphasizing not the individual's level of commitment, but the group's level of cohesion. Commitment is an individual-level variable, whereas cohesion operates collectively.

54. Leon Festinger, Stanley Schachter, and Kurt Back, *Social Pressures in Informal Groups: A Study of a Housing Project* (New York: Harper and Brothers, 1950), p. 164; William E. Piper, Myriam Marrache, Renee Lacroix, Astrid M. Richardsen, and Barry D. Jones, "Cohesion as a Basic Bond in Groups," *Human Relations,* 36 (1983): 93–108.

55. Neal Gross and William E. Martin, "On Group Cohesiveness," *American Journal of Sociology,* 57 (1952): 546–554; quotation from p. 553; Lawrence R. Brawley, Albert V. Carron, and W. Neil Widmeyer, "Exploring the Relationship between Cohesion and Group Resistance to Disruption," *Journal of Sport and Exercise Psychology,* 10 (1988): 190–213.

56. Social psychological research has, in practice, used cohesion either as an independent variable that produces outcomes on performance variables (Charles R. Evans and Kenneth L. Dion, "Group Cohesion and Performance: A Meta-Analysis," *Small Group Research,* 22 [1991]: 175–186; Susan A. Wheelan, *Group Processes: A Developmental Perspective* [Boston: Allyn and Bacon, 1994]) or as a dependent variable that is a function of membership composition, feedback, or group structure (Stuart Drescher, Gary Burlingame, and Addie Furman, "Cohesion: An Odyssey in Empirical Understanding," *Small Group Relations,* 16 [1985]: 3–30). Only rarely are the variables mediating the effects of cohesion, such as the salience of social norms, explored (Gregory K. Rutkowski, Charles L. Gruder, and Daniel Romer, "Group Cohesiveness, Social Norms, and Bystander Intervention," *Journal of Personality and Social Psychology,* 44 (1983): 545–552).

57. Jerome D. Frank, "Some Determinants, Manifestations, and Effects of Cohesiveness in Therapy Groups," *International Journal of Group Psychotherapy,* 7 (1957): 53–63.

58. Nancy J. Evans and Paul A. Jarvis, "Group Cohesion: A Review and Reevaluation," *Small Group Behavior,* 11 (1980): 359–370; Kanter, *Commitment and Community,* pp. 72–73.

59. Dorwin Cartwright and Alvin Zander, *Group Dynamics,* 2d ed. (New York: Harper and Row, 1960).

60. Muzafer Sherif, O. J. Harvey, B. J. White. W. R. Hood, and Carolyn Sherif, *Intergroup Conflict and Cooperation: The Robbers Cave Experiment* (Norman, Okla.: Oklahoma Book Exchange, 1961); Gary Alan Fine, "Small Groups and Culture Creation," *American Sociological Review,* 44 (1979): 733–745; William Foster Owen, "Metaphor Analysis of Cohesiveness in Small Discussion Groups," *Small Group Behavior,* 16 (1985): 415–424; Donna Eder, "Building Cohesion through Collaborative Narration," *Social Psychology Quarterly,* 51 (1988): 225–235.

61. Marvin Shaw, *Group Dynamics: The Psychology of Small Group Behavior,* 3d ed. (New York: McGraw-Hill, 1981), pp. 216–217.

62. Cartwright and Zander, *Group Dynamics,* p. 74.

63. Stebbins, *Amateurs, Professionals, and Serious Leisure.*

64. Goffman, *Encounters,* p. 17.

65. Turner, Hogg, Oakes, Reicher, and Wetherell, *Rediscovering,* p. 103.

66. In *Amateurs, Professionals, and Serious Leisure,* Stebbins notes that leisure activities differ in their collective character. Some, such as sports teams, theater troupes, or musical ensembles, demand group participation. In these activities, not only does the organization provide for training and sharing interest, but participation in the organization constitutes the doing of leisure. In contrast, mushroom clubs cater to individuals interested in activities that can be performed solo or in small groups.

67. Stebbins, *Amateurs, Professionals, and Serious Leisure.*

68. Aldrich, "Sociable Organization."

69. David Snow and Leon Anderson, "Identity Work among the Homeless: The Verbal Construction and Avowal of Personal Identities," *American Journal of Sociology,* 92 (1987): 1336–1371.

70. I do not make the extreme claim that all leisure groups have the same mix of trust and secrecy. Groups in which danger is recognized establish mechanisms for the establishment of trust. Groups that are grounded on the comparative ranking among members, which is based on achievement (competition), develop information preserves, preventing shared resources (mushrooms, caving routes) or keeping private styles of performance (parachuting, bungee jumping). Some risky groups may have relatively little secrecy, and the reverse, but my claim

is that groups involving risk typically have an achievement-based status hierarchy that involves protected information.

71. Some measure of trust is found in all organizations in which negative outcomes are possible. For example, in stamp collection, novices might trust others to inform them of stamp values or tell them how to preserve their collections. Bodily danger, and the edgework that goes with it, make the need for trust more explicit (Stephen G. Lyng, "Edgework: A Social Psychological Analysis of Voluntary Risk Taking," *American Journal of Sociology,* 95 [1990]: 851–886). Given the demands of edgework—exploring one's sense of an ordered existence—the amount and intensity of cohesion may be linked to the prominence of risk within an interactional arena.

72. The public, ritual demonstration of trust is linked to Schmalenbach's (*On Society and Experience,* pp. 83–86) construct of "communion," which he differentiates from Ferdinand Toennies's society (*gesellschaft*) and community (*gemeinschaft*) in altering an interest group into a brotherhood on the basis of emotional affiliation (see Ferdinand Toennies, *Community and Society* [New York: Harper, 1963]). For Schmalenbach, community is a "natural," "unconscious" bond (like family), whereas "communion" is contracted and voluntary. Leisure organizations represent an ideal type of "communion" in that they rely for their continued existence on the willingness, both cognitive and affective, of group members to trust one another. Commitment of individuals in leisure groups, because it is voluntary and contingent upon satisfaction, is different from that found in primary groups—even primary groups that are satisfying and time-consuming. This voluntary character makes the maintenance of allegiance critical for organizational stability.

73. Diego Gambetta, "Can We Trust Trust?" in Diego Gambetta, ed., *Trust* (Oxford: Basil Blackwell, 1988), pp. 213–237; quotation from p. 217.

74. Robert D. Putnam, *Making Democracy Work: Civic Traditions in Modern Italy* (Princeton: Princeton University Press, 1993).

75. J. David Lewis and Andrew J. Weigert, "Trust as a Social Reality," *Social Forces,* 63 (1985): 967–985; David Good, "Individuals, Interpersonal Relations, and Trust," in Gambetta, *Trust,* pp. 31–48.

76. Elizabeth W. McNulty, "Generating Common Sense Knowledge among Police Officers," *Symbolic Interaction,* 17 (1994): 281–294.

77. Peter Kollock, "The Emergence of Exchange Structures: An Experimental Study of Uncertainty, Commitment and Trust," *American Journal of Sociology,* 100 (1994): 313–345.

78. Beryl Bellman, "The Paradox of Secrecy," *Human Studies,* 4 (1981): 1–24.

79. Georg Simmel, *The Sociology of Georg Simmel* (New York: Free Press, 1950), p. 318.

80. Luhmann ("Familiarity, Confidence, Trust: Problems and Alternatives," in Gambetta, *Trust,* pp. 97–99) distinguishes between confidence and trust on the basis of whether potential negative consequences are considered (trust) or ignored (confidence). In English, at least, this flies in the face of the fact that the two words are often interchangeable, and in the uncertainty of whether danger is consciously recognized.

81. Annthony Giddens, *Modernity and Self-Identity* (Stanford: Stanford University Press, 1991).

82. Anthony Giddens, *The Consequences of Modernity,* (Stanford: Stanford University Press, 1990).

83. Heinz-Günter Vester, "Adventure as a Form of Leisure," *Journal of Leisure Research,* 6 (1987): 237–249; Peter Donnelly, "Take My Word for It: Trust in the Context of Birding and Mountaineering," *Qualitative Sociology,* 17 (1994): 215–241.

84. This assumes that the organization is seen as unified. In some instances, trust (and loyalty) to individuals in factionalized organizations may weaken the organization, while strengthening subgroups (Richard Lempert, personal communication, 1995).

85. Kanter, *Commitment and Community,* pp. 65–67.

86. S. N. Eisenstadt and L. Roniger, *Patrons, Clients, and Friends* (Cambridge, England: Cambridge University Press, 1984), p. 6; Ernest Gellner, "Trust, Cohesion, and the Social Order," in Gambetta, *Trust,* pp. 142–157.

87. Of the 129 members of the Minnesota Mycological Society who responded to my questionnaire, 94 percent said they had eaten wild mushrooms.

88. John Hewitt, "Stalking the Wild Identity," unpublished manuscript, 1984.

89. After one tasting sponsored by a club in Colorado, some members experienced gastrointestinal illness, although the club emphasized that it was uncertain that the *mushrooms* were to blame (Joan Betz, "The Future of Mushroom Tasting Meetings," *Spores Afield,* November 1984, p. 1).

90. This raises the delicate issue of relations among novices. Novices often announce their lack of expertise to avoid responsibility for expertise. This announcement is voluntary, however, and a novice could potentially harm others and weaken the bonds of trust. As a result, in most instances in which expertise is crucial, experts are assigned the task of monitoring information (and comestibles).

91. Holyfield, "Risk Talk."
92. Samuel R. Rosen. *A Judge Judges Mushrooms* (Nashville, Ind.: Highlander Press, 1982), pp. 18–19.
93. The number of mushroom fatalities in the United States is small, typically fewer than a half dozen a year. Only 2 of 129 Minnesota mushroomers reported becoming so ill from eating mushrooms that they had to be hospitalized. Only 15 percent had even become ill from eating mushrooms, however minor the discomfort.
94. Don Coombs, "The 1, 2, 3, 4, 5 of Starting Out," *Mushroom,* 4 (Spring 1986): 23–24; quotation from p. 23.
95. Bernard Williams, "Formal Structures and Social Reality," in Gambetta, *Trust,* pp. 3–13.
96. Hobson Bryan, "Leisure Value Systems and Recreational Specialization: The Case of Trout Fishermen," *Journal of Leisure Research,* 9 (1977): 174–187.
97. Everett Hughes, *The Sociological Eye* (Chicago: Aldine, 1971); Jack Haas, "The Stages of the High-Steel Ironworker Apprentice Career," *Sociological Quarterly,* 15 (1974): 93–108.
98. Letter to author.
99. Lorelei Norvell, "Which Are You?" *Mushroom,* 2 (Winter 1983–1984): 5–7; quotation from p. 7.
100. Stuller, "Birding," p. 92; Jennifer Hunt, "Divers' Account of Normal Risk," *Symbolic Interaction,* 18 (1995): 439–462.
101. Joseph Powell Stokes, "Components of Group Cohesion: Intermember Attraction, Instrumental Value, and Risk Taking," *Small Group Behavior,* 14 (1983): 163–173.
102. T. M. Luhrmann, "The Magic of Secrecy," *Ethos,* 17 (1989): 131–165.
103. Bellman, "Paradox of Secrecy."
104. David Nyberg, *The Varnished Truth* (Chicago: University of Chicago Press, 1993).
105. Erving Goffman, *Strategic Interaction* (Philadelphia: University of Pennsylvanis Press, 1967).
106. Lawrence J. Redlinger and Sunny Johnston, "Secrecy, Informational Uncertainty, and Social Control," *Urban Life,* 8 (1980): 387–397; Richard Wilsnack, "Informational Control: A Conceptual Framework for Sociological Analysis," *Urban Life,* 8 (1980): 467–489; T. M. Luhrmann, *Persuasions of the Witch's Craft* (Cambridge, Mass.: Harvard University Press, 1989).
107. Sissela Bok, *Secrets: On the Ethics of Concealment and Revelation* (New York: Vintage, 1983).
108. Bonnie Erickson, "Secret Societies and Social Structure," *Social Forces,* 80 (1981): 188–210.

109. A fine line exists between information that is termed private and that which is termed secret (Edward A. Shils, *The Torment of Secrecy* [Glencoe, Ill.: Free Press, 1956]; Carol Warren and Barbara Laslett, "Privacy and Secrecy: A Conceptual Comparison," *Journal of Social Issues,* 33 [1977]: 43–51; Bellman, "Paradox of Secrecy," pp. 1–24), with secret information often referring to information that is negatively valued by those from whom the information is shielded. In this case, the knowledge discussed here might be defined as private, although mushroomers themselves refer to their shielded information as "secret." In that the information I discuss is *in principle* public information and is information to which others wish access, I find that designating the shielding as secrecy is legitimate. My operational definition merely depicts the concealment of information to which others wish access, and which is potentially public.

110. The most obvious and acceptable context for secrecy is when a group member encounters an outsider, and doesn't tell or misleads the other. That other, by virtue of being a stranger, has no right to information. The legitimacy of secrecy toward outsiders is evident in the stories that mushroomers tell about deceiving anonymous others when asked what they are looking for and what they have found. These stories are relished when retold within the group. For example, Diane described meeting two well-dressed businessmen entering the woods to pick morels as she was exiting: "They asked, 'Did you find any?' and I said, 'No, there weren't any. This is a bad place.' And they got in their cars and left." The other club members laughed loudly at her story.

  Secrecy strengthens the organization by emphasizing its boundaries, which are necessary for collective identity. The members shield secret information from those who are excluded, emphasizing their mutual allegiance.

111. Richard Mitchell, Jr., *Mountain Experience* (Chicago: University of Chicago Press, 1983), p. 5; Stuller, "Birding"; Hummel and Foster, "Sporting Chance."

112. Bellman, "Paradox of Secrecy," p. 21.

113. Theresa Rey, "The Stories Are as Good as Collecting Mushrooms," *Mushroom,* 2 (Spring 1994): 16–17.

114. Laurel Richardson, "Secrecy and Status: The Social Construction of Forbidden Relationships," *American Sociological Review,* 53 (1988): 209–219; quotation from p. 209.

115. Thorolfur Thorlindsson, "Skipper Science: A Note on the Epistemology of Practice and the Nature of Expertise," *Sociological Quarterly,* 35 (1994): 328–346; Craig T. Palmer, "Telling the Truth (Up to a Point): Radio Communication among Maine Lobstermen," *Human Organization,* 49

(1990): 157–183; Carolyn Ellis, *Fisher Folk* (Lexington: University of Kentucky Press, 1986).

116. Donnelly, "Take My Word for It."

117. Because ownership is secret, it is possible that several people may have the same spot—a source of frustration when someone discovers that his or her spot has been picked.

118. This approach is taken by the Humboldt Bay Mycological Society:

> Beginning this year *Mycolog* will feature a regular article on what fungi are fruiting and where to collect them. This column will help novices follow the season and will provide "well-publicized" collecting places, for we know the old hands already have their secret spots. ("Is It Mushrooming Yet?" *Mycolog*, September 1983, p. 2)

119. Larry Lonik, *The Curious Morel* (Royal Oak, Mich.: RKT Publishing, 1984), p. 10.

120. Letter to author.

121. Ms. Mushroom, "Etiquette," *Mushroom,* 2 (Summer 1984): 28–29; quotation from p. 29.

122. Aldrich, "Sociable Organization."

123. Schmalenbach, *Society and Experience;* Kevin Hetherington, "The Contemporary Significance of Schmalenbach's Concept of the Bund," *Sociological Review,* 42 (1994): 1–25.

124. Stebbins, *Amateurs, Professionals, and Serious Leisure.*

125. Contra Lewis Coser, *Greedy Institutions* (New York: Free Press, 1974).

126. Putnam, *Making Democracy Work.*

127. Comparing the 1981 and 1982 membership lists, I found that 69 percent of members (sixty-four of ninety-three) who had been in the club at least two years in 1981 (that is, were not new members) continued their membership; only 48 percent (twenty of forty-two) of the new members continued their membership the following year. This figure undercounts the actual renewal rate, as many members did not renew their memberships until late in the year, although they continued to participate in club activities. By the end of most years, approximately two hundred members had paid dues. Twenty-nine members in 1982 remained members in 1992—a real core, given rates of mobility and morbidity. Members do disengage, partly if their interest in mushrooms is replaced by other activities, partly as a result of changes in temporal commitments, and partly when the organization itself does not meet their intellectual or emotional needs.

128. Barney G. Glaser and Anselm L. Strauss, "Awareness Contexts and Social Interaction," *American Sociological Review,* 29 (1964): 669–679.

6. FUNGUS AND ITS PUBLICS

1. Robert A. Stebbins, *Amateurs, Professionals, and Serious Leisure* (Montreal: McGill-Queen's University Press, 1992).

2. The North American Mycological Association publishes a quasi-scientific journal, *McIlvanea: Journal of American Amateur Mycology,* named after a turn-of-the-century American mycologist whose identification of mushroom species provided a basis for professional mycology in America. Articles in this journal may be written by professionals in relatively nontechnical language (often about mushroom taxonomy or distribution) or by amateurs systematically describing discoveries, taxonomic keys, poisoning, edibility, or the history of mycology. Similar publication outlets are found in other arenas of quasi-academic leisure, such as history, astronomy, or entomology (Ibid., p. 39).

3. Robert A. Stebbins, "Serious Leisure: A Conceptual Statement," *Pacific Sociological Review,* 25 (1982): 251–272.

4. R. Gordon Wasson, *Soma: Divine Mushroom of Immortality* (New York: Harcourt Brace Jovanovich, 1968).

5. Lynn Barber, in *The Heyday of Natural History* (Garden City, N.Y.: Doubleday, 1980), p. 13, notes of the early Victorian era in Britain:

   The public's tastes in natural history were unpredictable. One year they centered on mosses, the next madrepores. In the decade from 1845 to 1855 [public interest] moved successively from seaweeds to ferns to sea-anemones. In the next decade they switched bewilderingly to sea-serpents, gorillas and infusoria.

6. Suzanne Hamlin, "The Wild Mushroom: Exotic and Booming," *New York Times,* Oct. 19, 1994, p. C4.

7. "The Psychology of Mushroomers," *Mycofile,* 30 (Sept./Oct. 1989): 3.

8. Travis Dinoff, "Letter from Andrew Weil," *Spore Print,* 113 (Feb. 1984): 8–10; quotation from p. 8.

9. Sara Ann Friedman, "Blewitts That Bloom in the Spring . . . ," *New York Mycological Society Newsletter,* 5 (Spring 1981): 1.

10. See Robert A. Stebbins, *Amateurs* (Beverly Hills: Sage, 1979), p. 262. Any subculture that is not socially ratified faces this problem. As one collector notes, "When you tell people you collect spark plugs, they look at you like you've got about 12 ounces (of brain) to the pound" (Mark Kennedy, "If There's More Than One, Americans Will Collect It," *Star/Tribune,* Mar. 19, 1990, p. 5E). Boxers, too, face this problem—outsiders find their sport vicious and violent; they are unable to appreciate its social and emotional benefits (Loic J. D. Wacquant, "The Pugilistic Point of View: How Boxers Think and Feel about Their Trade," *Theory and Society,* 24 (1995): 489–535.

11. Heinz-Günter Vester, "Adventure as a Form of Leisure," *Journal of Leisure Research*, 6 (1987): 237–249; J. A. Walter, "Death as Recreation: Armchair Mountaineering," *Leisure Studies*, 3 (1984): 67–76, quotation from p. 68.

12. Allein Stanley, "Southern Forays," *NAMA XXV* (1985), pp. 19–21; quotation from p. 19.

13. Gary Alan Fine, *Kitchens: The Culture of Restaurant Work* (Berkeley: University of California Press, 1996), pp. 235–236.

14. Stephen Fox, *The American Conservation Movement: John Muir and His Legacy* (Madison: University of Wisconsin Press, 1981), p. 338.

15. Samuel R. Rosen, *A Judge Judges Mushrooms* (Nashville, Ind.: Highlander Press, 1982), p. 16.

16. "Warning: Mushrooming May Be Hazardous to Your Health," *Ohio Spore Print* (March–April 1984), p. 7.

17. Dianne Purce, "If It's a Disease, It's One with Pleasant Aspects," *Mushroom*, 4 (Spring 1986): 44.

18. No title, *Inky Captions: The Newsletter of the Tacoma Mushroom Society* (Jan. 1984), p. 2.

19. Diane Friedman, "Letter to the Editor," *New York Mycological Society Newsletter*, 5 (Fall 1981): 10–11.

20. Sara Ann Friedman, "The Meandering Mycophiles," *New York Mycological Society Newsletter*, 5 (Summer 1981): 1.

21. William Hay, *British Fungi* (London: S. Sonnenschein, Lowery & Co., 1887), p. 6.

22. Don H. Coombs, "Postma Helps Control the Mushrooms of Norway," *Mushroom*, 4 (Summer 1986): 5–6; quotation from p. 5.

23. Norm Strung, "The Greening," *Mushroom*, 1 (Fall 1983): 17–18; quotation from p. 17.

24. Maggie Rogers, "Keeping Up," *Mushroom*, 4 (Winter 1985–1986): 40–41; quotation from p. 40.

25. "Deadly Colors," *New York Times*, Oct. 6, 1981, p. A30.

26. A. D. Olmsted, "Morally Controversial Leisure: The Social World of Gun Collectors," *Symbolic Interaction*, 11 (1988): 277–287.

27. During the spring and summer of 1993, the "problem" of violence in the woods became widely publicized in Oregon (personal communication, Richard Mitchell, 1996). A Cambodian mushroom picker was murdered (probably in a robbery attempt) and reports spread of gunfire in the woods. Apparently much of this gunfire was designed to prevent fellow pickers from getting lost, but some may have involved warning shots, protecting pickers' personal spots. After the "panic" of 1993, exemplified by a string of articles in the *Portland Oregonian* in

1993 and early 1994, interest in activity in the woods subsided. Some speculated that the gunshots resulted from racial hostility, but this claim was never proven.

28. See Hamlin, "Wild Mushroom," and Don H. Coombs, "Profiteers and Common Thugs Trash Traditional Mushrooming?" *Mushroom,* 11 (Summer 1993): 13–14; quotation from p. 13. One estimate found that 3.9 million pounds of mushrooms with an economic value of $41.1 million were harvested in Oregon, Washington, and Idaho in 1992 (W. E. Schlosser and K. A. Blatner, "The Wild Edible Mushroom Industry of Idaho, Oregon, and Washington," *Journal of Forestry,* 93 [1995]: 31–36).

29. Joseph W. Schneider, "Social Problems Theory: The Constructionist View," *Annual Review of Sociology,* 11 (1985): 209–229; Gale Miller and James A. Holstein, "Reconsidering Social Constructionism," in James A. Holstein and Gale Miller, eds., *Reconsidering Social Constructionism* (New York: Aldine de Gruyter, 1993), pp. 5–23.

30. "Mushroom Conservation: The Camp Magruder Statements," *Mushroom,* 4 (Winter 1985–1986): 6–14; quotation from p. 6.

31. Peter J. Schmitt, *Back to Nature: The Arcadian Myth in Urban America* (New York: Oxford University Press, 1969), pp. 9–10; John F. Rieger, *American Sportsmen and the Origin of Conservation,* rev. ed. (Norman: University of Oklahoma Press, 1986), pp. 70–72; Steven R. Taylor, "Commercial Gathering: It's Time to Speak Out!" *Mushroom,* 11 (Summer 1993): 9–10, quotation from p. 10.

32. An officer of NAMA hoped to avoid this problem, and suggested a radical, if not entirely adequate, social constructionist argument:

> There are . . . people who morally disapprove of almost everything going on in this country, and will simply fix on something like mushroom commercialization, and it will end up meaning so much more than just selling chanterelles. It will be against all of the liberalization in society. I mean, for all you know, they may even be opposed to abortion, but they can't say anything about that, so they oppose the unlicensed selling of chanterelles. . . . This is one area that they feel they can do something about . . . alert the public. There are great alerters in mushrooming.

It is not clear why pro-lifers would choose the cause of the commercialism of the woods when so many potential problems exist.

33. Charles S. Richardson and Michael K. Richardson, "Warning: Your Days of Traipsing Off May Be Numbered," *Mushroom,* 12 (Spring 1994): 37–38; quotation from p. 37.

34. Tom Goff, "Ms. Nature, Take Another Memo to J. Muir," *Mushroom,* 11 (Fall 1993): 32–34; quotation from p. 33.

35. Sara Ann Friedman, *Celebrating the Wild Mushroom* (New York: Dodd, Mead, 1986), p. 173.
36. The label drug *abuse* has this feature—in contrast to drug use.
37. Linda Painter, "May and June Meetings," *Mush Rumor* (Apr.–Aug. 1985), pp. 1–3; quotation from p. 1.
38. Gary Menser, "Commercial Picking," *Mushroom*, 3 (Winter 1984–1985): 10–13; quotation from p. 11.
39. Sara Ann Friedman and W. K. Williams, "A Commercial Break," *New York Mycological Society Newsletter,* 7 (Spring 1983): 2–4; quotation from p. 3.
40. Stebbins, *Amateurs, Professionals, and Serious Leisure.*
41. "Conservation," *Mycophile*, 26 (Sept./Oct. 1985): 5.
42. Bob Burrell, "Collecting for Profit," *Boston Mycological Club Bulletin,* 38 (June 1983): 19.
43. Fox, *Conservation Movement*, p. 103.
44. Rebecca J. McLain and Eric T. Jones, "Creating Space for Mobile Wild Mushroom Harvesters in Community-Based Forestry in the Pacific Northwest," unpublished manuscript, 1996.
45. Friedman, *Celebrating*, p. 173.
46. Burrell, "Collecting for Profit," p. 19.
47. Jeff Hvid, "Letter," *Mycena News*, 33 (Spring 1983): 36.
48. Jeff Hvid, "Thoughts on Commercial Pick," *Mushroom*, 3 (Summer 1985): 5–7; quotation from pp. 6–7.
49. Larry Stickney, "Letter," *Mycena News*, 34 (Feb. 1985): 3.
50. Judy Roger, "The New Gold Rush," *Mycofile* (May–June 1983), p. 16.
51. Rebecca J. McLain, Margaret A. Shannon, and Harriet C. Chistensen, "When Amateurs Are the Experts: Amateur Mycologists and Wild Mushroom Politics in the Northwestern United States," unpublished manuscript, 1996.
52. This may be a function of the small number of mushroomers who have ever sold wild fungi (12 percent in Minnesota; 10 percent nationally). In a later survey of the Oregon Mycological Society, only 3 percent sold mushrooms, and a majority of the club's members favored some regulations (Richardson and Richardson, "Warning," p. 37).
53. Sara Ann Friedman and W. K. Williams, "Another Berkeley Protest," *New York Mycological Society Newsletter,* 7 (Spring 1983): 4–5; quotation from p. 4.
54. Steven Pencall, "FDS Proposal for Mushroom Regulation Called 'Ludicrous, Ill-Advised Idea,'" *Mushroom*, 5 (Winter 1986–1987): 4.
55. "Food for Thought," *Mush Rumor* (Dec./Feb. 1984–1985), p. 2.
56. The lobster mushroom (*Hypomyces lactifluorum*) is a mold that parasitizes species of *Lactarius* and *Russula,* transforming unpalatable

mushrooms into edible species. The problem is that occasionally this mold can parasitize a poisonous species, allegedly including amanitas, and so some expertise is required.

57. Leslie Prosterman, *Ordinary Life, Festival Days: Aesthetics in the Midwestern County Fair* (Washington: Smithsonian Institution Press, 1995), pp. 101–102.

58. Clubs differ to some degree on this; the Puget Sound and San Francisco clubs are known for their close working relationships with professionals, and the clubs provide scholarships for mycology students. These are both large clubs and are fortunate to have professional mycologists who enjoy the presence of amateurs. The Minnesota Mycological Society had few contacts with the professional mycologists at the University of Minnesota, although one did contribute to the mycological study group, in part at the request of a former student, and a second taught an evening course open to the public.

59. Friedman, *Celebrating*, p. 98.

60. One professional mycologist, specializing in large fleshy fungi, told me that he thought amateurs were a lot like professionals: the difference being that amateurs wanted to put a name on something, whereas professionals wanted to put a *correct* name on something.

61. Andrew Pickering, "The Mangle of Practice: Agency and Emergence in the Sociology of Science," *American Journal of Sociology,* 99 (1993): 559–589.

62. Anne Dow, "Looking Back," *Capital Mushrooms,* 5 (Sept.–Oct. 1984): 2–3; quotation from p. 2.

63. Michael R. Tansey and Donald J. Niederpruem, "Mycological Teaching Humor," unpublished manuscript, 1977, p. 21.

64. Harry Knighton, the founder and guiding spirit of NAMA, told me proudly that he collected *Pluteus cervinus* for Alexander Smith, a highly esteemed professional. Another serious amateur was proud to have one of her collections accepted by the herbarium at the Field Museum of Natural History in Chicago.

65. Helen V. Smith and Alexander H. Smith, "Amateurs Do Count," in *NAMA XXV.* Published by the North American Mycological Association, 1985, pp. 9–12; quotation from p. 12.

66. Stebbins, *Amateurs,* p. 266.

67. Lorelei Norvell, "Planning the Foray," *Mushroom,* 2 (Spring 1984): pp. 17–21.

68. See Margaret Dilly, "Remembering Dr. Stuntz," *Mushroom,* 11 (Summer 1993): 15–20. Some professionals worry about excessive involvement with amateurs. One told me that he wanted to support local amateurs, but "I've seen Dan Stuntz just get gobbled up with the need for

his expertise." Time with amateurs may take time from scholarly work or family life, and different scholars have different personal equations, leading some amateurs to speak with frustration of the "aloofness" of professionals. What is time management to one is aloofness to others.

69. J. E. S., "Dr. Thiers' Sierran Fungi Class," *Mycena News* (April 1984), p. 20.

70. Stebbins, *Amateurs,* p. 26.

71. Personal communication, Walter Litten, 1984.

72. Rod Tulloss, "How I Came to Amanita," *McIlvainea,* 7 (1985): 38–44; quotation from p. 43.

73. Ursula Hoffman, "On Boletes," *New York Mycological Society,* 5 (1981): 2–3; quotation from p. 2.

74. Don Stap, *A Bird without a Name* (New York: Knopf, 1990).

75. David Arora, *Mushrooms Demystified,* 2d ed. (Berkeley: Ten Speed Press, 1986).

76. According to one estimate from the mid-1970s, approximately 100 new genera of fungi and more than 1,000 new species were described annually (G. C. Ainsworth, *Introduction to the History of Mycology* [Cambridge, England: Cambridge University Press, 1976], p. 5)—increasing the number of potentially endangered species and the total species count.

77. See Gary Lincoff, "Mushroom Hunters Want Scientific Names They Can Pronounce and Understand," *Mushroom,* 10 (Summer 1992): 5–9; quotation from p. 8. In contrast, there are about 9,000 species of birds in fewer than 2,000 genera.

78. At one meeting, Brian and Jerry joked about turning English words into Latinized mycological words, by adding -oid, -id, and -aceous to their roots; for example, speaking of a mushroom as "purpleaceous."

79. Roman Stanley, "When We Have the Election, How Many Votes Should You Be Eligible to Cast?" *Mushroom,* 6 (Summer 1988): 4.

80. Berthold Horn, "In Defense of Common Names," *Boston Mycological Club Bulletin,* 37 (Dec. 1982): 12–13; quotation from p. 12.

81. Kent C. Ryden, *Mapping the Invisible Landscape: Folklore, Writing, and the Sense of Place* (Iowa City: University of Iowa Press, 1993), p. 78.

82. M. Prior, "Mushroom Slices . . ." *Mycelium* (Nov.–Dec. 1982), p. 11.

83. Harley Barnhart, "Incident on the Train," *Mushroom,* 11 (Spring 1993): 18.

84. The founding of the American Ornithologist's Union in 1883 served this purpose. By 1886 its committee on nomenclature published lists of the "official" names of American birds. These lists became widely

accepted within this natural domain (Schmitt, *Back to Nature,* p. 34). At one NAMA foray, Kent McKnight, the author of *Peterson's Field Guide to Mushrooms* (Kent H. McKnight and Vera B. McKnight, *A Field Guide to Mushrooms* [Boston: Houghton Mifflin, 1987]), suggested that NAMA set up a committee on common names, but apparently nothing was done.

85. Jack Goody, *The Culture of Flowers* (Cambridge, England: Cambridge University Press, 1993), p. xii.

86. Rene Pomerleau, "Mushrooms: A Late-Blooming Interest," *McIlvainea,* 6 (1984): 4–6.

87. Wendla McGovern, "Blewits and Man-on-Horseback Revealed," *Mycena News,* 34 (Jan. 1985): 1, 6.

88. Lorelei Norvell, "Every Mushroom, It Turns Out, Wasn't Named by the Supreme Being," *Mushroom,* 3 (Fall 1985): 14–15; quotation from p. 14.

89. Jack Parkin, "An Open Letter to Not One but Two People," *Mushroom,* 10 (Fall 1992): 37–38.

90. David S. Wilson, *In the Presence of Nature* (Amherst: University of Massachusetts Press, 1978), p. 14.

91. Kenneth W. Cochran, "Poisoning in 1984," *Mushroom,* 3 (Spring 1985): 30–33; quotation from p. 32.

92. Jeff Donaghue, "Hydnaceae," *Toadstool Review,* 10 (July 1985): 5.

93. Jorge Luis Borges, *Other Inquisitions, 1937–1952* (New York: Washington Square Press, 1966), p. 108.

94. Eleanor Rosch, "Principles of Categorization," in Eleanor Rosch and Barbara B. Lloyd, eds., *Cognition and Categorization* (Hillsdale, N.J.: Lawrence Erlbaum Associates, 1978), pp. 27–48; quotation from pp. 27–29.

95. Donald P. Rogers, "The Philosophy of Taxonomy," *Mycologia,* 50 (1958): 326–332; quotation from p. 328.

96. Cowan, quoted in Ainsworth, *History of Mycology,* p. 241.

97. Martha Singer, *Mycologists and Other Taxa* (Braunschweig: Verlag and J. Cramer, 1984), p. 115.

98. See Mark Derr, "The Politics of Dogs," *Atlantic Monthly* (March 1990), pp. 49–72; quotation from p. 51. I was told that there is a 97.5 percent overlap between the DNA of a chimp and that of a human. Is that 2.5 percent sufficient to make a difference, given the genetic variation among humans? Should both be in the same taxonomic family or different ones?

99. Stap, *Bird,* p. 84; D. L. Hawksworth, *Mycologist's Handbook* (Key, Surrey, England: Commonwealth Mycological Institute, 1974), p. 4.

100. Lincoff, "Mushroom Hunters," p. 7.

101. Brent Berlin, "Ethnobiological Classification," in Rosch and Lloyd, *Cognition and Categorization,* pp. 9–26; quotation from pp. 10, 17, 24.

102. Bruno Latour and Steven Woolgar, *Laboratory Life* (Beverly Hills: Sage, 1979), p. 64.

103. Edith Nelson, "Most Amateur Pleasure Comes from Alphas," *Mushroom,* 10 (Spring 1992): 5–6.

104. David Arora, *Mushrooms Demystified* (Berkeley: Ten Speed Press, 1979), p. 12; Lincoff, "Mushroom Hunters," p. 5; Scott Redhead, "Dear Gary," *Mushroom,* 10 (Spring 1992): 6–8; quotation from p. 7.

105. Bill Williams, "Taxonomic Tyranny or a Rose by Any Other Name Would Be More Difficult to Remember," *New York Mycological Society Newsletter,* 6 (Winter 1981–1982): 4–6, quotation from p. 5; Novell, "Every Mushroom," p. 15.

106. Latour and Woolgar, *Laboratory Life,* p. 176.

107. Gary Lincoff, "Yet Another Note on Names and Photographs," *Mushroom,* 9 (Fall 1991): 9–14, quotation from p. 14; Lincoff, "Mushroom Hunters," p. 9.

108. The naming of mountains has some of these same political features, as described by William R. Catton ("The Mountain with the Wrong Name," *Etc., 11* [1954]: 299–304) in his account of the dispute between supporters of the names Mount Rainier and Mount Tacoma.

109. Friedman, *Celebrating,* p. 19.

110. Hawksworth, *Mycologist's Handbook,* p. 125.

111. In 1967 a bill was proposed in Congress on behalf of the salmon industry to rename the salmonella organism. The Mycological Society of America and other biological organizations managed to defeat this governmental attempt to control their autonomy.

112. Hawksworth, *Mycologist's Handbook,* pp. 125–178; C. Jeffrey, *Biological Nomenclature* (London: Arnold, 1973).

113. There is a starting date from which earlier names are not considered: for gasteromycetes, this is from Persoon's *Synopsis methodica fungorum* of 1801, and for other fungi, Fries's *Systema mycologicum* of 1821. Previous names, including those in Linnaeus (the original taxonomist), are not considered valid.

114. Donaghue, "Hydnaceae," p. 5.

115. But see Stap, *Bird,* pp. 217–218.

116. Ellen O'Brien, "Once a Year, a Shared Love of Fungi Mushrooms," *Philadelphia Inquirer,* New Jersey/Metro, Aug. 18, 1984, pp. B1–B2; quotation from p. B2.

117. See Maggie Rogers, "Cooking: The Czarneckis and the Smiths Are Featured," *Mushroom,* 5 (Winter 1986–1987): 35–36; quotation from

p. 35. Sometimes this is an honor one wishes one could decline. One mycologist found a genus of stinkhorns named after him. He searched the literature, hoping that the name would not be valid, but the name stands (Singer, *Mycologists*, p. 19).

118. Hawksworth, *Mycologist's Handbook*, p. 50.

119. Ibid., pp. 116–123.

120. See C. B. Wolfe and Roy. E. Halling, "*Tylopilus Griseocarneus*, a New Species from the North American Atlantic and Gulf Coastal Plain," *Mycoloqia*, 81 (1989): 342–346. The person who collected the original specimens, K. Adamietz, is noted in the formal Latin description, but is not otherwise described.

121. Ibid., pp. 342, 344.

122. Wolfe and Halling (Ibid., p. 345) note: "We expect its distribution to be continuous throughout the Coastal Plain between Louisiana and New Jersey." This guesswork is impressive given that, until 1984, the mushroom was unknown, and has been found only in these two states. The assumption that the mushroom will be continuously found on the coast (rather than, say, in an arc through the Mississippi and Ohio Valleys, or beyond the endpoints of Louisiana and New Jersey) depends on the typification of climatic and ecological systems, but also on an aesthetic judgment of what a "proper" distribution looks like.

123. Ibid., p. 346.

124. Michael Lynch and Steve Woolgar, "Sociological Orientations to Representational Practice in Science," *Human Studies*, 11 (1988): 99–116; quotation from p. 103.

125. Personal communication, C. B. Wolfe, 1985.

7. NATUREWORK AND THE TAMING OF THE WILD

1. Bill McKibben, *The End of Nature* (New York: Random House, 1989).

2. Robert A. Stebbins, *Amateurs, Professionals and Serious Leisure* (Montreal: Queen's University Press, 1992), pp. 38–58

3. Andrew Abbott, *The System of Professions* (Chicago: University of Chicago Press, 1988).

Index